St. Louis Community College

Forest Park
Florissant Valley
Meramec

Instructional Resources
St. Louis, Missouri

GAYLORD

FORCED JUSTICE

FORCED JUSTICE

School Desegregation
and the Law

DAVID J. ARMOR

New York   Oxford
OXFORD UNIVERSITY PRESS
1995

Oxford University Press

Oxford   New York
Athens   Auckland   Bangkok   Bombay
Calcutta   Cape Town   Dar es Salaam   Delhi
Florence   Hong Kong   Istanbul   Karachi
Kuala Lumpur   Madras   Madrid   Melbourne
Mexico City   Nairobi   Paris   Singapore
Taipei   Tokyo   Toronto

and associated companies in
Berlin   Ibadan

Published by Oxford University Press, Inc.
198 Madison Avenue, New York, New York 10016

Oxford is a registered trademark of Oxford University Press, Inc.

Library of Congress Cataloging-in-Publication Data
Armor, David J.
Forced justice : school desegregation and the law /David J. Armor.
p.   cm.
Includes bibliographical references and index.
ISBN 0-19-509012-8
1. Segregation in education—Law and legislation—United States.
I. Title.
KF4155.A87   1995
344.73'0798—dc20
[347.304798]   94-13497

3 5 7 9 8 6 4 2

Printed in the United States of America
on acid-free paper

Preface

It was my intention to write a book on school desegregation more than a decade ago, and I actually began work on it in 1978. It seemed to be the right time, in that the national controversy over "forced busing" had peaked, and it appeared that the issue would fade away over the next several years. Other commitments intruded, however, and the book was set aside. The long delay would prove fortuitous because the busing issue did not disappear; indeed, many important events occurred in the desegregation field throughout the 1980s and early 1990s. Given these developments, coupled with further personal experiences and the maturation of my own views, this book offers a more complete discussion of school desegregation than I could have produced fifteen years ago.

My views on school desegregation have evolved considerably since my first research on the subject in the mid-1960s, shortly after I joined the faculty at Harvard. I was offered the unique opportunity to work with James Coleman and other social scientists on his now-classic study of equal opportunity. Like most of the project staff, I believed that the Coleman study would confirm two hypotheses widely supported in the social science and civil rights communities: that the schools attended by black students (most of which were segregated at that time) had resources and conditions inferior to schools attended by whites, and that these differences in "inputs" were responsible for the lower academic achievement of black students, once individual socioeconomic factors were taken into account.

The failure of the Coleman study to find systematic differences between the resources of black and white schools and to link these differences to academic achievement was both astonishing and controversial. These findings were so contrary to the conventional wisdom of the time that I decided to concentrate my research specifically on the effects of school desegregation, broaden the outcome measures, and use more rigorous research designs. Between 1966 and 1971, I developed additional analyses of the Coleman data, studied racial isolation for the U.S. Commission on Civil Rights, and evaluated a voluntary desegregation program in Boston called the METCO project. The results of these studies, along with reviews of other evaluations of desegregation programs, were reflected in my article "The Evidence on Busing," published in *The Public Interest* in 1972.

This essay on busing was one of the first academic studies to question the "harm and benefit" thesis—popular among both social scientists and civil rights advocates—which held that school desegregation would lead to social and academic benefits for black children. Even though the article challenged a key tenet of mainstream social science at the time, I was nonetheless startled by the emotional intensity of the controversy, especially by the strong reactions of some of my colleagues. A similar heated controversy occurred in 1975, when James Coleman published the first study of desegregation and white flight, which led to an unprecedented (and unsuccessful) attempt to expel him from the American Sociological Association.

My early work on school desegregation led to a number of appearances as an expert witness in school desegregation litigation. I testified mainly as a critic of comprehensive mandatory busing plans on the grounds that they were not educationally effective (e.g., the Detroit and Pasadena cases). As I learned more about the legal picture, however, it became clear that the courts were less concerned about educational issues than about the effectiveness of desegregation plans in producing racial balance. This led to a new research direction on the effects of desegregation plans on white flight and resegregation.

My research on the white flight problem, "White Flight, Demographic Change, and the Future of School Desegregation," was published in 1978 while I was a Senior Social Scientist at the Rand Corporation. The report concluded that certain types of mandatory busing plans were causing white flight, sometimes to the point of resegregation, and that voluntary plans could produce as much desegregation over the long run by stabilizing enrollments. At that time, I also became involved in several metropolitan school desegregation cases (including Atlanta and Kansas City), where I had the opportunity to study the causes of housing segregation. My research focused specifically on the role of black and white preferences in explaining housing segregation in larger cities.

During the 1980s and 1990s, I remained actively involved in desegregation policy and research. I have had the opportunity to test my research conclusions by helping to design several desegregation plans, including plans for Savannah–Chatham County, Georgia; Worcester, Massachusetts; Knox County, Tennessee; and Baton Rouge, Louisiana. Also, I have testified as an expert in several "unitary" cases in which districts are seeking termination of court supervision, including Norfolk, Virginia; Muscogee and DeKalb counties, Georgia; Topeka, Kansas; and Dallas, Texas.

My experience and research in desegregation cases have influenced the content and structure of this book in several ways. First, I have emphasized the linkages between social science research and the law on school desegregation. Many legal experts tend to oversimplify social science evidence or ignore it altogether, claiming that social science findings on white flight, academic achievement, and the causes of segregation are irrelevant to judicial doctrine. Having been asked to testify in numerous desegregation cases as a social scientist with expertise in these issues, I find it curious when legal scholars claim that there is little or no relationship between the law and social science research on these topics.

Second, the book presents some of the social science evidence on which I based my expert testimony in a variety of court cases; much of this evidence has not been published elsewhere. When testifying in a school desegregation case, I usually collect and analyze data specific to a school system and to the issues raised in the case. This evidence can include demographic analyses and projections, community and parent surveys, and academic achievement analyses. The objective of presenting this material here is twofold: to show how this research supports the argument in this book and to illustrate the relevance of this social science evidence to the fact-finding stage of desegregation cases.

Finally, after twenty-five years of experience and research in this field, I have arrived at some general conclusions about desegregation policy: where it has failed, where it has succeeded, and where it may be headed. Most of these conclusions, I believe, are based on a fair reading of scholarly studies, supplemented by case studies and courtroom experience on behalf of a considerable number of school systems. My purpose in writing this book is to describe and explain these conclusions, and especially to show how these viewpoints have evolved from legal doctrines, social science research (including my own), and extensive case experience.

My intention is not to review every study in the desegregation field. Other books offer comprehensive reviews of the literature, such as *Eliminating Racism*, edited by Phyllis Katz and Dalmas Taylor. Rather, my intention is to conduct a comprehensive review of desegregation policy that offers an alternative viewpoint about its efficacy. Most social science contributions in this field, such as the works of Gary Orfield (*Must We Bus*) and Judith Hochschild (*The New American Dilemma*), are more sanguine than I about the value of the compulsory policies that began after 1968. I contend that the limited educational and social benefits of desegregation must be weighed more carefully against its social, political, and economic costs.

In the realm of social policy and social research, one can never claim to have definitive proof for any conclusion. I do believe, however, that significant progress has been made since the 1960s and that we can now make more informed judgments about desegregation policy and its many aspects, including its rationale, its social and educational consequences, and its practicality than we could three decades ago. This book draws upon this knowledge and experience to offer conclusions and recommendations that are as consistent as I can make them with the best scientific evidence now available.

Sperryville, Virginia   D. J. A
December 1994

Acknowledgments

This book was written while I was a Senior Research Scholar of the Social Philosophy and Policy Center of Bowling Green State University, Ohio. Aside from these auspices, I am most grateful for the many contributions of Ellen Frankel Paul, Deputy Director of the center, and her staff during the writing and publication process, including very substantial editorial assistance and substantive suggestions for the manuscript.

Because this book depends heavily on research and experience I gained while working on school desegregation cases, I must express my sincere gratitude to the many school boards, school attorneys, and school administrators who have assisted me with my research, complied with innumerable requests for data, and endured my counsel at various times over the past twenty-five years.

Although I cannot list all of the individuals and school districts involved, I would like to offer special thanks to Alfred Lindseth (Atlanta, Charleston County, Savannah–Chatham County, Darlington County, and Knox County); Lee Paul and Henry Marcheschi (Pasadena); Donald Lincoln (San Diego); Tom Bartman, Bobbi Fiedler, and David Petersen (Los Angeles); George Feldmiller (Kansas City); Jim Stalneker (Norfolk); John Dudley (Yonkers); Gary Sams, Robert Freeman, Stanley Hawkins, and Charles Weatherly (DeKalb County); Robert Rosen (Charleston County); Steve Sheer and Geri Smith (Savannah–Chatham County); Gary Sebelius (Topeka); Richard Beeler and Sarah Simpson (Knox County); John Whelan (Hartford); Peter Collison, Celia Ruiz, and Mike Carven (San Jose); Robert Hammonds (Baton Rouge); John Milling (Darlington County), Michael Fields (Kansas City), Jim Humes (Muskogee County), and Charles Cooper (Wilmington).

Over the years I have received valuable intellectual assistance and advice from numerous social science colleagues, many of whom helped shape the research and the views presented in this book. My greatest debt is to Christine Rossell, who has offered ideas, data, and many discussions on many desegregation issues, including collaboration on a number of desegregation cases and studies (Yonkers, Savannah, Natchez, Knox County, Hartford, San Jose, Dallas, and the national desegregation and magnet school study by the American Institutes of Research). I have also benefited from my collaborations with William A. V. Clark (who coauthored chapter 3 in this book), Peter Morrison, Tony Pascal,

and Herbert Walberg. I received valuable comments on chapter 1 from desegregation attorneys Alfred Lindseth, Stanley Hawkins, and George Feldmiller;
on chapter 2 from Hugh F. Cline, Janet Schofield, Thomas Cook, and Larry
Feinberg; and on chapter 3 from Tony Pascal. Martin Patchen provided additional data from his Indianapolis study for chapter 2. Oxford University Press
reviewers and editors also greatly aided manuscript revisions, and Richard W.
White, Jr. suggested the book title.

Over the years I have received excellent professional assistance from Ron
Smith and the staff at Amrigon, who conducted the field work for most of the
surveys described in chapter 4.

I would like to offer special thanks to James Coleman and James Q. Wilson,
not only for their contributions to my intellectual growth but also for their
frequent encouragement and moral support for my research and writing in this
often-controversial field. I would also like to acknowledge a debt to Robert
Crain, Gary Orfield, and Karl Taueber; although we disagree about many desegregation issues, their work has always proven to be a constructive challenge
to my own.

Last, but certainly not least, I thank my family for their great love, patience,
and support during the years that I worked on this book. I am also grateful for
the many helpful editorial comments on various chapters offered by my wife,
Marilyn; my daughter, Adrienne Margolis; and my son, Daniel.

Contents

FORCED JUSTICE

Introduction: The
Desegregation Dilemma

Despite nearly four decades of controversy and debate over school segregation, the desegregation dilemma is still largely unresolved. The "busing" problem has received less national attention in recent years, and there are no riots, bus burnings, and school boycotts, as witnessed in earlier decades. Yet current events reveal the depth of a dilemma that has divided educators, parents, jurists, social scientists, and many other groups since the beginning of the civil rights movement.

Indicators of the current desegregation dilemma are numerous. Hundreds of school districts throughout the country still impose busing for desegregation purposes, many under court orders that are now more than twenty years old. Although the types of desegregation plans have evolved to some extent, with increased emphasis on school choice, many plans still compel children to attend schools that their parents would not choose, solely for the purpose of racial "balance."

Further, after a period of quiescence, school desegregation was again the subject of several major Supreme Court decisions in 1991 and 1992. The decisions affected the length of time and the conditions under which a school district has to maintain a court-ordered busing plan. Although these decisions dispelled a common misconception that school systems have to maintain desegregation plans "in perpetuity," it is still unclear how many school districts can or will end their busing plans.

Finally, new desegregation litigation and controversies continue to surface. In 1989 a lawsuit was initiated in a Connecticut state court by the National Association for the Advancement of Colored People (NAACP) to compel desegregation between the city of Hartford and its suburban districts. A similar city-suburbs desegregation strategy failed in the federal courts, but the Hartford lawsuit seeks to build on the success of school equal-finance cases under state constitutions. In 1991 the school board of La Crosse, Wisconsin, adopted a busing plan to equalize economic (rather than race) differences among schools. Reminiscent of the busing controversies of the 1970s, all board members who

3

supported the busing plan were voted out of office in a regular and a recall election, reflecting the widespread community opposition to busing for the purpose of achieving socioeconomic balance in schools.

Why, after years of debate and controversy, is the school desegregation dilemma still alive and well in so many communities? The answer is not simple, because it involves many different institutions, ideas, and players. It involves the courts and the complex and changing judicial doctrines about civil rights; it involves many years of social science theory and research, sometimes inextricably woven into judicial doctrines and court decisions; it involves educators, school boards, and theories of education; and above all, it involves strong ideological views by various advocacy groups about the rights of individuals and the obligations of institutions.

This book is about the desegregation dilemma. Although no single work can resolve a dilemma so durable and so deep, this inquiry is meant to shed light on its causes, its course, and its solutions. It will do so by considering the school desegregation problem from several perspectives, including judicial, social science, educational, and ideological viewpoints.

There are two major sources of school desegregation policies. One is desegregation law, beginning with the Supreme Court's 1954 decision in *Brown v. Board of Education*. The *Brown* decision sparked three decades of court decisions and legislative actions, including the Civil Rights Act of 1964, which sought to eliminate racial discrimination and promote (or require) desegregation. Desegregation law establishes the first and foremost justification for a school desegregation policy: to remedy past government-sponsored school segregation or related discriminatory practices. The application of desegregation law, either by a court or by a government agency, is responsible for the largest number of school desegregation plans today.

The second source of school desegregation policy is a social science theory, the "harm and benefit thesis." In short, this thesis holds that school segregation is harmful and desegregation is beneficial to the educational and social outcomes of schooling. Although the major tenets of this thesis are based on social science concepts and research, the thesis also has a long and important history in the evolution of desegregation law, with elements incorporated into major court decisions. For legislatures and school boards that have adopted desegregation policies in the absence of legal requirements, the harm and benefit thesis forms the major rationale.

Desegregation law goes far beyond simply ending official segregation. Its most controversial aspects have been over remedy, specifically the policies of racial balance and mandatory busing of students to attain racial balance. Policies that promote mandatory busing for racial balance have not only created public controversy but also have led to long-lasting disputes among educators and social scientists about educational benefits.

Another legal controversy concerns the relationship between housing segregation and school segregation, which arose because of well-entrenched policies and practices of assigning students to schools on the basis of residence, often called "neighborhood school" policies.* Social science research has also played a role in these controversies, with studies on the causes of housing segregation, the impact of desegregation on "white flight," and the effectiveness of alternative desegregation plans.

This book discusses all of these legal and social science concepts and issues: the evolution of desegregation law, the validity of the harm and benefit thesis, the causes of housing segregation and its relationship to school desegregation, and the effectiveness and feasibility of alternative desegregation plans— illustrating some of the practical problems raised when theory is translated into practice. The basic purpose of this review is to help resolve the desegregation dilemma by sorting out fact from fiction and social science theory from judicial doctrine and by trying to determine the ultimate validity and feasibility of the desegregation concept. Building on the legal and social science review, the book concludes with a look to the future of school desegregation and its implications for other related school policies, including the growing debate over school choice.

The evidence and data that provide the empirical basis for this book are of two types. First, the study draws on the major court decisions and federal laws that have created, maintained, and altered the judicial policies affecting school desegregation. Second, the book relies on both national and individual case studies relevant to the various desegregation policy issues raised. Some of these studies, particularly the case studies, I prepared in connection with hearings on school desegregation lawsuits, and they were introduced as expert testimony. Much of this case material has not been previously published.

Desegregation and the Law

In 1991 and 1992, the Supreme Court issued three decisions on school desegregation affecting Oklahoma City; DeKalb County, Georgia; and Topeka, Kansas. The last of these is a recent decision in *Brown v. Board of Education,* the famous case that launched the civil rights movement in 1954. Incredible as it may seem, this case still awaits a final court resolution after nearly forty years of litigation.

The decisions rendered in these three cases may signal an end to one of the most controversial incursions of the federal courts into the social policies of the twentieth century. Although the "activist" Supreme Court of the 1960s and 1970s delivered a host of controversial decisions on such social issues as abortion, school prayer, and affirmative action, the Supreme Court rulings on school desegregation have been among the most intrusive as far as institutions are concerned. Abortion and school prayer decisions have been limited to altering

---

*The term "neighborhood school" in this book denotes a policy in which students are assigned to schools by residence rather than some other criteria such as race. Such policies usually draw contiguous geographic zones so that students attend schools closest to them, but the zone might be large and might require transportation.

state or local laws; although affirmative action decisions have affected the hiring and promotion practices of firms, even here the judicial incursion is limited to a fairly narrow band of company activities.

In the case of school desegregation, court decisions have affected nearly every aspect of school policy and operations. Courts have ordered forced busing of students outside neighborhood schools, required changes to curriculum and resource allocation, ordered minority hiring and mandatory reassignment of faculty, decided what schools can be opened or closed, and even demanded relocation of public housing. In some of the more extreme cases, it is no exaggeration to say that local courts nearly replaced school boards and administrators in the running of school systems. Moreover, this intervention has not been brief; many school desegregation cases, such as Topeka, have extended over several decades.

This judicial intervention in school governance was not envisaged by the original *Brown* decision, which ended government-sanctioned segregation in the schools and other public institutions. Indeed, this treatise does not question the clearly necessary decision to end state-enforced segregation throughout American society. Rather, the major focus is the desegregation remedies initiated by later Supreme Court decisions, especially the 1971 decision, *Swann v. Charlotte-Mecklenburg Board of Education*, which endorsed a policy of "racial balance" for desegregating schools. A formula for student or faculty racial balance at individual schools is a type of racial quota, in which a student's or a teacher's race becomes a criterion for school assignment.

The evolution of desegregation law is complex and convoluted, and tracing the constitutional logic and principles that run through both higher and lower court cases is not easy. Frequently, lower court cases are interwoven with social science theories and with interpretations not obviously justified by Supreme Court doctrine. Moreover, desegregation law is not monolithic; many desegregation policies stem from lower or appellate court decisions that are never challenged or, if challenged, are not reviewed by the Supreme Court. Therefore, desegregation law that applies to one school district or a group of districts might not resemble that applied to others, and it can even be inconsistent with Supreme Court decisions. Finally, the Supreme Court itself has changed over time, and it is no secret that the major philosophical changes and divisions on the high court during the past four decades have affected civil rights decisions.

Although some legal analysts have emphasized changes in Supreme Court doctrines on desegregation, I contend that Supreme Court decisions are consistent with respect to (1) the definition of unconstitutional segregation, (2) the minimum requirements for desegregation plans, and (3) the process of terminating court orders and being restored to "unitary" status.

While the *Brown* decision declared state-promoted segregation unconstitutional and pronounced any such laws or policies null and void, it did not actually prescribe what formerly segregated school systems must do to attain "de-" segregation, other than ending laws and other practices that promoted segregation. Not until a series of later decisions on remedy did the Supreme Court create such concepts as affirmative desegregation, racial balance, mandatory busing, and racial quotas for teacher and staff assignments. In short, these later decisions changed the meaning of desegregation from prohibiting forced segregation to requiring forced integration. Instead of embracing race-neutral remedies, which the original *Brown* decision seemed to do, the federal courts ultimately sanctioned race-conscious policies wherever remedies were imposed.

The impact of *Brown* and later Supreme Court decisions on school desegregation went far beyond the federal judiciary. Court actions gave moral legitimacy to the growing civil rights movement and greatly enhanced its political influence. The combination of court decrees, pressures from civil rights groups, and justification by social scientists provided the necessary political muscle for legislative actions to promote school desegregation at all levels, including the federal government, state governments, and local school boards. Some of these legislative actions went far beyond the narrower doctrines of the Supreme Court, enacting desegregation remedies regardless of the original cause of segregation.

Were its overall effects beneficial or even benign, this monumental judicial intervention into the public schools would itself be a significant issue, given its implication for the separation of powers and for American democratic principles in general. Indeed, just as some despots are enlightened, some court decrees—being free of political constraints—have undoubtedly improved the quality and equity of educational services, at least for some students. That judicial and other governmental policies for school desegregation have been effective is by no means clear, however; indeed, some argue that the more extreme desegregation remedies such as mandatory busing have been counterproductive in attaining the original goals of *Brown*.

How did the federal courts become enmeshed in such a drastic policy in the first place? How did the judicial doctrine that abolished forced segregation end up requiring forced integration? Have recent Supreme Court decisions made major changes in desegregation law or signaled an end to the era of mandatory busing? What is the status of legislative initiatives for school desegregation, and how do they relate to judicial doctrine? What are the implications of changing judicial policies for the growing school choice movement, whose critics claim it will have adverse effects on minorities and desegregation?

These and other questions are addressed in chapter 1, which reviews the evolution of desegregation law and explains its origins, rationale, and current status. I argue that social science theory and research have played important roles in the evolution of desegregation law, at various times providing an important intellectual basis for court decisions or legislative actions that might otherwise be lacking a clear legal foundation. I am not saying, of course, that social science has played a determining role or that legal doctrines and ordinary political processes are unimportant.

An understanding of desegregation law also requires knowledge of several legal concepts as applied to school desegregation, some of which are unique to federal judicial doctrine. These concepts include the distinction between liability and remedy phases of a desegregation case, the distinction between de jure (official) and de facto segregation, and the distinction between dual and unitary school systems. Other important considerations are that the judicial doctrine in desegregation cases has changed over time and that lower courts have frequently been in conflict over the interpretation of these doctrines. Some but not all of the changes in desegregation law occur through Supreme Court decisions, which resolve conflicts among lower courts by "clarifying" or reinforcing principles embraced in earlier decisions.

Perhaps the most widely misunderstood or misconstrued legal doctrine is the conditions under which schools with differing racial makeups constitute illegal (de jure) segregation. Another judicial doctrine that has been difficult to understand, partly because it has changed over time, is the appropriate desegregation remedy, given a condition of illegal school segregation. Finally, there has been considerable confusion and conflict, among jurists and laymen alike, over the long-term obligations of a school system after it has implemented a desegregation plan to remedy illegal segregation. All of these judicial concepts and doctrines are discussed and interpreted in chapter 1.

The Harm and Benefit Thesis

The social science theory that has played the greatest role in the evolution of school desegregation policy, both inside and outside the courts, is the harm and benefit thesis. In the absence of a legal requirement, most school districts that maintain or adopt desegregation plans use this thesis as their major rationale. Indeed, even if the legal mandates for school desegregation were to vanish, belief in the harm and benefit thesis by educators, social scientists, and civil rights groups would create powerful pressures for school desegregation.

Legal scholars have debated whether the Supreme Court adopted a version of the harm and benefit thesis in the original *Brown* decision, and this debate has been the source of much discussion and misunderstanding. Although some Supreme Court justices and some lower courts invoked various forms of the harm and benefit thesis in the past, it has not been cited explicitly in any Supreme Court decisions after *Brown* (which is not to say it had no role in decision-making for individual justices). Regardless of its role in Supreme Court doctrine, the mention of psychological harm in the *Brown* decision, coupled with strong ideological and scientific endorsements, transformed this thesis into a powerful force in the desegregation movement. Aside from its role in legislative initiatives, the harm and benefit thesis is still invoked by plaintiffs in lower federal court hearings (e.g., for obtaining unitary status), and it has been raised as the central premise in the Hartford desegregation case that is being pursued under the Connecticut state constitution.

In its broadest form, the thesis has two components. The first component holds that segregated schools harm the education and academic achievement of minority children, in part by reinforcing negative racial stereotypes and damaging personal self-esteem. The second component is a reasonable corollary to the first: Desegregation benefits the self-esteem, academic achievement, and long-term educational and occupational outcomes for minority children while improving race relations for everyone. According to social science theory, the harm and benefit thesis applies regardless of the cause of the segregation—whether the segregation was due to state action—and therefore it applies to all school systems with racially imbalanced or isolated schools, not just those covered by the legal doctrine of *Brown*.

Chapter 2 reviews evidence on both components. Considerable social science research exists on the social, psychological, and educational differences of students who attend segregated versus desegregated schools, and some of this research allows inferences about whether desegregated schools can improve educational outcomes for minority students. The most widely studied educational outcome is academic achievement, as measured by standardized reading and mathematics tests. The academic evidence reviewed includes both national assessments, such as the National Assessment of Educational Progress (NAEP), and case studies of academic achievement in a number of school districts undergoing desegregation.

Research on other social and psychological outcomes is also reviewed. A major subcomponent of the harm and benefit thesis is "contact theory," which postulates that interracial contact—under the right conditions—improves race relations and the self-esteem of minority children. As applied to school settings, contact theory implies that school segregation promotes racial ignorance, stereotypes, and bigotry and that under the right conditions school desegregation can improve interracial understanding and reduce racial prejudice. Although race relations goals have not been prominent in the development of desegregation law, contact theory is usually cited by social scientists and civil rights groups, as well as many other citizens, who support school desegregation policies. A number of social science studies have examined the effects of desegregation on self-esteem, racial attitudes, and race relations. Although such characteristics are important outcomes in their own right, they may also be important as mechanisms that can affect academic achievement.

Some social scientists have suggested that long-term outcomes like college attendance, employment status, and income are more important than short-term outcomes like self-esteem or achievement test scores. A few studies have also assessed the impact of desegregation on these longer-term outcomes, and they are reviewed as well. Unfortunately, much less information on long-term outcomes is available.

At the time of *Brown*, the harm and benefit thesis enjoyed almost unanimous support from the social science community. In more recent years the thesis has been challenged by a number of social science studies, and many of its stronger assumptions—especially the impact of desegregation on academic achievement—have been subjected to intense scrutiny. Although the harm and benefit thesis may have a diminished role in the federal courts, it is still the single most important rationale for proponents of desegregation policies and opponents of increased school choice. The outcome of the debate over the harm and benefit thesis will therefore influence the future course of school desegregation, especially after legal necessity has expired, as well as contribute to the debate over school choice.

Housing Segregation and School Desegregation

Another rationale for school desegregation policies is to overcome school segregation caused by residential patterns. With the exception of the former dual
school systems in the South, most school districts have historically employed a
neighborhood school policy, whereby students are assigned to school on a geographic basis according to where they live. Given the housing segregation in
most communities, a neighborhood school policy in larger school districts usually leads to segregated schools. If housing segregation is caused mainly by a
combination of public and private discrimination, as maintained by many social
scientists and civil rights advocates, then a neighborhood school policy becomes
a vehicle for translating one form of discrimination into another, thereby challenging the legitimacy of neighborhood schools.

From a legal standpoint, housing segregation has played a complex and
changing role in the evolution of school desegregation law over the past twenty
years. Several different and conflicting legal doctrines have been embraced by
the federal courts over this period, especially in the lower courts, and its proper
role in school desegregation law is still debated by legal scholars today. Significantly, the issue of housing segregation has been a major topic in the two most
recent desegregation decisions by the Supreme Court in the Oklahoma City and
DeKalb County cases.

In the years leading up to the 1971 *Swann* decision, many lower courts found
that segregated schools and other government policies had contributed significantly to housing segregation, thereby rendering neighborhood school zones—
the most common method for assigning students to schools—suspect as a
racially neutral policy for student assignment. Some of these lower courts declared neighborhood school policies unconstitutional. The Supreme Court did
not embrace this model, however, and it has never permitted the use of housing
segregation as the sole basis for a school desegregation remedy. Still, by endors-
ing racial balance and mandatory busing in *Swann,* the Supreme Court in effect
held that a neighborhood school policy could not be used in a former dual school
system if it perpetuated segregated schools.

The issue of housing segregation and its relationship to school segregation has
been most prominent in interdistrict or metropolitan cases, where lawsuits have
sought to consolidate city and suburban school districts to foster school desegregation. Social science research on the causes of housing segregation has been
heavily involved in these cases, with expert testimony playing a significant role.

In its first major decision in an interdistrict case, which involved the Detroit
and its suburbs, the Supreme Court held in 1974 (*Milliken I*) that an interdistrict
desegregation remedy can be adopted only if government actions, including
those that promote housing segregation, are a major cause of the school segregation between a city and its suburbs. That allegation was not proven in Detroit,
and government-induced housing segregation has not been the sole basis for an
interdistrict remedy in any other metropolitan case. In more recent decisions,
the Supreme Court has emphasized that school boards should not be held
accountable for housing patterns or demographic changes not caused by school

board actions. It has also clearly stated that neighborhood school policies are not unconstitutional simply because they reflect segregated housing patterns.

Although the role of housing segregation in a school desegregation case may be settled in the federal courts, the battle is far from over. Civil rights groups have recently challenged metropolitan school segregation in the state courts, with Hartford, Connecticut, being the first test case. If housing segregation is caused primarily by a combination of public and private discrimination—such as location of public housing, "steering" by real estate agents, landlord refusals to rent—then a state court or other agency might find it reasonable to overcome the effects of housing segregation by ordering an interdistrict busing plan. By contrast, if housing segregation is caused primarily by a combination of non-discriminatory factors such as economics differences, convenience, and personal preference, then it might be hard for a state court to order an interdistrict desegregation plan.

Chapter 3 discusses the relationship between housing segregation and school desegregation from both legal and social science perspectives. Considerable social science research has been conducted on the causes of housing segregation, and it is now possible to estimate the relative contributions of both discriminatory and nondiscriminatory actions and policies to residential segregation. Some of this research has been conducted in connection with desegregation litigation and has been cited in court decisions. A resolution to the debate over the causes of housing discrimination could have a significant impact on future interdistrict desegregation policies and lawsuits.

Desegregation Remedies

If a school board has intentionally caused or contributed to school segregation, according to federal laws, the board or a court must devise an effective remedy consistent with the scope of the federal violation. In some cases, new remedies must be fashioned if earlier desegregation plans were not effective or if vestiges of a former segregated system still remain. In other cases, a school board may simply desire a desegregation policy for educational purposes. The question then becomes what type of desegregation plans or techniques are feasible, effective, and permissible.

The first challenge in designing a desegregation plan is to define *desegregation*. The options are somewhat more limited for a court-ordered plan than for a board-initiated plan, but even in federal case law no single standard defines a desegregated school. The most common formulas refer to some form of racial balance, which means comparing each school to the systemwide racial composition, with each school falling within some allowable range of the system racial makeup.

The second question is the selection of specific desegregation techniques. Desegregation plans can include a number of options, but in general each technique can be classified as a mandatory technique or a choice technique. The most common mandatory techniques are pairing, satellite or pocket zoning, and contiguous rezoning. The most common choice techniques are magnet schools and voluntary integrative transfers. A more recent type of plan, "controlled choice," combines both mandatory and voluntary elements. There has been much debate within both legal and social science circles as to the appropriateness and relative effectiveness of mandatory versus choice methods.

Without question, the most controversial issue in school desegregation policy has been the use of mandatory busing, promulgated by the Supreme Court's 1971 decision in *Swann*. This decision was a critical turning point in the evolution of school desegregation law, when the court finally abandoned race-neutral remedies and endorsed race-conscious standards for attaining school desegregation. The driving principle for remedy became racial balance, in which each school reflected the total district composition—usually within a narrow range. In effect, a racial balance formula is a type of racial quota for the assignment of students to schools. Given the existence of housing segregation in most larger school districts, racial balance could be attained only by abandoning neighborhood schools and using mandatory busing to attain the prescribed quotas. After the *Swann* decision, many thousands of parents in dozens of school districts came to realize they no longer had a right to attend their neighborhood school.

The federal courts, with the endorsement of many social scientists, believed that mandatory busing was the only feasible way to desegregate schools in larger districts. Little weight was given to community protests over the loss of neighborhood schools or to the possibility that this opposition could lead to white and middle-class flight from school districts. White flight was discounted by early courts because of the widespread belief that it was a manifestation of racist attitudes—part of the very problem needing remedy.

Accordingly, during the 1970s, racial balance and mandatory busing became the dominant theme of court-ordered desegregation; indeed, even today mandatory busing techniques still predominate in school systems that maintain desegregation plans. Although controlled choice techniques have begun to replace more traditional mandatory pairing or satellite zoning, in larger districts controlled choice can lead to considerable mandatory busing and hence remains a controversial desegregation technique.

The issue of white flight generated much controversy among social scientists, and numerous studies were undertaken to determine its causes, its magnitude, and its consequences for the long-term effectiveness of a desegregation plan. Although mandatory busing clearly produced a high degree of short-term racial balance within districts where it was adopted, there was concern that white flight over the longer run could accelerate demographic changes and ultimately increase the segregation between central cities and their suburbs or between public and private school systems.

Social science research has not only examined the extent of white flight but also evaluated the causes of white flight and the effectiveness of mandatory versus voluntary plans, particularly the use of magnet schools to attract white students to predominantly minority schools. Studies have also surveyed parents to determine attitudes toward various desegregation remedies, the reasons for support or opposition, and estimated participation (or nonparticipation) rates.

Some of this research revealed that, under certain conditions, a choice plan can lead to greater desegregation over the long run than a mandatory busing plan.

Expert studies and testimony by social scientists on the effectiveness and white flight problems became commonplace in desegregation cases during the late 1970s, and by the early 1980s this evidence began to shift judicial opinion about the appropriate role of white flight in designing a desegregation plan. Although mandatory busing has lost some favor in the lower courts because of the white flight problem, it is still the most commonly used technique for school desegregation. In part because of concerns about white flight, some courts have turned to the newer methods of controlled choice, although these techniques do involve mandatory busing in a somewhat different form. The Supreme Court, however, has still not modified the dictates of *Swann* for attaining desegregation or commented on the appropriateness of mandatory versus choice plans.

Chapter 4 discusses the general problem of desegregation remedies and their effectiveness from both legal and social science perspectives. The evolution of case law regarding definitions, desegregation techniques, and the white flight problem is traced, showing the role (or lack of role) for social science evidence on these topics. Social science findings are presented on such topics as general attitudes toward desegregation, support for or opposition to various desegregation techniques, white flight and its causes, and the effectiveness of alternative desegregation plans.

While the introduction of social science evidence on effectiveness has influenced court decisions in a number of school desegregation cases, many other school systems adopted desegregation remedies before this evidence was available and disseminated. For these systems, as well as those school systems planning a desegregation policy for the first time, the evidence on the effectiveness and consequences of different desegregation techniques should inform decision-makers about the type of desegregation plan most likely to work under their conditions.

The Future of School Desegregation and Choice

The evolution of desegregation law and the accumulation of social science knowledge reviewed in chapters 1 to 4 offer a number of insights and lessons learned about desegregation policies that can inform future policy-making in this area. Some of these observations also apply to the school choice debate, particularly certain legal issues and the educational impact of school choice on minority students. The objective of chapter 5 is to suggest future directions in desegregation and choice policies that meet legal requirements, that are consistent with current social science knowledge, and that maximize those goals in common to both policies, namely, those that enhance the quality of education.

From the standpoint of individual school districts, the future of school desegregation policy depends initially on several legal conditions. Although new federal school cases are becoming less common, hundreds of school systems throughout the country currently operate under a federal court–ordered deseg-regation plan. The school boards running these systems face at least two ques-tions: First, should they seek unitary status in order to have the court order dismissed, particularly if mandatory busing is involved? If this quest is success-ful, a school district can usually eliminate or reduce mandatory busing, given that the change is done for educational purposes. In most communities this move would be popular, although some school boards see a downside to losing the "protection" of a court order, under which unpopular policy decisions can be blamed on the court.

Second, if unitary status is not possible or desirable, should a desegregation plan be modified? Changing a desegregation plan may be necessary before unitary status can be pursued, especially if any "vestiges" of the former dual school system remain. In some cases a school district may wish to modify a plan because of cost or political considerations, without necessarily terminating the court order. One of the more common changes is to convert a mandatory plan to a voluntary or choice plan of some type, usually for reasons of community support or perceived educational benefits. Such changes have been approved by federal courts in several instances.

School systems not subject to desegregation orders have considerably more latitude to design school desegregation or choice programs, although they must take care not to instigate litigation by adopting policies that create a new consti-tutional violation. A violation of the Fourteenth Amendment for school systems depends on both the purpose of a policy as well as its effects. If the principal purpose of a policy is to enhance education, rather than to cause segregation, its consequences for racial balance might well be ignored. Because discrimina-tory purpose is usually problematic in the courts, however, any new policy that adversely affects the racial composition of schools always carries some risk.

For school boards that are contemplating a desegregation plan for the first time or trying to decide whether to seek unitary status, the uppermost ques-tions for a board and a community are educational quality and racial equity. In other words, a school board has to evaluate the validity of the harm and benefit thesis, along with other considerations such as cost. Does desegregation en-hance social and academic outcomes? Do positive effects depend upon the type of plan, such as whether it is mandatory or voluntary? What is the cost—both financial and political—of a desegregation plan compared to alternative strate-gies for improving educational quality, especially for minorities? If a desegrega-tion policy is being considered for educational reasons rather than legal neces-sity, then clearly decisions about the type of desegregation plan—or whether there should be a plan at all—depend on how the benefit and cost questions are answered.

The connections between desegregation and choice policies may not be im-mediately apparent. Although their overall purpose is similar—to improve the quality of education—and they both focus on how students are assigned to schools, their assumptions about educational quality and their approach to stu-dent assignment are dissimilar if not antithetical. Proponents of the new school choice movement seek to improve educational quality through maximizing school choice at all levels and without constraints: within a public school system, between different public school systems, and between both public and private schools. This policy could lead to an increase in school segregation unless certain precautions are undertaken. Several states have passed school choice laws that expand interdistrict public school choice, Wisconsin has established a private school choice program for minority students in Milwaukee, and comprehensive school choice proposals (including vouchers for private and parochial schools) are on the ballots in several states.

Proponents of school desegregation, in its traditional mandatory forms, believe that educational quality is promoted through racial balance and mandatory busing, which usually restrict the choice of schools. On the one hand, the restriction applies most clearly to middle-class parents, who view neighborhood schools as schools of choice because they can afford to choose their neighborhood of residence. On the other hand, mandatory desegregation plans have been more popular among low-income minority parents because the plans provide increased access to desirable schools in neighborhoods they could not afford.

Clearly, both points of view cannot be true. A common ground for both school desegregation and school choice has been developing, however, in the recent emergence of voluntary desegregation programs, where a combination of incentives (e.g., magnet schools) and choice are the main vehicles for desegregating a school district. Indeed, some of the most successful intradistrict and interdistrict choice programs in operation today were designed for the purpose of school desegregation, and federal courts and agencies have been increasingly willing to allow choice options in place of mandatory busing techniques. A new type of desegregation plan—"controlled choice"—tries to combine both racial balance and choice concepts in order to promote high quality, equity, and desegregation, although it still contains some mandatory busing.

Like debates over school desegregation policy, the debate over school choice also raises its own version of the harm and benefit thesis. Does school choice enhance educational outcomes by allowing parents or students to choose among a number of public or private schools? Can benefits for choice students be realized without harming the students who do not choose and who are left behind in their existing schools, which might become increasingly segregated? Can a choice policy be configured that benefits minority students as well as nonminority students?

Of course, desegregation and choice policies may have other benefits not directly related to the kinds of educational outcomes that can be readily assessed and evaluated. The advocates of both of these policies generally lay claim to direct educational benefits, however, as indeed they must if they hope to mobilize support for these policies and foster the participation of parents and students. If neither choice nor desegregation policies *by themselves* offer clear educational benefits to the affected students, school boards or legislatures have less reason to adopt such policies in view of their potential costs, monetary and otherwise.

Then again, if a particular type of desegregation or choice policy allows parents or students to select an enhanced or improved school program, or at least a school that is objectively better than their current assigned school, then educational benefits might be more likely. The important question of educational benefits and costs needs much greater emphasis in the public dialogues about both desegregation and choice policies.

1

Desegregation Policy and the Law

Between the landmark *Brown v. Board of Education* decision in 1954 and Supreme Court decisions in 1991 and 1992, civil rights laws and policies, especially those affecting schools, have undergone dramatic transformations and fluctuations.[1] After the elegantly straightforward but unprecedented principles propounded in *Brown*, which have not been seriously challenged in their application to schools, the Court entered what might be called the conceptual swamp of remedy.

In a series of major school desegregation decisions during the 1970s, the Supreme Court grappled with a host of complex legal issues involving the definition of desegregation, the nature of remedies, the obligations of school districts, and the remedial powers of the lower courts. The period was marked by divided Supreme Court panels; conflict among numerous lower courts; intense debate among political groups, legal scholars, and social scientists; and heated controversy—and sometimes violence—in affected communities. These battles and disputes were not over the basic principles of *Brown* but over how school segregation should be remedied. In view of the difficult and often emotional questions involved, it is not surprising that the evolution of school desegregation law has followed a tortuous and convoluted path.

Given the basic constitutional principle of nonracial classifications promulgated by *Brown* and related cases, there was little indication that the principle would be turned on its head in 1968 by *Green v. New Kent County* and the concept of affirmative integration and, even more explicitly, by the 1971 decision in *Swann v. Charlotte-Mecklenburg Board of Education*, which fostered policies of racial balance and racial quotas—in effect, a race-conscious policy of forced integration.[2] In 1973 many people were surprised, if not shocked, when the Supreme Court applied the *Swann* concepts of mandatory busing and racial balance to northern school systems, most of which never had the state-mandated "dual" school systems of the South (*Keyes v. Denver*).[3] Then, when mandatory busing appeared likely to become commonplace and permanent throughout the country, the 1974 decision in *Milliken v. Bradley* severely restricted remedies by excluding the white suburbs surrounding the predominantly black Detroit schools.[4] This ruling was followed two years later by the *Spangler v. Pasadena* decision, which freed districts from the obligation to

17

maintain racial balance in perpetuity.[5] Finally, following a ten-year period of mainly circuit court action, the 1991 decision in *Dowell v. Oklahoma City* brought desegregation doctrine full circle by allowing a school district, once desegregated, to return to neighborhood schools and the inevitable resegregation caused by segregated housing patterns.[6]

This evolutionary sequence requires some explaining. Although probably no single set of consistent legal principles can account for all these judicial swings over the past thirty-five years, there is more constitutional logic behind these events than meets the eye. Some of the doctrinal shifts do, indeed, reflect differing philosophical orientations of new justices on the Court, although not as much as some critics of the Court have argued. Most of the changes reflect a constant thread of basic constitutional principles coupled with increasing knowledge about the causes and effects of segregation and desegregation, some of which has accumulated because of the very Court actions at issue.

Although saying that social science research has been the deciding factor in any one of the major decisions by the Supreme Court would be an exaggeration, I argue and document here that the evidence generated during three decades of school desegregation experience and research has had a cumulative impact on lower and higher court decisions as well as on the formulation of government desegregation policies in general.

The *Brown* Decision and the Civil Rights Act

The Fourteenth Amendment, which commands, "No State shall . . . deny to any person within its jurisdiction the equal protection of the laws," became part of the U.S. Constitution in 1868, not long after the Civil War. Its purpose was widely viewed as barring state laws that could disadvantage black citizens after the abolition of slavery. Shortly thereafter, the Supreme Court began interpreting the Fourteenth Amendment as prohibiting state-imposed discrimination against racial minorities in regard to political and property rights.[7]

During this early period, the Supreme Court did not view state-imposed segregation in public facilities (including schools) as a form of racial discrimination prohibited by the Fourteenth Amendment. This interpretation was formalized in the "separate but equal" doctrine articulated in *Plessy v. Ferguson*, an 1896 decision upholding a Louisiana law requiring separate railway cars for black and white passengers.[8] The Supreme Court stated that the Fourteenth Amendment was designed to create equality under the law, not to "abolish distinctions based on color, or to enforce social, as distinguished from political, equality" or to abolish "separate schools for children of different ages, sexes, and colors." Rejecting the argument that enforced separation stamps the black race with a "badge of inferiority," the Court said that such a view arises "solely because the colored race chooses to put that construction upon it."[9]

The test then became whether state-imposed segregation in various public facilities and services was or was not equal in tangible respects. As long as the public facilities and services provided were equal for all citizens, even though separated by race, then no constitutional violation arose. This doctrine governed segregation and discrimination lawsuits in education for nearly fifty years.

Public education was not commonplace when the *Plessy* doctrine was adopted, and not until nearly 1920 had compulsory education laws had been enacted by all states. Even then, the compulsory attendance period under such laws was brief, and during the first half of the century most persons of both races left school before receiving a high school diploma. Hence, the issue of segregated education was a less salient issue until at least World War II.

The change of doctrine in *Brown* was presaged by two 1949 Supreme Court decisions involving admission and treatment of black students in graduate schools, *Sweatt v. Painter* and *McLaurin v. Oklahoma State Regents*.[10] Both decisions ruled against segregation policies involving less tangible but no less important aspects of education. In *Sweatt* the Court declared that denying admission of a black student to a white law school violated the equal protection provision because the black student could not achieve an equal education without the opportunity to commingle with and experience the same education as his future peers (there was no separate law school for blacks in Oklahoma). The same principle was articulated in *McLaurin,* in which the Court held that separating a black graduate student from white peers in classrooms and other facilities impaired his ability "to study, to engage in discussions and exchange views with other students, and, in general, to learn his profession."[11] These two decisions clearly undermined the separate but equal doctrine as applied to public elementary and secondary schools.

Just five years later the Court, in *Brown v. Board of Education,* finally confronted the question of whether state-imposed segregation of public schools constitutes discrimination against black students, even if equal in all tangible respects. The *Brown* decision was actually a consolidation of four separate cases, including the school districts of Topeka, Kansas; Clarenden County, South Carolina; Prince Edward County, Virginia; and New Castle County, Delaware.[12] The *Plessy* doctrine was overruled in *Brown* with the following declaration:

> To separate [black children] from others of similar age and qualifications solely because of their race generates a feeling of inferiority as to their status in the community that may affect their hearts and minds in a way unlikely to ever be undone. . . . We conclude that in the field of public education the doctrine of "separate but equal" has no place. Separate educational facilities are inherently unequal. (347 U.S. at 494–495)

With these brief, eloquent words, the *Brown* decision overturned more than fifty years of Court precedent and set in motion one of the most controversial judicial interventions into local government affairs in U.S. history. Although the initial controversy over the decision was mainly in the South, whose state-sponsored segregation (so-called Jim Crow) laws were the main target of *Brown,* within fifteen years the controversy became nationwide as school desegregation law was applied to cities in the North that had no history of state laws that required segregated or "dual" school systems.

The *Brown* decision raised three interrelated questions that have generated intense debates among jurists, political groups, policy makers, and social scientists for nearly forty years. First, does the decision apply only to state-enforced or de jure segregation, or does it also encompass de facto segregation not brought about by state action of some type? Second, to what extent does the opinion rely on a finding of psychological harm, and does the harm finding apply only to state-enforced segregation or to any type of segregation regardless of cause? Third, what are the appropriate remedies for school systems found in violation of the *Brown* ruling, and should the nature of those remedies depend on the answers to the first two questions?

The history of the school desegregation controversy, whether in the courts, in the political arena, or in academia, is a history of shifting answers to these critical questions. To a large extent, the political and legal battles on civil rights issues are between those who take opposite sides on all three questions. On one side are those who believe that *Brown* applies only to de jure segregation, that whatever harm accrues to minorities stems only from official segregation, and that remedies should be constructed narrowly to eliminate only that segregation clearly traceable to state action. On the other side are those who believe that *Brown* should encompass all segregation, regardless of cause, because all segregation is harmful and that remedy for this harmful condition demands complete integration—usually defined as racial balance—in all schools and their staffs.

De Jure versus De Facto Segregation

During the first ten years or so after *Brown*, the distinction between de jure and de facto segregation was not a major issue. Until the late 1960s, nearly all desegregation cases arose in states that had required or permitted official school segregation as of 1954, most of which were in the South.[13] Indeed, courts did not even discuss the issue in this early period, and courts, legal scholars, government agencies, and even civil rights groups generally assumed that, whatever the desirability of dealing with de facto segregation, the *Brown* decision applied only to de jure or state-enforced racial segregation.

The distinction was reinforced in a far-reaching decision in 1966 by the Fifth Circuit Court of Appeals, *U.S. v. Jefferson County Board of Education*, which at that time was overseeing desegregation in the states of Texas, Louisiana, Mississippi, Alabama, Georgia, and Florida.[14] The decision dealt with the slow progress in school desegregation since the *Brown* decision and with the applicability of the U.S. Department of Health, Education, and Welfare (HEW) guidelines for desegregation deriving from the 1964 Civil Rights Act. Since the Civil Rights Act had defined school desegregation as excluding student assignment for "overcoming racial imbalance," the Fifth Circuit panel offered the interpretation that this phrase was not intended as a restriction on remedy but rather was intended to limit the law to de jure cases.

In later years, however, the de jure–de facto distinction and the related issue of discriminatory "intent" became a matter of considerable debate not only among political and policy groups but also within the Supreme Court itself. Ultimately, as discussed in more detail in a later section, the concept of de jure segregation was clarified in cases without explicit segregation laws to include two components of official action: a policy or action that *intends* to segregate by race (discriminatory intent) and that has a significant segregative *effect*.

The Psychological Harm Thesis

There has been much disagreement among legal scholars and social scientists on the issue of psychological harm in the *Brown* decision, regarding both the extent to which the decision depended on this conclusion and the adequacy of supporting evidence in the opinion. The supporting authority is cited in its famous "footnote 11," which listed a number of social science studies of the effects of segregation on children.

The psychological harm issue had been raised explicitly in testimony at the district court level, and a statement on this subject, signed by a group of social scientists, was submitted as part of the appeal briefs to the Supreme Court in the *Brown* case.[15] The Court was, of course, under no obligation to address this issue in its opinion.

Indeed, many legal scholars believe that a finding of psychological harm was not necessary for the opinion and that the adequacy of social science evidence cited is not an important consideration.[16] The best evidence in support of this view is actions of the Court over a ten-year period following *Brown*, during which it declared a myriad of segregation laws unconstitutional—affecting public beaches, golf courses, transportation, and parks—all without hearings, evidence about harmfulness, or written opinions.[17] Moreover, the most important of *Brown's* declarations—that separate facilities are *inherently* unequal—can be viewed as a prima facie declaration that does not require demonstration of harm or negative effects. Something that is inherently unequal by definition violates the equal protection clause of the Fourteenth Amendment.

Why, then, did the Court feel a need to state conclusions about psychological harm in the opinion? The harm finding was not merely a footnote; in addition to the previous statement, the Court went out of its way to quote and endorse a finding of the lower court in the Topeka case:

> Segregation of white and colored children in public schools has a detrimental effect upon the colored children. The impact is greater when it has the sanction of the law, for the policy of separating the races is usually interpreted as denoting the inferiority of the negro group. A sense of inferiority affects the motivation of a child to learn. Segregation with the sanction of law, therefore, has a tendency to [retard] the educational and mental development of negro children and to deprive them of some of the benefits they would receive in a racial[ly] integrated school system.[18]

This quote was followed by the statement, "Whatever may have been the extent of psychological knowledge at the time of *Plessy v. Ferguson*, this finding is amply supported by modern authority" (referenced by footnote 11).[19] Never before had a popular social science theory found its way into such a momentous decision by the Supreme Court. It should be noted here that the quote emphasizes "segregation with the sanction of law," thereby stressing the harms deriving from de jure rather than de facto segregation.

There are at least two reasons why the Court may have wanted to forge a link between segregation and harm. First, the Court was overturning a long-standing judicial standard of separate but equal, on which most southern states had based a great deal of legislation and custom. A majority of the Court may have felt the need to justify this abandonment of precedent, based in part on accumulated knowledge in the social sciences, to avoid the appearance of a sudden and capricious change in constitutional principles.

A second reason may be that most justices actually believed in the psychological harm thesis and were looking ahead to the difficult challenge of imposing remedies. It is one thing to declare a law null and void, and something else again to create desegregated schools. Justifing some of the massive and controversial remedies imposed in later years, especially mandatory busing, is easier if one believes that the policy is actually going to improve the self-concept, motivation, and intellectual development of disadvantaged black children.

Whatever the reason for its appearance in *Brown,* the psychological harm thesis has played a significant role in the evolution of desegregation law, both judicial and legislative. Numerous lower courts have heard testimony on the educational harms of segregation and the benefits (or lack thereof) of desegregation and have incorporated various versions of the harm thesis into their factual findings and decisions. The harm thesis has also been invoked by many civil rights groups and social scientists to justify and defend both comprehensive racial balance remedies and an extension of these remedies to de facto situations. Finally, the harm thesis has also played a role in governmental policy formulations, particularly the development of the Civil Rights Act and associated regulations.

The most prominent and probably the most influential appearance of the harm thesis in governmental deliberations was in a 1967 report of the U.S. Commission on Civil Rights, *Racial Isolation in the Public Schools.*

> The central truth which emerges from this report and from all of the Commission's investigations is simply this: Negro children suffer serious harm when their education takes place in public schools which are racially segregated, whatever the source of such segregation may be. . . . The conclusion drawn by the U.S. Supreme Court about the impact upon children of segregation compelled by law—that it "affects their hearts and minds in ways unlikely ever to be undone"—applies to segregation not compelled by law.[20]

The main thrust of this report was to invoke the harm thesis as justification for federal policies to end all school segregation, whether de facto or de jure.

The Supreme Court never again explicitly considered the psychological harms of segregation or the benefits of desegregation. In later Court decisions, both in school and other civil rights cases, the concept of de jure segregation evolved into a more general federal doctrine covering racial classifications and discriminatory actions (which is discussed in a subsequent section).

   The harm and benefit thesis remains, however, as a major issue in social science, educational policy, and legislative arenas (including some state courts). Given the general desire to improve the academic performance of minority groups, and given limited resources, a critical policy question becomes how to improve educational opportunities for disadvantaged students. Desegregation policies can be both costly and controversial, depending upon how a desegregated school is defined and the particular techniques used to attain desegregation (see chapter 4). Desegregation clearly becomes a more or less desirable option depending on its potential to improve minority education in an effective and feasible manner when compared to other reforms, such as compensatory education.

Early Remedies: *Brown II*

The original controversy over *Brown* in the South and the broader controversy when *Brown* was applied to school segregation in the North would not have been so severe or so long-lasting but for the adoption of such controversial desegregation remedies as racial balance and the mandatory busing needed to attain it in larger school districts. There are few hints in *Brown* of the types of remedies that would be imposed fifteen years later.

   The first Supreme Court decision on school desegregation remedy, known as *Brown II*, was issued one year after the original decision.[21] It was surprisingly short and remarkably free of detail, a circumstance seen by some legal scholars as contributing to the delay, confusion, and controversy over remedy that characterized the next fifteen years.[22] One reason for the brevity may have been a lack of consensus among the justices about just how far remedy should go. Another reason appears to have been to give local courts maximum flexibility in responding to local situations. A key proviso in the decision was to delegate remedy to local courts, on the grounds that they were best suited for solving "varied local school problems. . . . because of their proximity to local conditions."[23]

   The only information on remedy offered in *Brown II* was very general and lacked specific definitions and guidelines. The sketchy remedial guidance can be summarized as follows:

   1. The guiding principle will be equity, but public disagreement is not a consideration.[24]
   2. Students must be admitted "to public schools as soon as practicable on a nondiscriminatory basis."
   3. Remedies can deal with administration, physical facilities, transportation, personnel, and "revision of school districts and attendance areas into compact units to achieve a system of determining admission to the public schools on a nonracial basis."
   4. The court will evaluate the adequacy of a school board's plan "to effectuate a transition to a racially nondiscriminatory school system."
   5. "During this period of transition, the courts will retain jurisdiction of these cases."[25]

The only definition of desegregation is found in the phrases "admission . . . on a nondiscriminatory [or nonracial] basis" and "transition . . . to a racially nondiscriminatory school system." The repeated use of the term *non-discriminatory* was not very helpful, for this term is merely the opposite of discrimination, which was state-enforced separation. The only other information about student assignment policies occurs in the statement about revising "attendance areas into compact units," which could be taken to mean some form of geographic or neighborhood zoning.

Given this guidance, it is not surprising that for the next ten years the dominant form of remedy, for those states and school districts that attempted to comply with these rulings, was to nullify laws and practices that mandated separate schools and to employ various "nonracial" policies for assigning students to schools. The two most common desegregation techniques during this period were geographic zoning and "freedom of choice." Under freedom of choice, students or parents could theoretically select any school to attend, subject only to capacity constraints.

Justifications for the freedom of choice policies were found in numerous lower court decisions following the remand order of *Brown*. Perhaps the most influential of these was *Briggs v. Elliott*, a 1955 district court decision affecting Clarendon County, South Carolina (one of the companion cases in *Brown*). The district court interpreted *Brown II* as simply forbidding the state from enforcing separation and requiring only that children be allowed to attend any school they wished:

> It is important that we point out exactly what the Supreme Court has decided and what it has not decided. . . . It has not decided that the states must mix persons of different races in the schools or must require them to attend schools or must deprive them of the right of choosing the schools they attend. What it has decided . . . is that a state may not deny to any person on account of race the right to attend any school that it maintains . . . if the schools which it maintains are open to children of all races, no violation of the Constitution is involved even though the children of different races voluntarily attend different schools. . . . The Constitution, in other words, does not require integration. It merely forbids discrimination. [26]

This statement is one of the earliest and strongest expressions of the judicial doctrine that segregation arising from voluntary actions of individuals is not prohibited by the Constitution. The *Briggs* decision was not appealed, and for many years it was cited by lower courts in the South as a reasonable interpretation of *Brown* and *Brown II*.

Although at first glance, freedom of choice appears to be a race-neutral policy of student assignment, it was more often used to preserve racially separate schools than to promote integration. Given the residential dispersion of black communities in many parts of the South, particularly in smaller cities and in rural areas, geographic attendance zones were uncommon, and students were frequently bused some distance in order to attend designated black and white schools. In such cases a geographic or "neighborhood" assignment method would have produced considerable desegregation. Many of these school districts refused to draw attendance zones, however, and instead opted for freedom of choice, which allowed students to attend their existing segregated schools. As a result, some white schools gained small numbers of black students, but virtually no white students enrolled in black schools.

The major problem of remedy in these early years, however, went beyond freedom of choice or the failure to adopt geographic zoning policies. Rather, it was the outright rejection of any type of school integration policy throughout the South, particularly in the Deep South states of Louisiana, Alabama, Mississippi, and Georgia. Many states passed laws to thwart virtually all school integration, including freedom of choice policies, either by closing public schools or by setting up rigid eligibility requirements for blacks who wanted to attend white schools, such as requiring approval by a state agency. In one famous case, Governor Faubus of Arkansas called out the National Guard to prevent black students from entering a Little Rock high school. In most of these states, even freedom of choice was rejected as a legitimate and reasonable policy for desegregation.

If the Deep South had embraced policies of geographic zoning and some integrative forms of school choice rather than resisting all methods for school integration, the history of school desegregation might have taken a different course. Unfortunately, that did not happen, and partly as a result of this resistance, lower courts and the Supreme Court eventually moved on to stronger forms of remedy.

Government Actions: The Civil Rights Act of 1964

Generally speaking, little or no local or federal legislative activity promoted school desegregation in the years immediately following the *Brown* decision, and most legislative efforts in the South were designed to frustrate and obstruct school desegregation. Legislatures at that time were content to let the federal courts take the lead as well as the heat in school desegregation efforts.

The general political climate changed in the late 1950s and early 1960s, with a growing grassroots civil rights movement that promoted sit-ins, boycotts, and demonstrations to protest continuing segregation policies. President Eisenhower sent federal troops in 1957 to prevent violence during the desegregation of Central High School in Little Rock, President Kennedy dispatched military troops to protect James Meredith's entrance into the University of Mississippi, Governor Wallace tried personally and unsuccessfully to block integration of the University of Alabama, and there were mass demonstrations in Birmingham, Alabama, against segregation of public facilities. The strength and depth of the civil rights movement were illustrated in the dramatic 1963 March on Washington, during which 250,000 demonstrators heard the Reverend Dr. Martin Luther King, Jr., deliver his stirring "I have a dream" speech.

The civil rights movement was met with increasingly violent white responses, both official and unofficial, especially in the Deep South. This violence included the killing of Mississippi civil rights leader Medgar Evers; the bombing of a black church in Birmingham, Alabama, that killed four Sunday school students; and the murders of three civil rights activists in Mississippi.

Prodded by the growing political strength and legitimacy of the civil rights movement, the U.S. Congress passed its first major law on racial segregation and discrimination, the Civil Rights Act of 1964. Two titles dealt with schools. Title IV authorized the secretary of Health, Education, and Welfare (HEW) to render technical assistance in the preparation and implementation of school desegregation plans. Desegregation was defined as "assignment of students to public schools . . . without regard to race . . . but . . . shall not mean the assignment of students to public schools in order to overcome racial imbalance." Title IV also authorized the attorney general to initiate class-action lawsuits following legitimate complaints of racial discrimination by parents or individuals, but excluded orders for "achieving a racial balance by requiring the transportation of . . . students from one school to another." Title VI states simply that "no person in the United States shall, on the ground of race, color, or national origin, be excluded from participation in, be denied the benefits of, or be subjected to discrimination under any program or activity receiving Federal financial assistance." The law empowered the secretary of HEW to deny federal funds to any school district found in violation of Title VI after appropriate complaints, investigations, and hearings.

Although the majority of subsequent school desegregation actions were still handled by the courts, the passage of the Civil Rights Act added another weapon to the arsenal of civil rights groups in the war over remedies. This weapon was strengthened with the preparation of specific HEW guidelines for school desegregation remedies in 1965. Using the new HEW guidelines, courts were able to rely on specific federal standards for desegregation rather than the rather ambiguous remedial provisions of *Brown II*. Indeed, the Court of Appeals for the Fifth Circuit did just that in a 1966 decision affecting school districts in Alabama, Louisiana, and Mississippi.[27] The appellate court ordered implementation of HEW guidelines, which established timetables, policies for school choice and geographic student assignment, equalization of facilities and programs, and integration of faculties and staff. Significantly, the student assignment guidelines were aimed at removing state-imposed restrictions limiting choice and moving to a true freedom of choice policy for all students. Those not choosing a school were to be assigned to the school nearest their homes, in other words, their neighborhood school. The concepts of racial balance and mandatory busing were not raised in these early guidelines.

The Evolution of Remedy from *Green* to *Keyes*

In spite of growing debates and controversy over school desegregation remedies, the Supreme Court had surprisingly little to say about specific remedy issues between 1955 and 1968, particularly regarding student assignment to schools. Most Supreme Court decisions during this period dealt with speeding up the process, perhaps implying but not explicitly stating how to do so.[28] Only one case during this period dealt with student assignment, which invalidated a student transfer policy that allowed transfers among schools that increased segregation.[29] In another case the Supreme Court approved an Alabama pupil placement law that was designed to limit freedom of choice; it set up criteria, such as achievement tests, for admission of black students to white schools.[30] The Court seemed determined to follow its original decision in *Brown II* to leave remedy entirely in the hands of local courts.

Given the lack of specific guidance as to appropriate remedies, many lower courts defined remedies in the narrowest possible terms. Delays were granted and plans were approved that amounted to only token desegregation. Throughout the Deep South, black and white students were still assigned to their original separate black and white schools, and the faculties of those schools were still white schools and the faculties of those schools were still all black or all white. Neither geographic zoning nor meaningful choice plans were the order of the day.

In defense of these lower court actions, throughout this period opinion was deeply divided as to the meaning of remedy ordered by *Brown II*, which, significantly, had not used the term *desegregation*. At one end was the view of *Briggs*, which interpreted *Brown II* as requiring only the abolition of compulsory segregation laws and adoption of freedom of choice; at the other end was the view of the Fifth Circuit Court of Appeals cited previously, which explicitly criticized *Briggs*, decried the tokenism of plans to date, and adopted the HEW guidelines as a court-ordered remedy. Even the Fifth Circuit Court of Appeals stopped short of anything approaching racial balance and mandatory busing policies.

The confusion and disagreements were sustained by the Supreme Court's silence on various lower court actions, such as the *Briggs* interpretation of *Brown II*, and indeed by its few affirmative decisions, such as approving the Alabama pupil placement law. It was as though the Supreme Court was avoiding involvement in these very complex and contentious issues, hoping that they would somehow be worked out to everyone's satisfaction in the lower courts.

The Supreme Court's silence finally ended with a series of decisions between 1968 and 1973 that completely changed the landscape of desegregation law and ordered new definitions of both liability and remedy under the Fourteenth Amendment. These decisions formulated the rule of affirmative integration, equated that integration with racial balance, replaced neighborhood school policies with mandatory busing, and effectively extended these novel remedies to northern school segregation, much of which arose from residential patterns.

Green and Affirmative Duty

The first change in Supreme Court doctrine on school desegregation occurred in 1968 with the *Green* decision involving a small school district in Virginia.[31] New Kent County had only two schools, a kindergarten through twelfth grade (K–12) school designated for blacks on the west side of the county and a K–12 school designated for whites on the east side. Both blacks and whites were dispersed throughout the county and most had to ride buses to their respective schools—a form of mandatory busing to maintain segregation. For ten years after *Brown*, no changes had been made in New Kent County's dual school assignment policy, in part because of a Virginia pupil placement law, adopted after *Brown*, that required students to petition a state board to change schools. No students had done so, and each school remained all white or all black until 1964.

In 1965, after the lawsuit had been initiated and in order to remain eligible for federal aid under the Civil Rights Act, the school board finally adopted a freedom of choice plan but not geographic attendance zones, which would have desegregated its two schools. By 1967, 15 percent of black students had chosen the white school, but no whites had chosen the black school.

The strongly worded unanimous decision, written by Justice Brennan, reflects a Court that had tired of the active resistance to desegregation by many southern school districts. The thrust of the opinion is an interpretation of the obligations imposed by *Brown II*, although very little of the specific *Green* directions can be found in that earlier decision:

> School boards . . . operating state-compelled dual systems were nevertheless clearly charged [by *Brown II*] with the affirmative duty to take whatever steps might be necessary to convert to a unitary system in which racial discrimination would be eliminated root and branch . . . it is relevant that this first step [of freedom of choice] did not come until some . . . 10 years after *Brown II* directed the making of a "prompt and reasonable start." This deliberate perpetuation of the unconstitutional dual system can only have compounded the harm of such a system. Such delays are no longer tolerable. . . . Moreover, a plan that at this late date fails to provide meaningful assurance of prompt and effective disestablishment of a dual system is also intolerable. . . . The Board must be required to formulate a new plan . . . which promises realistically to convert promptly to a system without a "white" school and a "Negro" school, but just schools.[32]

This is the first decision of the Supreme Court that declared an affirmative duty to desegregate and, more important, that defined desegregation not as ending compulsory separation but rather as the abolition of white and black schools. From this point on, desegregation plans would be judged by their effectiveness in eliminating formerly white and black schools; in other words, courts would have to apply a "results" test based on the racial composition of schools. The decision also reiterates the harm thesis of *Brown*, albeit only the brief passage quoted, as part of the justification for speeding up remedies.

Contrary to some views, the *Green* opinion did not find freedom of choice itself unconstitutional and, in fact, stated that it might be one option in a desegregation plan. But the Court also said such a policy had to be judged by its effectiveness and could not be the only device in the face of more effective alternatives. Moreover, the *Green* decision did not endorse the concept of racial balance and the technique of cross-district busing. In fact, the Court noted that desegregation could be attained in this small rural school district by straightforward geographic zoning. Adoption of freedom of choice rather than the common technique of geographic zones led the Court to conclude, in this instance, that freedom of choice was simply a means to perpetuate the dual school system.

Nevertheless, *Green* laid the foundation for stronger interventions by emphasizing effectiveness and elimination of "white" and "Negro" schools. While racially identifiable schools can be eliminated in smaller communities by simply changing neighborhood zone lines, the elimination of predominantly black or white schools is not so easily accomplished in larger school districts, especially when residential segregation exists. Even so, *Green* gave no indication that the effectiveness of plans and the elimination of black and white schools would be judged ultimately by attainment of equal racial ratios in each school.

Finally, the *Green* decision emphasized that desegregation remedies had to deal with all aspects of school operations and not just with student assignment. A complete remedy had to address such factors as hiring and assignment of faculty and staff assignment, equity of facilities, and nondiscrimination in transportation and extracurricular activities. These became the six "*Green* factors" that a school district had to address in its desegregation plan in order to attain "unitary" status.

Swann: Mandatory Busing for Racial Balance

The *Green* decision did not resolve all disagreements and confusion over remedy in the lower courts. While most lower courts by this time acknowledged that desegregation meant more than simply ending separate school assignment policies and that plans would be judged by their effectiveness in accomplishing integration, there was still a great deal of latitude regarding the actual type and degree of remedies.

With its 1971 *Swann* decision, involving the Charlotte–Mecklenburg County, North Carolina, school district, the Supreme Court finally put an end to the debate. If *Brown II* was notable for its ambiguity and lack of detail, *Swann* was exceptional for its clarity and specificity, which ended much of the legal confusion at that time. Unfortunately, it did nothing to quell the controversy over school desegregation; indeed, the controversy was exacerbated because of the unprecedented remedies it endorsed.

Charlotte–Mecklenburg was a large county school district with an enrollment of more than 80,000 students. There was substantial residential segregation; most of the black students lived in the city of Charlotte, and the suburban portions of Mecklenburg County were predominantly white. In 1965 the school board adopted a geographic zoning plan and a freedom of choice transfer provision that were approved by the Fourth Circuit Court of Appeals. Because of residential segregation, many schools remained predominantly black or white. In 1968 plaintiffs requested further relief in light of the *Green* decision. The local district court did so by ordering a massive cross-county busing plan to attain racial balance; in each school the racial composition would equal the systemwide ratio of black and white students.

The district court decision, which the Supreme Court eventually ratified, is especially instructive because it justified its sweeping remedy in part on findings and conclusions about several controversial factual issues being reviewed here: the causes of housing segregation, the harm thesis, and community opinion. Specifically, the district court found that:

1. Housing segregation "is the result of a varied group of elements of public and private action, all deriving their basic strength originally from public law or state or local governmental action."[33]
2. Students in black schools have lower scores on achievement tests than students in white schools, and these differences are "the tangible results of segregation."[34]
3. Evidence from public opinion polls and testimony that parents oppose busing should be excluded because it reflects political pressures.[35]

The findings on housing segregation, academic achievement, and community opposition (which raises the white flight issue) were common in many lower court opinions of this era. Although courts could have defended extensive mandatory busing without such findings, this formidable intervention is clearly easier to justify in an equity hearing if a court believes that housing segregation, like school segregation, is a product of state action; that continued school segregation is harming the academic achievement of black children; and that public opposition (and ultimately white flight) is not a legitimate issue in the balancing of interests.

The Supreme Court agreed to review the lower court decision after the Fourth Circuit Court of Appeals reversed that part of the plan calling for busing of elementary students on the grounds that it failed a "test of reasonableness."[36] Reviewing the history of desegregation actions since *Brown II*, the Court acknowledged the problems encountered to date, that "many difficulties were encountered in implementation. . . . Nothing in our national experience . . . prepared anyone for dealing with changes . . . of the magnitude and complexity encountered since then. Deliberate resistance of some to the Court's mandates has impeded the good-faith efforts of others to bring school systems into compliance."[37]

The Supreme Court also finally but somewhat grudgingly acknowledged that it was time to clarify remedy: "The problems encountered by the district courts and courts of appeals make plain that we should now try to amplify guidelines, however incomplete and imperfect, for the assistance of school authorities and courts."[38] The guidelines offered, however, were anything but incomplete, especially in light of the Supreme Court's tradition of dealing only with broad legal principles. The guidelines were also remarkable for the extent to which they called for a unprecedented judicial intervention into school operations and policies.

The guidelines touched on all areas of school operations where segregation must be remedied. In the areas of transportation, supporting staff, extracurricular activities, maintenance, and equipment, school authorities were ordered to "eliminate invidious racial distinctions" to "produce schools of like quality, facilities, and staffs"; for teacher assignment, each school was to have "a ratio of

white to Negro faculty members substantially the same throughout the system";
regarding school construction, school districts and the courts were to "see
to it that future school construction . . . do[es] not serve to perpetuate or reestablish the dual system."[39]

The longest and most important section of the decision is devoted to student
assignment, always the most controversial aspect of a school desegregation plan
and subject to much divided opinion in the lower courts. The Court addressed
the issues of racial balance, one-race schools, attendance zones, and transportation, as follows:

1. *Racial Balance or Racial Quotas* . . . the District Court has imposed a
   racial balance requirement of 71%–29% [white to black] on individual
   schools. . . . The constitutional command to desegregate schools does
   not mean that every school . . . must always reflect the racial composition of the school system as a whole. . . . We see therefore that the use
   made of mathematical ratios was no more than a starting point in the
   process of shaping a remedy, rather than an inflexible requirement.[40]

2. *One-race Schools.* . . . Schools all or predominantly of one race in a
   district of mixed population will require close scrutiny to determine that
   school assignments are not part of state-enforced segregation. . . . The
   district judge or school authorities should make every effort to achieve
   the greatest possible degree of actual desegregation and will thus necessarily be concerned with the elimination of one-race schools. . . . [T]he
   burden upon the school authorities will be to satisfy the court that their
   racial composition is not the result of present or past discriminatory
   action on their part.[41]

3. *Remedial Altering of Attendance Zones.* . . . Absent a constitutional
   violation there would be no basis for judicially ordering assignment of
   students on a racial basis . . . [and] it might well be desirable to assign
   pupils to schools nearest their homes. But all things are not equal in a
   system that has been deliberately constructed and maintained to enforce
   racial segregation. . . . "Racially neutral" assignment plans proposed
   by school authorities . . . may fail to counteract the continuing effects
   of past school segregation. . . . We hold that the pairing and grouping
   of noncontiguous school zones is a permissible tool and such action is to
   be considered in light of the objectives sought.[42]

4. *Transportation of Students* . . . we find no basis for holding that the
   local school authorities may not be required to employ bus transportation
   as one tool of school desegregation. Desegregation plans cannot be limited to the walk-in school.[43]

Whether or not the Supreme Court fully intended it, these guidelines essentially invalidated those desegregation remedies based on neighborhood or geographic zoning that did not produce adequate racial balance. For most larger
school districts, *Swann* ushered in an era of extensive cross-district busing to
attain racial balance in virtually every school within a school district. Soon after
the *Swann* decision was issued, plaintiffs in many other cases were back in court

demanding remedies tailored according to these new guidelines. Mandatory busing for racial balance was soon implemented in numerous cities across the South, almost all by court order, even in those that had already adopted geographic zoning policies. Among the larger southern school districts affected were Little Rock, Arkansas; Duval (Jacksonville) and Hillsborough (Tampa) counties, Florida; Muskogee (Columbus) and Chatham (Savannah) counties, Georgia; Louisville–Jefferson County, Kentucky; Prince Georges County, Maryland; Charlotte–Mecklenburg and New Hanover counties, North Carolina; Oklahoma City, Oklahoma; Memphis and Nashville, Tennessee; Dallas, Fort Worth, and Waco, Texas; and Norfolk, Virginia.

The Court was careful to point out that racial quotas were only a "starting point" and not an "inflexible requirement" and that every school did not have to be balanced. In spite of these caveats, however, many lower courts not only started with a narrow racial balance requirement for each school (e.g., plus or minus 5 or 10 percentage points from the systemwide percent black) but also ordered periodic adjustments in attendance zones to maintain rigid racial quotas for long periods of time, sometimes over ten years. By converting a starting point into a long-term policy, many lower courts acceded to the desires of civil rights groups to have a permanent policy of school desegregation, in which desegregation is defined as racial balance in all schools.

The *Swann* decision is also noteworthy for clarifications on several other legal issues that had divided lower courts. Some of these statements became increasingly important during later eras of desegregation policy. On the issue of de facto versus de jure segregation, for example, the Court made it clear that the racial quotas being approved in this decision were appropriate only where de jure segregation had been found and that the remedy was dictated by the extent of the constitutional violation. In addition to the third guideline previously quoted, the Court said:

> School authorities . . . might well conclude, for example, that . . . each school should have a prescribed ratio of Negro to white students. . . . [A]bsent a finding of a constitutional violation, however, that would not be within the authority of a federal court. As with any equity case, the nature of the violation determines the scope of the remedy.[44]

Needless to say, the statement about the match between remedy and violation seems almost gratuitous here, given the rest of the opinion. It has always been clear that a high degree of racial balance in larger school districts is almost impossible to attain under any standard geographic zoning policy because of residential segregation, and it was by no means clear at this point whether, and to what degree, a school district should be held accountable for such housing patterns. Therefore, a court-ordered remedy that creates a high degree of racial balance—greater than what housing segregation would dictate—is highly likely to exceed the scope of school board violations, unless a board is also held liable for all housing segregation as well.

On this issue, the Court noted that the district court had found housing segregation arising in part from federal, state, and local government action and that the court of appeals had accepted these findings. Agreeing that decisions about school openings and closings could affect residential segregation and, coupled with a neighborhood school policy, could further aggravate school segregation, the Court said, "Upon a proper showing a district court may consider this in fashioning a remedy."[45] Still, the Court also said that its decision in this case and the remedial guidelines being offered did not settle the issue of school district liability for government-induced residential segregation, in the absence of school district violations:

> We do not reach in this case the question whether a showing that school segregation is a consequence of other types of state action without any discriminatory action by the school authorities, is a constitutional violation requiring remedial action by a school desegregation decree. This case does not present that question and we therefore do not decide it.[46]

Finally, the Supreme Court took up the question of what happens after a school district implements a desegregation plan and attains "unitary" status, and in particular what the future responsibilities might be for school districts and courts:

> At some point, these school authorities . . . should have achieved full compliance. . . . The systems would then be "unitary" in the sense required by our decisions in *Green* and *Alexander*. It does not follow that the communities served by such systems will remain demographically stable. . . . Neither school authorities nor district courts are constitutionally required to make year-by-year adjustments of the racial composition of student bodies once the affirmative duty to desegregate has been accomplished and racial discrimination through official action has been eliminated. . . . [I]n the absence of a showing that the . . . State has deliberately attempted to fix or alter demographic patterns to affect the racial composition of the schools, further intervention by a district court should not be necessary.[47]

It seems clear from this statement that a school district does not have to maintain permanent racial balance, once it attains unitary status, in the face of demographic changes. In their supervision of desegregation plans, however, many lower courts have tended to overlook this portion of the *Swann* decision and required long-term maintenance of racial balance policies and mandatory busing. As a result, there has been much confusion as to the long-term obligations of school boards regarding remedies, and indeed it has been unclear what their constitutional responsibilities are once they have attained unitary status. There has been some clarification of these obligations in the more recent Supreme Court decisions for Oklahoma City and DeKalb County, which are discussed later.

Interestingly, *Swann* did not address the issue of community opinion and possible flight from the public schools. In claiming that racial balance formulas and cross-district busing were reasonable and feasible remedies, they clearly did not examine the possibility that opposition to such policies could undermine their effectiveness and create resegregation between a city and its suburbs or between public and private schools. This oversight might be excused because of lack of good evidence at that time, as well as lack of experience with successful voluntary plans. The issues of feasibility and resegregation became serious as more school districts were ordered to adopt mandatory busing plans (see chapter 4).

Although the *Swann* decision resolved questions about appropriate remedies for former de jure school systems, the consequence of requiring racial balance for state-enforced segregation presented the Court with a new problem. Nearly all larger school districts, southern or northern, have highly segregated housing patterns. If racial balance and mandatory busing were required for southern de jure segregation but not for northern de facto segregation, then complete school integration would exist only in the South. This result was clearly not acceptable to those who believed that any type of school segregation was harmful and should therefore be illegal, regardless of its causes.

Moreover, some argued that, even though the South had official segregation policies, it was not fair to impose desegregation on one region of the country but not on other regions, given that one of the major underlying causes of segregation, housing patterns, was similar in both regions. This dilemma was noted by legal scholars, at least one of whom forecast that the Court would ultimately have to create a more uniform policy for desegregation liability and remedy.[48] It did so within two years, but at the cost of consensus. *Swann* was the last unanimous decision of the Supreme Court on the difficult problem of school desegregation.

Keyes and the Northern Cases

After *Swann*, the Supreme Court could have established a more uniform policy on school segregation between the North and the South in several ways. One would have been to abandon the *Swann* racial balance remedies because they exceed the scope of most school violations; in most school systems, some degree of school segregation is caused by housing segregation. Another approach, advocated by many civil rights groups and social scientists, was to declare all school segregation from all causes—de facto or de jure—unconstitutional. A third approach, which the Supreme Court eventually chose, was to broaden the legal standards for de jure violations, thereby making it easier for a court to find a dual school system.

Perhaps more than any other case, the *Keyes* decision, affecting Denver, Colorado, marks a manifest departure from the basic principles established by *Brown*. While *Swann* endorsed a new remedial standard of busing for racial balance, the liability requirements of *Brown* were undisturbed. According to *Swann*, the remedy of racial balance could be applied only to state-mandated school segregation, a condition that could have contributed to housing segregation. In *Keyes* the liability principle was modified to such an extent that school boards could, in effect, be held liable for school segregation arising mainly from de facto housing segregation, unless they could prove, definitively, that they did not cause it.

Before discussing details of the *Keyes* case, some other historical developments are worth noting. The move away from the liability principles of *Brown* actually began with several lower court decisions affecting the northern school districts of Pasadena and San Francisco, California, and Pontiac, Michigan, none of which was appealed to the Supreme Court. These early decisions reveal district court judges who reflected the views of many social scientists and civil rights groups, including the U.S. Commission on Civil Rights, that any form of school segregation was harmful, regardless of cause, and that racial balance would remedy these harms. The main goal of these courts appears to have been a racial balance policy, justified by blurring the distinction between de jure and de facto conditions, by finding neighborhood school policies suspect, and by ignoring the relationship between constitutional violations and the scope of the remedy.

The earliest of these actions took place in Pasadena, California, which in 1970 became the first non-southern city with extensive court-ordered busing for the purpose of attaining racial balance. The district court in Pasadena found that (1) the schools were racially imbalanced, which was caused in part by a neighborhood school policy; (2) the school board had approved boundary changes, student transfer policies, and school construction that were in some instances racially motivated and that "contributed to and intensified" this imbalance; (3) some schools had racially imbalanced faculty and staff; (4) housing segregation was caused mostly by racial discrimination (e.g., racially restrictive covenants and real estate agency practices); and (5) segregation "imposes a badge of inferiority" and integration removes this stigma and provides educational benefits.[49] In its legal analysis, the Court said the significance of *Brown* was its finding that "segregation is inherently unequal" and "detrimental to school children." It also asserted that "use of a strict neighborhood school policy and a policy against cross-town bussing take on constitutional significance as a violation of the Fourteenth Amendment."[50]

The opinions in the Pontiac and San Francisco cases followed similar lines of reasoning. The district courts found that the schools were racially imbalanced in both enrollment and faculty, that decisions about new construction or boundary changes had perpetuated and enhanced this imbalance, that segregation was educationally and psychologically harmful to black children, and that a neighborhood school policy was improper when it perpetuates or continues segregation.[51] Most important, both lower courts concluded that actions that knowingly maintain or exacerbate racial imbalance are sufficient to create a de jure segregated condition. Like Pasadena, both of these courts ordered extensive mandatory busing to attain complete racial balance in all schools.

The most noteworthy aspect of these three decisions, other than the emphasis on conditions not clearly caused by the state or the school board, was the total lack of concern about the relationship between remedy and the specific violations cited (discriminatory boundary changes or new school sitings). The only possible violation whose effect could justify a systemwide desegregation plan is segregated housing and the school segregation caused by a board's conscious maintenance of a neighborhood school policy. The Supreme Court had never gone this far, and even though *Swann* endorsed the racial balance concept, it did so only for the de jure condition of state-mandated segregated schools. In fact, the Supreme Court has always rejected the thesis that housing segregation alone, coupled with a neighborhood school policy, is a violation of the Fourteenth Amendment.

Ironically, the district court in *Keyes* did precisely what these other northern courts did not do: It clearly distinguished de jure and de facto conditions and then conducted a careful analysis of school board actions applying both effect and intent criteria. The court concluded that a group of schools in one section of Denver, the so-called Park Hills area, met the de jure segregation standard. It found that the school board, by virtue of new school sitings and attendance boundary decisions, had deliberately acted to create and maintain segregated schools in this part of the city. By contrast, it decided that another group of "core area" schools were segregated by virtue of residential patterns coupled with a neighborhood school policy; as such it did not meet the de jure criterion of intent or purpose to segregate.[52]

The district court did find, however, that these core area schools were not offering educational programs equal to white schools, and in that respect they were found in violation of the Fourteenth Amendment. Relying on the testimony of several expert witnesses, including Professor James Coleman of the University of Chicago, the district court concluded that "improvement in the quality of education in the minority school can only be brought about by a program of desegregation and integration."[53] In spite of finding the school board innocent of causing segregation in the core area schools, the district court ordered a racial balance plan for both the Park Hills and core area schools.

The Tenth Circuit Court of Appeals accepted the findings and remedy for the Park Hills area schools, but reversed on the remedy for the core area schools. The appeals court was sympathetic with the finding that segregated schools produced lower achievement for minority students, but it said that a neighborhood school policy was constitutional and that the federal courts were powerless to "resolve educational difficulties arising from circumstances . . . outside state action."[54]

The Supreme Court rejected the legal reasoning and conclusions of both lower courts. Instead, it expanded the de jure doctrine by adopting a new standard for evaluating de facto segregation within a school district. If there was some de jure segregation in the district, the burden of proof for the de facto segregation was shifted to the school board:

> . . . a finding of intentionally segregative school board actions in a meaningful portion of a school system . . . creates a presumption that other segregated schooling within the system is not adventitious. It . . . shifts to those [school] authorities the burden of proving that other segregated schools within the system are not also the result of intentionally segregative actions.[55]

The case was returned to the district court to reevaluate the causes of segregation in the core area schools by this new standard. In effect, the school board would be liable for all school segregation, including that arising from the combination of neighborhood schools plus de facto housing segregation, unless it could prove that none of its policies or actions had been a significant cause of housing segregation. The school board was not able to meet this difficult burden of proof, and ultimately a racial balance and busing plan was ordered for the entire school system. While the *Keyes* decision left the de facto–de jure distinction alive in theory, it had much less practical significance because few school districts at that time could meet a burden of proving that they had not contributed to housing segregation or had not intentionally adopted a neighborhood school policy.

Unlike the major Supreme Court school decisions from *Brown* to *Swann*, which were decided by a unanimous Court, the *Keyes* decision marked the beginning of a divided Court on the critical issue of de facto–de jure distinction and the scope of remedies. The majority opinion, authored by Justice Brennan, was joined by Justices Burger, Blackmun, Marshall, and Stewart; three justices wrote separate concurring or dissenting opinions, and Justice White did not participate. Justices Douglas and Powell both thought that the de jure–de facto distinction should be ended, but for very different reasons and with very different results.

Justice Douglas, taking a position popular with civil rights groups, favored treating de facto segregation the same as de jure segregation on the grounds that neighborhood school policies simply build on housing patterns, which are in turn influenced by state actions, and that segregation arising from neighborhood school policies should therefore be unconstitutional. Justice Powell agreed that the de jure–de facto distinction had outlived its usefulness, but mainly because of the "affirmative integration" standard adopted by *Swann*. Justice Powell's dissent openly acknowledged that the meaning of desegregation had changed between *Brown* and *Swann* and that the remedies imposed by the latter were not carefully tailored to the actual effects of constitutional violations (because some racial imbalance is caused by de facto housing patterns, even in southern districts). Unlike Justice Douglas, he found nothing unconstitutional about a neighborhood school policy that leads to predominantly black or white schools, as long as the school system was integrated and nondiscriminatory in all other respects (such as faculty, resources, maximization of integration when opening or closing schools). In other words, Justice Powell would have abandoned the de jure–de factor distinction, but at the same time he would have nullified the *Swann* student assignment requirements of mandatory busing and racial balance.

Justice Rehnquist, in a strongly worded dissent, agreed with Justice Powell's assessment of the changes in the meaning of desegregation from *Brown* to *Green* and *Swann*. Rather than agreeing with the doctrinal change to "affirmative integration," however, Justice Rehnquist called for a more rigorous adherence to the de jure standard of deliberate or intentional discriminatory actions. He argued that intent need not be determined for every school in a southern dual school system because state laws mandated separate schools for all schools in a system. Regarding a system like Denver with no history of state-mandated dual schools, however, a careful analysis was necessary to determine whether state or school board action caused segregation in individual schools, and there was no basis for shifting the burden of proof just because the question concerned individual schools rather than a system as a whole. He also noted the difficulty any school board would have proving it did not cause or contribute to housing segregation and said that the new "evidentiary rules . . . make it more likely that the trial court will on remand reach the result which the Court apparently wants it to reach."[56]

The *Keyes* decision stimulated a series of other northern lawsuits ultimately leading to comprehensive mandatory busing plans in such cities as Los Angeles and Stockton, California; Wilmington, Delaware; Indianapolis, Indiana; Boston and Springfield, Massachusetts; Detroit, Michigan; Minneapolis, Minnesota; Omaha, Nebraska; and Dayton, Columbus, and Cleveland, Ohio.

Milliken and the Limits of Liability and Remedy

The divided opinion in *Keyes* grew to a full-fledged split in the Supreme Court just one year later in its *Milliken v. Bradley* decision affecting Detroit (*Milliken I*).[57] The split in *Milliken I* was a turning point of sorts, revealing the emergence of two factions with fundamental doctrinal differences about both liability and remedy. The "liberal" or "activist" faction, led by Justices Brennan and Marshall (and Justice Douglas before his retirement in 1975), generally favored broader grounds for liability and more intrusive desegregation remedies. The "conservative" or "traditionalist" faction, led by Justices Rehnquist and Powell, generally favored more rigorous determinations of liability, especially the requirement of proving de jure discrimination, and a strict tailoring of remedy to specific constitutional violations.

Despite turnover in justices, the philosophical and doctrinal division revealed in the *Milliken I* opinion dominated Supreme Court decisions on civil rights issues for the next fifteen years. Because the split led to close votes and numerous split decisions, and a shift by one justice could change the outcome, many of the decisions on civil rights issues during this era appeared to lack consistency in basic legal principles and doctrine. In fact, the inconsistency was simply a manifestation of an underlying rift that was first revealed in *Keyes*.

The *Milliken I* case was the first major "metropolitan" lawsuit to be decided by the Supreme Court, although it was not the first major metropolitan case to be heard by the Court. (A metropolitan case is one where liability or remedy encompasses a group of adjacent but separate school districts, usually those suburban school districts surrounding a central city school district.) The first major metropolitan case to be reviewed by the Supreme Court involved Richmond, Virginia. In 1972 a district court had ordered consolidation of the predominantly black Richmond school district with two predominantly white suburban school districts, even though all three districts had complied with earlier desegregation decrees and had been declared "unitary" systems. The basis of this order included findings that (1) meaningful desegregation could not be accomplished solely within the city of Richmond; (2) a combination of state, other government agencies, and private discrimination had contributed to housing segregation; and (3) expert testimony of Harvard psychologist Thomas Pettigrew had established that schools should have an "optimum" racial composition between 20 and 40 percent black enrollment in order to realize the educational and social benefits of integration.[58]

This ruling was reversed by the Court of Appeals for the Fourth Circuit on the straightforward grounds that they could find no constitutional violation in the existence of three independent school districts that happened to have different racial compositions.[59] Although the appellate court accepted the lower court finding that state actions had contributed to housing segregation, they asserted that other economic, demographic, and social factors were also at play and that primary responsibility for this problem could not be attributed to either the state or the school districts. The appellate opinion relied on declarations in *Swann* that there is no inherent right to a prescribed ratio of blacks to whites in schools and that school districts are not responsible for demographic changes or patterns not caused by official discriminatory conduct. The appellate decision was subsequently reviewed by the Supreme Court, but no Supreme Court decision was rendered because of a 4–4 split opinion (Justice Powell did not participate) that left the appellate decision as the final disposition of the case.

The Detroit case began at about the same time as the Richmond metropolitan case. In 1971 a district court concluded that the Detroit school board had created and was maintaining a segregated system in violation of the Fourteenth Amendment. The constitutional violations were similar to those found in the other pre-*Keyes* northern cases: racially imbalanced schools, a neighborhood schools policy building on housing segregation caused by public (state) and private discrimination, use of optional attendance zones and other zone changes that had the foreseeable effect of perpetuating segregation, and avoiding integration policies because of community opposition.[60] The findings on housing segregation were based largely on the expert testimony of University of Wisconsin demographer Karl Taueber.

The case diverged dramatically from its northern cousins, however, in the matter of remedy. Because Detroit was a majority-black (64 percent) school district at the time of trial, and projected demographic trends indicated that it would become increasingly black in the near future, the district court concluded that an effective remedy could not be attained within the confines of the Detroit system. In arriving at this conclusion, the court relied upon expert testimony that a desegregation plan involving only the city of Detroit would cause substantial white flight and would have the effect of accelerating the transition of Detroit to a predominantly black school district. The district court had also found that the State of Michigan had contributed to Detroit school segregation in some of its policies, including failure to subsidize transportation of Detroit students, approval of the locations of new schools, and legislation aimed at barring some voluntary programs for improving the integration of Detroit schools.

Concluding further that school districts are creations of the state and subject to state authority, the Court ordered a massive metropolitan remedy whereby Detroit would be consolidated with fifty-three independent suburban districts and students would be bused between the city and suburbs to attain racial balance in all schools. This remedy would have created the second largest school district in the country, with 750,000 students compared to Detroit's 250,000, and with hundreds of thousands of children being subjected to mandatory busing for the purpose of racial balance.

Significantly, none of the suburban school districts was allowed to intervene in the Detroit proceedings during the liability phase of the case, which played an important role during appeals to higher courts. The Court of Appeals for the Sixth Circuit agreed with all aspects of the district court decision except the exclusion of the suburban districts from the liability proceedings. Most important, they agreed with the extension of remedy beyond the city of Detroit: "We reject the contention that school district lines are sacrosanct and that the jurisdiction of the District court . . . is limited to the geographic boundaries of Detroit. We reiterate that school districts and school boards are instrumentalities of the State."[61]

The case was subsequently reviewed by the Supreme Court, which reversed both lower courts in a lengthy and deeply divided opinion. The majority opinion was delivered by Chief Justice Burger who was joined by Justices Stewart, Blackmun, Powell, and Rehnquist. Three dissenting opinions authored by Justices Douglas, White (joined by Brennan), and Marshall were together longer than the majority opinion. Justice Stewart wrote a brief concurring opinion, motivated by "some of the extravagant language of the dissenting opinions."[62]

The majority opinion did not take issue with any lower court finding on liability and, in fact, explicitly confined their inquiry to the issue of the remedy, "to determine whether a federal court may impose a multi-district, areawide remedy . . . absent any finding that the other included school districts have failed to operate unitary school systems . . . or . . . that the boundary lines of any affected school district were established with the purpose of fostering racial segregation . . . [or] that the included districts committed acts which affected segregation within the other districts."[63]

The Court majority was clearly bothered by the scale of this massive and unprecedented judicial intervention. The opinion mentioned the myriad of administrative and logistical problems that would confront the lower court in creating this "vast new super school district," including reorganizing more than fifty independently elected school boards, problems of tax levies and finance, differences of curriculum and programs, and large-scale transportation. Resolving these and other complex problems and implementing their solutions would, in the view of the Court, convert the district court into a de facto "legislative authority" and "school superintendent" for the new school system. The decision probably did not turn on the issue of scale, however; the Court was also divided on the Richmond case, which involved only three school systems and a much smaller total enrollment. Rather, these two cases reveal a high Court split on more fundamental principles of liability and remedy.

The fundamental principles cited by the majority in *Milliken I* were similar to those offered by the appellate court in the Richmond case. The Supreme Court said:

The controlling principle . . . is that the scope of the remedy is determined by the nature and extent of the constitutional violation . . . it must first be shown that there has been a constitutional violation within one district that produces a significant segregative effect in another district. Specifically, it must be shown that racially discriminatory acts of the state or local school districts . . . have been a substantial cause of interdistrict segregation.[64]

Since there was no evidence that the suburban districts had caused Detroit's school segregation—indeed, this had not even been alleged during the initial trial—or that any unconstitutional actions by the Detroit school board or the State of Michigan had interdistrict effects, the inclusion of the suburban districts in a metropolitan remedy was not warranted.

Milliken I was the first major Supreme Court decision since *Brown* to limit (rather than expand) the scope of desegregation remedies, and the dissents illuminate the very different views of the "activist" faction and the extent to which desegregation had come to mean a particular degree of racial balance rather than an elimination of discriminatory practices. The most forceful argument in this regard was made by Justice Douglas, who again called for abandoning the difference between de jure and de facto segregation so that any form of segregation (or racial imbalance) would have to be eliminated irrespective of whether there were any deliberate discriminatory laws or policies that caused the segregation.

The dissents by Justices White and Marshall did not question the requirement of de jure segregation, but once de jure violations are shown, they argued against significant limits on remedy. At that point the only consideration should be "effectiveness," that is, whether the remedy attains the maximum feasible degree of desegregation. Effectiveness necessarily requires attention to the ratio of blacks to whites; because Detroit is majority black and the suburbs are majority white, the lower courts were justified in reaching out to include suburban districts in order to "effectively" desegregate the entire region. In other words, the match between violation and remedy was of secondary importance to the effectiveness of a desegregation plan.

While the majority continued to stress the *Swann* requirement of tailoring remedies to violations, Justice White cited another *Swann* dictate that local authorities "should make every effort to achieve the greatest possible degree of actual desegregation," and Justice Marshall said the purpose of the *Swann* rule is simply to guarantee "a remedy which effectively cures the violation." For some of these dissenting justices, the racial balance rule first propounded by *Swann* was not merely a starting point but also an important goal of a desegregation plan. Justice White's dissent also suggested the familiar harm and benefit thesis as a rationale for this goal, citing the "social, economic, and political advantages which accompany a desegregated school system."[65]

Washington v. Davis and Discriminatory Intent

Although *Milliken I* arose over a dispute about remedy, the most important long-term implication of the decision concerns liability and the relationship between liability and remedy, at least for litigation among separate school systems. It reaffirmed the de jure principle that a court can impose a desegregation remedy upon a school system only when official discriminatory conduct is proven, as well as the remedial principle that the scope of the remedy must match the extent of the proven discrimination.

These principles of liability and remedy seemed clear enough when applied to Detroit and subsequent metropolitan cases (to be discussed shortly), but the principles, especially the distinction between de jure and de facto segregation, were becoming muddled in many northern intradistrict cases. Some lower courts, such as those in the Pasadena, Pontiac, and San Francisco cases, had argued against any distinction between de jure and de facto actions, finding all segregative policies, such as neighborhood schools, to be unconstitutional regardless of the origin or purposes of those actions. This broader basis for mandatory busing was derailed by *Keyes,* when the Supreme Court stated that "the differentiating factor between de jure and so-called de facto segregation . . . is *purpose* or *intent* to segregate."[66]

A more difficult issue arising uniquely in the North was the standard used to judge discriminatory purpose or intent. Neither the *Keyes* nor *Milliken I* decisions explicitly endorsed a "foreseeable effects" standard for evaluating discriminatory intent, but later lower courts argued that the high Court had adopted the foreseeable effects standards used by the district courts in these cases.[67] By this standard, which was articulated most clearly by the Sixth Circuit Court of Appeals in 1974, "A presumption of segregative purpose arises when plaintiffs establish that the natural, probable, and foreseeable result of public officials' action or inaction was an increase or perpetuation of public school segregation."[68] If this presumption was established, then a school board would have the burden of proving that they had not acted with an intent to segregate. Other appellate courts endorsed the foreseeable consequence standard, including an important appellate decision leading to a mandatory busing plan in Omaha, Nebraska.[69]

The notion of "perpetuating" segregation apparently comes from the *Swann* decision (also restated in *Keyes*), which spoke of remedies such as neighborhood zoning that "maintained" state-sponsored segregation. The use of this concept in *Swann,* however, clearly applied to the adequacy of remedies once intentional segregation had been established; the Supreme Court had never said that perpetuation of nonofficial segregation was itself evidence (presumptive or otherwise) of discriminatory intent.

Because housing segregation can exist without official action, by the combination of normal demographic forces and private residential decisions, then the foreseeable consequences test could render a neighborhood school policy unconstitutional in that it is a policy that purposely perpetuates a condition of segregation. In other words, if a school board failed to work affirmatively against de facto segregation in housing, that failure could become a de jure school violation, triggering a court-imposed school desegregation remedy for an otherwise legal condition of housing segregation. The foreseeable consequences standard eviscerated the distinction between de facto and de jure segregation, rendering it of little practical significance.

The Supreme Court tried to address the erosion of the de facto–de jure distinction in a key 1976 decision, *Washington v. Davis*.[70] Although the case involved the issue of discriminatory intent in employment discrimination, the majority of a divided Court also applied the ruling to school segregation. The case concerned a verbal skills test used to screen potential police recruits in the District of Columbia. Plaintiffs complained that the test was discriminatory and therefore unconstitutional under the Fourteenth Amendment because black recruits failed the test at a higher rate than whites; no claim of intentional racial discrimination was made by the plaintiffs.

The district court did find that the racially disparate failure rates were sufficient to shift the burden of proof to the defendants. But it also found the verbal test to be reasonably job related and to have no discriminatory purpose, and therefore the testing policy was constitutional.[71] The court of appeals reversed the district court on the grounds that Title VII of the Civil Rights Act (which deals with discrimination in employment) did not require a showing of discriminatory intent.[72] Although examining the legislative and constitutional issues in employment discrimination would take this discussion too far afield, suffice it to say that the Supreme Court has applied different standards for determining racial discrimination under Title VII, mainly on grounds of the Congress's legislative authority and intent.[73]

On appeal, the Supreme Court reversed the court of appeals, stating that the standards for illegal discrimination under the Constitution differ from those approved for Title VII. The majority opinion, delivered by Justice White and joined by Chief Justice Burger and Justices Blackmun, Powell, Rehnquist, and Stevens, declared that a policy with a racially disparate impact is not sufficient to establish a constitutional violation: "Our cases have not embraced the proposition that a law or other official act, without regard to whether it reflects a racially discriminatory purpose, is unconstitutional *solely* because it has a racially disproportionate impact."[74] In describing the proper test for a constitutional violation, the Court cited the rule as used in various contexts, including school cases:

> The school desegregation cases have also adhered to the basic equal protection principle that the invidious quality of a law claimed to be racially discriminatory must ultimately be traced to a racially discriminatory purpose. That there are both predominantly black and predominantly white schools in a community is not alone violative of the Equal Protection Clause.[75]

Justice Stevens wrote a concurring opinion and Justice Brennan, joined by Justice Marshall, wrote a dissenting opinion.

Although the *Washington v. Davis* case did reaffirm the distinction between de facto and de jure segregation and equated the latter to discriminatory intent, it did not settle the disputed constitutional issues in northern desegregation cases. On the one hand, *Washington v. Davis* and a closely related housing decision known as *Arlington Heights* are cited in several Supreme Court decisions that reversed lower court desegregation orders on grounds that proof of discriminatory intent was insufficient.[76] In the Omaha case, for example, these cases were cited by the Supreme Court as partial grounds for reversing the appellate court and its formulation of the "foreseeable consequences" rule.[77] They were also cited in Supreme Court reversals of lower court decisions in the Dayton and Pasadena cases, as described later in this chapter.

In spite of these Supreme Court rulings, *Washington v. Davis* did not stop the systemwide busing plan in Omaha. The court of appeals, on remand, simply reiterated its earlier findings of discriminatory intent based on foreseeable consequences, which were not rebutted by the School Board, and the systemwide mandatory busing order remained in effect. Likewise, *Washington v. Davis* did not stop mandatory busing orders in Dayton or, Pasadena. Busing was eventually terminated in Pasadena, but this required yet another Supreme Court decision (in a case to be discussed later).

The Columbus and Dayton Cases

In the context of judicial disagreement about the meaning of de jure segregation and the standards by which it should be judged, the 1976 and 1979 Supreme Court decisions in the Dayton and Columbus cases deserve special emphasis.[78] Although these opinions can be viewed as extending the *Keyes* doctrine as it applies to de facto segregation in the North, they again reflect a divided court on the issues of both liability and remedy. The 1979 opinions in these two cases were the last major Supreme Court opinions on the issue of school desegregation until 1991.

Neither Columbus nor Dayton was subject to southern-style segregation laws after the late 1800s, but both districts had a number of predominantly black schools at the time of *Brown,* and both systems had large numbers of predominantly white or black schools at the time of their trials in the early 1970s. Both district courts found a series of school board actions that had contributed to the existence of segregated schools at various times, such as faculty assignments, use of optional attendance zones, transfer policies, and new school siting and construction patterns. The district court in the Dayton case, however, did not order a systemwide racial balance and busing plan on grounds that the limited violations justified only a limited remedy, whereas in the Columbus case the district court believed that the violations did justify a comprehensive mandatory busing plan. Both decisions were appealed, and both cases were ultimately reviewed by the Supreme Court.

In the Dayton case, the court of appeals accepted the district court's findings on liability but ordered a systemwide remedy based on their view of the scope of the violations. The Supreme Court, in *Dayton I*, reversed the appellate court on the grounds that (1) some violations found by the lower courts, such as racially imbalanced schools, were not constitutional violations in light of *Washington v. Davis* and (2) the few actual constitutional violations did not justify a systemwide remedy. The district court was ordered to hold new hearings to first determine whether there was any action [by the school board] . . . which are intended to, and did in fact, discriminate against minority pupils, teachers, or staff. . . . If such violations are found, the District Court . . . must determine how much incremental segregative effect these violations had on the racial distribution of the Dayton school population as presently constituted . . . compared to what it would have been in the absence of constitutional violations . . . and only if there has been a systemwide impact may there be a systemwide remedy.[79]

Following further hearings, the district court decided that most school board actions did not satisfy both intent and effect criteria for a constitutional violation, and the violations that were found did not justify a systemwide racial balance remedy. The court of appeals reversed again, on the grounds that the district court did not follow the *Keyes* standard of shifting the burden of proof to the school board, and the case went to the Supreme Court for a second review (*Dayton II*). This time a badly split Supreme Court voted 5 to 4 to affirm the appellate decision and the systemwide busing plan that had been ordered by the appellate court. The majority opinion, delivered by Justice White, was joined by Justices Brennan, Marshall, Blackmun, and Stevens. Chief Justice Burger and Justices Stewart, Powell, and Rehnquist dissented. The Burger and Stewart dissents emphasized deference to the district court as the finder of fact on the complex issues of discriminatory intent and incremental effects.

A significant difference in the Columbus case, reviewed by the Supreme Court at the same time as *Dayton II*, is that the district court found that a series of similar school board actions did satisfy the intent and effect requirements of a de jure violation, and this finding was upheld by the court of appeals. Again, the Supreme Court was split, but in this case Chief Justice Burger and Justice Stewart concurred with the majority, again deferring to the trial court. Interestingly, the Chief Justice indicated agreement with part of Justice Powell's dissent, saying he was becoming increasingly doubtful that massive public transportation (busing) is an effective remedy for desegregation.

The dissents by Justices Powell and Rehnquist echoed the growing disenchantment in the society at large with the effectiveness of massive busing remedies and the disparity between these systemwide remedies and the types of violations found. Justice Powell lamented the lack of convincing evidence, as well as credibility, that all of the segregation in the Columbus and Dayton schools could be attributed to discriminatory conduct by their school boards. He also pointed out that the experience with massive busing was having the negative consequences of white flight, resegregation, and loss of community support for the public schools, citing works by James Coleman and other social scientists.[80]

In addition to the weak relationship between the violations found and systemwide busing remedies, the dissent by Justice Rehnquist also discussed the standards of proof for a finding of intentional segregation. In particular, he took issue with a "foreseeable effect" standard that had been adopted by the court of appeals, which held that discriminatory intent could be inferred if "the natural, probable, and foreseeable result of public officials' action or inaction was an increase or perpetuation of public school segregation."[81] For Justice Rehnquist and many legal scholars, a foreseeable effect standard eliminates the distinction between intent and effect by inferring discriminatory purpose simply by awareness of a likely segregative effect. Hence, maintenance of a neighborhood school policy, which is known to perpetuate school segregation because of underlying housing segregation, can become intentional discrimination under a foreseeable effect test.[82] Justice Rehnquist concluded that such a procedure "would all but eliminate the distinction between de facto and de jure segregation and render all school systems captives of a remote and ambiguous past."[83]

Metropolitan Cases in the Post-*Milliken* Era

After Richmond and Detroit, a number of other metropolitan school desegregation lawsuits were initiated during the late 1970s and 1980s. Some were brought by individual black plaintiffs, represented by the National Association for the Advancement of Colored People (NAACP) or the American Civil Liberties Union (ACLU); others were brought by predominantly black central city school districts against their neighboring suburban districts. All of these plaintiffs attempted to prove the essential elements required by *Milliken* for bringing about a metropolitan, interdistrict remedy: that actions of the states and local school districts had the intent and effect of causing significant interdistrict segregation. Most of these lawsuits included allegations that the state, local districts, or both had contributed to housing segregation between the city and the suburbs.

Only a few of these metropolitan cases led to metropolitan desegregation plans. Metropolitan plans were implemented for Wilmington, Delaware; Indianapolis, Indiana; and St. Louis, Missouri; the first two were by court order, and the last was settled out of court but only after indications that a court order might be forthcoming.[84] In all three cases, lower courts had found state laws or other actions to be partial causes of interdistrict segregation, thereby justifying an interdistrict remedy.

Of the three cases, only Wilmington was ordered to implement a comprehensive two-way mandatory busing plan to attain complete racial balance in all schools. All original city and suburban school districts were dissolved and replaced by one large school district, and black students were bused from the city to the suburbs while white students were bused from the suburbs into the city to accomplish desegregation. Ironically, the Wilmington case was similar to the Detroit case in most respects, but in 1980 a split Supreme Court declined to review it on appeal (Justices Stewart and Powell dissented, but Chief Justice Burger sided with the majority).[85]

The remedy for Indianapolis involved a one-way busing plan for blacks to attend predominantly white suburban schools; suburban whites were not required to attend the Indianapolis city schools, and the original district boundaries and governance remained intact. In St. Louis, after protracted litigation and a court-ordered *design* of a mandatory interdistrict busing plan, the city and suburban school districts settled out of court (prior to a finding of liability). They agreed to implement a voluntary plan that allowed city blacks to enroll in suburban schools and suburban whites to enroll in city magnet schools.

Similar metropolitan lawsuits were filed involving the cities and suburbs of Atlanta; Kansas City, Missouri; Goldsboro, North Carolina; Milwaukee, and Cincinnati. In the Atlanta, Kansas City, and Goldsboro cases, the plaintiffs failed to prove interdistrict constitutional violations, including allegations of housing segregation caused by public and private discrimination (see chapter 3).[86] In both the Milwaukee and Cincinnati cases, the suburban school districts agreed to out-of-court settlements for voluntary interdistrict plans, whereby black students could voluntarily transfer to suburban school districts up to a specified percentage. Another metropolitan lawsuit in Little Rock, Arkansas, resulted in a portion of a county suburban district being annexed to the city school district, as well as a program of voluntary interdistrict transfers.[87]

Of all of these metropolitan cases, only the Atlanta case was reviewed by the Supreme Court, and it was affirmed without a written opinion. With the possible exception of the Wilmington case, the basic principles of *Milliken I* were not substantially eroded by any of the lower court decisions. If anything, lower court decisions have tended to reinforce the principles of *Milliken I*, particularly regarding the requirement that remedies must be tailored to specific constitutional violations.

From Mandatory Busing to Choice

For the first five or six years after the 1971 *Swann* decision, nearly all desegregation plans emerging from federal court or federal government actions involved the mandatory reassignment of students to attain a fairly high degree of racial balance. In smaller school districts, racial balance was attained by simply redrawing school attendance boundaries, sometimes accompanied by carefully chosen school closures. In larger school districts, however, racial balance usually requires cross-district busing of both white and black students, which came to be known as "mandatory busing" plans. These plans frequently led to significant white flight and, in some cases, to resegregation.

Initially, there was little interest in desegregation plans relying on voluntary or choice techniques, that is, voluntary in the sense of parental choice of schools. One reason was that early choice methods, such as "freedom of choice," did not control for adverse racial impacts and frequently hampered rather than improved desegregation. Moreover, if white flight was ignored—as was done by most early courts—mandatory plans promised faster and greater racial balance "on paper" than any voluntary plan could.

As social science studies began documenting the phenomenon of white flight and the possibility of resegregation (see chapter 4), some courts began accepting voluntary or "choice" plans in place of mandatory busing plans. San Diego adopted one of the first comprehensive voluntary plans in 1978, which was approved by a California state court and has been in effect since that time.[88] The plan integrated schools by attracting minority students to predominantly white schools with a voluntary transfer program and by attracting white students to specialized "magnet" schools in predominantly minority schools. In 1979 Milwaukee implemented one of the first comprehensive choice plans to be approved by a federal court; it also relied on voluntary transfers and magnet schools, although some black students were mandatorily reassigned away from their neighborhood schools to make room for magnet programs.[89]

During the 1980s, choice programs became more commonplace. Federal courts approved a form of "controlled" choice programs for desegregation remedies in Yonkers, New York, and San Jose, California.[90] A pure controlled choice program eliminates all attendance zones, and parents or students select schools of preference; some schools have specialized magnet programs. The school administration assigns students to schools according to capacity and racial balance constraints and tries to maximize parents' first choices. Because of racial constraints, however, sizeable numbers of students are mandatorily assigned or bused to schools they did not choose; therefore, controlled choice also involves some mandatory busing, although sometimes less extensive than a traditional busing plan.

In some cases, school districts still under court supervision have been permitted to replace a failed mandatory busing plan with a voluntary plan. A good example is Savannah, Georgia, where in 1988 a district court approved a return to neighborhood schools with a voluntary magnet plan in place of a mandatory busing plan that had failed because of white flight and demographic changes. The plan was challenged but upheld by the Court of Appeals for the Eleventh Circuit.[91]

To date there has been no Supreme Court review of a school case in which strictly voluntary techniques were used to remedy a dual school system, and the high Court has not issued any rulings since *Swann* on the degree of racial balance required in a desegregation remedy. District courts are likely to continue to have wide latitude in approving definitions of desegregation and specific desegregation techniques (see chapter 4).

The Issue of Unitary Status

One of the more exasperating problems throughout the history of the school desegregation movement concerns how former "dual" school systems attain "unitary" status and obtain release from judicial supervision, and what obligations remain on school districts once this status is achieved. Contributing to the general frustration has been the relatively little attention paid to this issue by the Supreme Court, other than brief mentions in *Green* and *Swann*, until its 1976 *Spangler* decision involving Pasadena.[92] Even after *Spangler*, there was still much disagreement and inconsistency among lower courts—including the court supervising the Pasadena desegregation plan—over the meaning and applicability of the *Spangler* decision. There was no further Supreme Court action on this issue until the 1991 *Dowell* decision for Oklahoma City.

According to the brief mention in *Green*, a unitary system is one in which racial discrimination has been completely eliminated. *Swann* took this concept a step further in stating that, once desegregation is accomplished and discrimination has been eliminated, and absent deliberate (nondemographic) actions to alter racial composition of schools, annual adjustments in school composition are not required and "further intervention by a district court should not be necessary."[93]

The problem is that neither of these opinions addressed the question of whether a school district can change or abandon a desegregation plan after attaining unitary status and, in particular, whether it must maintain some degree of racial balance forever. Although the *Swann* decision implies that permanent racial balance is not required, most civil rights groups, many lower courts, and individual Supreme Court justices have equated a nondiscriminatory system with nonsegregated schools. If housing segregation remains after a desegregation plan has been in effect for a number of years, and if neighborhood schools that reflect such segregation are violations of the Constitution, then obviously a mandatory busing plan to attain racial balance may be a permanent, not a temporary, requirement.

The *Spangler* Case

One of the earliest examples of the permanent racial balance viewpoint is illustrated by the district court in the Pasadena case. In 1974, after the court-ordered racial balance plan had been in effect for four years, the Pasadena board petitioned the district court to allow adoption of a voluntary integration plan, including magnet schools, and to be released from court supervision. Although the new plan was not a traditional neighborhood school policy, the school board acknowledged it would yield less racial balance than the court-ordered plan, and some schools would become majority black. The board argued that it had maintained the court-ordered plan for four years and had thereby attained unitary status in the sense described by *Green* and *Swann*.

The district court denied the motion on the grounds that (1) the school board had not been sufficiently supportive of the court-ordered plan, (2) by the 1973–1974 school year five of the thirty-two schools had fallen out of compliance with the original requirement that no school have a majority of black students (although four of the five were only a few points above 50 percent and the district had risen to 40 percent black), and (3) the alternative voluntary plan would produce a large number of racially imbalanced schools.[94] In spite of clear Supreme Court language to the contrary in *Keyes*, this district court also stated in a footnote, "There appears to be, in logic, no distinction between de jure and de facto segregation for our purposes. 'De jure' and 'de facto' are only adjectives that give some attempted 'legal' distinction to the aims of *Brown*."[95] The Court of Appeals for the Ninth Circuit upheld the district court, with the exception of a statement by the district court judge during the lower court hearing that "at least during my lifetime there would be no majority of any minority in any school in Pasadena," which the appellate court said was contrary to *Swann's* prohibition of annual adjustments for racial balance.[96]

The Supreme Court reversed both lower courts, again relying heavily on

Swann. Noting the local judge's statement that no school would have a majority of any minority in his lifetime, the high Court said this view was in conflict with *Swann* insofar as it meant a "constitutional right to a particular degree of racial balance or mixing" and an "inflexible requirement" applied each year rather than as a "starting point" in devising a remedy:

> The district court was not entitled to require the School District to rearrange its attendance zones each year so as to ensure that the racial mix desired by the court was maintained in perpetuity. For having once implemented a racially neutral attendance pattern . . . to remedy the perceived constitutional violations, the district court had fully performed its function of providing the appropriate remedy.[97]

In other words, remedy should fix only the conditions caused by a school board. The Supreme Court relieved the board of any responsibility to alter attendance zones in response to demographic changes, and it returned the case to the district court for further proceedings.

The 6–2 majority opinion was delivered by Justice Rehnquist, with Justices Brennan and Marshall dissenting (Justice Stevens did not participate). In dissent, Justices Marshall and Brennan pointed out that the *Swann* rule about annual adjustments to school boundaries applied only when "racial discrimination through official action is eliminated" and that they would defer to the district court's opinion about whether nondiscriminatory status had been attained. Until the district court decided that discrimination had ended, it had broad discretion to modify a desegregation plan, including altering attendance zones.

Despite this rather explicit Supreme Court ruling, the district court continued supervision of the Pasadena school district and its desegregation plan for three more years, mainly on the grounds that the school board would attempt to change or abandon the desegregation plan once it was free of court supervision. Finally, in 1979 the Ninth Circuit Court of Appeals issued a direct order to the district court to terminate the case.[98] By this time Pasadena had become a predominantly (more than 70 percent) minority school district, and in 1990 it was more than 80 percent minority. Thus by the time the case was finally terminated, Pasadena had become largely resegregated.

Dowell, Pitts, and Postunitary Issues

Although *Spangler* did not deal comprehensively with the issue of unitary status, it was the first Supreme Court decision to address the limits of desegregation decrees and racial balance remedies in an intradistrict case. After *Spangler*, there were no further Supreme Court decisions on the issue of unitary status until *Dowell* in 1991 and *Pitts* in 1992, when the Court issued some very important clarifications about the requirements and obligations of unitary status.

During the 1980s, unitary status issues were settled by appellate court decisions that were at times in sharp disagreement with one another. The first of these involved Norfolk, Virginia, which had implemented a comprehensive desegregation plan in 1970 and 1971, including cross-district busing for racial balance. After maintaining the plan for several years, in 1975 the district court declared Norfolk "unitary" and dismissed the case. Norfolk maintained the busing plan for ten more years, with periodic adjustment of attendance zones to maintain racial balance.

In 1983 the Norfolk school board decided to return to neighborhood schools at the elementary level only, with a voluntary transfer program for integration purposes. It justified this decision on several grounds: (1) Mandatory busing had not improved the academic achievement of black students relative to white students; (2) a neighborhood school policy with voluntary options would stop white flight and produce more long-term desegregation; and (3) neighborhood schools would improve the quality of education by increasing parental involvement in the schools.[99] The board acknowledged that this action would reestablish several predominantly black schools.

A new lawsuit was filed in 1984 to stop Norfolk on the grounds that a neighborhood school plan was racially motivated and would resegregate the elementary schools. The district court found no constitutional violation by the school board and approved the return to neighborhood schools at the elementary level. The court's reasoning was that, given a unitary district, the plaintiffs had the burden of showing discriminatory intent in the return to neighborhood schools. The court was satisfied that the reasons cited by the board were legitimate educational concerns supported by the evidence, and that the plaintiffs had failed to prove any discriminatory intent on the part of the board.[100] The Fourth Circuit Court of Appeals affirmed the district court decision upon appeal, agreeing that reestablishment of a neighborhood school policy for the purposes of reducing white flight and improving parental involvement is not proof of discriminatory intent.[101] The Supreme Court declined to review the appellate decision.

A similar outcome occurred for a case involving Austin, Texas. Austin adopted a court-ordered cross-district busing plan in 1980 and maintained it until 1986 in accordance with a consent decree. As part of the consent decree, Austin was declared unitary in 1983, and the case was dismissed. In 1987 the Austin school board proposed to return to a neighborhood school plan with voluntary integration options, which would reestablish sixteen racially identifiable elementary schools of a total of sixty-five. The United States, as plaintiff, brought suit asking the district court to enforce the consent decree, and another group of plaintiffs brought a new suit charging the school board with discrimination on grounds that some of the new neighborhood schools would be racially identifiable. The district court, as well as the Fifth Circuit Court of Appeals, found that the consent order could not be enforced because it had expired; moreover, enforcement of the consent decree would be improper since the district had been declared unitary. Both courts also concluded that plaintiffs had failed to prove discriminatory intent in the board's decision to return to neighborhood schools, even though a large number of schools would be racially identifiable.[102]

The third major postunitary decision, involving Oklahoma City, had a different outcome. During the 1960s, Oklahoma City had implemented a court-ordered desegregation plan relying primarily on geographic zoning. In 1972, after new hearings in light of the *Swann* decision, the district court concluded that state and school district actions had contributed to housing segregation and that the neighborhood school system had not eliminated the dual school system.[103] A mandatory busing plan was ordered for elementary schools, and this plan was maintained until 1985. In 1977 the school board moved to dismiss the case; in granting the motion, the district court stated it did not foresee board actions that would dismantle the plan or "undermine the unitary system." In 1984, the school board voted to abandon the busing plan for kindergarten to grade four and return to neighborhood schools; this plan would create predominantly white or black schools in approximately half of its sixty-four elementary schools. One of the reasons for the new plan was demographic changes that had increased transportation burdens on black students.

A new motion was filed by plaintiffs to reopen the case on the grounds that the new neighborhood plan was a return to illegal segregation. In ruling against the motion, the district court concluded that the school district had been declared unitary, that it had a fully integrated staff, that resources and programs were equal, and that there was no basis for maintaining the original busing plan.[104] In a later decision the district court also found that the current residential segregation was largely the result of private decisions and economics and not a vestige of the earlier dual school system, and therefore the neighborhood school plan was not a discriminatory action on the part of the school board.[105]

The Tenth Circuit Court of Appeals reversed the decision on the grounds that, although the school district had been declared unitary, the district court had not lifted the 1972 decree ordering the busing plan.[106] In a later decision, the court of appeals ruled that the decree has a "life of its own" and that the district court could not dissolve the original decree because the school board had a continuing duty not to take any action that would "impede the process of disestablishing the dual system and its effects."[107]

The Supreme Court accepted the second appellate decision for review, acknowledging the need to resolve the conflict between this decision and appellate decisions in the Pasadena, Norfolk, and Austin cases. Its 1991 decision reversed the appellate court and offered the first comprehensive ruling on the issue of unitary status, although the 5–3 vote reflected a continuing division on the Court.[108] Drawing on its decisions in *Swann, Milliken I,* and *Spangler,* the majority opinion emphasized that federal court supervision of desegregation is only a temporary measure and did not agree with the appellate court that a desegregation decree could be imposed on a school district for the "indefinite future." The Court also defined the conditions for dissolving a desegregation decree (or attaining unitary status) as (1) good faith compliance with a desegregation decree from its onset, and (2) elimination of vestiges of past discrimination to the extent "practicable." In addition to student assignment, a review of vestiges should look at all facets of school operations (e.g., the other *Green* factors of faculty assignment, administration, transportation, facilities, and extracurricular activities). Finally, the Court said that, once a school district is released from a decree, it no longer needs court authorization for student assignment or other school operations but that the Equal Protection Clause of the Constitution still applies.[109]

The dissent by Justice Marshall is especially noteworthy, not only because it was his last opinion in a school case before his retirement but also because it represents one of the strongest endorsements of the harm and benefit thesis by a sitting justice. Quoting the original psychological harm statements in *Brown*, he argued that racially identifiable schools are harmful and cause "stigmatic injury" and that a desegregation remedy should remain in place not only until discrimination is eliminated but also until the *effects* of that discrimination are also eliminated. Although he does not define these effects in detail, academic performance is implied by mention of a second Supreme Court decision in the Detroit case (*Milliken II*) which endorsed remedies such as compensatory education for improving black academic skills.[110]

The *Dowell* decision appears to settle the obligations of a school board regarding the duration of court-imposed desegregation plans. After a school district meets the requirements of good faith compliance and elimination of vestiges, it can be declared unitary. After unitary status is attained, it has no obligation to maintain a mandatory busing and racial balance plan indefinitely. If a return to geographic or neighborhood attendance zones is motivated by legitimate educational concerns, as opposed to a racially motivated intent to separate the races, then no constitutional violation should be found.

Although *Dowell* clarified postunitary obligations and the general requirements for unitary status, it left at least two other remedial questions unanswered: First, does a school district have to satisfy all *Green* factors simultaneously or incrementally? That is, can it be declared unitary and released from supervision in one area, say, student assignment, while the court retained jurisdiction in another area, say, faculty assignment? Second, is a school district responsible for maintaining school racial balance in the face of demographic changes until it is declared unitary? This question is especially critical for school districts that, prior to being declared unitary, stopped making changes in student assignment in order to maintain racial balance. The importance of having a unitary declaration was not appreciated until at least the mid-1980s.

Both of these questions appeared to be answered by the Supreme Court in its 1992 *Pitts* decision affecting DeKalb County, Georgia.[111] DeKalb County is a suburban school system adjacent to Atlanta, one of the largest in the state, and it adopted a court-ordered desegregation plan in 1969. At the time the school district was only 5 percent black, and all schools were desegregated by means of a neighborhood zoning plan. Starting in the early 1970s, DeKalb County experienced dramatic population growth, including heavy immigration of blacks from Atlanta. By the mid-1980s, DeKalb was nearly 50 percent black; most blacks had settled in the southern end of the county, converting many formerly white schools into predominantly black schools. During this time DeKalb County adopted a voluntary integrative transfer program and some magnet schools, but no attempt was made to racially balance all schools by means of mandatory busing or other techniques.

In 1986 DeKalb County filed a motion for unitary status and final dismissal from court supervision. In 1988 the district court granted that motion with regard to student assignment, transportation, facilities, and extracurricular activities but not with regard to faculty and principal assignment, which the Court concluded needed further improvements.[112] On appeal the Eleventh Circuit Court of Appeals reversed, holding that all six *Green* factors had to be met simultaneously before a unitary declaration and that until that time DeKalb County must take "affirmative steps" to maintain desegregation in all schools regardless of demographic changes, including consideration of mandatory busing techniques.[113]

The Supreme Court reversed the appellate court on both counts. Drawing on the principle that the nature of a violation determines the scope of a remedy, the decision authorizes a federal court to withdraw its supervision or control over the six *Green* factors incrementally or partially, providing that the requirements of unitary status are met for each one. The only additional consideration, in the discretion of the local court, is whether supervision has to be retained on one factor (e.g., facilities) to ensure attainment of another factor (e.g., student assignment).

The Supreme Court also stated that a district is not responsible for subsequent racial imbalance due to purely demographic factors: "Once the racial imbalance due to the de jure violation has been remedied, the school district is under no duty to remedy imbalance that is caused by demographic factors."[114] In support of this conclusion, the Court emphasizes the numerous causes of demographic change and residential patterns, including the role of personal preferences and private choices that have no "constitutional implications" (see chapter 3).

The *Pitts* ruling is unusual in that it is one of the few major desegregation decisions since *Swann* without a dissenting opinion. The majority opinion was delivered by Justice Kennedy, joined by Chief Justice Rehnquist and Justices White, Scalia, and Souter. Separate concurring opinions were written by Justices Scalia, Souter, and Blackmun, the latter being joined by Justices Stevens and O'Conner. Justice Thomas did not participate.

The possibility of future limitations on partial unitary rulings was raised in the concurring opinions of Souter and Blackmun, both of which placed greater emphasis on the potential interrelationships among the *Green* factors. In particular, they suggested that one of these factors (such as faculty assignment) might have a causal impact on another (such as student imbalance), thereby raising another condition that should be investigated before a court relinquishes control over any of the factors. They also emphasized the possibility that a dual school system might itself cause demographic or residential changes, which, if proven, could be the basis for holding a school responsible for housing segregation (see chapter 3).

A Summary of Desegregation Law

This overview has tried to trace and describe the complex evolution of desegregation law from *Brown* to *Pitts*. Although there have been significant changes and even conflicts in the case law over this period, the conflict arises more from ambiguity in key Supreme Court decisions rather than inconsistency. The ambiguity leads to different interpretations and different results from one lower court to another, compounded by the fact that the Supreme Court does not and could not review every lower court decision that strays from its main doctrinal principles. Indeed, Supreme Court justices themselves cite different parts of the same opinion to arrive at opposite conclusions. The *Swann* opinion has been the most vulnerable in this respect, with both majority and dissenting factions relying on various portions to defend their conflicting positions in *Milliken* and *Spangler*.

Documenting these changes is one matter; explaining why they have occurred is something else. Some commentators believe they can be reduced to ideological swings—a shift in the balance of "judicial activists" or "strict constructionists" sitting on the bench. While ideological changes are undoubtedly part of the explanation, they cannot carry the entire burden. In addition to philosophical principles, judicial doctrine must have a knowledge base—a factual view of what is, as opposed to what should be. Changes in this knowledge base, whether by scientific study or by ordinary experience, in turn have an impact on doctrine.

Unquestionably, the evolution of school desegregation law and policy has been influenced in part by changes in social science knowledge, generated by social scientists who study and write on race and desegregation issues and who frequently impart this knowledge as expert witnesses. The best examples are the research and testimony on the harm and benefit thesis (both old and new versions), the causes of housing segregation, and the problem of white flight, all of which have numerous citations in both lower and higher court opinions.

The most important philosophical changes on the Court, from the standpoint of school desegregation law, concern the standards to be applied when judging the discriminatory intent of official actions and the tailoring of remedy to the proven discrimination. The Supreme Court divisions began when desegregation cases moved out of the South to regions without a history of state-imposed segregation, where state-enforced segregation was not automatic.

More activist jurists have been willing to impose stronger and more permanent remedies in all desegregation cases and to apply these same remedies outside the South, where most segregation arises from housing patterns and not state action. Activist and constructionist jurists are most likely to divide on those standards that rely on foreseeable consequences and shifting the burden of proof, which were the main mechanisms for extending desegregation in the North.

As indicated in Justice Marshall's dissent in *Dowell*, one of the reasons for this division may well be a belief in the general harm and benefit thesis, a belief more prominent among jurists during the 1960s and 1970s than during the 1990s. Whatever the views of the harm and benefit thesis today, clearly fewer Supreme Court justices in 1990 than in 1970 are willing to blur the distinction between de jure and de facto segregation or to permit a loose relationship between remedy and violation.

The evolution in desegregation law, whether due to changes in ideology or

knowledge, is not over. Social science research will continue to play an important role in the future of desegregation law and policies, particularly in legislative settings and school board deliberations, where such concepts as the harm
and benefit thesis are still very much at issue. To set the stage for the following
chapters, the next section summarizes desegregation law today, considers
which issues are settled and which are not, and considers the types of social
science evidence relevant to each of these issues.

Legal Standards

De jure versus de facto segregation. It is relatively settled that only de jure
segregation violates the Constitution, which means policies or actions by public
officials or agencies that meet two critical conditions: significant segregative
effects and discriminatory *intent;* that is, a policy or action must not only cause a
significant degree of segregation, but it must also be motivated by an intent to
cause segregation, such as the Jim Crow laws of the Old South. A policy or
action motivated by a legitimate educational purpose that incidentally causes
segregation and has no segregative purpose is not unconstitutional by this rule.

The standards by which segregative intent are judged, however, are not
completely settled. The standards of foreseeable effects and shifting the burden
of proof—which can make a school board prove that segregative intent is not a
factor—are the most problematic. The foreseeable effect rule appears to be less
important in light of the *Dowell* and *Pitts* decisions, in which school boards were
permitted to reestablish or maintain racially imbalanced schools.

Scope and types of remedy. Another principle that seems fairly well settled by
the Supreme Court is the equity and compensatory aspects of desegregation
remedies. Once a constitutional violation is established, a remedy should be
designed to eliminate the effects of the violation so that victims are restored to
the position they would have occupied without the violation. In practical terms,
a remedy has only to fix what the violation causes, which should involve only
those individuals, schools, or segments of school systems actually affected by
the violations found.

Given a constitutional violation with systemwide effects, less settled are the
specific types of desegregation plans required. In particular, the definitions of a
desegregated school, the time allowed to attain plan goals, and specific techniques used (mandatory or voluntary student assignment to schools) are up to
the discretion of lower courts. The main concern of a lower court is the effectiveness of a desegregation plan in remedying the constitutional violations.

The most troubling issue here, both in the past and at present, is the degree
of racial balance that must be attained by a desegregation plan. *Swann* is the
only case that offered detailed remedial guidelines by the Supreme Court, and
it clearly approves numerical quotas and cross-district busing to attain racial
balance in all or nearly all schools. Although *Swann* clearly saw numerical
quotas as a starting point, the fact is that many lower courts have used racial
balance as a definition and goal of desegregation, rather than as a temporary

guideline. Presumably, *Spangler, Dowell* and *Pitts* have changed this outlook to some extent, although the later decisions have yet to be fully interpreted and implemented by the lower courts.

Unitary status. The final set of established principles has to do with attaining unitary status. After complying with a desegregation decree and eliminating the vestiges of unconstitutional segregation "to the extent practicable," a school district can be declared unitary and relieved of court supervision. At this point a school district can modify or even abandon a previous court-approved desegregation plan; it can revive neighborhood schools that are racially imbalanced, providing the change is not made with a discriminatory purpose.

There is likely to be much debate and possibly disagreement among the lower courts about the legitimacy of returning to a neighborhood school system that reestablishes predominantly one-race schools. Under a foreseeable consequences rule, some courts might demand that the burden of proof be on the school board that a neighborhood policy in those circumstances is not motivated in part by a segregative purpose.

Social Science Issues in Desegregation

The harm and benefit thesis. The desire of some educators, social scientists, and jurists and most civil rights groups to expand desegregation to de facto situations appears motivated primarily by a belief in the harm and benefit thesis: that segregation of any kind is harmful while desegregation (defined as racial balance) is socially and educationally beneficial. Evidence on the harm and benefit thesis has been a factor in earlier court decisions, particularly by lower courts wanting to justify integration for de facto housing segregation. Given the evolution of a relatively firm de jure rule, the harm and benefit thesis is less relevant to future court deliberations. Given the current status of constitutional law, policies that address de facto segregation must emerge from legislatures and school boards, and in these contexts the harm and benefit thesis is still relevant to the general debate. Indeed, without a legal requirement to remedy de facto segregation, and absent proof that housing segregation is a de jure violation, the harm and benefit thesis is about the only justification for encouraging legislatures and school boards to overcome the very obstinate if not intractable condition of residential segregation.

Residential segregation. The Supreme Court has never ruled explicitly on the relationship between housing and school segregation, although they have stated that a school district is not responsible for segregation arising from demographic factors alone. The evaluation of residential patterns has been left up to district courts, many of which have ruled against neighborhood school policies on the grounds that governmental discrimination contributes significantly to segregated housing. Therefore, social science knowledge about the causes of housing segregation has been and continues to be an important basis for determining the future viability of neighborhood school policies.

Effectiveness of remedies. There are two major interrelated issues concerning desegregation plans that determine the effectiveness of a desegregation remedy. One is the definition of a desegregated school in terms of its racial composition, particularly how far it can deviate from perfect racial balance. The second is whether a mandatory student assignment plan is more or less effective in attaining long-term desegregation than a voluntary or choice plan. Although in principle both mandatory and choice plans can meet the legal requirements for a remedy, there is still much contention over which is the most effective in particular circumstances. Both of these issues have been the subject of substantial social science research, in which the issue of white flight has been a major consideration. These expert studies and testimony have been important in many court cases and will continue to play a major role in the future evolution of desegregation law.

2

The Harm and Benefit Thesis

Of all the social science theories that have been applied to school desegregation policy, none has a longer or more important history than the harm and benefit thesis. In its simplest form, the thesis holds that school segregation is harmful to the social, psychological, and educational development of children, both minority and white, and that school desegregation is beneficial for undoing or at least ameliorating the damages from segregation and discrimination. While the harm and benefit thesis began as a purely social science theory, its apparent endorsement by the Supreme Court in *Brown* gave the thesis an enormous boost, elevating it from academic theory to moral authority.

From *Brown* to the present time, the harm and benefit thesis has played a curious and bifurcated role in the evolution of school desegregation policy. Although it began as a social science theory that had apparently found its way into judicial doctrine, its role in the courts soon parted from its role among educators, social scientists, and civil rights groups.

On the judicial front, a number of lower court decisions in the early 1970s stressed the harms of school segregation and the benefits of integration remedies. The Supreme Court itself never again explicitly addressed the harm and benefit thesis after *Brown*, however, and its judicial relevance diminished over the next three decades as the high Court majority restricted the application of *Brown* to government-enforced school segregation. For this reason many constitutional scholars have long maintained that the psychological harm finding in *Brown* is not an essential part of constitutional law. To the extent that a harm thesis can be inferred from current judicial doctrine, then, harm arises only if school (or other) segregation is sanctioned by law or official action.

For many other actors on the desegregation stage, however, the harm and benefit thesis has had a far broader applicability. During the periods when the earliest formulations began to appear, such as that by Gunnar Myrdal in 1944 or the famous doll studies of Kenneth and Mamie Clark in the late 1930s, most existing segregation was in fact sanctioned by law, and thus most social science research on this issue of necessity reflected the effects of official segregation.[1] Indeed, the original social science statement submitted by appellants in the *Brown* case (signed by thirty-two social scientists) explicitly limited the thesis to cases of official segregation.[2]

By the late 1960s, however, when school desegregation remedies were becoming more widespread and the distinction between de facto and de jure
segregation was emerging in the law, the harm and benefit thesis had evolved to
a more comprehensive form. One of the earliest and most influential versions of
this expanded proposition was found in the 1967 report by the U.S. Commission
on Civil Rights, which concluded that the effects of segregation compelled by
law also applied to segregation not compelled by law.[3] This broader formulation
has been embraced by most civil rights groups and several Supreme Court
justices, and it continues to be supported by many social scientists and educators. The most recent manifestation of this thesis is another social science statement, signed by fifty-two social scientists, included in an amicus curiae brief
submitted by the NAACP and other civil rights organizations to the Supreme
Court for its review of the *Pitts* (DeKalb County) case.[4]

Although more social scientists signed the 1991 statement than the 1952 statement, there was far less unanimity about the harm and benefit thesis in 1991
than at the time of *Brown*. One reason is that the latest thesis is much broader
and more complex than the original thesis, which had dealt only with the effects
of official or de jure segregation. The latest thesis covers de jure and de facto
segregation; the presumed harmful effects cover a wider range of social and
educational outcomes; and the presumed benefits of desegregation are conditional on other features of school systems (that is, if certain conditions are not
present, there may be no benefits as all).

Moreover, by 1991 a large research literature had accumulated on the effects
of segregation and desegregation, and major studies of school desegregation
challenge some of the central premises of the harm and benefit thesis. Although
many educators and social scientists continue to support the modern version of
the thesis, others believe that it should have a diminished role in educational
policy and particularly that it does not justify some of the more drastic desegregation remedies such as mandatory busing.

Given the diminished importance of the harm and benefit thesis in federal
court proceedings, some might question whether the thesis is relevant to
present-day discussions and debates over school desegregation and civil rights
policies. On the contrary, if anything, the harm and benefit thesis will play an
even greater role in the future of school desegregation, albeit in a different
context and on a different stage. Since the federal courts have limited school
desegregation remedies to official segregation, and even former de jure districts
can reestablish neighborhood schools following attainment of unitary status, the
role of federal courts in school desegregation matters is on the decline.

Yet de facto school segregation continues to grow because of a combination of
demographic factors, housing patterns, neighborhood school policies, and
boundaries that separate city and suburban school districts. Thus the debate
over school desegregation will of necessity shift to legislatures, school boards,
and even state courts, where the harm and benefit thesis is very much a live
issue.

For example, in 1993 Connecticut became the first state to adopt legislation
encouraging school desegregation between cities and suburbs, the rationale for
which draws heavily from the harm and benefit thesis. Not coincidentally,

Connecticut is also the first state to be sued by the ACLU and the NAACP to bring about desegregation between a city and its suburbs on the grounds of equal opportunity clauses in the *state* constitution. The lawsuit relies heavily on the harm and benefit thesis: that segregation between city and suburban schools is the cause of poor educational outcomes among minority children, and that desegregation across district boundaries will remedy this condition.

Many school boards still debate the relative benefits and costs of school desegregation initiatives, even when they are not under threat of lawsuits, and the harm and benefit thesis is usually invoked by those who support such initiatives. In 1992 the school board of La Crosse, Wisconsin, adopted a controversial desegregation plan to bring about economic (and racial) balance in its schools, which led to a successful recall election. The primary justification for the desegregation plan, again, was the harm and benefit thesis, in this case promoted by the local teachers' union.

Finally, the harm and benefit thesis surfaces in the debates over new school choice proposals, where numerous states are considering or have passed laws increasing the choice of schools, including interdistrict choice and even vouchers for private schools. One of the most common arguments against such proposals is that they will cause the middle class (or what is left of it) to leave city schools, increase segregation, and leave only disadvantaged minority children in central city school districts. The contention is that higher concentrations of poor or minority students lead to inferior education, which is another version of the harm and benefit thesis.

The discussion and evaluation of the harm and benefit thesis are offered in several stages in this chapter. First, it is important to describe how the thesis has evolved and changed, from its earliest formulations in social science research to its more recent versions, along with its application in various court decisions and federal policy formulations. The four major components of the thesis are academic achievement, self-concept and aspirations, race relations and prejudice, and long-term educational and vocational attainments. Second, some of the major social science research on each component is discussed, emphasizing those studies introduced as part of expert testimony in school desegregation cases. This discussion draws on several comprehensive studies that have played a central role in the policy debate over school desegregation.

The purpose of this chapter is not to provide a comprehensive review of the entire social science literature on the effects of segregation and desegregation. Rather, the aim is to understand the nature of the harm and benefit thesis, the way it has been used in court decisions and in the policy debate, and the extent to which it forms a valid and credible basis for influencing school desegregation or school choice policies.

History of the Harm and Benefit Thesis

Just as school desegregation law has evolved and changed over the past thirty-five years, so has the content and scope of the harm and benefit thesis. Although some changes in the thesis derive from the substantial research undertaken since *Brown* on the effects of desegregation, other changes, including its scope of application, have been in response to changes in judicial doctrine and law.

The history of the harm and benefit thesis can be broken into several stages. The first is the social science work leading up to the 1954 *Brown* decision and culminating in the first social science statement submitted to the Supreme Court on the topic of school desegregation. The second is marked by publication of the 1967 U.S. Commission on Civil Rights report, *Racial Isolation in the Public Schools*, just before the era of large-scale mandatory busing. The third stage is best represented by the social science statement submitted to the Supreme Court during the *Pitts* (DeKalb County) appeal in 1991. Unlike the first social science statement submitted in *Brown*, this most recent statement reflects a more comprehensive theory of the harms of segregation and the benefits of desegregation, along with a more complex dynamic of the conditions under which the benefits of desegregation occur.

The Harm and Benefit Thesis before *Brown*

The body of research on segregation and desegregation before *Brown* was not vast, and the studies that did exist were quite limited, either by methodology or scope. Because segregation was pervasive in those parts of the country where most blacks resided, the opportunities to study desegregation, especially in schools, were restricted, and the possibility of comparing the effects of segregation and desegregation with rigorous experimental designs was virtually nonexistent.

One of the most prestigious early studies of segregation and discrimination against blacks was that sponsored by the Carnegie Corporation in the late 1930s. A team of social scientists led by Swedish economist Gunnar Myrdal conducted a comprehensive study of the condition of blacks in America, documenting the social, legal, and political forces that caused and maintained a state of inequality between blacks and whites. The study, published as *An American Dilemma* in 1944 and *Negro in America* in 1948, formulated the famous vicious circle theory that explained the interdependence between prejudice, discrimination, and inequality: "White prejudice and discrimination keep the Negro low in standards of living, health, education, manners, and morals. This, in its turn, gives support to white prejudice. White prejudice and Negro standards thus mutually 'cause' each other."[5]

They also postulated that the vicious circle process could work in reverse; that is, if black standards could be raised in some area such as employment or education (presumably by changes in government policies), then white prejudice and discrimination would be lessened and pave the way for further increases in standards for blacks. The causal link between white prejudice and black-white inequality, given scientific credibility by this comprehensive study, has been a long-standing tenet of civil rights groups and forms a integral component of the harm and benefit thesis.

The research by Myrdal and his colleagues focused on the broad social causes and correlates of black discrimination and inequality; it did not deal specifically with the psychological harm arising from segregation and discrimination. The psychological harm tenet emerged from research on black children by psychologists, the most influential of which were the doll studies of Kenneth and Mamie Clark. These studies showed that young black children (ages three to seven) were aware of racial differences, that they tended to associate negative characteristics with black dolls and positive characteristics with white dolls, and that, when asked to choose a doll like themselves, a substantial proportion incorrectly chose the white doll.[6] This last finding was replicated in other studies and was widely interpreted by psychologists as indicating racial self-rejection and low self-esteem, hence an example of psychological harm or damage. It was generally agreed that this psychological harm was caused by the long history of prejudice and discrimination against blacks, of which state-mandated segregation was the most prominent form.

Interestingly, one of the Clarks' earliest findings raised a question about whether segregation was one of the mechanisms that caused this psychological harm. Although all black children had substantial rates of incorrect racial identification, those in the segregated South were more likely to make correct self-identifications than those in northern desegregated environments. This finding did not receive much attention at the time, and it was clearly ignored in the earliest versions of the harm and benefit thesis. Subsequent and more sophisticated research corroborated this finding, setting the stage for a challenge to the thesis that school desegregation would reverse these psychological harms, if, indeed, segregation had caused them in the first place (as contrasted, for example, with the effects of more than two hundred years of slavery).

The final component in the early harm and benefit thesis concerned the probable effects of desegregation. Because segregation policies were entangled with many other social and economic conditions of blacks, that the mere elimination of official segregation would overcome all of the forces that might be contributing to psychological damage was by no means clear. In particular, no theory provided specific social and psychological mechanisms to enable desegregation to undo damages caused by decades (if not centuries) of discrimination and segregation. The key development here was yet another set of psychological hypotheses, "contact theory."

The best-known progenitor of contact theory was Gordon Allport, who described it in *The Nature of Prejudice*. This seminal study synthesized the work of various social scientists who had studied desegregation in such areas as public housing, employment, and the military and provided a conceptual foundation for the theory:

> Contacts that bring knowledge and acquaintance are likely to engender sounder beliefs about minority groups. . . . Prejudice . . . may be reduced by equal status contact between majority and minority groups in the pursuit of common goals. The effect is greatly enhanced if this contact is sanctioned by institutional supports (i.e., by law, custom, or local atmosphere), and if it is of a sort that leads to the perception of common interests and common humanity between members of the two groups.[7]

For many social scientists, contact theory became the key to breaking the vicious circle of prejudice, discrimination, segregation, and inequality. If blacks and whites were brought together in a desegregated environment under the conditions posited by contact theory, then white prejudice could be reduced. Reduced prejudice would then lead to reduced discrimination and segregation, which would, in turn, ultimately reduce inequalities in education, employment, and income.

Although the earliest expressions of the harm and benefit thesis were not quite this comprehensive, the social science statement submitted as part of the 1952 appeals process in *Brown* had many of the critical elements, particularly regarding the harms of segregation. Citing the social science research of Myrdal, the Clarks, Allport, and many others, the first part of the statement summarizes a report from a White House Conference on Children and Youth (authored by Kenneth Clark), which documented the psychological harms of segregation:[8]

> As minority group children learn the inferior status to which they are assigned—as they observe the fact that they are almost always segregated and kept apart from others . . . they often react with feelings of inferiority and a sense of personal humiliation. Many . . . become confused about their own personal worth. . . . The minority group child is thrown into a conflict with regard to his feelings about himself and his group. . . . This conflict and confusion leads to self-hatred and rejection of his own group. . . . Minority group children . . . often react with a generally defeatist attitude and a lowering of personal ambitions. This . . . is reflected in a lowering of pupil morale and a depression of the educational aspiration level. . . . Segregated schools impair the ability of the child to profit from the educational opportunities provided him.

The causal chain here starts with white prejudice toward blacks, reflected in segregated schools and other activities, which leads to black internalization of the negative attitudes of whites, which ultimately leads to poor self-esteem and lowered educational expectations. Low esteem and aspirations were widely believed to be among the major psychological causes of lower academic achievement.

Another part of the statement addressed the effects of school desegregation. It first argued that desegregation does not have negative side effects such as lowering educational standards for whites, putting blacks at an educational disadvantage, or promoting interracial conflict. Those concerned about negative educational effects, it claimed, were influenced by the false belief that blacks were intellectually inferior to whites, a belief contradicted by the research available at that time. The concern about interracial conflict was assuaged by reference to studies documenting the successful implementation of desegregation (in the army, public housing, employment, and so forth) without serious racial incidents or violence.

Finally, the statement points out that under the right circumstances, desegregation can not only proceed smoothly but also lead to the "emergence of more favorable attitudes and friendlier relations between the races." It mentioned the kinds of conditions posited by Allport's contact theory, including firm enforcement by authorities, absence of competition between racial groups, and equal positions and functions (status) among those persons being desegregated. The statement said that these conditions could be generally satisfied "in the armed services, public housing developments, and public schools."[9] Moreover, the favorable outcomes being stressed here, racial attitudes and relations, were beneficial to both blacks and whites.

This first expression of the harm and benefit thesis did not specifically ascribe the lower academic achievement of black students to the psychological harms flowing from segregation or assert that the academic achievement of black students would be improved by desegregating the schools. Such a connection was certainly implied, however, and it was asserted in expert testimony in lower court hearings, which was cited by the Kansas district court in *Brown:* "Segregation with the sanction of law, therefore, has a tendency to [retard] the educational and mental development of Negro children and to deprive them of some of the benefits they would receive in a racial[ly] integrated school system."[10]

It should also be noted that the social science statement—as well as the Supreme Court decisions in *Brown*—very clearly claimed that the psychological and educational harms at issue were those arising from segregation compelled by law. The social science statement actually defines segregation as "restriction of opportunities" arising from official actions and emphasizes that "we are not here concerned with such segregation as arises from the free movements of individuals which are neither enforced nor supported by official bodies. . . ."[11]

The fact that the social science statement restricts the harm thesis to de jure segregation, in line with the Supreme Court's ultimate decision, does not appear coincidental. There is nothing in the early research to indicate that the effects of segregation depended on sanctions by law because most of the key mechanisms thought to cause and maintain white prejudice—lack of communication, stereotyping, reinforcing negative attitudes—were fostered by any type of separation, with or without the force of law. The definition of segregation in the social science statement is very carefully crafted to limit harmful effects to government-sponsored segregation, which may have been motivated by a concern to keep the social science research consistent with legal issue at hand.

The Harm and Benefit Thesis between *Brown* and *Swann*

Whatever the reasons for the limited harm and benefit thesis before *Brown*, it did not last long. During the legal debate over the constitutionality of de facto segregation in the 1960s, new social science research was underway that would become the basis for a significant expansion of the harm and benefit thesis.

Without question, the most important social science study during this period was sponsored by the U.S. Office of Education (USOE), which had been commissioned by the Civil Rights Act of 1964 to survey the "lack of availability of equal educational opportunities for individuals by reason of race" in public schools throughout the country. The massive survey and study, the largest of its kind at that time, was conducted by a team of social scientists led by sociologist James Coleman. The 1966 report, *Equality of Educational Opportunity* (also dubbed the "Coleman Report"), was at once powerful and controversial.[12] Its findings and policy implications were debated for years, and many secondary analyses of the data were carried out to revalidate, refine, or extend the original findings.[13]

Most of the reassessments failed to shake the major conclusions of the report, which are summarized here:

- Twelve years after *Brown,* the overwhelming majority of white students attended predominantly white schools and a majority of black students attended schools that were majority black.
- Contrary to expectations, within regions of the country the distribution of school facilities and resources—expenditures, teacher background, equipment, textbooks—were largely equal between black schools and white schools, and where there were differences, they tended to be small and could favor blacks or whites.
- The academic achievement of blacks lagged substantially behind whites at all grade levels, and the small differences in school resources contributed very little to these achievement differences; however the achievement levels of both blacks and whites were strongly associated with the socioeconomic characteristics of their families.
- Black students in desegregated schools had higher achievement levels than black students in predominantly black schools, although this difference was reduced substantially when family socioeconomic levels were taken into account (that is, blacks in desegregated schools were from families with more education, income, and so forth).

The conclusions about the extent of segregation, racial differences in academic achievement, and the relationship between desegregation and academic achievement were generally in line with expectations and not controversial. However, the lack of major differences in school resources for blacks and whites and, especially, the lack of a relationship between school resources and academic achievement were extremely controversial and led to intense debates in educational policy circles, debates that have continued up to the present. Many of the controversies were methodological in nature, with critics arguing that the data were limited in various ways and would not support some of the stronger conclusions about school versus family effects.

For example, critics pointed out that the USOE survey assessed facilities and teacher characteristics rather than program characteristics such as curriculum content or academic standards, and therefore it was improper to conclude that school characteristics had *no* impact on academic outcomes. In addition, the USOE study was not an experimental design, whereby equivalent groups of students would be exposed to various school conditions and outcomes would be assessed over time. This second limitation was frequently cited in connection with the fourth finding about the relationship between desegregated schools and achievement because desegregated blacks at that time were clearly drawn from different socioeconomic strata than segregated blacks.

In spite of these limitations, the USOE data and findings were used repeatedly in the debate over the educational effects of segregation and desegregation, sometimes in court settings and sometimes by government agencies or school boards. It was used extensively in the second version of the harm and benefit thesis, which was advanced in an important report issued in 1967 by the U.S. Commission on Civil Rights, *Racial Isolation in the Public Schools*.[14] This report was based on extensive analyses of the USOE data on the relationship between school desegregation and a variety of social and educational outcomes, including student achievement, aspirations, and self-esteem. It became the first government-sponsored study to conclude specifically that school segregation, whatever its source, lowered the educational achievement of black children:

> Negro children who attend predominantly Negro schools do not achieve as well as other children, Negro and white. Their aspirations are more restricted that those of other children and they do not have as much confidence that they can influence their own futures. When they become adults, they are less likely to participate in the mainstream of American society, and more likely to fear, dislike, and avoid white Americans.[15]

These results led the commission to decide that "the conclusion drawn by the U.S. Supreme Court about the impact upon children of segregation compelled by law . . . applies to segregation not compelled by law."[16] The report did not specifically state that desegregation would cure all these harms, but such a conclusion was implied in that black students in desegregated classrooms had higher academic achievement than those in segregated classrooms. The *Racial Isolation* report acknowledged that the federal courts were not likely to impose desegregation remedies in cases of de facto segregation, so instead it called on Congress to pass legislation compelling schools to eliminate racial isolation and establishing a racial balance standard of not more than 50 percent black in any public school.

The timing of this broader version of the harm and benefit thesis was propitious. School desegregation litigation was about to escalate on several fronts: the adoption of mandatory busing, a shift of focus to northern de facto segregation, and the expansion to metropolitan school segregation. Some but not all of these enlarged efforts were successful, and in many cases the broader harm and benefit thesis played an important role in the lower courts. Some lower court judges were sufficiently impressed by the harm and benefit thesis, bolstered by testimony of social scientists as expert witnesses in their courtrooms, that they incorporated it into their rulings. As reviewed in chapter 1, specific findings on the harmful effects of segregation on educational outcomes—or the beneficial effects of desegregation—were found in lower court decisions in Charlotte–Mecklenburg, North Carolina (the seminal *Swann* case); Pasadena and San Francisco, California; Pontiac, Michigan; Denver, Colorado (the *Keyes* case); and Richmond, Virginia.

The fact that the Supreme Court itself did not rule on the harm and benefit issue in any of these cases (some of which did not reach the high Court on appeal) does not diminish the importance of the issue in the lower courts. Moreover, for many civil rights groups such as the NAACP and the ACLU, the harm and benefit thesis has always been a major reason for initiating litigation, and it continues to be a factor in their pursuit of school desegregation in other forums.

The Harm and Benefit Thesis after *Swann*

By the late 1960s, there was overwhelming consensus among social scientists and many others about the harm and benefit thesis, and this consensus led to widespread support for court or government intervention to foster school desegregation. Most social scientists also supported the new policies of mandatory busing promulgated by the *Swann* decision, in spite of overwhelming public controversy and community opposition. Most of the opposition to busing came from whites and was thought to be racially motivated, and most of the academic community felt opposition should not stand in the way of a truly beneficial policy for disadvantaged blacks.

This consensus was about to end. Prior to *Swann*, a major limitation common to desegregation studies was that very few reflected the type of comprehensive desegregation policies implemented after 1970, particularly mandatory busing plans. During the 1960s most desegregated schools either reflected housing decisions or voluntary "freedom of choice" plans, and thus desegregated black students were a highly self-selected group. Desegregation studies were also of more limited design, such as the one-shot USOE survey. After the onset of large-scale desegregation plans, a much greater cross-section of students was exposed to desegregation, and more rigorous experimental studies became possible.

Moreover, cross-district busing plans added yet another dimension to the harm and benefit thesis: the possibility of white flight. White flight meant that large-scale desegregation plans might increase racial balance within one district at the expense of greater segregation between cities and suburbs or between public and private schools. The white flight problem threatened to undermine the harm and benefit thesis by increasing segregation for minority children. Unpopular desegregation plans also threatened community support for public education, which was manifested in opposition to bond issues or tax increases for important educational improvements.

The number of social science studies of school desegregation multiplied rapidly during the 1970s and early 1980s, coinciding with the increase in court-ordered desegregation plans after *Swann*. Most of these studies evaluated some aspect of the harm and benefit thesis as applied to self-esteem and aspirations, academic achievement, and race relations; a number of studies also addressed the white flight issue. In contrast to the pre-*Swann* era, many of these new studies raised serious questions about the effectiveness and viability of large-scale desegregation programs. For example, various studies found that black students in segregated schools did not have serious self-esteem problems, that desegregation had not raised the achievement levels of black students, that desegregation either failed to improve or actually worsened racial attitudes and race relations, and that desegregation was causing white flight and the segregation between cities and suburbs.

Some of these studies are reviewed in more detail in subsequent sections or chapters, but a partial listing of studies critical of the harm and benefit thesis is appropriate here.

- In 1972 I published a study of a Boston voluntary city-suburban busing program and a review of six other studies of desegregation which concluded that achievement, self-esteem, and aspirations had not improved and that race relations had declined after desegregation. [17]
- In 1975 Harold Gerard and Norman Miller published a comprehensive long-term study of desegregation in Riverside, California, concluding that neither academic achievement nor self-esteem of minority children had improved, and that racial attitudes (stereotyping) and race relations had worsened after desegregation. [18]
- A 1975 review of 120 desegregation studies by Nancy St. John concluded that desegregation had not closed the achievement gap significantly, that black self-esteem and aspirations may have declined, and that changes in racial attitudes were "sometimes positive but often negative."[19]
- In 1975 James Coleman published a national study of the relationship between desegregation and white flight, in which he concluded that desegregation was causing white flight and was, under certain conditions, increasing the segregation between cities and their suburbs. [20]
- In 1978 Walter Stephan published an evaluation of predictions made in *Brown* and "tentatively" concluded that school desegregation does not improve black self-esteem, "sometimes" increases black academic achievement, does not reduce white prejudice toward blacks, and increases black prejudice toward whites as often as it is reduced. [21]
- In 1982 Martin Patchen published a major study of race relations following desegregation in Indianapolis, which concluded that race relations worsened in classrooms as the percent black increased from 10 to 50 percent and improved only when classrooms became majority black. [22]
- In 1983 Christine Rossell, who had criticized Coleman's 1975 study of white flight, published a study of 113 school districts and concluded that mandatory busing plans caused significant long-term white flight. In later studies she concluded that, because of the white flight problem, voluntary desegregation plans could be more effective than mandatory plans. [23]

- In 1984 the National Institute of Education published a review of the most rigorous studies of desegregation and the academic achievement of blacks, concluding that desegregation had no effects on math achievement and only small effects on reading achievement.[24]

Many other social science studies appeared in support of the thesis, and some of these studies expanded the harm and benefit thesis by adding new types of outcomes or stressing the conditions under which positive effects would occur. Some of the more significant works in this category are as follows:

- A 1977 review of seventy-one studies of desegregation and black achievement by Meyer Weinberg concluded that a majority of the studies showed positive effects.[25]
- In 1982 Robert Crain published the first formal meta-analysis of ninety-three studies of the effects of desegregation on black achievement, concluding that desegregation did benefit black achievement although large effects were confined those students in kindergarten or the first grade.[26]
- A series of longitudinal studies in the 1980s by Jomills Braddock and James McPartland found that students who attended desegregated schools were more likely to attend desegregated colleges or to be employed in desegregated workplaces (but not necessarily more likely to have attended college or to hold white-collar jobs).[27]
- Several studies by Robert Slavin during the 1980s concluded that a new instructional technique used in desegregated classrooms, "cooperative learning," had positive effects for lower-achieving students and for intergroup relations.[28]
- A sixteen-year follow-up study of black students in a Hartford voluntary city-suburban busing program by Robert Crain and others concluded that those who graduated from desegregated schools were more likely to attend college, to complete more years of college, to hold higher status jobs, and to work in more desegregated work environments than those students who attended segregated schools in Hartford.[29]

The conclusions of other social scientists who have written extensively on school desegregation policies, especially Gary Orfield and Willis Hawley, generally support the harm and benefit thesis and question the seriousness of the white flight problem.[30]

In light of the large number of research reviews that find considerable variation in desegregation effects—even the most positive reviewers acknowledge studies without positive outcomes—many writings on school desegregation have focused on the conditions under which positive outcomes can occur.[31] Unlike the research behind the original thesis, which tended to find desegregation benefits across the board, modern research tends to find that effects are not uniform but vary from one study (and presumably one set of conditions) to another. Inconsistencies in research findings have even led some writers to suggest that some of the original objectives of desegregation as well as the social science theory underlying the benefit thesis may well be oversimplified and in need of major rethinking.[32]

Another interesting development in the post-*Swann* research on the harm and benefit thesis is the fading emphasis on benefits to white students. In the original thesis, whites benefit from desegregation by a reduction in racial prejudice and an improvement in race relations, ultimately paying off in less discrimination and segregation. Ironically, although there is little question that white prejudice toward blacks has declined since *Brown* (see chapter 3), improvement in racial attitudes is the one area where the benefits of school desegregation have been hardest to demonstrate, indeed, where some of the most negative effects have been found.

Moreover, virtually all studies of desegregation and achievement have found little or no change in achievement or other educational outcomes for white students. Some desegregation researchers present this as a positive finding, either as refuting a view that desegregation is harmful to white achievement or because the only way the black-white achievement gap will close is if black students outgain white students. Most white parents are unlikely to view this result as beneficial, especially if they are being asked to accept mandatory busing away from their neighborhood school.

What distinguishes social science research in the post-*Swann* era from earlier eras, then, is a lack of consistent research findings and therefore a lack of consensus about the specific benefits of school desegregation. Depending on the particular harm or benefit being assessed, some studies find that desegregation has positive effects (often small), some studies find no effects, and some studies find negative effects. There is generally more consensus that desegregation (particularly mandatory busing) causes white flight, but there is no consensus on whether this flight is extensive enough to cause resegregation.

The 1991 Harm and Benefit Thesis

The lack of consistency in research findings is reflected in the most recent articulation of the harm and benefit thesis, which is the 1991 social science statement submitted to the Supreme Court as part of the NAACP brief in the DeKalb County case (*Pitts*).[33] While the statement endorses several across-the-board benefits of school desegregation and cites few studies to the contrary, the statement also says, "Merely placing black and white children together in schools, however, does not achieve these goals."[34] Nearly half of the statement is devoted to specifying the "conditions of successful desegregation."

The statement is divided into several sections. The first section deals with the relationship between housing and school segregation, concluding that school segregation fosters residential segregation and that school desegregation plans have contributed to desegregated housing (which is taken up in chapter 3). It acknowledges an intense debate among social scientists over "white flight," but goes on to say that "plans can produce long-lasting integration" and cites Charlotte–Mecklenburg, North Carolina, as a case in point.[35]

The second part of the statement is titled "Desegregation's Impact on Students" and expresses its main benefit propositions.

> Desegregation is generally associated with moderate gains in the achievement of black students and the achievement of white students is unaffected. . . . Desegregation has clear benefits for black students. It does not harm the academic achievement of white students and may well be beneficial in their future work. Its benefits extend beyond the classroom to the larger issues of integration in employment, higher education, and housing.[36]

Unlike earlier expressions of the harm and benefit thesis, the statement makes no specific claims about beneficial effects of desegregation on self-esteem and race relations, and, with the exception of St. John's study, none of the major studies that have questioned the harm and benefit thesis is cited. It does acknowledge the existence of negative findings indirectly by stating that school desegregation alone does not guarantee benefits: "There is nothing to suggest that brief exposure to whites, in schools that do nothing else to produce equal opportunity, will cure the harms created by a history of segregation."[37]

Another departure from the first social science statement is a section on the "necessary conditions for effective desegregation." Claiming that "assigning minority and white students to the same school is no panacea for educational inequality," the statement posits three general conditions for successful desegregation: "(1) desegregate as many grades as possible at the same time, concentrating especially on the youngest students; (2) cover as large a geographic area as possible to include a broad spectrum of socio-economic classes as well as races; and (3) persevere with the long-range goal of desegregation, despite opposition."[38]

With the exception of the age at which desegregation starts, which reflects findings from the Crain achievement study, most of the remaining conditions are aimed at minimizing the possible effects of white flight. In support of these conditions, the statement makes the rather surprising claim of enrollment stability in Charlotte–Mecklenburg, Atlanta, Dallas, Boston, Denver, Riverside, and San Jose. Four of these cities experienced dramatic loss of white enrollment after desegregation; by 1990 Atlanta was less than 10 percent white, Dallas was at 18 percent white, Boston at 23 percent, and Denver at 34 percent white.

The statement also says that a number of within-school conditions are necessary for realizing the benefits of desegregation, including structured cooperative learning strategies, parental involvement in planning and monitoring desegregation, utilization of multiethnic textbooks, elimination of ability grouping and tracking (which can cause resegregation in classrooms), avoidance of discipline for "cultural differences," recruiting "substantial" numbers of minority teachers and administrators, and teacher support for the desegregation plan.

Finally, the statement concludes with a section on the influence of desegregation on educational reforms. The basic thesis here is that desegregation often promotes new looks at curriculum, teacher training and assignment, organizational issues, and other programmatic innovations. The statement cites one of the best examples of an innovation spawned by desegregation to be the magnet school concept, which has proven popular in many desegregation programs (to be discussed further in chapter 4).

In its concluding section, the statement offers another perspective on successful or unsuccessful desegregation plans:

> School districts who adopt desegregation in good faith are able to use it as an opportunity to increase the achievement of their students, promote racial harmony in the classroom and the community, experiment with innovative educational reforms, and influence integrated housing patterns. On the other hand, a weak or inadequate plan or local officials opposed to the process of desegregation can resegregate students within the schools, cling to established ways of teaching, speed neighborhood resegregation, foster interracial tensions within a desegregated school, or create racially identifiable schools that lack key advantages of desegregation.[39]

Although the overall tone of the statement is positive and generally optimistic about the chances for successful desegregation, the concession that success depends upon fulfilling a number of conditions, some not under the control of local authorities, represents a major departure from earlier versions of the harm and benefit thesis. The moral authority of the thesis is also weakened by raising the possibility that, if certain conditions are not met, desegregation will fail to deliver the promised benefits.

A conditional harm and benefit thesis raises several questions about the certainty of the conditions and the feasibility of meeting them. Regarding their certainty, virtually all desegregation researchers have underscored the methodological problems of research in this field, many concluding that they account for the variation in outcomes.[40] Even for those outcomes that have received the most attention, such as academic achievement, consensus has been elusive on the overall effect of desegregation—much less on specific conditions that mitigate its effects. For most desegregation effects, including academic achievement, there are no more than a handful of studies on which to base a conclusion about conditional effects. More is said about the evidence on conditional effects in later sections and in chapters 4 and 5.

Regarding the feasibility of implementing any of the proposed conditions for successful desegregation, a distinction must be made between implementation by federal courts and by other decision-making bodies. From a federal court standpoint, most desegregation plans focus on accomplishing the six factors identified in *Green* and *Swann*, such as desegregating student bodies and faculties or equalizing facilities. Indeed, the Eleventh Circuit Court of Appeals has specifically held that one of the important conditions cited in the 1991 statement, tracking or grouping students by ability levels, is not unconstitutional even if it contributes to racial imbalance in classrooms.[41] Even if social scientists attain consensus about the academic or social harms of tracking or ability grouping or any other condition identified in the 1991 statement, it is by no means clear that federal courts will see a constitutional necessity to add this component to desegregation decrees, if for no other reason than that they are not bound by the dictates of the harm and benefit thesis.

From the standpoint of other groups that decide desegregation policies, including school boards and legislatures, these conditions could represent potential barriers to the adoption of desegregation plans. For example, some conditions may not be under the control of local policy makers, such as parental involvement (if parents oppose a particular type of desegregation plan), the number of minority teachers available (which is declining in many regions), and teacher support (sometimes problematic when a plan reassigns teachers to attain racial balance).

Even those policies that are under a school board's direct control—such as ability grouping, multiethnic textbooks, disciplinary practices, or cooperative learning—pose clear trade-offs between the costs of changing such policies and the promised benefits of desegregation. School boards or school staff may oppose changes in any one of these areas for reasons unrelated to desegregation, and far more consensus about the educational value of desegregation may be necessary before school boards would be willing to change long-standing policies in these other areas on the promise that they will enhance the benefits of desegregation.

Parents may also oppose changing some of these policies, particularly in the areas of ability grouping, tracking at the secondary level, and changing disciplinary practices. Parents of all races may well be concerned about the potential weakening of disciplinary practices, in that discipline is frequently mentioned by parents in national surveys on major problems in public schools. White middle-class parents in particular might understandably oppose a desegregation plan that first abandons neighborhood schools and then bars accelerated classes (because of classroom segregation), when informed that the academic benefits of desegregation accrue primarily to minority children and not to their own.

The issue of perceived costs and benefits for white parents raises a potentially significant condition not considered in the 1991 statement, which is the issue of voluntary versus mandatory racial balance plans. Its omission is puzzling since it has been the most divisive issue in desegregation policy, and since it could affect some of the conditions for successful desegregation, such as parental involvement, community support, and white flight. Indeed, given the strong opposition to mandatory busing by most white and a growing proportion of minority parents (see chapter 4), a plan involving extensive mandatory busing can generate sufficient opposition from citizens and local officials to harm local revenue-generating efforts.

The statement does endorse the use of voluntary magnet schools as an acceptable part of a desegregation plan "when used on a large scale," but the statement does not define a comprehensive desegregation plan or offer recommendations about specific plan techniques. Given the number of signatories to the statement, perhaps consensus on this difficult issue was not possible.

Whatever the opinions of social scientists and educators, ultimately the importance of the harm and benefit thesis will be determined by its credibility in the eyes of the public and their elected officials, who ultimately decide desegregation policies. In this regard, the harm and benefit thesis must overcome some very strong beliefs in the community about the importance of desegregation in relation to other school attributes.

For example, Table 2.1 shows the results of a parent survey in a large southern school district about the importance of a number of school features in determining student success in school. The school district, serving the East Baton Rouge Parish in Louisiana, has been under a comprehensive court-ordered desegregation plan since 1982. For all but one of the attributes in the list, racial balance, the unanimity is impressive; over 80 percent of both black and white parents believed each one was *very* important for a student's success in school (as opposed to somewhat or not important). Maintaining racial balance in school stands in stark contrast to all the other factors, with only 28 percent of white parents and 61 percent of black parents saying it was very important; 41 percent of white parents said it was *not* important. Although black parents are more likely than white parents to value racial balance, it is not nearly as important to them as other school attributes.

Belief in the harm and benefit thesis has generally been more widespread among blacks than whites, which probably explains stronger black support for desegregation. Nonetheless, opposition to certain types of desegregation methods, such as mandatory busing, has been increasing among blacks (see chapter 4), which may reflect growing disenchantment with the thesis as more blacks experience desegregation. Given the personal hardships often endured to participate in a desegregation plan (long bus rides, distance from school, an unfamiliar and possibly hostile environment), community support for a plan must depend on a belief that children will benefit educationally or socially, at least in comparison with other educational programs.

Thus research on the effects of school desegregation and the status of the harm and benefit thesis is still very much relevant to the debate over desegrega-

Table 2.1. School Attributes Rated Very Important for Student Success

Attribute	White Parents (Percent)	Black Parents (Percent)
Teacher training and commitment	97	97
Maintaining order and discipline in classrooms	97	94
Student's own ability and motivation	89	92
Leadership of the principal	88	93
The content of the curriculum	89	90
Size of classrooms	84	85
Maintaining racial balance	28	61

Based on a sample of approximately 600 white and 600 black parents in Baton Rouge surveyed in June 1993.

tion. Having relied for many years on the federal courts to promote school desegregation, proponents must turn to other decision makers for continued progress. Given the current state of public opinion, many parents, voters, and legislative bodies will require solid evidence if they are to be convinced that school desegregation has sufficient educational payoffs to justify its costs, both personal and budgetary.

Desegregation and Achievement

In spite of voluminous research and writing on this topic, there is still no definitive study of the relationship between school desegregation and academic achievement, and no group of studies has generated consensus among social scientists who have conducted reviews of the research literature.

Perhaps the best illustration of the elusive consensus on this issue is a 1984 review of desegregation and black achievement sponsored by the National Institute of Education (NIE).[42] A panel of experts named by NIE developed a common methodology and selected a set of the most rigorous studies of desegregation and black achievement. Half of the panelists decided not to use the selected set at all, preferring other selections instead or preferring to compare desegregation to other educational interventions. Of the panelists who used the selected set, each applied other methodological criteria and eliminated additional studies, so that all panelists ended up analyzing different groups of studies. Not surprisingly, each panelist came to different conclusions about the effects of desegregation on achievement.

The review of desegregation and achievement offered here makes no pretense of succeeding where panels of experts have failed. Indeed, experience with this issue suggests that there may never be consensus among social scientists on an emotional issue with so much policy at stake, with so many methodological problems to overcome, and with such major variations in the results of individual studies. Although much of the research reviewed here fails to support the achievement benefit thesis, the goal of this section is not to convince the reader that there is no relationship between desegregation and achievement. Rather, the aim is to demonstrate that the lack of consensus stems from the inconclusive nature of the research itself and that decisions about school desegregation by policy makers or individual participants must be reached without a definitive answer about whether and how much desegregation aids academic achievement.

The review begins with several unpublished studies of desegregation and achievement that I have conducted in connection with school desegregation litigation and that were presented in court hearings. These studies illustrate the way in which the harm and benefit thesis has been introduced and used at the trial court level. The discussion also revisits several of the more comprehensive research reviews of desegregation and achievement, including a new study based on data from the U.S. Department of Education's National Assessment of Educational Progress (NAEP).

Achievement in Pasadena, California

One of the more prominent cases in which the relationship between desegregation and achievement arose was in Pasadena, a suburban school district in the
Los Angeles area (*Spangler*). The Pasadena case led to one of the first comprehensive mandatory busing programs in the nation, and it is best known for the
1976 Supreme Court decision that imposed limits on federal court supervision
of desegregation plans and, in particular, limited the requirement to maintain
strict racial balance for long periods of time. It is less well known for being one of
the earliest non-Southern cases in which a lower court relied on the harm and
benefit thesis. In its 1970 decision ordering a cross-district busing plan for racial
balance, the district court said that any type of segregation, de jure or de facto,
has adverse effects: "Racial integration provides positive educational benefits. . . . In addition, racial segregation imposes a badge of inferiority on minority students; integration is necessary to remove that badge."[43]

There was heated community controversy over busing in Pasadena. For several years during the late 1960s, the local school board had rejected various
proposals from its own staff and from citizen groups to adopt an affirmative
integration plan, which the board maintained arose primarily from de facto
housing patterns. Eventually a suit was filed, and in early 1970 the district court
ordered a mandatory busing program to create racial balance in all of its schools.
There followed an unsuccessful recall election for school board members who
voted to oppose an appeal to the Supreme Court, but ultimately new board
members were elected who opposed the strict racial balance and busing plan.
After several years of maintaining the plan, which had produced a high degree
of racial balance in all schools in the district, the school board went back to court
in 1974 to ask that mandatory busing at the elementary level be replaced with
voluntary magnet schools. The school board offered two studies in support of its
petition, one study concluding that mandatory busing had caused white flight
and the other concluding that desegregation had failed to improve the academic
achievement of black children. This author conducted the achievement study
and testified in the district court hearing for the school board.

The reading achievement trends shown in Figure 2.1 are adapted from one of
the court exhibits. The chart shows results from a longitudinal analysis that
followed the same students over four years, from first grade to fourth grade,
between 1970 and 1974. At the beginning of the desegregation plan in 1970,
first-grade white students scored at the 59th percentile on average. Black students scored at the 27th percentile, about one standard deviation below white
scores, which corresponded to the average reading achievement differential
between blacks and whites at that time.[44] White achievement remained constant over the first four years of desegregation, contrary to predictions of some
critics of mandatory busing in Paradena that white achievement would decline.
Although black achievement (as measured by percentiles) increased significantly in the second grade, by the third and fourth grades it had fallen back to
first-grade levels or below. Analyses for other grade levels and for math achievement showed similar trends.[45]

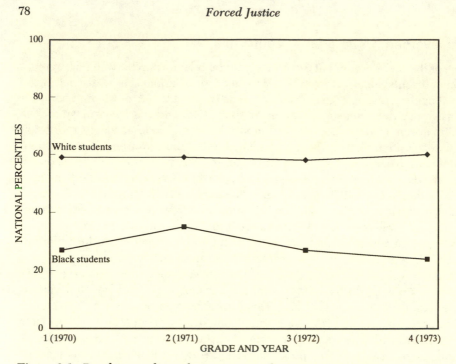

Figure 2.1. Pasadena reading achievement trends, 1970–1973 (CTBS).

After four years of desegregation, then, the Pasadena plan had failed to deliver the educational benefits postulated by the district court. Black student achievement had not improved relative to national norms, relative to white students in the same schools, or relative to their beginning scores, in spite of a high degree of racial balance in the schools. At the same time, the combination of mandatory busing, black in-migration, and other demographic changes caused an accelerated loss of white students, and the district was rapidly becoming a predominantly minority school district.

Neither the achievement study nor the white flight study was sufficient to convince the district court that mandatory busing was not an effective remedy. The expert for plaintiffs, sociologist Jane Mercer, testified that the lack of a growing achievement gap should be interpreted as a positive result since some national data showed a growing gap between black and white students over time. The district court took a position similar to that expressed in the 1991 social science statement regarding support from local officials, asserting that "it takes little educational expertise to recognize that the Pasadena Plan has not had the cooperation from the Board that permits a realistic measurement of its educational success or failure."[46] Because school board members in Pasadena had clearly been elected specifically for their opposition to mandatory busing, it is hard to conceive of conditions under which that school board could have supported the plan. As was true for many communities across the country during the 1970s, the Pasadena school board was simply representing a community opposed to mandatory busing.

During the appeals process, neither white flight nor academic achievement played a role in higher court decisions. Rather, the legal issue became how long a school district had to maintain a specific desegregation plan. While the school board ultimately prevailed in the Supreme Court in 1976, by the time the Ninth Circuit Court of Appeals finally ended court supervision in 1979, the community had become overwhelmingly minority, the controversy over busing had ended, and the issue of meaningful desegregation became moot. As of the 1989–1990 school year, the Pasadena schools were still racially balanced, but the system as a whole had only 19 percent white students remaining, and all but one school was predominantly minority.

Achievement in Norfolk, Virginia

Like Pasadena, the Norfolk public schools also implemented a court-ordered desegregation plan in 1970 that relied primarily on mandatory busing to maintain strict racial balance. Unlike Pasadena, the Norfolk school board supported the mandatory busing plan and maintained a very high degree of racial balance for many years after the original court order, even after the school system was declared unitary and the case dismissed by a federal district court in 1975. The school board did not try to change the desegregation plan in any major way until 1982, after white enrollment had declined to less than half its level before busing and the racial composition had reached 60 percent black.

In 1983, concerned about becoming a predominantly black school district, the school board voted to return to neighborhood schools at the elementary level with options for voluntary integrative transfers (a majority-to-minority program). Not surprisingly, a new lawsuit was filed to prevent the return to neighborhood schools on the grounds that a number of schools would become predominantly black under the plan.

During 1982 I conducted a study for the school board to assess the current and alternative desegregation plans.[47] The study investigated the problem of white enrollment losses, academic achievement, and community attitudes toward various desegregation methods. The achievement study was in response to an earlier study for the school board by sociologist Robert Green that argued against returning to segregated neighborhood schools on the grounds that desegregation improves black achievement; it relied partly on local data and more heavily on national studies by Robert Crain.[48] The results of these various studies were presented in a district court hearing in 1984.

My achievement study for the school board focused on total Norfolk achievement trends for fourth graders (combined scores for reading, math, and language arts). Fourth-grade achievement had been assessed for nearly twenty years with various forms of the same test. The achievement trends for black and white students between 1965 and 1982 are shown in Figure 2.2. Unfortunately, there was no socioeconomic data over this same time period with which to examine the possibility of changing socioeconomic status (SES) makeup and its potential impact on achievement trends.

Prior to the start of mandatory busing in 1970, fourth-grade white achieve-

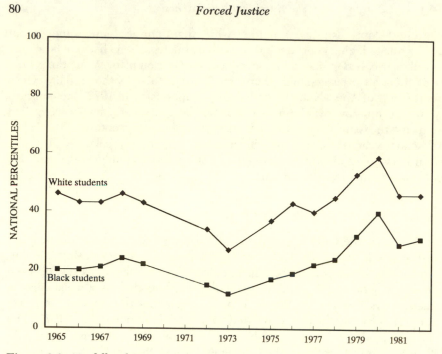

Figure 2.2. Norfolk achievement trends, 1965 to 1982 (grade 4, SRA Total Battery).

ment hovered around the 45th percentile, and the average level for blacks averaged at about the 21st percentile, a differential somewhat smaller than the national black-white gap. Testing was not administered every year during the early years of desegregation, but testing in 1972 and 1973 showed clearly that fourth-graders of both races were achieving considerably below their prede-segregation counterparts. The low point occurred in 1973, when white fourth-graders scored at the 27th percentile and black fourth graders scored at only the 12th percentile.

In 1975, when fourth-graders would have spent all their years in desegre-gated schools, achievement scores had still not reached their predesegregation levels. The achievement of both blacks and whites did not recover prede-segregation levels until 1978, nearly eight years after the start of desegregation. Although the decline in white scores might be attributed to the flight of middle-class whites, that explanation is less likely for the decline in black scores. Although these achievement declines are probably not attributable to deseg-regation itself—that is, to the racial balance in schools—the disruption caused by the implementation of a mandatory busing program may have reduced the achievement of Norfolk black (and white) students during the first five or six years of the plan.

In 1979 Norfolk implemented an intensive instructional program for basic skills, "competency challenge." The program appeared to have positive effects for both black and white achievement in 1979 and 1980, but an internal study revealed that some teachers were improperly teaching test content or coaching on the test. This problem was confirmed in 1981, when a new form of the same test was administered, and average scores declined appreciably for both blacks and whites.

In 1981 and 1982, white scores fell back to their predesegregation levels, but black achievement remained higher than during the predesegregation years. In fact, these two years are the first indications of a significant closure of the black-white gap, which (ignoring 1972 and 1973) had remained just over 20 percentile points from the late 1960s until 1978. Given the timing of changes in these trends, it is unlikely that racial balance by itself caused the improvement in black achievement since no significant improvements occurred in the achievement gap until 1981. Other factors are more likely explanations, such as the basic skills program adopted in 1979 or socioeconomic gains by black families (a subject that is taken up later).

Several other experts testified on the achievement issue, including Herbert Walberg, Robert Green, and Robert Crain. Walberg testified for the school board that school desegregation did little to improve achievement in comparison with program enhancements at the classroom level, Green testified for plaintiffs about his original study emphasizing black gains in the late 1970s and attributing this to desegregation, and Crain testified for plaintiffs based on his national review and meta-analysis of ninety-three studies of desegregation and achievement cited earlier.[49] However, the district court did not rely on any of the achievement testimony in reaching its decision to approve the return to neighborhood elementary schools. The court stated that the white flight issue precluded the necessity of deciding which side was right. Even assuming that desegregation improves achievement, the court said:

> If the Proposed Plan is *successful* and the racial composition of the school population stabilizes, the school administration will have considerably more white students for the purpose of integrating the system. . . . [If] the Proposed Plan *fails* to stem the tide of "white flight" . . . the failure . . . would produce a result no different from that of the continued operation of the present plan.[50]

The district court decision was upheld on appeal to the Fourth Circuit Court of Appeals, and the Supreme Court denied an appeal for further review.[51] Accordingly, Norfolk became one of the first school districts to end a mandatory busing plan and return to a system of neighborhood schools at the elementary level. Although the Norfolk achievement studies did not play an important role in the ultimate court decisions, the Norfolk case is another illustration of how the harm and benefit thesis has been invoked at the trial level to defend school desegregation policies, in this case to defend maintenance of a mandatory busing and racial balance plan. The Norfolk achievement analysis also illustrates the persistence of the black-white achievement gap, even after many years of following a strict racial balance policy.

Achievement in Charleston, South Carolina

In Pasadena and Norfolk, all schools were racially balanced after busing was implemented, and thus there were no segregated black students who could serve as a comparison group once the desegregation plan had begun. The desegregation plan implemented in Charleston County, South Carolina, followed a different course, thus allowing a comparison between segregated and desegregated black students in a special achievement study done for that case.

The Charleston County school district has an unusual structure. It was created in 1965 by consolidating a much larger group of school districts, most of which were very small, into eight constituent school districts including the city of Charleston. The state law that created the consolidation delegated student and teacher assignment to elected school boards for each constituent district, whereas general school policy and school finance powers were delegated to a countywide school board. Since student assignment is controlled by constituent districts, desegregation was implemented on a within-district basis rather than on a countywide basis. As a result, all of the schools in the city of Charleston and in two outlying rural districts were predominantly black, even though the total county school population was about 50 percent black in 1980. The other five districts had varying racial compositions, some majority white, and by 1980 most of their schools were desegregated according to each constituent district's black-white ratio. A new lawsuit filed by the U.S. Department of Justice in 1981 alleged that the state law reserving the power of student and teacher assignment to constituent districts was unconstitutional and that school desegregation should be accomplished on a countywide rather than district basis.[52]

I conducted an achievement study as part of a broader study of whether black students were receiving equitable programs and resources throughout Charleston County. Since some schools were racially balanced and some were not (according to a countywide criterion), it was possible to examine academic achievement for blacks in schools that were predominantly black, predominantly white, or balanced.

A summary of the Charleston achievement study is shown in Figure 2.3. Longitudinal achievement trends were tracked for students who were third-graders in 1980 and fourth-graders in 1981; scores are average grade equivalents according to national norms for the test used. Results for reading achievement are presented for black and white students in three groupings of schools: predominantly black schools were over 65 percent black (the bulk of which were over 80 percent black), predominantly white schools were less than 25 percent black, and balanced (or desegregated) schools were between 25 and 65 percent black. In this study, all scores were adjusted for students' socioeconomic status by using eligibility for the federal free/or reduced-price lunch program, which is determined by whether a family is at or below the official poverty level. This step was necessary to control for the possibility that black students in desegregated or predominantly white schools might be of higher SES, thereby yielding higher test scores than black students in predominantly black schools.

The achievement trends and differences in Figure 2.3 show clearly that the reading achievement of black elementary students in Charleston—whether absolute level or one-year gains—was not significantly related to the racial composition of their schools, once poverty differences were taken into account. Although white students in Charleston generally scored about one grade level

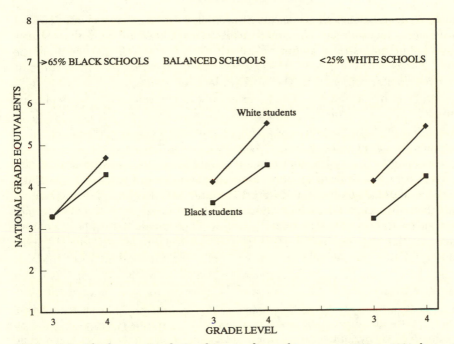

Figure 2.3. Charleston, South Carolina, reading achievement, 1980 to 1981, by racial composition of school (CTBS).

higher than black students, blacks scored at about the same level and gained about one grade equivalent whether they were in predominantly black, balanced, or predominantly white elementary schools. White students show slightly larger gains, and although whites in predominantly black schools have lower scores, there are no achievement differences between whites in desegregated versus predominantly white schools.[53]

The plaintiffs did not present their own study of achievement, and the achievement results discussed here were not cited by the district court in its final decision. The court did find, however, that school facilities and resources were distributed throughout Charleston County on an equitable basis. It denied the Justice Department's petition for further relief, approved the constitutionality of desegregation on a within-district basis, and declared the district unitary.[54] This decision was upheld on appeal to the Fourth Circuit Court of Appeals.[55]

Achievement in Hartford, Connecticut

Although educational achievement has diminished as an issue in most federal desegregation cases, it has become a central issue in the Hartford, Connecticut, metropolitan desegregation case.[56] In 1989 the State of Connecticut was sued by minority children and parents (represented by the Connecticut Civil Liberties Union) for maintaining racially and ethnically segregated education in the Hartford area in violation of the *state* constitution. The Hartford city school district is predominantly black and Hispanic, and it is surrounded by more than twenty small suburban districts, all but one of which was predominantly white at the time the lawsuit was filed.[57] It was well documented that suburban students enjoyed greater success than Hartford students on numerous educational indicators, including achievement test scores and dropout rates; the same would be true for most larger American cities. The disputed issue was the cause of these differences and whether the state violated the state constitution by failing to mitigate the lower achievement of Hartford students.

The plaintiffs invoked the modern form of the harm and benefit thesis, maintaining that de facto racial and economic isolation was the primary cause of the lower academic outcomes for Hartford students and that school desegregation was the only way to assure educational equity for minority students. The motivation for the lawsuit was a legal theory involving several interrelated contentions: (1) that the state constitution guaranteed equality of educational opportunity, (2) that unequal educational outcomes for white and minority students were caused by racial and ethnic school segregation, (3) by allowing this result the state government was in violation of the state constitution, and (4) the state had an obligation to remedy this condition of inequality by desegregating schools throughout the metropolitan region. The plaintiffs relied heavily on an earlier decision by Connecticut Supreme Court relating to the equality of public school financing.[58]

A superior court trial in early 1993 brought together perhaps the largest number of education and desegregation experts ever to testify on the harm and benefit thesis in a school desegregation hearing. Although numerous experts and state officials testified about general education and desegregation issues, only a few experts conducted studies and testified about the educational achievement of Hartford area students.[59]

Gary Natriello testified for plaintiffs concerning results of the state Mastery Test (a standardized achievement test) and high school dropout rates, and Robert Crain testified about his earlier studies on the long-term educational and vocational outcomes for Project Concern students, who were part of a voluntary city-to-suburb busing program. This author was hired by the state to conduct an analysis of state Mastery Test results and dropout rates, as well as a secondary analysis of the Project Concern data. The Project Concern studies are discussed in a later section on the long-term outcomes of desegregation.

The Natriello study consisted simply of a comparison of Mastery Test results and other achievement indicators between Hartford students (at various grade levels) and suburban school districts. The Natriello study did not distinguish achievement results by race or attempt to control for possible socioeconomic differences between city and suburban students. He acknowledged during cross-examination that some of the differences between city and suburban students were due to individual differences in race and poverty, which were not caused by actions of the state, but he did not quantify the contribution of race or measurable socioeconomic factors to city-suburban achievement differences. As such, the Natriello findings about differences between Hartford and suburban students were not contested by the state or disputed here. The critical legal question is the cause of those differences, especially the extent to which they are caused by de facto racial and ethnic segregation versus socioeconomic differences.

My study also focused on Mastery Test results and dropout rates, but it differed from the Natriello study by introducing the factors of race, ethnicity, and socioeconomic levels into the analysis. Although Hartford students were mostly black and Hispanic and suburban students were mostly white, there were white students in Hartford and a substantial number of minority students in the suburbs; indeed, one suburban school district (Bloomfield) was predominantly black. Moreover, as in most metropolitan areas, there were significant variations in socioeconomic levels within the city, among the different suburbs, and even within racial groups in these communities. These variations allowed a quantification of the contribution that race, segregation, and socioeconomic factors have on achievement differences between Hartford and the suburbs.

The analysis of Mastery Test scores used regression techniques to examine the effects of race, location (Hartford versus suburbs), segregation, and several socioeconomic factors on academic achievement for fourth- and sixth-grade students in the Hartford metropolitan area.[60] After controlling for both race-ethnicity and socioeconomic factors, neither location nor segregation had a statistically significant impact on black, Hispanic, or white achievement; that is, most of the differences in achievement between the city and the suburbs could be explained by a combination of race, ethnicity, and socioeconomic factors.

Figure 2.4 is one of the defendant's exhibits presented during the court hearing. It shows an analysis of sixth-grade reading scores for black students in communities with at least ten sixth-grade black students; it compares actual achievement scores to those predicted from black socioeconomic (SES) characteristics alone. The actual averages correspond quite closely to those predicted from SES levels, especially the comparison for Hartford, which has the lowest black SES levels of all communities.[61] Those suburban communities with the highest SES blacks (Bloomfield, Vernon, and Windsor) have both actual and predicted average scores near 50, compared to Hartford's actual and predicted average scores near 42. By contrast, East Hartford is a desegregated but lower socioeconomic suburban district, whose black students have a predicted score of 46 and an actual average score of 43—only one point higher than Hartford's actual black average.[62] Similar results were obtained for white students, Hispanic students, and fourth-graders.

In other words, Hartford black and white students do score lower than their suburban counterparts, but they also come from families with greater poverty, less education, and a higher percentage of single parents than suburban students. These factors, not segregation or attending school in Hartford, explain the higher academic performance of suburban students.

These relationships between segregation, socioeconomic status, and location can be illustrated without relying on statistical regression techniques that require a number of assumptions. One of the suburban communities, Bloomfield, is almost as segregated as Hartford (averaging only 20 percent white enroll-

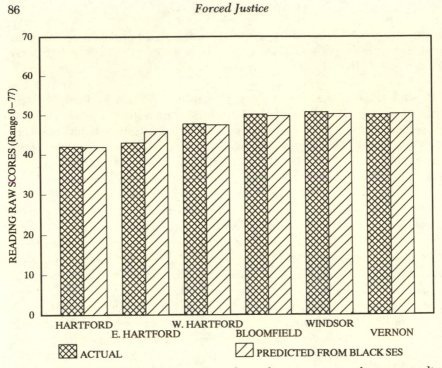

Figure 2.4. Hartford area black sixth grade reading scores, actual versus predicted. (SES characteristics include individual poverty level, percent black college grads, percent single parent families).

ment), but its black families have a much higher SES than Hartford blacks: twice the mean income, more than double the rate of college graduates, and less than half the rate of single-parent families. East Hartford blacks, by comparison, are desegregated (averaging 70 percent white enrollment) but are only slightly better off than Hartford blacks in average income, education, and family structure.

If segregation is more important than socioeconomic status in causing the poor performance of Hartford students, Bloomfield would have scores closer to Hartford, and East Hartford would have scores relatively higher. In fact, Bloomfield is one of three suburbs with the highest test scores for blacks (50), while East Hartford has the lowest scores (43), only one point higher than Hartford. Thus socioeconomic status of black families in the Hartford area, not school segregation, is largely responsible for differences in academic performance.

The National Institute of Education Review

One of the most comprehensive reviews of the relationship between desegregation and black achievement was carried out in 1984 under the auspices of the National Institute of Education (NIE), which at that time was the research arm of the U.S. Department of Education. Although the NIE review was not done in conjunction with a school desegregation lawsuit, it and the earlier Crain review of ninety-three studies are the two most cited studies of the relationship between desegregation and black achievement, and they are both cited frequently by experts who testify on the achievement issue in desegregation cases.

The purpose of the NIE review was to bring together a group of experts in school desegregation research or research methodology to review the research on school desegregation and black achievement. By appointing experts with diverse viewpoints and asking them to develop a common methodology for selecting the best studies, the NIE thought that greater consensus might be attained on this important and controversial topic. The panelists included six experts known for their research on school desegregation, most of whom had published studies with differing conclusions about the achievement issue, and one additional expert in research methodology who had not studied school desegregation and who would act as a neutral "referee."[63]

The panel agreed on a set of criteria for selecting the most rigorous studies of the relationship between school desegregation and black achievement. Generally, the most important criteria corresponded to the basic requirements of an experimental or "quasi" experimental research design, including (1) existence of a contemporaneous group of segregated black students who could serve as a control or comparison group for desegregated black students, (2) existence of predesegregation and postdesegregation achievement measures, and (3) the same standardized test used in both the pretest and the posttest. The majority of the panel rejected a requirement that students be randomly assigned to segregated and desegregated conditions (a pure experimental design) because it would severely reduce the number of available studies. This rejection increased the importance of predesegregation measures so that adjustments could be made for potential pretest differences between desegregated and segregated students. A total of nineteen separate "core" studies met the methodological criteria established by the panel. Because some of the studies tested more than one grade level and most panelists treated each grade level as a separate observation, there were a total of thirty-five observations from the nineteen studies.[64]

Several panelists decided not to use the nineteen studies and the others used slightly different subsets of the nineteen selected studies (as well as somewhat different calculation methods), so it is not surprising that complete consensus was not obtained on the key question of whether and how much desegregation raises black achievement. For this reason, the analysis and conclusions of the referee, Thomas Cook, are of special importance. Before discussing his synthesis of the other analyses and his own conclusions, the results from the nineteen core studies are briefly reviewed.

A summary of the effects of desegregation on black reading achievement from the nineteen core studies is presented in Figure 2.5. (See the Appendix for a description of the nineteen studies and other technical details.)[65] The effects are differences in achievement gains for desegregated versus segregated black students, expressed in standard deviation units. Because the average elementary student gains about one standard deviation (and one grade level) in achievement per school year, the effects can also be interpreted as the fraction of school year

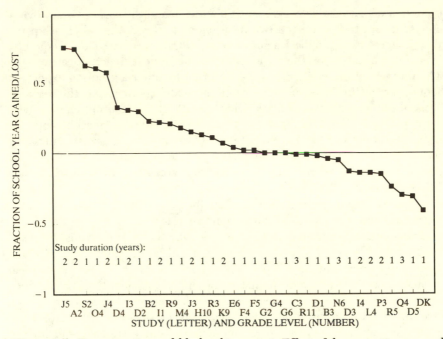

Figure 2.5. Desegregation and black achievement: Effect of desegregation on reading achievement (NIE Review).

gained or lost because of desegregation. Thus a study that shows a gain of 0.1 means that desegregated black students gained about a tenth of a school year (about one month) more than segregated black students.

Results are tabulated separately for each study–grade level combination; each study is identified by a letter (on the horizontal axis) followed by a number indicating the grade level. The duration of each study in years (the period over which the gain is calculated) is shown in the lower portion of the graph.

The considerable variation in study results is immediately striking. Eight study-grade combinations show declines in reading achievement greater than one month of a school year, twelve show very small effects of less than one month (some positive, some negative), and fifteen show gains in reading achievement of more than one month. It is no wonder that researchers who look at different combinations of studies might come to different conclusions about the effects of desegregation.

Five of the positive cases in Figure 2.5 show very large gains of more than six-tenths of a school year. These five observations (from four separate studies) have a significant impact on conclusions about the overall effect of desegregation. As pointed out by Cook, the outliers cause the distribution of effects to be skewed, so that the arithmetic mean is considerably higher than the median (the value exceeded by half of the cases). Summarizing the studies in common to the panelists who used the core studies, Cook estimates the mean effect for reading achievement from 0.13 to 0.16, which corresponds to about six weeks of a school year, while the median effect ranges from only 0.03 to 0.08, or less than one month.[66] When distributions are skewed, the median is often preferred over the mean as the best summary of an "average" effect.

The effects of desegregation on math achievement from the core studies is shown in Figure 2.6. Only sixteen of the core studies assessed mathematics achievement, for a total of twenty-five observations. Again, there is considerable variability in study outcomes, although in the case of math achievement the results are balanced more evenly between positive, neutral, and negative effects (with at least one outlier showing a large negative effect). Seven studies show losses in math achievement greater than one month, eight show effects less than one month either way, and ten show gains of more than one month. Using the common studies, Cook computed means ranging from 0.07 to 0.12 and medians ranging from zero to 0.06.

Most panelists investigated the possibility that the variability of outcomes could be explained by one or more conditions of the study or the desegregation program, such as the duration of study, grade level, or the mandatory or voluntary nature of the program. No consensus emerged on these alternative explanatory factors, however, primarily because of the small number of cases that satisfy one condition or another.

For example, it has been argued that it takes time to overcome possible "disruption" effects of desegregation, and therefore the full benefits would not be realized until desegregation was in operation for several years. If so, studies

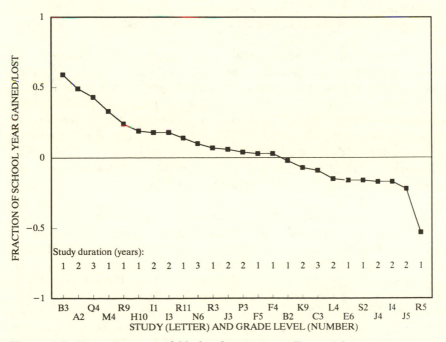

Figure 2.6. Desegregation and black achievement: Effects of desegregation on math achievement (NIE Review).

with longer evaluation periods should show larger effects. In fact, the average reading gains of the two-year studies in Figure 2.5 are higher than the one-year studies, but the hypothesis breaks down for three-year studies, one of which shows no effect and two of which show negative effects. For mathematics, the three-year studies show two positive effects and one negative effect, but the two-year studies show five positive and five negative effects.

Another possible cause of variations investigated by some panelists was mandatory versus voluntary desegregation plans. Four of the NIE core studies evaluated mandatory desegregation plans: studies D, Q, F, and L (Ann Arbor and Flint, Michigan, and Fort Worth and Dallas, Texas, respectively). All of the remaining studies evaluated voluntary desegregation plans in which black students volunteered to leave their segregated home school to attend a desegregated school. Interestingly, the studies of mandatory desegregation account for five of the eight larger reading losses in Figure 2.5 (studies D, L, and Q), and the other mandatory plan (F) has an effect near zero. These negative or neutral effects are also consistent with the Pasadena and Norfolk analyses shown in Figures 2.1 and 2.2, both of which were mandatory desegregation plans. It is possible, then, that voluntary but not mandatory desegregation plans benefit reading achievement, although there are not enough cases for a statistically significant result.

An equally plausible explanation is the inevitable self-selection problem that arises in voluntary plans, which no amount of analysis can remove entirely; that is, those black students with more ability, more motivation, or better home environments may be the ones who volunteer for desegregation, and these initial conditions, not the desegregation experience, explain the modest gains shown.

A third possible explanation of variations in desegregation effects is the grade level at which desegregation began, an important factor because studies by Crain have emphasized that desegregation has large effects only if it begins in kindergarten or first grade. He finds effects on the order of 0.3 at these grade levels, or about one-third of a school year, but his overall effects for all grades resemble those of the other NIE panelists. Unfortunately, most of the kindergarten and first-grade studies Crain uses have no pretest measures with which to control for bias due to self-selection or attrition, and these studies did not meet the methodological criteria to be included in the NIE core studies.

The NIE core studies do include one observation for kindergarten (D), two for first grade (D,I), and five observations for second grade (A,B,D,G, and S). If study D is eliminated, as some of the panelists chose to do, then the one remaining first-grade observation and three of the four second-grade observations show positive effects. However, this positive effect is based on only four observations and does not reach statistical significance.

What conclusions can be drawn from the NIE review? Some of Thomas Cook's conclusions may well speak for a number of social scientists who have examined the issue of school desegregation and black achievement:

Desegregation did not cause any decrease in black achievement. On the average, desegregation did not cause an increase in achievement in mathematics. Desegregation increased mean reading levels. The gain reliably differed from zero and was estimated to be between two and six weeks [of a school year] across the studies examined. . . . The *median* gains were almost always greater than zero but were lower than the means and did not reliably differ from zero. . . .

Studies with the largest reading gains can be tentatively characterized . . . [as having] small sample sizes . . . two or more years of desegregation, desegregated children who outperformed their segregated counterparts even before desegregation began, and desegregation that occurred earlier in time, involved younger students, was voluntary, had larger percentages of whites per school, and was associated with enrichment programs. None of the above factors can be isolated, singly or in combination, as causes of any of the atypically large achievement gains. . . .

Because of the small samples and apparently non-normal distributions, little confidence should be placed in any of the mean results presented earlier. I have little confidence that we know much about how desegregation affects reading "on the average" and, across the few studies examined, I find the variability in effect sizes more striking and less well understood than any measure of central tendency.[67]

The cautious tone of Cook's conclusions about desegregation and black achievement differs substantially from the much more optimistic tone of the 1991 social science statement, whose assessment relies heavily on the findings of a single research review. Of course, the social science statement also includes the caveat that educational benefits flow only if a number of other conditions are met, such as absence of ability grouping and broad socioeconomic integration. Although all NIE studies with positive effects might have met these conditions while those with negative or neutral effects did not, no information from the core studies—or any other group of desegregation studies—would enable a systematic and definitive test of these conditions.

Although the NIE review suggests a small positive *average* effect of desegregation on reading (but not mathematics), perhaps the most relevant finding for policy purposes is the variability of results as noted by Cook. Some individual studies show large positive gains in black reading skills, but slightly more than half show either no effect or negative effects. According to the NIE review, then, policy makers cannot be confident that a desegregation policy by itself has a high probability of increasing the achievement of minority students.

National Achievement Trends

In 1966, when most students attended segregated schools (either de facto or de jure), the Coleman equal opportunity report documented the large difference in academic achievement between black and white students at all grade levels. This very difference fueled the belief in the late 1960s that segregation was harmful to black education. Since considerable school desegregation has taken place since that time, especially beginning in 1970, one obvious way to approach this issue is to examine achievement trends for blacks and whites over the last twenty years or so. This strategy may be especially valuable, given the lack of consensus about the conclusions of smaller experimental studies.

The best data available for examining the overall trends and differences between black and white achievement are from the National Assessment of Educational Progress (NAEP), which has been collecting academic achievement data on large national samples of students since the early 1970s. The NAEP data have several advantages over other assessments: The samples are representative of the total U.S. population of students and schools, several age levels are assessed, and test content is held constant in subsamples used for long-term trend analysis.[68]

Figure 2.7 shows black and white reading achievement between 1971 and 1990 for thirteen-year olds (most of whom are eighth-graders). In 1971, when most blacks in this age group had been educated in segregated schools, black thirteen-year-olds trailed whites by 39 points. Over the next two decades, white scores remained virtually constant, starting at 261 and ending the period at 262 points. In contrast, black scores rose steadily for most of the period, starting at 222 and ending at 242 points (following a drop of a point in the latest assessment). By 1990 there was still a reading achievement gap between blacks and whites, but it had been reduced by almost half, from 39 to 20 points.

Figure 2.8 shows a similar trend and pattern for mathematics achievement. In 1973 black thirteen-year-olds were 46 points behind whites in math achievement. Again, white scores remained relatively constant over the next seventeen years, increasing slightly from 272 to 276, but black math scores rose by 21 points, from 228 to 249. At the end of the interval, black thirteen-year-olds were only 27 points behind whites in math achievement, reducing the black-white mathematics gap by nearly half.

These patterns of black gains are replicated for seventeen-year-olds, with similar reductions in the black-white achievement gaps. The black-white achievement gap in reading fell from 52 to 30 points; the gap was actually down to 21 points in 1988, but black achievement fell 7 points in 1990. In mathematics the gap has fallen from 40 to 21 points, with most of the reduction taking place between 1986 and 1990.

The achievement gap has also been reduced for black nine-year-olds, but the magnitude of the reduction is much smaller. The gap in reading has been reduced by only 9 points, largely because black reading achievement fell 7 points between 1988 and 1990. The gap in mathematics was reduced by only 8 points, mainly because white math achievement increased by 8 points between 1986 and 1990. This is one of the few sizeable increase in white achievement documented by the NAEP.

Likewise, the achievement gap between white and Hispanic students has fallen in the past twenty years, but, with two exceptions, the reductions are much smaller in magnitude. The reduction in the white-Hispanic reading gap is less than 10 points for nine- and thirteen-year-olds (but is 19 points for seventeen-year-olds), and the reduction in the math gap is less than 10 points for

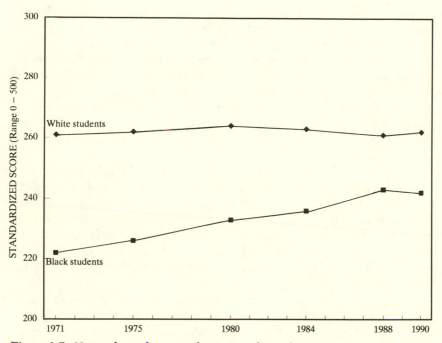

Figure 2.7. National trends in age-thirteen reading achievement. *Source:* National Assessment of Educational Progress.

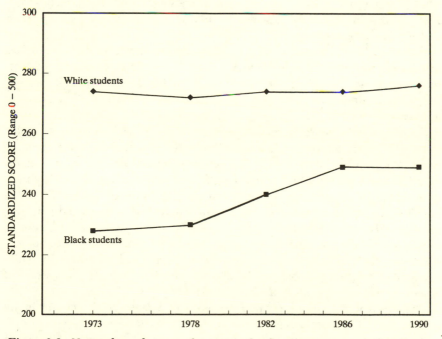

Figure 2.8. National trends in age-thirteen math achievement. *Source:* National Assessment of Educational Progress.

nine- and seventeen-year-olds (but is 14 points for thirteen-year olds). Because black achievement gains have been the largest and most consistent, however, the explanation of black gains demands the greatest attention.

A number of studies and several noted educators have invoked the harm and benefit thesis by suggesting that black achievement gains observed in the NAEP might be attributed in part to school desegregation. Such suggestions have been offered by the president of the Educational Testing Service, the research organization that currently administers the NAEP; the first director of the NAEP project; and a comprehensive study on race sponsored by the National Academy of Science.[69]

The desegregation theory is also attractive because the achievement gains correspond to the era of greatest increases in the proportion of desegregated black students. According to federal statistics, in 1968 about 77 percent of black students attended schools that were more than half minority; by 1988 the black enrollment in predominantly minority schools had declined to 63 percent.[70] Further, in 1968 a majority of black students—about 64 percent—attended schools that were more than 90 percent minority; in 1988 that figure had shrunk to 32 percent.

Ironically, the desegregation explanation has never been tested by examining the relationship between achievement and racial composition of schools using the most appropriate source of data, the NAEP itself. Since the NAEP established achievement trends for blacks in the first place, it makes sense to test the desegregation theory by comparing achievement trends for blacks in segregated versus desegregated schools. If the desegregation theory is correct, larger achievement gains would be expected for blacks in desegregated schools than for blacks in segregated schools.

Achievement trends for blacks in desegregated versus segregated schools has only recently become available for NAEP data. The definition used for a desegregated school in the NAEP analysis is one that has a majority-white enrollment; a segregated school is one that has a majority of black or other minority students.[71]

Figure 2.9 shows trends in reading achievement for black thirteen-year-olds according to the racial composition of their schools. The desegregation theory is clearly not supported by the NAEP data. While blacks in majority-white schools generally score somewhat higher than blacks in predominantly minority schools (although not in every year), the trend in reading between 1975 and 1988—when the largest black gains occurred—shows that thirteen-year-old blacks in predominantly minority schools have gained virtually the same as blacks in majority-white schools. In the case of math trends, blacks in predominantly minority schools actually gain 10 points *more* than blacks in majority-white schools. By 1990 there was only a 2-point difference between the math scores of segregated and desegregated black students.

This pattern of gains for segregated versus desegregated black students in the NAEP is replicated for other age groups as well. Over these assessment periods, age-nine blacks in segregated schools gained 12 points in reading and 17 points in math, compared with 11 points and 16 points, respectively, for blacks in

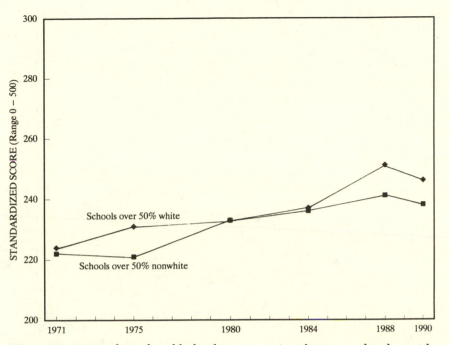

Figure 2.9. National trends in black achievement: Age-thirteen reading by racial composition of school. *Source:* National Assessment of Educational Progress.

desegregated schools. For age-seventeen blacks, those in segregated schools gained 34 points in reading and 22 points in math compared to 21 and 17 points, respectively, for those in desegregated schools. By 1990 age-nine black students in segregated schools were only a few points lower in reading and math achievement than desegregated black nine-year-olds, and there was virtually no difference for black seventeen-year-olds.

The NAEP data can also be used to compare black achievement trends according to four types of community in which a school is located, including its socioeconomic status. Two categories of this typology, in particular, encompass about 85 percent of all black students: "Disadvantaged Urban" and "Other" urban and suburban schools. Although type of community is defined in geographic and economic rather than racial terms, the average racial composition for schools in each type of community can be determined. Not surprisingly, disadvantaged urban schools average about 30 percent white, while other urban (and nonrural) schools average about 80 percent white.[72]

Reading achievement trends by type of community are shown for age-thirteen black students in Figure 2.10. Black students in nondisadvantaged urban and suburban communities generally average about 6 points higher than blacks in urban disadvantaged communities, with the exception of 1971, when they are 3 points lower. If this inconsistent data point is ignored, age-thirteen blacks in disadvantaged urban communities gained 18 points between 1975 and 1990, while their counterparts in nondisadvantaged urban and suburban schools

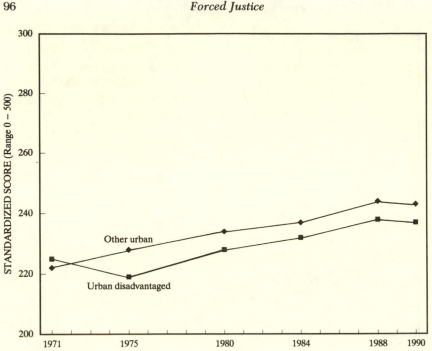

Figure 2.10. National trends in black achievement: Age-thirteen reading by type of urban setting. *Source:* National Assessment of Educational Progress.

gained 15 points (or 21 points between 1971 and 1990). The pattern is similar for math scores, with age-thirteen blacks in disadvantaged urban schools gaining 21 points compared to 19 points for those in nondisadvantaged communities.

Because the NAEP finds that gains for segregated black students are as large or larger than for desegregated blacks, and that blacks in disadvantaged urban communities gain as much as blacks in nondisadvantaged communities, school desegregation is unlikely to have contributed significantly to national black achievement gains. This statement does not mean that school desegregation has no educational benefits to black students under any conditions, but it does mean that school desegregation is probably not a major explanation of the black achievement gains documented by the NAEP.

If desegregation does not explain black achievement gains, what does? One obvious candidate is the significant increase in compensatory programs for disadvantaged students, such as Head Start and Chapter 1, which have expanded greatly since 1970.[73] Another possibility is improvement in black family socioeconomic status. In most national studies of academic achievement, beginning with the Coleman report, socioeconomic factors have been the strongest correlates of both black and white achievement levels, with such factors as parents' education, income, and job status the most prominent. It is reasonable to ask, therefore, whether black achievement gains are due in part to the improved educational and economic conditions of the black family.

The NAEP data base does not contain information about compensatory programs, but it does allow a test of the socioeconomic hypothesis. The NAEP data include information about various family characteristics, and new tabulations allow a comparison of trends in parents' education for blacks and whites between 1971 and 1990. Figure 2.11 compares the percentage of black and white thirteen-year-olds who report one or more parents with some post–high school education. The trends show a remarkable reduction in the gap between black and white parents' education.

In 1971, when the achievement gap was large, only 21 percent of age-thirteen black students had parents with post–high school education compared to 41 percent for white students. By 1990, when the achievement gap had been reduced by half, the parents' education gap had been reduced by more than half. During this time the rate of post–high school education for black parents rose to 49 percent, while it rose to only 53 percent for white parents. Thus, according to the NAEP, the education gap between parents of age-thirteen black and white students narrowed from 21 points to 3 points between 1970 and 1990.

The student-report measures of parent education in the NAEP may be subject to some bias, either by a desire to enhance the status of one's parents or by lack of knowledge. Nonetheless, U.S. Census data indicate that the education and economic status of black adults increased substantially between 1970 and 1990. For example, according to statistical abstracts for the United States,

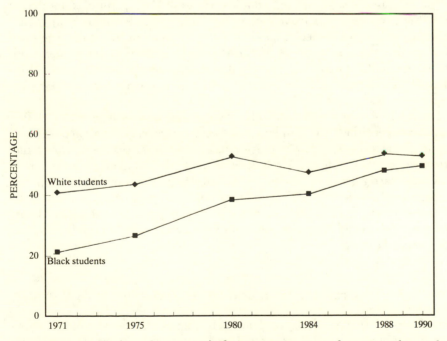

Figure 2.11. National trend in parents' education: Percentage of parents with post–high school education (age-thirteen students). *Source:* National Assessment of Educational Progress.

among black adults age thirty to forty-four—the approximate age range for parents with thirteen-year-old children—the proportion with post–high school education rose from 12 percent in 1970 to 38 percent in 1989. Although this is not a strictly comparable population because there is no breakout for parents, the size of the educational gain is similar to the NAEP: 26 percentage points compared to 28 points.[74]

Because black students with more highly educated parents also have higher achievement, the improvement in black parents' education alone can explain a significant portion of black achievement gains. In reading, for example, the aggregate shift in black parents' educational level between 1971 and 1990 can explain about 8 points, or about 42 percent, of the 19-point gain during this period.[75] A similar result can be demonstrated for mathematics achievement.

The fact that there are achievement gains beyond that explained by parents' education suggests a role played by other factors, such as other socioeconomic characteristics or improvements in school programs. Such characteristics as income, poverty level, and family structure (e.g., single-parent household) are known to have effects on educational achievement. There is also evidence that compensatory education has had some effect on increasing black achievement. For example, a study by the Congressional Budget Office estimated that federal Chapter 1 programs had reduced the black-white achievement gap by about 10 percent.[76] Although this impact is smaller than that for the improved education of black parents, it is larger that shown for desegregation in the NAEP data.

The increased educational or economic status of black parents is not necessarily the direct cause of achievement gains. Rather, socioeconomic status probably stands for a host of specific family behaviors and attitudes—such as motivation, educational aspirations, childrearing practices, enforcement or help with homework, and so forth—that become the mechanisms by which parents' educational status is translated into actual academic improvement for their children.

The NAEP data are consistent with a great deal of social science research that finds academic achievement to be strongly related to the educational and economic characteristics of families. Although some studies show a correlation between desegregation and black achievement, the relationship is generally weak and inconsistent compared to the effect of educational and economic factors. To the extent that black achievement has improved since 1970, the improved socioeconomic condition of the black family and federal compensatory programs appear to be considerably more important contributors than school desegregation.

Desegregation and Other Outcomes

The effect of desegregation on academic achievement has received more attention in social science research than other outcomes, in part because standardized achievement tests are widely administered in schools and in part because achievement is viewed by many as the most important outcome of the formal educational process. But the harm and benefit thesis, particularly in its earlier formulations, postulates other harms of segregation and benefits of de-segregation, and many of these effects have also been studied by social scientists in the years since *Brown*. In particular, studies have evaluated the impact of desegregation on self-esteem, on racial attitudes and race relations, and on various long-term outcomes such as educational and occupational attainment. With some exceptions, this body of research has generally offered no more support for the harm and benefit thesis than the achievement research, and in some cases the evidence has been more negative than positive.

Self-Esteem

The research on black self-esteem is of particular historical interest, given the original emphasis on this issue by the 1952 social science statement and the Supreme Court's decision in *Brown*. At that time low self-esteem was seen as the major psychological mechanism contributing to lower academic perfor-mance of black children (or any group of children, for that matter), and that view is still popular among many educators and some social scientists today.

The early versions of self-esteem theory, as applied to racial segregation, emerged from studies that used indirect or projective measures of self-esteem (the doll-playing techniques of Kenneth and Mamie Clark being the most prominent). During this period black children's preferences for white dolls were interpreted as rejection of their race and hence rejection of themselves. As the research on self-esteem became more extensive and more sophisticated during the 1960s, studies came to rely more on direct (self-report) measures of self-esteem, and earlier interpretations gave way to what came to be seen as a much more complex process. A distinction evolved between racial self-esteem (attitude toward one's racial group) and personal self-esteem (one's sense of personal worth), and personal self-esteem is generally agreed to be the more important potential determinant of academic performance. Although many studies have replicated the finding that preschoolers prefer to play with white dolls, this fact alone no longer justifies an inference of low personal self-esteem, and indeed some psychologists have concluded that it may have more to do with an evaluation of colors than with either racial or personal self-esteem.[77]

There are two types of studies on black self-esteem. One type addresses the potential harms of segregation by comparing the personal self-esteem of blacks and whites, and the other addresses the potential benefits of desegregation by comparing the personal self-esteem of segregated versus desegregated black students. There have been several comprehensive reviews of both types of studies, and these reviews constitute a substantial basis to evaluate the self-esteem aspects of the harm and benefit thesis. Unlike the early indirect mea-sures of self-esteem based on doll choices, most studies of personal self-esteem after 1960 rely on direct self-report measures based on interview or question-naire methods.

The results of two research reviews comparing the self-esteem of black and white children are summarized in Table 2.2. The review by Rosenberg and

Table 2.2. Studies of Black versus White Self-esteem

Results	Number of Studies Reviewed	
	Rosenberg and Simmons*	Porter and Washington
Black self-esteem higher than white	9	10
No difference	1	9
White self-esteem higher than black	3	4
Total studies	13	23
Years of studies	1963–1970	1967–1977

*Includes results of a separate study by Rosenberg and Simmons in addition to the twelve other studies reviewed.

Simmons covered a number of early studies as well as their own comprehensive study of self-esteem in the Baltimore public schools; the Porter and Washington review covered more recent studies.[78] None of the studies reviewed by Rosenberg and Simmons was included in the Porter and Washington review, with the exception of Rosenberg and Simmons's own study of Baltimore students, so that the two reviews cover thirty-five independent studies altogether. The vast majority of these studies find that black self-esteem is either higher than or equal to white self-esteem; only seven showed that black self-esteem was lower than white self-esteem.

Some social scientists have speculated that black self-esteem was lower than that of whites during the era of state-sanctioned segregation but that the relationship changed after the 1954 *Brown* decision. While such a change might have occurred, it has never been documented. The transition would have had to happen very rapidly because many of the negative studies reviewed by Rosenberg and Simmons were conducted during the early to mid-1960s when the *Brown* decision was still new (and controversial) and de jure school segregation was still widespread.

Indeed, in their own study of Baltimore, which found substantially higher self-esteem among black students at all grade levels, Rosenberg and Simmons report that more than 80 percent of the black students were in segregated black schools (most of which were 100 percent black and had been so for many years). Possibly the results of the early doll studies were misinterpreted, and segregated black students did not in fact have lower personal self-esteem than white students at the time of *Brown*. Unfortunately, the theory than black self-esteem differed before *Brown* cannot be tested because no known studies using direct assessment of personal self-esteem were conducted during that period. What is known, with considerable certainty, is that from at least mid-1960s forward there is little evidence that black students have lower self-esteem than white students.

If school segregation does not create low black self-esteem in the first place, then the question of whether desegregation raises black self-esteem may be somewhat academic. Nonetheless, numerous social science studies have compared the self-esteem of segregated and desegregated black students, and several reviews of these studies have been compiled. Summaries of two of the more careful reviews, both of which have been frequently cited, is provided in Table 2.3.[79] These reviews have fourteen studies in common, but there is no overlap for the studies showing positive effects. Of nearly fifty studies of desegregation and black self-esteem identified by these reviewers, only six had consistently positive effects. A much larger number—seventeen separate studies—found that school desegregation has adverse effects on black self-esteem.

The research on black self-esteem over the past thirty years not only fails to support the harm and benefit thesis, then, but indeed seems to turn the thesis on its head. First, school segregation appears not to harm self-esteem of black students in the first place, at least in the post-*Brown* era, and in many cases segregated black students have higher self-esteem than white students. Second, desegregation not only fails to improve black self-esteem but may in fact lower it.

Several theories have been advanced to explain the adverse effects of desegregation on self-esteem. Most explanations rely on one of two possibilities: a social comparison phenomenon or racial prejudice. Desegregated black students may for the first time find themselves at a disadvantage academically or economically in comparison with white students, and these unfavorable comparisons lead to a lowered personal sense of worth. Desegregated black students may also experience racial prejudice or acts of discrimination for the first time, which may also have an impact on their personal self-esteem. Whatever the ultimate explanation may be for these adverse effects on black self-esteem, such an outcome is clearly inconsistent with the harm and benefit thesis and indeed demands new theories about the relationship of segregation, desegregation, and blacks' self-esteem.

Table 2.3. Studies of Black Self-Esteem in Segregated versus Desegregated Schools

	Number of Studies Reviewed	
Results	St. John*	Stephan
Black self-esteem higher in segregated schools (total 17 separate studies)	14	7
No differences or mixed results	16	19
Black self-esteem higher in desegregated schools (total 6 separate studies)	5	1
Total studies	35	28
Years of studies	1966–1973	1963–1981

*General self-esteem combined with academic self-esteem.

Race Relations and Attitudes

By definition, in a completely segregated society, contact between the races is infrequent and of a socially limited nature. It is reasonable to conclude, therefore, that desegregated schools generate more interracial contact than segregated schools. The critical assumption behind the harm and benefit thesis is that increased interracial contact can lead to "more favorable attitudes and friendlier relations between the races" rather than increased hostility or reinforcement of stereotypes; that is, interracial contact can lead to a reduction of racial prejudice and, most important, a reduction of white prejudice toward blacks.

The importance of this component of the harm and benefit thesis cannot be overemphasized. According to early versions of the thesis, school desegregation promised not only improvement in black self-esteem and academic achievement, in effect remedying the damages inflicted by past discrimination and segregation, but also a reduction in one of the root causes of racial discrimination and segregation—white prejudice. Thus school desegregation was supposed to relieve the psychological harms of segregation and at the same time eradicate or at least diminish its source.

In fairness to the original harm and benefit thesis, the 1952 social science statement did recognize that increased racial contact did not guarantee improved race relations, and in fact it clearly outlined certain conditions that must be met before contact could benefit race relations and reduce prejudice. Generally, the conditions necessary for success resembled those listed in Allport's contact theory, such as absence of competition for scarce benefits, treatment as equals, and full support of local authorities. The social science statement also asserted without qualification or cautions, however, that these conditions can generally be satisfied in the public schools. In retrospect, one might wonder how some of the Allport conditions could be attained, given some of the more drastic school busing plans implemented after 1970. For the next twenty years, however, there were few warnings by social scientists that massive desegregation plans might be violating these conditions; indeed, numerous social scientists who were fully aware of the conditions of contact theory either wrote or testified in favor of such busing plans.

Like the research on self-esteem and achievement, the research on race relations since 1970 has generally failed to provide consistent support for the race relations component of the harm and benefit thesis. Again, the comprehensive reviews of individual studies all come to generally the same conclusions. The St. John and Stephan reviews also evaluated studies on race relations, and their results are summarized in Table 2.4. Like the achievement studies, these reviews find great variation in individual study findings. Eliminating studies in common to the two reviews, the total set of independent studies yields almost equal numbers of studies finding positive effects, negative effects, and inconclusive effects of desegregation on race relations for both black and white students.

Summarizing the results of a large number of research reviews on desegregation and race relations, Janet Schofield, another psychologist who has studied

Table 2.4. Studies of Desegregation and Racial Attitudes

	Number of Studies Reviewed	
Results	St. John*	Stephan
White Students		
Increased prejudice	11	11
No differences or mixed results	13	9
Decreased prejudice	11	4
Number of studies	35	24
Black students		
Increased prejudice	10	5
No differences or mixed results	12	8
Decreased prejudice	6	4
Number of studies	28	17

*Studies using attitude measures combined with studies using sociometric (friendship) choice measures.

race relations extensively, concluded, "In general, the reviews of desegregation and intergroup relations were unable to come to any conclusion about what the probable effects of desegregation were . . . virtually all of the reviewers determined that few, if any, firm conclusions about the impact of desegregation on intergroup relations could be drawn."[80]

Before discussing the implications of these results, it might be helpful to illustrate the complexity of the findings on desegregation and race relations by using examples from actual case studies. Two of the case studies often cited for their sophistication and thoroughness are the evaluations of desegregation in Riverside, California, and Indianapolis.[81]

The Riverside evaluation is one of the most comprehensive of its kind; it covers a six-year period following implementation of a desegregation plan in 1966. The desegregation plan closed three predominantly minority elementary schools and reassigned their students to attain approximate racial balance. At that time the Riverside school population was about 16 percent minority (10 percent Hispanic and 6 percent black), but the minority proportion grew to 27 percent by 1973. As part of an evaluation of race relations, elementary students were asked to name up to three fellow students whom they would prefer as their friends, and this assessment was repeated each year for six years after desegregation was implemented.

Figure 2.12 shows the average number of friendship choices received by white, Hispanic, and black classmates of fourth-grade to sixth-grade white students in the years following desegregation of the Riverside school system.[82] Not surprisingly, the study found that white students received more choices from whites than either minority group, and the white rate did not change. More important, however, was the trend over time for choices received by minority

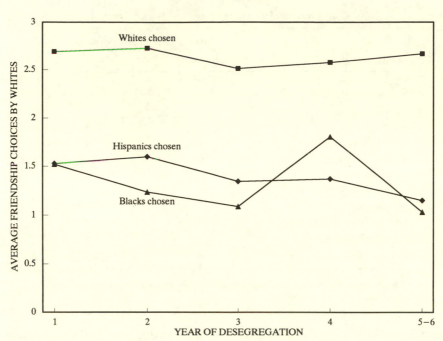

Figure 2.12. Race relations in Riverside: Friendship choices from whites by race/ethnic group, grades 4–6. *Source:* Harold Gerard and Norman Miller, *School Desegregation*, Table 10.2B.

students: the number of friendship choices received by both Hispanic and black students actually declined over the six-year period after desegregation.

After five years of desegregation and after most of the fourth- to sixth-graders had been desegregated from the beginning of their schooling, minority children were *less* likely to be chosen as friends by whites than at the beginning of desegregation. The same basic pattern was repeated at other grade levels and for other types of choices, such as work partners or play partners, even when socioeconomic and academic differences were taken into account. The authors concluded, "Little or no real integration occurred during the relatively long-term contact situation represented by Riverside's desegregation program. If anything we found some evidence that ethnic cleavage became somewhat more pronounced over time."[83]

The Indianapolis evaluation of race relations was conducted in twelve high schools during the 1970-1971 school year. Indianapolis high schools had been undergoing desegregation for several years, mostly by means of attendance zone changes and new feeder patterns, and by 1970 all but four high schools ranged from 13 to 53 percent black. Two other high schools were predominantly white, one was almost all black, and another was about 71 percent black. Among the many analyses of race relations in the study, one of the most important findings concerned the relationship between race relations and the racial composition of classrooms.

Figure 2.13 plots a measure of racial attitudes toward opposite-race students according to the average percentage of blacks in their classrooms; higher scores indicate more positive attitudes toward the other race.[84] For both black and white students, racial attitudes dropped to their lowest point when classes reached 20 to 40 percent black. For blacks, attitudes toward whites improved significantly when classes either became predominantly white or majority black. Other indicators of race relations, such as unfriendly interracial contacts or avoidance of the other race, showed similar patterns.

Moreover, the Indianapolis study also found that, like the original Coleman report, the highest academic outcomes for both black and white students were found in classes that were majority white. The author thus concludes, "Where there was a small black minority . . . social frictions between the races were relatively low . . . and academic outcomes for both races were relatively good. Where there was a larger black minority . . . frictions between the races generally increased considerably, but academic outcomes (especially effort) remained relatively high for both races. . . . And finally, when there was a clear black majority . . . social relations between the races generally were at their best while academic outcomes generally were low."[85] In other words, the racial composition best for race relations was worst for academic performance!

No version of the harm and benefit thesis has contemplated the complex possibility that one type of benefit such as race relations would fare best under conditions that hamper another benefit, and the thesis has not encompassed the

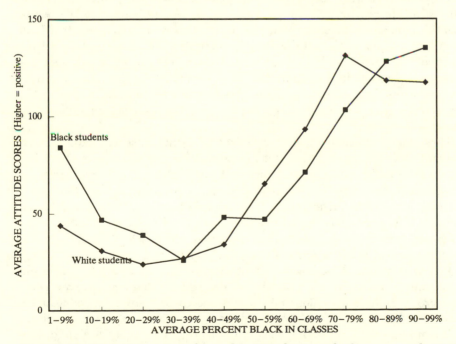

Figure 2.13. Race relations in Indianapolis: Attitudes toward other race, grades 9–12. *Source:* Martin Patchen, *Black-White Contact in Schools*, Figure 7.4.

possibility that race relations would be worse when black students were a sizeable minority in classrooms and best when blacks were in the majority. In fact, the 1967 statement of the U.S. Commission on Civil Rights argued that schools should be considered segregated and inferior when their composition exceeded 50 percent black.

Most reviewers of this body of research offer two explanations for the failure to demonstrate consistent benefits of desegregation for race relations and attitudes. One is methodological: Most studies are impaired by a host of technical problems such as nonstandardized measures of race relations and attitudes; lack of experimental designs; failure to assess important student, school, or desegregation plan characteristics; and short periods of observation. The other is substantive: Many desegregated schools may not meet the conditions for success demanded by contact theory, and when that happens contact can produce adverse effects on race relations and attitudes. St. John clearly spelled out this second problem:

> Allport . . . concluded that contact between ethnic groups leads to reduced prejudice only if such contact is prolonged, is between equals in the pursuit of common goals, and enjoys the sanction of those in authority. . . . Reflection suggests, however, that classroom contact is often short run, competitive, and between unequals, and, though formally sanctioned, may be informally resented and bypassed by those in authority.[86]

Many other reviewers offer similar explanations. Stephan, citing the conclusions of another reviewer, says, "S. Cook . . . has suggested that the reason that the optimistic predictions of the social scientists who participated in *Brown* have not been fulfilled is that the conditions required for desegregation to have positive effects have rarely been present."[87] Schofield, in her most recent review, says, "Researchers often tip their hats to contact theory in the introductory passages of a research report and then fail entirely to give information on topics that it suggests should be vital to predicting the probable outcomes of the contact experience."

Thus, many researchers have acknowledged that desegregation has not brought about the expected benefits in race relations and attitude changes, but the reason is not the fault of social science theory. Rather, the fault lies with the designers of desegregation plans—including, presumably, courts that order their adoption—who did not create the conditions necessary for successful racial contact. This approach is also taken in the 1991 social science statement of the harm and benefit thesis, which lists numerous within-school conditions that must be present if the benefits of desegregation are to be realized.

It is by no means clear, however, that all conditions necessary for successful racial contact are under the control of desegregation planners or, even when they are, that these conditions take precedence over many other educational policies and priorities with which school boards must grapple. The most serious problem arises if "equal-status" contact means relatively equal academic abilities or socioeconomic levels among students, as St. Johns suggests. If so, then few comprehensive desegregation plans will produce equal-status contact for most white and minority students. If the "absence of competition" standard is violated by the normal academic competition for grades, then most American educational practices would require major overhauling before this condition could be met.

In this regard, one major new movement in educational policy, "cooperative learning," seeks to eliminate or reduce traditional competitive grading practices. Cooperative learning strategies are based on a teamwork philosophy by which heterogeneous groups of students of differing abilities and races study as a team and work as much for group as for individual academic rewards. Some social scientists believe that these cooperative learning strategies better satisfy the requirements of contact theory and, when incorporated into a desegregation program, have had positive impacts on both academic achievement and race relations.[88]

Others believe that cooperative learning strategies, by de-emphasizing specialized or accelerated programs for higher ability students, might offer advantages for the lower achieving students but only at the expense of higher achieving and especially gifted students.[89] It is too early to say whether this teaching strategy will always fulfill the conditions of contact theory, and it is also too early to say whether cooperative learning will have lasting positive effects on achievement and intergroup relations for all types of students. It seems fairly clear, however, that cooperative learning strategies may have limited applicability where black achievement is lowest, which are the predominantly minority inner-city school districts. Here there are insufficient numbers of middle class and white students to create the heterogeneity required by cooperative learning theory.

Long-Term Outcomes

Most social scientists who have reviewed the research on desegregation have emphasized a major limitation of many studies: The effects of desegregation are studied for relatively short periods of time, frequently only one or two years after the onset of desegregation. Given the many changes and adjustments demanded by most desegregation plans, some social scientists argue that the benefits of desegregation may not occur for some years after a desegregation plan has been implemented and that the most important benefits might be realized in longer-term outcomes such as educational attainments, occupational outcomes, and residential decisions.

In recent years a number of social science studies have focused on these potential long-term outcomes of school desegregation. The number of available studies is much smaller than those for achievement, self-esteem, and race relations, and most of the studies must overcome several methodological hurdles to isolate the effects of desegregation from other factors. Nonetheless, this body of research has become of increasing importance to the harm and benefit thesis, as indicated by the emphasis it received in the 1991 social science statement.

Before examining this research, a comment is necessary on a methodological problem that is especially troublesome in many long-term outcome studies. The problem is isolating the effect of school desegregation from the effects of self-selection (if the desegregation was voluntary) or from the effects of natural residential desegregation. Minority students who volunteer for a desegregation plan or whose families already live in desegregated communities may differ from those who remain in segregated schools along a number of dimensions, including ability, motivation, family socioeconomic levels, and family preference for integrated environments. Most long-term studies are conducted retrospectively with national data bases of various sorts, and therefore they cannot determine the type and source of school desegregation. Even though they may have adequate controls for socioeconomic differences, such studies cannot compare the effects of school desegregation with the effects of self-selection or the effects of residential integration; in particular, they cannot control for minority family preferences for integrated environments.

With this caveat in mind, the studies can be grouped into three basic types of long-term outcomes. One group of studies has found that students who attended desegregated K-12 schools were more likely to attend four-year desegregated colleges rather than two-year or segregated colleges, particularly in the North.[90] Another group of studies has concluded that attending desegregated K-12 schools leads to different types of occupations (not necessarily better-paying) and more desegregated work settings.[91] A third group of studies finds that desegregated blacks attain more years of education than segregated black students, although the strength and consistency of the relationship is in question.[92]

Of these studies, the reports by Robert Crain and his colleagues on educational and occupational attainment are especially noteworthy because of their unique research design. The reports are based on a sixteen-year follow-up study of minority (mostly black) students who enrolled in Project Concern, a voluntary busing program in Hartford, Connecticut. Project Concern, which began in the late 1960s, enables minority children from segregated Hartford city schools to transfer to predominantly white schools in the suburbs. The study not only separates the effects school desegregation from residential integration, but it also employs a quasi experimental design that allows comparison of Project Concern (PC) students with a control group of minority students who remained in the Hartford public schools. Although not all students were assigned randomly to the PC and control conditions (one subgroup was), an attempt was made to match control students with PC students on a number of relevant characteristics. The study also distinguishes those students who remained in PC until they finished school from those who dropped out of PC and returned to segregated schools in Hartford, a factor that offers a unique opportunity to assess self-selection effects.

The difficulty of sorting out the effects of school desegregation from the effects of self-selection is illustrated in Figure 2.14.[93] The first and third set of bars (labeled stayins) in the figure compare all Project Concern students who remained and completed their education in the suburbs with the control group students who stayed and completed their schooling in Hartford. These bars show that the PC stayins had significantly higher educational attainment than

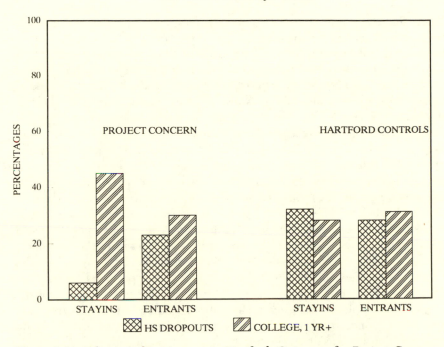

Figure 2.14. Educational attainment in Hartford: Outcomes for Project Concern and Hartford controls, by stayins versus all entrants. *Source:* Robert Crain et al., "Finding Niches," Tables 2 and B.1.

the Hartford controls; that is, 45 percent of the PC stayins have attended one or more years of college compared to only 32 percent of the control stayins. The high school dropout rates also differ dramatically; only 6 percent of the PC stayins dropped out of high school, versus 28 percent of the Hartford controls.

From this single comparison one might be tempted to conclude that desegregation had substantial educational benefits for Project Concern students. The problem, however, is that about half of Project Concern students left the program before finishing school, and most returned to Hartford schools to complete their education (most of the Hartford controls remained in the Hartford schools). The key question becomes, then, whether the higher education realized by the Project Concern stayins was caused by desegregation or rather is simply a manifestation of better outcomes from a subgroup that was more academically motivated and talented in the first place.

Crain and colleagues recognized the potential bias stemming from this very high withdrawal rate. Quite aside from the potential self-selection effects of volunteering for Project Concern in the first place (Project Concern students had somewhat higher socioeconomic profiles than the control group), survey results showed that those who withdrew from the program were having more academic and behavioral problems than the stayins, which raises the possibility of biased results. The study team attempted to deal with this problem in an appendix that showed educational attainment for all students who entered the PC or Hartford control groups initially (called *entrants*).

The second and fourth columns of Figure 2.14 show the educational attainment of all those who entered Project Concern or the original control group (labeled entrants), additionally adjusted for various initial ability and socioeconomic background differences between PC entrants and controls. The college attendance rates for all PC entrants is nearly the same as all controls (30 versus 31 percent), while the high school dropout rate is somewhat higher for all controls (23 percent versus 28 percent), but the difference is not statistically significant. In other words, when all original Project Concern and Hartford control students are compared, regardless of the length of stay in the program, educational outcomes for Project Concern are not significantly better than for Hartford schools. The difference between this comparison and the first comparison, of course, is due to the dramatically different outcomes for Project Concern students who stayed in compared to those who withdrew from the program.

Inferences about the effects of desegregation here depend heavily on how the PC withdrawals are handled and interpreted. In his report and in his 1993 testimony in the Hartford case, Crain put heavy emphasis on the importance of staying in and completing the program to realize the full effects of desegregation (most Project Concern students began in an early elementary grade). Crain views the withdrawals as not receiving the full "treatment" effect of desegregation. Acknowledging the possible selection effects of withdrawing, however, Crain testified that the true effects of desegregation were probably somewhere "in between" the results for the stayin and the entrant samples.

Conventionally, when evaluating an intervention program that is designed to change behavior (e.g., treatment for substance abuse), dropping out of the program is usually considered a treatment failure and the program dropouts would normally be included with the treatment group when assessing long-term outcomes. This strategy may not be appropriate for evaluating desegregation, but nonetheless the fact that, for a variety of reasons, half of a group of volunteers chose not to continue their desegregation experience must be taken into account.[94]

There is one other source of information to help decide whether the difference between the two groups is desegregation or self-selection. Figure 2.15 compares the education outcomes for PC withdrawals and stayins, classifying the withdrawals by how long they remained in the PC program. If the length of desegregation was the critical difference for the stayins, then one might expect that the withdrawals who stayed the longest had higher attainment that those who withdrew early on. In fact, if anything, those withdrawing after one or two years had slightly better outcomes than those who stayed in Project Concern for six to ten years (although the differences were not statistically significant). None of the withdrawal groups has educational attainment as high as the stayins, regardless of their length of stay.

One has to question, then, whether the length of the desegregation experience itself generates the better outcomes for the stayins. Rather, other student characteristics—which might have been present before they entered the

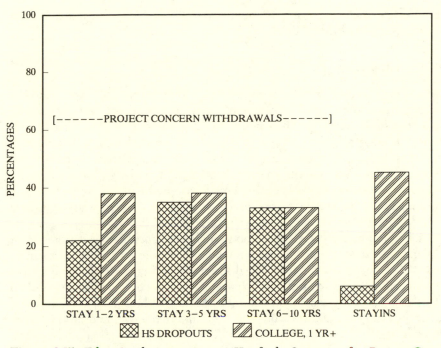

Figure 2.15. Educational attainment in Hartford: Outcomes for Project Concern withdrawals and stayins, by length of stay.

program—may cause some students to stay and some to leave. It is also possible, of course, that for a whole variety of reasons desegregation was not experienced uniformly by all students. Some stayins might have had very positive experiences; other stayins might have had negative experiences but decided to stay anyway for the perceived benefits. The withdrawals might have had negative experiences that were not balanced by perceived benefits, and so they decided to leave.

While one cannot gainsay the very positive outcomes for the Project Concern students who stayed with the program, at the same time one must somehow factor in the high withdrawal rate and the much poorer outcomes for the withdrawals, regardless of how long they experienced desegregation. At the very least, one has to conclude from this important study that the benefits of desegregation are not uniform, even for those who volunteer for it, and for reasons not fully understood at this point some students received long-term benefits from Project Concern while many others did not.

Status of the Harm and Benefit Thesis

The status of the harm and benefit thesis can be evaluated in several different contexts. First, how valid are its various tenets in light of social science research? Second, what is its future role in judicial proceedings, both federal and state? Finally, what role should it play in educational decision making, at both institutional and individual levels?

Validity of the Thesis

Although the harm and benefit thesis has changed in the past forty years and has been revised in response to new research and new legal doctrines, no major component of the thesis receives unequivocal support from the available evidence. While virtually all social scientists would agree that forced racial segregation is both unconstitutional and immoral, it has not been demonstrated that attending de facto segregated schools is harmful to black or other minority students that desegregated schools by themselves produce consistent social and educational benefits; in some cases the consequences of desegregation may be harmful to race relations and black self-esteem.

This does not mean that there are no benefits of school desegregation or that the policy should be abandoned by school boards or other government agencies. What it does mean is that some social scientists and civil rights groups have oversold the policy, promised more than it can produce, and thereby implied that its benefits always outweigh its costs. Whatever the role of the harm and benefit thesis in judicial proceedings, it is definitely relevant to other branches of government and to citizens who must decide on desegregation plans and on their participation in them. Decisions about school desegregation, whether by governments or individuals, should be made after a sound assessment of its costs and benefits and a careful consideration of alternatives.

The most prominent theme from the evidence on school desegregation is the great variation in outcomes in academic achievement, self-esteem, race relations, or long-term attainments. The variations occur not only from study to study but also for different individuals within a study. Some variations may well be spurious, arising from technical problems with the research, and some variations may be real but cannot be explained, given current social science knowledge. Other variations have reasonable explanations, however, and these explanations might form the basis for rational decision making about school desegregation for both individuals and government agencies. Before commenting on variations in outcomes, a few broad summary statements are in order about each of the major components of the thesis.

First, whatever the state of black self-esteem at the time of *Brown*, there is little evidence of a black self-esteem problem between the early 1960s and 1990. Most studies show that blacks have the same or higher self-esteem than whites. Given the black-white academic achievement gap, the absence of a black-white self-esteem gap suggests that self-esteem does not explain achievement differences between black and white children. Of course, individual minority students (and individual white students) can have low self-esteem that might affect their performance in school. As a *group*, however, minority students do not have a self-esteem problem that requires remedy. Moreover, school desegregation may cause declines in self-esteem for some minority students, either as a result of white prejudice or unfavorable academic competition with white students. Adverse effects are most problematic for minority students whose academic skills are lower than those of white students in the desegregated school.

Second, interracial exposure by itself cannot be assumed to improve race relations and attitudes in a desegregated school, at least as most desegregation plans have been implemented. By definition, desegregated schools generate more interracial contact than segregated schools, and therefore they undoubtedly increase the knowledge about the behaviors, attitudes, and characteristics of different races and ethnic groups. This increased knowledge, however, does not automatically lead to better race relations, better attitudes, and lowered prejudice. Improvements have been documented for some desegregation programs, but just as many show worse outcomes and a number of others produced no observed changes. Many suggestions have been offered for these wide variations in results, but there is no definitive research that explains why positive or negative results occur.

Third, perhaps the greatest misconceptions among parents are the perceived effects of segregated or desegregated schools on academic achievement. Minority parents frequently believe that desegregated schools alone benefit minority achievement (compared to segregated minority schools), whereas white parents frequently believe that desegregated schools harm white achievement (compared to segregated white schools). Neither of these views is supported by the available research. Instead, sometimes achievement is higher in desegregated schools and sometimes it is lower, but in most cases the differences in achievement between desegregated and segregated schools are small once socioeconomic differences are taken into account. Enhanced academic achievement is probably the last reason why any agency or individual should endorse desegregation policies.

Of all the research done on the harm and benefit thesis, the research on long-term outcomes offers the strongest argument for desegregated schools, although even here the research is not consistent, and the benefits may well be confined to voluntary desegregation plans. Some national studies show that minority students who attended desegregated schools are more likely to live and work in desegregated environments as adults, but the exact mechanism for this outcome is not well understood. In particular, these studies do not distinguish between natural residential desegregation and the induced school desegregation that takes place from court or legislative actions. Therefore, the positive results shown in these studies might simply be a family preference for desegregated environments being passed on from one generation to the next.

One of the few long-term studies that does distinguish residential from induced school desegregation is the Project Concert evaluation. This study shows that minority students who voluntarily transfer to *and remain* in a desegregated school do well educationally, socially, and vocationally. This positive finding is tempered, however, by the high program dropout rate; large numbers of initial transfers left the program for various reasons and returned to segregated schools. Some of these program dropouts come away with more negative attitudes about desegregation in general and whites in particular.

Finally, some judgment is needed about the considerable variation in desegregation outcomes, especially those for achievement, race relations, and long-term educational and vocational attainment. One explanation is simply that the variations are not related to desegregation policies at all, but simply arise from any number of uncontrolled conditions that are extraneous to desegregation: technical study problems including use of different outcome measures, differences in school policies and programs, and differences in student and family background characteristics. A second and competing explanation is offered by the 1991 social science statement on desegregation: that positive benefits accrue only if certain conditions are met by a desegregation plan.

Although the 1991 social science statement offers one possible explanation for the lack of across-the-board desegregation benefits, no one comprehensive study or group of studies allows one to decide between the two explanations for variation in outcomes. Such a study would have to assess systematically the relationship between multiple benefits (e.g., academic achievement, race relations, long-term attainments) and the postulated conditions for positive outcomes (e.g., community and parental support, staff attitudes, type and scope of desegregation plan, ability grouping, multiethnic textbooks, grade and length of implementation). Such a study may not even be possible because it presumes some control over conditions that may be mutually contradictory, such as lack of community and parental support or negative staff attitudes for large-scale mandatory busing plans.

In the absence of definitive studies, what can be said about controllable conditions that might optimize the benefits of desegregation and that might be supported by more than a single study? To the extent that desegregation can improve educational achievement and race relations, most desegregation experts might agree that benefits are optimized if desegregation is voluntary, if it can be started at the earliest grades, and if students with similar values, interests, and skills are targeted for desegregation. Voluntary plans not only create more community and parental support (see chapter 4) but also allow parents and students to seek out those schools most compatible with their interests and skills and then allow students to return to their original school if benefits are not forthcoming. Children have steeper learning curves at younger ages, and therefore whatever school factors might enhance achievement—racial contact, curriculum, or other factor—should generally have larger effects at earlier grades. Finally, the similarity condition may be an important prerequisite for avoiding possible negative effects postulated by contact theory, and it also may be necessary for maximizing the achievement of highly talented students.

The Judicial Process

Many legal scholars have asserted that the psychological harm thesis was never fully embraced by the Supreme Court in *Brown* and that it was unnecessary for their decision that state-imposed segregation is unconstitutional. Subsequent Supreme Court decisions seem to validate this interpretation because the thesis was never discussed again. In light of subsequent social science research, this outcome is propitious; the harm and benefit thesis has too many flaws and too many "conditions" to be a sound basis for jurisprudence. Not only has mandatory desegregation failed to produce educational and social benefits for most minority children but also research shows it can lead to adverse consequences for some.

While the thesis never became permanent Supreme Court doctrine, its appearance in *Brown* was not completely without meaning and effect. Because some justices (e.g., William Douglas and Thurgood Marshall) embraced it, it probably influenced such later decisions as *Swann, Keyes,* and *Columbus,* in which considerable de facto segregation was fused with de jure segregation in comprehensive mandatory busing remedies. The thesis had even greater judicial consequences in lower federal courts, which ordered mandatory busing plans in such cities as San Francisco, Pasadena, and Pontiac with explicit references to the educational harms of segregation and benefits of desegregation.

Although no recent lower court decisions invoke the harm and benefit thesis, it remains very much an active issue in desegregation litigation. Plaintiffs now argue in federal courts that the minority-white achievement gap is a vestige of former dual school systems and that unitary status should not be granted until and unless the gap is closed or reduced appreciably (e.g., Wilmington, Delaware; San Jose, California). In at least one state court (Hartford), plaintiffs contend that achievement differences reflect unequal educational opportunity and are hence illegal educational practices. It remains to be seen whether any federal or state court accepts these arguments, but until decisions are rendered and appeals exhausted, the harm and benefit thesis is still playing a role in the judicial process.

Educational Policy Decisions

Decisions about desegregation are not confined to the courts. Many desegregation plans are adopted by school boards without litigation (e.g., Seattle; Knox County, Tennessee; La Crosse, Wisconsin), and in many of these situations the harm and benefit thesis is invoked as a primary justification. State legislatures have also passed laws requiring or encouraging some type of desegregation policies (e.g., Massachusetts, Connecticut, and New Jersey) with a similar rationale. Finally, parents are asked to make decisions about desegregation, especially when a voluntary plan has been adopted by a school board for whatever reason.

At the government level, the lack of across-the-board benefits for desegregation suggests that mandatory methods may not be cost-effective. For example, community opposition to large-scale mandatory busing and the potential loss of support for raising revenue may outweigh the minimal gains that might be realized in social and educational outcomes. Even if the community supports the plan in general, it is also possible that mandatory busing can produce negative outcomes (race relations) that neutralize positive outcomes (achievement), depending on certain other factors such as the racial composition of the district and the similarities in student backgrounds. Given these uncertainties, voluntary or choice plans might be more feasible and more likely (although not guaranteed) to produce social and educational benefits. Further discussion about cost-effectiveness issues appears in chapters 4 and 5.

Voluntary desegregation or choice plans also have the advantage that individual parents can evaluate the likely benefits (or potential harms) for their children, both before and during a desegregation program. Because the research suggests that some students benefit educationally while others do not, parents, especially minority parents, ought to be in a position to decide whether their children should attend and remain in a desegregated school. Further, parents are likely to differ in their own personal cost-benefit equation, so that for some parents the benefits of increased racial contact and knowledge in desegregated schools may well outweigh lack of achievement benefits or the risk of increased racial hostility. A voluntary desegregation plan allows these individual variations and decision-making processes to take place.

Someday social scientists may be able to design a comprehensive desegregation plan proven to benefit all students, such as that described in the 1991 social science statement; if so, that policy might appropriately be made mandatory. Unless that happens, parents are in the best position to decide whether a given desegregation plan is consistent with their long-term goals and will benefit their children's academic progress.

3

Housing Segregation and School Desegregation*

The issue of residential segregation has had a long history in the development of school desegregation laws and policies. Most social scientists and jurists would agree that school segregation is closely associated with racial segregation in housing, particularly in larger school systems. Residential segregation can give rise to school segregation between school systems, such as that existing between a predominantly minority city school system and its predominantly white suburban systems, and within a single school system when a neighborhood school policy reflects segregated residential patterns. The debate over the relationship between housing and school segregation arises, however, not from the mere fact of association, but from the causal interpretations applied to this association.

Two major issues have framed the debates over this relationship. One issue concerns the causes of housing segregation itself, whether it arises primarily from discriminatory actions, either public or private, or from a complex set of social, economic, and demographic forces in which discrimination plays only a secondary role. The second issue focuses on the causal connections between school segregation and housing segregation and the direction of the causal relationship: the extent to which a neighborhood school policy actually contributes to housing segregation (rather than simply reflecting it) and the extent to which school desegregation contributes to integrated housing choices. On these points there is sharp disagreement between and within the social science and legal communities.[1]

The debates within the social science and legal communities have had reciprocating influences. On the one hand, a considerable amount of research on housing segregation has been generated by school desegregation litigation. On the other, a number of court decisions about the role of housing in school desegregation cases have been influenced by social science research and expert testimony. Thus the relationship between judicial policy and social science research is well illustrated by the housing segregation issue.

The role of residential segregation in school desegregation law has itself

*This chapter was coauthored by William A. V. Clark.

117

passed through several stages during the past thirty years of school desegregation litigation. During the first era of school desegregation cases, before *Swann v. Charlotte–Mecklenburg* justified mandatory busing on broader grounds, some lower courts found that neighborhood school policies were themselves unconstitutional because of housing segregation.[2] These courts accepted a view propounded by some social science experts that housing segregation was largely caused by—or at least heavily influenced by—governmental and private discrimination of various types; neighborhood school policies that mirrored the housing segregation were thereby tainted. Early courts could thereby link the segregation associated with neighborhood schools to unconstitutional state actions and impose mandatory busing programs as remedies.

After the *Swann* decision, which endorsed a general requirement for racial balance and mandatory busing without relying on the housing argument, housing segregation played a diminishing role in most intradistrict desegregation cases. The issue of housing segregation surfaced again, however, in a series of interdistrict desegregation lawsuits, the "metropolitan" cases, beginning in the late 1970s. Many of these cases tried to take advantage of language in part of the *Milliken v. Bradley* decision suggesting that, if housing segregation (and hence segregation arising from neighborhood schools) could be traced primarily to state action, then the segregation between cities and suburbs might be found unconstitutional.[3] If so, a court could order an interdistrict desegregation plan, including metropolis-wide busing and racial balancing between city and suburban school systems. The studies and testimony of social scientists in these metropolitan cases was generally more extensive than those in the pre-*Swann* cases.

Although none of these metropolitan cases led to a major Supreme Court opinion on the issue of housing segregation, the high Court did affirm a 1980 lower court decision that had found no school district responsibility for housing segregation in the Atlanta metropolitan area (*Armour v. Nix*).[4] More recently, the issue of housing segregation was discussed in two Supreme Court decisions dealing with unitary issues, *Dowell v. Oklahoma City* in 1991 and *Freeman v. Pitts* in 1992.[5] Like the Atlanta case, the lower courts in *Dowell* and *Pitts* had found that housing segregation was caused by a complex set of social and economic factors rather than government action. Thus questions about the relationship between housing and school segregation continue to arise in desegregation litigation.

Quite aside from the constitutional questions raised by housing segregation and its causes, the fact of housing segregation is not in question. In contrast to the considerable racial integration that has taken place in public facilities, in schools, and in the workplace, racial segregation in housing remains pervasive and resistant to change. Housing segregation remains one of the reasons why many school boards continue to debate school desegregation policies, even in the absence of legal necessity, simply because traditional geographic methods for assigning students to schools so frequently yield segregated schools. In the face of residential segregation, many educators argue that schools should ameliorate the conditions of racial isolation that prevail at home, particularly when they believe that the residential racial isolation is caused by prejudice and discrimination rather than by choice or economic necessity.

The social science evidence on the causes of housing segregation and its relationship to school segregation is therefore relevant both to legal questions and to the general policy debates over school desegregation. Like evidence on the harm and benefit thesis, the social science evidence is complex and often marked by conflicting interpretations. Before discussing the social science research on this issue, however, a more detailed review of the legal history is in order to set the stage for evaluating the role of housing issues in school desegregation law and policies.

Housing Segregation in School Desegregation Cases

The history of housing segregation in school desegregation cases can be divided into several broad categories that correspond to the eras described in chapter 1. Generally, the way in which housing segregation has been used in school litigation depends on the period of time and whether the case was intradistrict or interdistrict (metropolitan). The first category covers intradistrict cases before the *Swann* decision, the second category includes metropolitan cases up to and including the *Milliken I* decision, the third category covers metropolitan cases in the post-*Milliken* era, and a fourth category covers more recent intradistrict cases. Most of the research on the causes of housing segregation described in this chapter was not generated or used in school desegregation cases until the post-*Milliken* era.

Early Housing Issues

The housing segregation issue arose in a number of early intradistrict school desegregation cases in which lower courts were struggling with the problem of neighborhood school policies and the fact that housing segregation operates through such policies to produce or at least aggravate school segregation. Before the *Swann* decision, no established Supreme Court doctrine permitted overturning a neighborhood school policy, even in the South, without some tie to unconstitutional conduct.

A number of lower courts invoked housing discrimination as part of the basis for altering or abolishing neighborhood school policies and ordering some type of busing plan. Some of the more significant intradistrict decisions include the Oklahoma City, Pasadena, and Charlotte–Mecklenburg litigation.[6] These lower court decisions cite various types of government or government-related discrimination in housing, such as racial zoning, racially restrictive deeds and covenants, and racial "steering" by real estate agents. These decisions also acknowledged the role of private discrimination, but little attempt was made to distinguish between public and private discrimination. For these early cases, most of the evidence on housing discrimination was introduced as historical documents or by fact witnesses such as real estate agents; no comprehensive studies or testimony by social scientists evaluated the weight of discriminatory versus nondiscriminatory factors or separated the impact of private versus public actions.

None of these early court decisions reached the Supreme Court except *Swann*. Later lower court decisions in the Oklahoma City and Pasadena cases were reviewed by the Supreme Court, and the 1990 *Dowell* decision for Oklahoma City does raise the issue of residential segregation, but these later decisions do not disturb the original findings of housing discrimination and its impact on school segregation. Thus the *Swann* case became the first Supreme Court review of a decision that had used housing discrimination as one reason for voiding a neighborhood school policy.

It is significant that all these lower court decisions, including *Swann*, also found that school policies and actions had contributed to school segregation, so that their conclusions about constitutional violations and remedy were not based solely on housing discrimination. In *Swann* the Supreme Court did, in fact, validate a connection between residential segregation and school policies, although not necessarily the same one used by the lower courts. Commenting on school construction policies, the Supreme Court said:

> The location of schools may thus influence the pattern of residential development of a metropolitan area. . . . It may well promote segregated residential patterns which, when combined with "neighborhood zoning," further lock the school system into the mold of separation of the races. Upon a proper showing a district may consider this in fashioning a remedy.[7]

Then again, as cited in chapter 1, the *Swann* decision did not rule on the question of whether discriminatory actions (including, presumably, housing discrimination) by other state agents, absent discrimination by school authorities, would justify a school desegregation remedy. Therefore, housing segregation and its relation to school actions can be considered by a court in designing a desegregation plan, but it would not necessarily serve as the sole basis for a desegregation plan. In short, *Swann* did not rule out neighborhood school policies that might mirror illegal housing segregation, unless significant school policies also contributed to school segregation.

Housing Issues Leading to *Milliken I*

Prior to *Milliken* there were relatively few metropolitan desegregation cases, and not all were reviewed by the Supreme Court. Two of the earliest interdistrict cases that reached the Court involved the relatively small school districts serving Emporia, Virginia, and Scotland Neck, North Carolina. The principal issue in both cases was the creation of two new segregated school districts from a single county district, and both actions were ruled unconstitutional because they frustrated the dismantling of dual systems in those counties.[8] The issue of housing segregation or discrimination was not raised in either case.

The first major metropolitan case to reach the Supreme Court that had invoked housing discrimination involved Richmond, Virginia, and two surrounding county school districts. Borrowing language from *Swann*, the district court used housing segregation as part of its basis for ordering consolidation of the three school districts. The lower court found that school and housing segregation were "interdependent," with school segregation building upon and contributing to housing segregation between the city and suburban counties. By choosing between the city and county, new residents were guaranteed both a segregated neighborhood and a segregated school. The district court also cited various discriminatory housing practices and policies including restrictive covenants, discrimination by real estate agents, and exclusion of low-income housing by county governments.[9] Like most of the pre-*Swann* cases, there were no comprehensive housing studies or testimony by housing experts.

In overturning the district court, the Fourth Circuit Court of Appeals acknowledged the existence of housing discrimination in the Richmond area, but it was "unable to determine whether such discrimination . . . has had any impact upon movement by blacks out of the city and into the counties." In other words, no interdistrict effects of housing discrimination were proven. It also said that "what little action, if any, the counties may seem to have taken to keep blacks out is slight indeed compared to the myriad reasons, economic, political, and social, for the concentration of blacks in Richmond."[10] The Supreme Court reviewed this decision on appeal, but the appellate decision was upheld by virtue of a 4–4 deadlock on the Supreme Court.

The district court decision in Detroit's *Milliken I* case also invoked housing discrimination and segregation, but it was the first to rely on extensive testimony and studies by Karl Taeuber, a demographer and housing segregation expert.[11] Taeuber distinguished between the three causes of housing segregation discussed in the previous section: economics, choice, and discrimination. He concluded that economics explains only a small part of housing segregation, that choice is not an important explanation because blacks express a preference for integrated neighborhoods (without specifying the degree of integration or the preferences of whites), and that discrimination was the predominant cause of housing segregation in Detroit. He included both private and public discrimination in his conclusions; examples of public discrimination included location of public housing, zoning and urban renewal, restrictive covenants, lending practices of financial institutions, and real estate practices. He also concluded that school segregation itself was a reciprocal cause of housing segregation through the "beacon" effect. With the exception of some economic and demographic analysis, however, his conclusions were not based on a quantitative evaluation of the relative contributions of each of the main causes of housing segregation, either in Detroit or elsewhere.

The district court embodied Taeuber's testimony in its conclusions, including both public and private forms of discrimination:

> While the racially unrestricted choice of black persons and economic factors may have played some part in the development of this pattern of residential segregation, it is, in the main, the result of past and present practices and customs of racial discrimination, both public and private, which . . . restrict the housing opportunities of black people. . . . Governmental actions and

inaction at all levels . . . have combined with those of private organizations, such as loaning institutions and real estate associations . . . to establish and to maintain the pattern of residential segregation throughout the Detroit metropolitan area. . . . And we note that just as there is an interaction between residential patterns and the racial composition of the schools, so there is a corresponding effect on the residential pattern by the racial composition of the schools. [12]

Like other pre-*Swann* cases, the district court decision included a number of other findings of discriminatory practices by both Detroit school authorities and the State of Michigan. Also, *Milliken I* did not start out as a metropolitan case, and the order to merge Detroit with fifty-three suburban districts for the purpose of a metropolitan desegregation plan was not based on the conclusions about housing segregation. Rather, the metropolitan order emerged from a later hearing on remedy, at which the district court concluded that a Detroit-only plan would result in a racially identifiable school district that would be worsened by white flight. [13] In other words, the constitutional violations found by the lower court applied only to Detroit and the State of Michigan, and housing segregation between the city and suburbs was not raised as an issue.

The Court of Appeals for the Sixth Circuit upheld the lower court order in most respects, but it also emphasized that its conclusions were based on specific unconstitutional actions of school authorities and the state and that "we have not relied at all upon testimony pertaining to segregated housing except as school construction programs helped cause or maintain such segregation." [14] School construction was, of course, one type of housing evidence that the Supreme Court had explicitly allowed in *Swann*.

The majority opinion in the Supreme Court's *Milliken I* decision cited the appellate court's caveat on housing segregation in a footnote. It then stated: "Accordingly, in its present posture, the case does not present any question concerning possible state housing violations." [15] As in *Swann*, then, the Supreme Court bypassed the question of whether housing discrimination alone could form the basis for a desegregation remedy, in this case a remedy crossing school district boundaries. As discussed in chapter 1, the majority opinion overturned the district and appellate court decisions on the grounds that no interdistrict constitutional violation had been proven that justified a metropolitan remedy.

Given the high Court's explicit avoidance of the broader housing issues in two major decisions, one might wonder why housing segregation became such a major focus of several major metropolitan lawsuits in the late 1970s and early 1980s. At least one major reason has to do with the 5–4 split on *Milliken I* and with a concurring opinion by Justice Stewart. Although siding with the majority, Justice Stewart's concurring opinion opened the door for a housing strategy. Emphasizing that the only issue decided by the majority opinion was the failure to prove interdistrict violations, Justice Stewart wrote:

This is not to say, however, that an interdistrict remedy of the sort approved by the Court of Appeals would not be proper, or even necessary, in other factual situations. Were it to be shown, for example, that state officials had contributed

to the separation of the races by . . . purposeful, racially discriminatory use
of state housing or zoning laws, then a decree calling for transfer of pupils across
district lines or for restructuring of district lines might well be appropriate.[16]

Because the four dissenting justices were ready to support a metropolitan
remedy without requiring proof of interdistrict violations, numerous constitutional scholars reasoned that a housing discrimination strategy might well deliver a Supreme Court majority favoring metropolitan school desegregation.[17]
Indeed, a number of metropolitan desegregation lawsuits were initiated partly
on the basis of this interpretation, and some subsequent lower court decisions
cited Justice Stewart's remarks about housing discrimination in *Milliken I*.

Housing Issues in Post-*Milliken* Metropolitan Cases

During the first few years following *Milliken I*, there were indications that
metropolitan remedies might become more commonplace under these newly
articulated standards for interdistrict violations. The first two metropolitan desegregation lawsuits to be decided under the *Milliken I* standards involved
Indianapolis and Wilmington, Delaware, and both ultimately led to metropolitan busing plans that were either affirmed or allowed to stand by the Supreme Court. Housing discrimination arose in both of these metropolitan cases
and became part of the constitutional violations, but the lower courts also found
other interdistrict violations that alone might have justified metropolitan remedies.

In the Indianapolis case, the final district court decision (following remands of
earlier decisions in light of *Milliken* and *Washington v. Davis*) cited only two
interdistrict violations to justify an interdistrict remedy: (1) repeal of a state law
that would have made the city school boundaries coterminous with a countywide municipal government, thereby preventing merger of Indianapolis with
ten virtually all-white suburban districts within that county, and (2) location of
all low-income public housing projects within the city school district.[18] The
metropolitan remedy involved only the transfer of black students from the city
to the suburban districts; school district mergers were not required. The metropolitan desegregation plan was ultimately upheld by the Seventh Circuit Court
of Appeals, and an appeal to the Supreme Court was denied. Although no
Supreme Court review is available, the boundary violation alone might have
justified the relatively modest metropolitan remedy imposed here.

The Wilmington case was decided on similar grounds. Although housing
discrimination was also raised in this case, the primary interdistrict violation
found by the district court appears to have been exclusion of the predominantly
black Wilmington school district from a 1968 state school consolidation law,
which could have led to a merger of Wilmington with ten predominantly white
suburban districts.[19] Unlike Indianapolis, however, the Wilmington remedy
required merger of the eleven former city and suburban districts into one large
metropolitan district, and mandatory busing was used for racial balance in all
schools in the new district. A majority of the Supreme Court denied a review
petition, but a strong dissenting opinion was written by Justice Rehnquist,

joined by Justices Powell and Stewart, suggesting that the metropolitan busing remedy exceeded the scope of the violation.[20]

This brief trend was brought to an end by the first metropolitan lawsuit that relied primarily on housing discrimination. The case involved Atlanta and nine suburban city and county districts. Although the lawsuit also alleged other discriminatory school policies with interdistrict effects, the major thrust of the complaint concerned government-induced housing discrimination and segregation. The district court recognized this strategy in its opinion: "Inasmuch as the court has found no evidence that . . . [actions of] the defendant school systems . . . constitute constitutional violations, plaintiffs must succeed on their housing evidence if they are to prevail in the liability portion of this trial."[21]

The principal expert on housing segregation for the plaintiffs was Karl Taeuber, who presented analysis and testimony similar to his testimony in the Detroit case and concluded that the present school segregation within and between school districts in the Atlanta metropolitan area was caused principally by housing discrimination. As in the Detroit case, his conclusions were based primarily on an analysis of specific discriminatory anecdotes and historical documents; very little quantitative analysis was presented to assess the relative effects of economics, preferences, discrimination, and school policies on housing segregation. The experts on housing segregation for the defendant school districts were Anthony Pascal, David Armor, and William Clark, who testified about economic factors, racial preferences, demographic-geographic factors, and discrimination. The testimony was based on quantitative analyses and simulations using existing U.S. Census and survey data.

The district court agreed with plaintiffs that, historically, government actions at all levels had contributed to housing segregation both within and between the city and suburban school districts. Specifically, the court found that (1) "local government units outside of the City of Atlanta discouraged movement of blacks into those areas and discouraged the continuation of black enclaves already located there" and (2) "Location of public housing has tended to concentrate the black population of the metropolitan area within the City of Atlanta."

Still, the court did not agree with plaintiffs that *present* levels of housing segregation were caused principally by government discrimination. Whereas the court stated that "the causes of residential patterns can never be fully explained," it also concluded that "of the factors which influence housing decisions, economic restraints and personal preference appear to be the strongest" and that "the court was impressed by defendants' expert testimony as to the role of personal preference in housing decisions." The court also concluded that "governmental discrimination is not presently a cause of segregated housing patterns. . . . Government discrimination played a significant role in the past, but plaintiffs have not shown that any of them has sought and been denied any housing because of governmental discrimination."[22] In short, the district court concluded that the plaintiffs had failed to prove that official discrimination in housing met the *Milliken I* requirements for current interdistrict effects on school segregation. The district court decision was affirmed by the Supreme Court without comment in 1980.

Following Atlanta, no major metropolitan desegregation order has been based primarily on housing discrimination. Of the several metropolitan cases ongoing or initiated at about the same time as Atlanta, only the Kansas City case led to further rulings on the interdistrict effects of housing discrimination. As described in chapter 1, metropolitan lawsuits in Cincinnati, Milwaukee, and St. Louis ultimately settled out of court, with suburban districts agreeing to participate in voluntary student transfer programs between the city and suburban school districts.

In the Kansas City metropolitan case, the plaintiffs argued in part that government-sponsored housing discrimination was responsible for the school segregation between Kansas City and its suburbs, and this position was supported by extensive testimony from numerous school and housing experts, including Gary Orfield, John Kain, Yale Rabin, and Gary Tobin. The district court disagreed and dismissed the suburban districts as defendants following plaintiffs' presentation; the defendants therefore did not present their own expert studies on housing segregation. In its opinion, the district court said:

> [N]o [suburban school district] in any significant way influenced the housing patterns in the Kansas City metropolitan area . . . [T]he Court rejects plaintiffs' "effect" theory that liability may be placed on the [suburban school districts] for being the recipients of people moving for whatever reason. Absent a nexus between conduct of the defendant [suburban school districts] and the housing actors, the Court will not find the [suburban school districts] liable for racial imbalance that may be attributed to policies or practices of independent housing actors.[23]

Unlike the Atlanta court, which evaluated contrasting testimony on the relative contributions of discriminatory versus nondiscriminatory causes of housing segregation, the Kansas City court adopted a narrower approach requiring proof that the suburban districts themselves—not just any official person or agency—contributed to interdistrict housing segregation. In any event, this ruling was upheld on appeal, and the Atlanta and Kansas City decisions remain as the last major federal court rulings on the role of housing discrimination in a metropolitan school segregation case.

Housing Issues in Post-*Swann* Intradistrict Cases

Although the housing discrimination issue was most prominent in metropolitan cases after *Milliken I*, it was raised again in several other intradistrict cases (including the Columbus and Dayton, Ohio, cases) but in basically the same way as in the pre-*Swann* cases. A different application of housing discrimination arose in a Yonkers, New York, case in which a district court found that significant intradistrict school segregation had been caused by intentional concentration of public housing projects in one part of the city. The city council was ordered to construct subsidized housing units in other sections of the city, and, because of separate school violations, a school desegregation plan was also ordered.[24]

The issue of housing segregation was also raised again in the 1991 Supreme Court decision on *Dowell*. Although the district court had found that housing discrimination contributed to school segregation in its 1965 decision, it came to a different conclusion after unitary hearings in 1987 and after expert testimony about the causes of housing segregation. Based on a detailed case study of Oklahoma City and some of the evidence gathered in other metropolitan cases, William Clark testified that the present housing and school segregation in Oklahoma City was not due largely to government discrimination; using other sources of data, including audit studies conducted by the Department of Housing and Urban Development, (HUD), Rabin testified that it was. As noted by the Supreme Court, the lower court found that "present residential segregation was the result of private decisionmaking and economics, and that it was too attenuated to be a vestige of former school segregation." In a footnote the Court said it was unsure if the Court of Appeals had held this finding to be "clearly erroneous" and ordered the lower courts to consider the housing issue once again on remand.[25]

Finally, the Supreme Court took up the issue of housing segregation in its *Pitts* decision affecting DeKalb County, Georgia. The district court had decided that the current school segregation in DeKalb County was caused primarily by demographic changes and private residential decisions of both whites and blacks, not by school district actions or the prior dual school system. The district court relied in part on testimony by Armor and Clark on the causes of housing segregation.

The Supreme Court endorsed the district court's view of the causes of school and housing segregation in DeKalb County and offered one of the strongest statements to date on the obligations of school districts regarding housing segregation.

> The findings of the District Court that the population changes which occurred in DeKalb County were not caused by the policies of the school district, but rather by independent factors, are consistent with the mobility that is a distinct characteristic of our society. . . . The District Court in this case heard evidence tending to show that racially stable neighborhoods are not likely to emerge because whites prefer a racial mix of 80% white and 20% black, while blacks prefer a 50%-50% mix. Where resegregation is a product not of state action but of private choices, it does not have constitutional implications.[26]

The Court went on to say that demographic changes are not necessarily caused by the earlier de jure violation and that the passage of time, along with demographic changes, makes the racial imbalance less likely to be a vestige of the former dual school system.

It would appear, then, that a former dual school system is not responsible for countering the effects of demographic changes or segregated residential patterns, provided that it implemented a desegregation plan in good faith and can show that current racial imbalance is a product of housing segregation rather than vestiges of the prior de jure segregation.

The Causes of Residential Segregation

Residential segregation is endemic in the United States and has proven highly resistant to change. In cities or communities with a significant black population, white families and black families tend to live in neighborhoods that are almost completely separate. These patterns of housing segregation existed forty years ago, at the beginning of the civil rights movement, and they remain entrenched today with only slight improvements. This static picture stands in stark contrast to very substantial changes in racial attitudes and to increased tolerance for integrated settings in most other economic and social sectors, to be described shortly.

Indeed, the contrast between integration in housing and in such areas as schools and employment requires an explanation. Most social scientists agree that housing segregation is influenced by a myriad of factors, but there are basically two schools of thought on the weight to be given to each of these factors. One school emphasizes the role of racially discriminatory actions, both private and governmental (including schools), and argues that housing segregation is largely the product of intentional discrimination to exclude persons from certain areas on the basis of race alone.[27] While not denying the existence of racial discrimination in housing, the other school argues that housing segregation is caused primarily by a series of objective factors such as cost and affordability (economics), convenience (to friends, jobs, and shopping), and personal preferences for racially homogeneous neighborhoods.[28]

Although all racial discrimination in the sale or rental of housing is illegal under Title VIII of the 1968 Civil Rights Act, the distinction between public and private discrimination is important for the purpose of school desegregation law. A public school system, as an agency of the state, might be held accountable for actions of other public officials or agencies (although this is not a settled issue), but under the existing de jure doctrine schools cannot be held responsible for the discriminatory actions of private citizens.

By now a sizeable number of studies and sources of data support one view or another. The strongest empirical support for the racial discrimination thesis generally comes from "audit" studies, the largest of which are sponsored by HUD.[29] Most of the data for the opposing viewpoint are derived from special housing surveys and simulations conducted by the authors and colleagues in connection with ten school desegregation cases: Atlanta; Omaha; Kansas City and St. Louis, Missouri; Milwaukee; Cincinnati; Little Rock; Los Angeles; Nash County, North Carolina; and Hartford, Connecticut.

The Extent of Housing Segregation

There are numerous ways to measure racial segregation, but one of the most common summary measures is the index of dissimilarity. This index ranges from a high of 100, indicating total segregation, to a low of zero, indicating perfect racial balance. For housing segregation, the index is usually calculated for census tracts or smaller groups of blocks (for school segregation, the unit of analysis is a school). A value of zero is attained only when every tract in an area has an identical racial composition; a value of 100 is attained when all persons in every tract or school are of the same race. (See chapter 4, note 14.)

The housing segregation of blacks versus nonblacks in the twenty-one largest cities and counties with more than 50,000 blacks is shown in Table 3.1. The first two years, which are calculated for blacks versus whites, are not strictly comparable to the second two years, which are calculated for blacks versus nonblacks

Table 3.1. Housing Segregation in the Twenty-One Largest Counties with over 50,000 Blacks and with Central Cities[a]

City/County	Index of Dissimilarity[b]			
	1960	1970	1980	1990
Mostly black minority				
Chicago	93	93	90	86
Philadelphia	87	84	85	84
Detroit	84	82	84	86
Washington, D.C.	80	79	77	76
Boston	84	84	79	73
Atlanta	89	88	80	81
St. Louis	90	90	76	74
Baltimore	90	89	82	80
Pittsburgh	85	86	79	77
Cleveland	91	90	88	85
Newark	72	76	79	79
Kansas City, Mo.	91	90	83	76
Cincinnati	89	84	79	75
Milwaukee	88	88	81	79
Averages	87	86	82	79
Black and Hispanic				
Los Angeles	82	90	78	66
Houston	94	93	79	66
Dallas	95	96	81	63
Oakland	73	70	71	63
Tampa	94	92	76	65
Miami	98	92	81	74
San Francisco	69	75	65	61
Averages	86	87	76	65

[a] 1960 and 1970 from Sorensen, Taeuber, and Hollingsworth, "Indexes of Racial Residential Segregation for 109 Cities," *Sociological Focus*, 1975, 128–130; 1980 and 1990 figures from Reynolds Farley, "Neighborhood Preferences and Aspirations among Blacks and Whites," University of Michigan, May 20, 1991, Table 3.

[b] For 1960 and 1970, the index is for cities and for whites versus blacks. For 1980 and 1990, the index is for counties and for the black versus nonblack population. All indices are computed from census block or block group data.

and can reflect changes due to growth in the Hispanic population. For this reason the cities with predominantly black minorities are grouped separately from those with both black and large Hispanic populations.[30]

For cities whose minority population is predominantly black, the average segregation level was high (87) in 1960 and remains high (79) in 1990. Even the small reduction shown may reflect growth of nonblack minorities rather than an improvement in black-white balance. Historically, residential segregation has been high in these cities and counties, and it remains high as of the most recent U.S. census.

For cities and counties with large Hispanic (and sometimes Asian) populations, the 1960–1970 figures are not comparable with the 1980–1990 figures. Considering just the last ten-year period, the average black-nonblack segregation in these cities and counties dropped 11 points between 1980 and 1990, with the southwestern cities of Los Angeles, Houston, and Dallas showing the largest declines. Most of this change reflects growth of Hispanic and Asian populations in these cities rather than increased housing integration between blacks and whites.

Housing segregation has remained high in this country in spite of very substantial changes in general racial attitudes, especially in the willingness of whites to accept blacks as neighbors.[31] Numerous national attitude surveys have shown that, before the *Brown* decision in 1954, white Americans exhibited very high levels of racial prejudice toward blacks, and these attitudes were consistent with high levels of actual segregation in employment, housing, schools, and social relationships. Since that time, especially during the civil rights protests and the passage of civil rights laws during the 1960s, similar surveys have shown increasing tolerance of blacks and greater support for integration in nearly every sector of society, including schools and housing.

By 1990 white support for civil rights and the principles of racial integration was far greater than it had been thirty years before, and along with that increased support there has been considerable actual desegregation in schools, work settings, and other areas (although not without significant court interventions). The continuing high levels of housing segregation in the face of these attitudinal changes and progress in other spheres has engendered various social science theories to explain the discrepancy. Some theories attempt to downgrade the importance of these attitudinal changes, while others emphasize the importance of factors other than general racial tolerance to explain the persistence of housing segregation.

The Role of Economics in Housing Segregation

One potential cause of black-white housing segregation investigated by social scientists and economists is the substantial economic difference between black and white households. On the average, black households have lower incomes and lower net assets than white households, and they are more likely to rent than to own their homes. Moreover, the average rent paid by renters and the average home value for home owners are lower for blacks than for whites.

Because homes and apartments of varying costs are distributed unequally throughout a metropolitan area, economic differences alone should account for some racial separation in residential patterns.

Table 3.2 compares black and white households on several economic indicators from the 1980 U.S. Census. The comparison is made for the nation as a whole as well as for several large metropolitan statistical areas (MSAs) that have experienced metropolitan desegregation litigation and for which special housing segregation studies have been conducted.

Nationally, the average black household in 1980 received only about 60 percent of the income enjoyed by the average white household. One reason for this difference, of course, is that blacks have a higher proportion of single heads of households than whites. The percentage of blacks owning their own homes is substantially less than for whites (44 versus 68 percent), and for those who do own homes, the average value of white homes is nearly twice that of black homes. The race difference in rents is smaller, with black rents averaging about 80 percent of white rents, but, of course, there are proportionately more black renters than white renters. This national pattern of disadvantage for blacks holds up in each of the metropolitan areas listed in Table 3.2; in fact, the disparities are frequently larger than the national figures.

Two other economic differences between black and white households should be noted. Nationally, the average black household in 1980 had only $678 in net financial assets, such as savings or investments (excluding home equity), compared to $8,082 for white households. The lack of financial assets is probably one

Table 3.2. Selected Economic Indicators for White and Minority Households, 1980

MSA		Income ($)	Percent owners	Median home value ($)	Median rent ($)
Atlanta	B	11,232	42	29,200	201
	W	20,654	67	51,000	260
Cincinnati	B	10,652	35	36,600	163
	W	19,020	67	48,300	220
Kansas City	B	12,162	52	19,100	193
	W	19,948	69	45,800	248
Los Angeles	B	12,427	39	59,100	202
	H	14,645	37	71,200	208
	A	—	51	96,900	371
	Wa	18,962	52	92,500	261
Milwaukee	B	12,187	35	29,600	158
	W	20,899	58	61,400	214
National	B	10,943	44	27,200	208
	W	17,680	68	48,600	251

aIncludes Hispanic.

Source: U.S. Bureau of the Census, *1980 Census of Population and Housing*, Washington, D.C.

of the main reasons why blacks are less likely to be home owners; they are less likely to have the available cash on hand for making a down payment. In addition, it has been documented that black and white workers tend to work in different parts of a metropolitan area. For example, in the greater Kansas City area, nearly 80 percent of black workers worked in the central city in 1980, compared to only 54 percent of white workers.

Blacks in inner cities also may have greater difficulty obtaining home mortgages because of red lining, whereby banks or mortgage brokers declare certain portions of a city to be high risk. In such cases it is difficult for black families to obtain home financing even if they have the personal assets to qualify for a mortgage loan.

Given substantial economic differences between black and white households, one question becomes how much housing segregation can be attributed to economic factors alone. Obviously, the answer depends on the costs of rented and owned housing units and their distribution throughout a metropolitan area. Several different methodologies have been used to relate these economic differences to housing segregation, and the results have not always been in agreement.

One of the earliest analyses of economic factors in housing segregation was carried out by Taeuber and Taeuber in 1965.[32] Using data from the 1960 U.S. Census, the Taeubers concluded that ownership status, rents, and home values accounted for only about 10 to 39 percent of the index of dissimilarity, depending on the city being studied. Using a different approach, Farley computed desegregation indices for economically homogeneous populations (homeowners versus renters and differing income or home value levels) and concluded that racial segregation is nearly as high among economically homogeneous groups as it is in the population as a whole.[33] More recently, a study by Kain showed that income differences alone account for only a small fraction of housing segregation in Chicago.[34] The thrust of these studies is to argue that blacks' ability to pay for housing, if it was the only constraint operating, would lead to greater dispersal of black households throughout a metropolitan area than what is actually observed.

A different approach was used by Pascal to study the importance of economic factors in housing segregation in the Atlanta and Kansas City metropolitan school desegregation cases.[35] He employed a simulation technique to reallocate all black households in a metropolitan area according to rent, home value, and job location. The simulation assumes that, but for economic differences and job locations, and in the absence of any other factor including discrimination, blacks and whites would be dispersed throughout a metropolitan region in proportion to their numbers. Therefore, blacks and whites were allocated among census tracts so that each tract would have a proportionate share of black and white households within each economic category equal to the black-white ratio (for that category) in the metropolitan area and so that the percentage working in the central city would also be equal for blacks and whites.[36] The index of dissimilarity was then compared before and after the reallocation to determine the effect of these economic and job location factors on segregation.

Table 3.3. Degree of Segregation Due to Economic Factors in
Atlanta and Kansas City

	Index of dissimilarity		
Metropolitan area	Actual	Simulation	Percent
Atlanta (1970)			
Housing + job location	86	59	67
Kansas City (1980)			
Housing only	80	46	58
Housing + job location	80	57	72

Source: Exhibits prepared by Anthony Pascal for the Atlanta and Kansas City
metropolitan school desegregation lawsuits (*Armour v. Nix* and *Jenkins v. Missouri,* respectively).

The results of the Pascal simulations for Atlanta and Kansas City are shown in
Table 3.3. The Atlanta simulation is based on the 1970 U.S. Census, and the
Kansas City simulation is based on the 1980 U.S. Census. Considering both
housing costs and job locations together, economic factors accounted for about
two-thirds of the 1970 housing segregation in Atlanta and nearly three-fourths of
1980 housing segregation in Kansas City.

One of the important differences between the Pascal simulations and the
Taeuber method, other than the more recent census data used in Pascal's
studies, is the inclusion of job location. Considering housing costs alone, which
is available only for the Kansas City study, the cost of housing by itself accounts
for 58 percent of the housing segregation in that metropolitan area. This figure is
not that different from the upper end of the distribution found by Taeuber and
Taeuber. The important point is that ability to pay for housing by itself accounts
for considerably less housing segregation in the Kansas City area than when
both ability to pay and job location are considered simultaneously. The job
location factor could be argued to be a result rather than a cause of housing
segregation; that is, if more blacks moved to the suburbs according to their
ability to pay, they would be able to find jobs in those locations. Then again,
many black workers are employed in state and local government offices, which
are usually located in central city areas.

Some but not all housing segregation appears attributable to such economic
factors as home ownership and cost of rent or home payments. Leaving aside job
location, the cost of housing by itself explains some degree of the housing
segregation in some large urban areas. If job location is included, a larger
portion of housing segregation can be explained by economic factors.

The Role of Preferences in Housing Segregation

A second major cause of housing segregation studied by social scientists is the
preference for and choice of various neighborhood racial compositions. The
preference thesis holds that housing segregation arises because persons of a
given racial or ethnic group prefer to live in neighborhoods where their race or

ethnicity predominates. Under this theory, blacks, whites, and members of other groups tend to choose racially homogeneous neighborhoods for housing moves, and they also tend to leave a neighborhood if their racial group diminishes beyond a certain point.

Some social science studies have evaluated the preference thesis primarily as a question of whether blacks segregate themselves by choice, therefore focusing primarily on the preferences of blacks rather than whites.[37] The de-emphasis of white attitudes in these studies stems from the concern that some white preferences—for example, for predominantly white neighborhoods—may indicate racial prejudice and should be considered a type of discrimination rather than personal preference. Indeed, some researchers have also diminished the importance of black preferences on the grounds that they could reflect expectations based on past discriminatory experiences, rather than simply an own-race preference.[38] At least one major study has produced some evidence that black preferences are influenced to some extent by perceived white hostility.[39]

Although some preferences for neighborhood composition may have their origins in prejudicial attitudes or discriminatory experiences, in the context of federal desegregation policies or antidiscrimination laws they should be considered an independent social factor. Moreover, although preference for an all-white neighborhood might suggest some underlying racial prejudice, it seems unreasonable to characterize white preference for a 10–20 percent black neighborhood as prejudiced if that approximates the racial composition of a metropolitan area. Even the preference for a mostly white or mostly black neighborhood could reflect nonprejudicial reasons based on past personal experiences.

Racial preferences that are based explicitly on prejudice toward or erroneous perceptions about another race are morally reprehensible but not illegal under existing federal laws or judicial doctrines. Provided that racial preferences operate simply in the context of a person's own housing choice—as opposed to denying others' housing choices—preferences would not be considered a form of discriminatory behavior. From the standpoint of school desegregation and fair housing laws, therefore, the degree of housing segregation arising from the personal preferences and choices of housing seekers should not be tallied on the discrimination side of the ledger.

Racial preference in housing choice is but one aspect of a larger array of attitudes on race-related issues that have been studied extensively by social scientists over the past half-decade. As mentioned earlier, recent studies of long-term trends have documented very significant changes in many racial attitudes since the 1954 *Brown* decision, especially white prejudice toward blacks. These changes are reflected in attitudes toward housing integration.

Changes in white attitudes about housing integration are illustrated in Figure 3.1 (taken from the Schuman study) which shows the trend in white responses to two questions about having blacks as neighbors.[40] One question was asked by the National Opinion Research Center for thirty years: "If a Negro with the same income and education as you moved into your block, would it make any difference to you?" The second question is similar and has been asked by the Gallup Poll for more than twenty years: "If black people came to live next door,

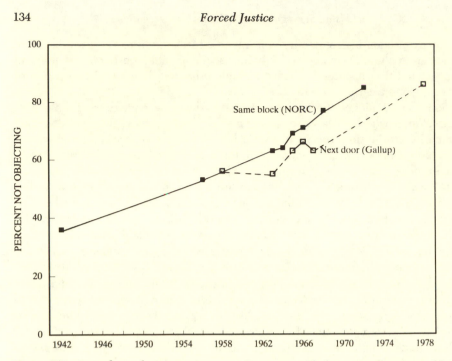

Figure 3.1. Attitudes on housing integration: Percentage of whites not objecting to black neighbors. *Source:* H. Schuman, C. Steeh, and L. Bobo, *Racial Attitudes in America*, Table 3.3.

would you move?" The chart plots the percentage saying "no" to each of these questions.

Prior to the *Brown* decision, a majority of white Americans objected to blacks as neighbors. By the 1970s, however, there had been a complete reversal in white attitudes; more than 80 percent of whites said they would not object or would not move if a black family lived nearby. The Schuman study also documented similar changes for other white racial attitudes, such as increased support for open housing principles and increased tolerance of blacks in various settings such as attending school with blacks, having a black as a dinner guest, and interracial marriage.

Nevertheless, not all white attitudes on racial matters have changed. The Schuman review documented that significant proportions of whites say that they would move out "if black people came to live in great numbers" in their neighborhood (33 percent in 1978), that they would object to sending their children to a school "where more than half of the children are black" (see Figure 4.1), and that they would oppose a variety of federal government interventions in the civil rights arena. Perhaps most important for this discussion, large majorities of whites remain strongly opposed to busing children out of neighborhood schools for the purpose of school integration, in spite of the widespread adoption of busing techniques during the 1970s. A more detailed discussion of attitudes toward school desegregation and busing for integration is taken up in the next chapter.

Because Figure 3.1 deals only with white attitudes about a single black family in their neighborhood, the trends depicted there do not convey the full range of racial preferences in housing. A better assessment of both black and white racial preference for integrated or segregated housing is offered in Figure 3.2, which shows the results of a 1978 national survey of central city populations.[41] The question asked was "Would you personally prefer to live in a neighborhood that was all white, mostly white, mostly black, all black, or half and half?"

The most striking result in Figure 3.2 is the contrast in the preferences of blacks and whites. While a majority of urban whites express a preference for all or mostly white neighborhoods, only 10 percent of blacks express a preference for all or mostly black neighborhoods. Instead, nearly 70 percent of blacks expressed a preference for a mixed half-and-half neighborhood; less than a third of the whites preferred this mix. Almost no blacks or whites expressed a preference for being in a mostly opposite-race neighborhood.

These survey results have important implications for the prospects of integrated housing. Black disinterest in majority white neighborhoods is important because if all neighborhoods were racially balanced throughout a typical metropolitan area, most of them would be predominantly white. More important, while a majority of black and white citizens express a preference for some degree of racial mix in housing, their preferences differ sharply on the definition

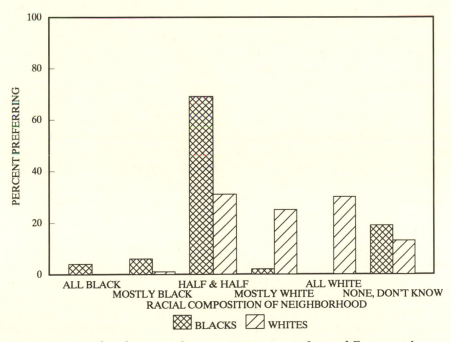

Figure 3.2. Racial preferences in housing: Percentage preferring differing racial compositions. *Source:* National survey of urban populations, *New York Times*, February 26, 1978.

of that mix. Black and white preferences for different racial mixes play an important role in the persistence of housing segregation.

The first social science study to examine the consequences of these asymmetric preferences was conducted by Farley at the University of Michigan's Population Studies Center.[42] The study was conducted in the Detroit area, where large random samples of both blacks and whites were interviewed in detail about their housing preferences. In addition to asking about preferred racial compositions, the study also asked whites about whether they would try to leave neighborhoods of various racial compositions.

The Detroit area study found that (1) only 15 percent of Detroit blacks would choose a majority-white neighborhood as their first choice, and 76 percent would choose fifty-fifty or majority-black neighborhoods first; (2) 73 percent of Detroit whites would not be willing to move into a neighborhood that was one-third or more black; and (3) 64 percent of whites would try to move out of a neighborhood that became half black. The authors concluded that "these data indicate that the likelihood of achieving stably integrated neighborhoods in the Detroit area is small."[43] The authors also faulted white choices of all-white or majority-white neighborhoods, rather than black choices of fifty-fifty neighborhoods, for being responsible for the maintenance of housing segregation.

Are the Detroit findings unique, or do they hold up for other cities as well? The methodology of the Detroit study was adapted for housing surveys conducted by the authors in connection with a series of eight school desegregation cases.[44] Telephone surveys were conducted with large representative samples of white and minority respondents throughout each metropolitan region; the first survey was conducted in 1978, and the last was conducted in 1991.

Respondents were asked detailed questions about preferences for neighborhoods of varying racial compositions as well as responses to racially changing neighborhoods. A typical preference question was "I would like you to assume you have been looking for a house or apartment and have found a nice place which you can afford. It could be located in several different types of neighborhoods. If you could have any racial mix you wanted, which would you be most likely to choose?" In most of the surveys, racial composition was defined in 10 percentage-point intervals—10 percent black, 20 percent black, and so forth—in order to make finer distinctions about racial preferences than earlier studies. Following the preference question, respondents were asked, "If your present neighborhood changed to become [various percentages] white [or black], would you try to move out or stay where you are?"

The responses to the preference questions were averaged across the eight cities, and the results are tabulated in Figures 3.3 and 3.4 for white and black respondents, respectively.[45] The results are quite similar from one city to another, despite differing geographic regions and different time periods. They also resemble the results for the 1978 national survey in Figure 3.2, with the exception that, as in the Detroit study, fewer whites in these eight cities select the fifty-fifty category (possibly because more alternative composition categories were offered to the respondents). The vast majority of whites prefer majority- white or all-white neighborhoods, and 65 percent of whites on the aver-

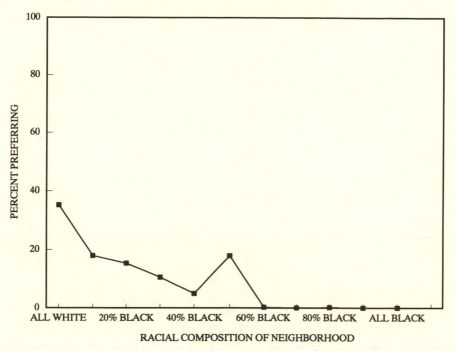

Figure 3.3. Housing preferences of whites in eight cities [Omaha, Kansas City (MO), Cincinnati, Little Rock (AR), Milwaukee, Los Angeles, Nash County (NC), and Hartford], average percentage preferring differing racial compositions.

age prefer some black neighbors compared to 35 percent who prefer all-white neighborhoods. The average percent black preferred by whites (across all composition categories) is approximately 20 percent, which, interestingly, approximates the percent black in most of these metropolitan areas.

The racial preference pattern for blacks in Figure 3.4 also resembles the 1978 national survey and again stands in significant contrast to white preferences. Large majorities of blacks in all of these cities choose the fifty-fifty category. Only about 18 percent of blacks on the average prefer majority-white neighborhoods, and the same percentage prefer majority-black neighborhoods. There is remarkably little variation from city to city, and the average black respondent prefers a 50 percent black neighborhood.

These survey results are inconsistent with two commonly held assumptions about the role of preferences in housing segregation. First, they clearly refute the notion that segregation is caused by black preferences for predominantly black neighborhoods because blacks strongly prefer mixed neighborhoods. Second, they also fail to support the theory that segregation is caused mainly by white preferences because a majority of whites claim to prefer neighborhoods in the 10–50 percent range, and only a minority prefer all-white neighborhoods. A large proportion of both blacks and whites prefer some degree of racial integration in their neighborhoods, but the preferred mix differs sharply for each

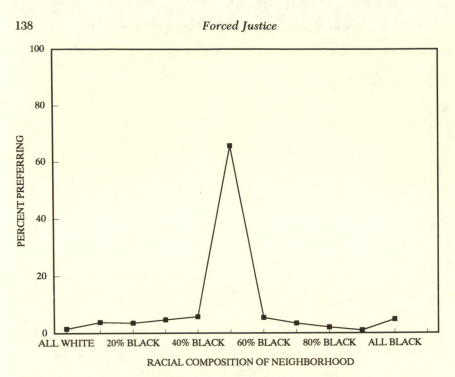

Figure 3.4. Housing preferences of blacks in eight cities, average percentage preferring differing racial compositions. (See Fig. 3.3. for cities.)

group, with blacks preferring a higher proportion of blacks in their neighborhoods than whites do.

Of course, the preferences recorded in these surveys cannot necessarily be assumed to reflect what blacks and whites actually do when choosing a neighborhood or community. Nevertheless, the survey results presented here—even though they may exaggerate preference for integrated neighborhoods—can explain a very large amount of the existing residential segregation in these communities.

Before discussing the relationship between preferences and actual residential segregation, one more issue must be addressed. Aside from people's racial preferences in choosing a neighborhood, what about responses of blacks and whites to changes in their present neighborhood compositions? One of the key findings in the Detroit study was that a majority of whites said they would try to leave neighborhoods that became 50 percent black or greater. In the eight separate city studies, similar questions were asked about the responses of blacks and whites to racially changing neighborhoods.

Figure 3.5 shows the average cumulative percentage of whites who say they would try to move if their current neighborhood changed to become increasingly black. On the average, more than one-third of whites say they would try to move if the neighborhood became 50 percent black, and about half would try to move if their neighborhood became majority black. Of course, if a neighborhood becomes majority black and loses half of its white population, then it

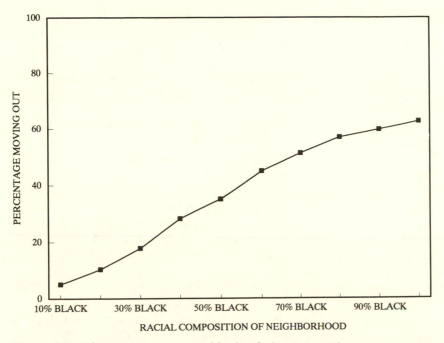

Figure 3.5. White responses to neighborhood change in eight cities, percentage of whites who would move out if neighborhood changed. (See Fig. 3.3. for cities.)

becomes even blacker and therefore loses more whites. According to the average survey results, a neighborhood could expect to lose somewhat more than 60 percent of its white residents if it became virtually all black. These survey results probably understate the actual losses of whites in a 90 percent black neighborhood.

Black responses to changing racial composition are very different from white responses. Very few blacks say they would try to leave their neighborhood regardless of the change in racial composition. Therefore, although most blacks are not likely to choose a majority-white neighborhood, they would not try to leave if their current neighborhood became majority white. In contrast, a majority of whites are willing to choose a neighborhood with some black residents, but most want to leave their current neighborhood if it becomes predominantly black.

These preference and avoidance results can be used to explain the dynamics of housing segregation. Housing choice simulations were constructed for Atlanta and Kansas City in connection with their metropolitan desegregation cases.[46] For the Atlanta simulation, black preferences were estimated from a 1971 national survey and white preferences were taken from the 1978 Detroit study. The Kansas City simulation utilized preference results from the Kansas City survey included in the averages shown in Figures 3.3 to 3.5.

The Kansas City simulation, which was the more complete of the two, was carried out in three stages. At the first stage, households were reallocated so that blacks in majority-black neighborhoods received their preferred neighborhood composition based on survey results; blacks already in majority-white neighborhoods were not moved. This first stage essentially creates neighborhood compositions in accordance with black preferences. For the second stage, whites were reallocated out of the newly integrated neighborhoods in accordance with the survey's estimate of white responses to changing neighborhood compositions.

The results of the simulations, shown in Table 3.4, are quite similar for the two cities. In both Atlanta and Kansas City, black preferences alone account for a substantial amount of the housing segregation observed there, 82 percent and 76 percent, respectively (according to the index of dissimilarity). When white responses to neighborhood change are added to the simulation, 91 percent and 86 percent of the housing segregation can be explained in Atlanta and Kansas City, respectively. Preferences explain somewhat higher segregation in Atlanta than Kansas City, mainly because the older survey data used for the Atlanta simulation had somewhat higher proportions of blacks choosing majority black neighborhoods than the Kansas City survey.

Simulations were not carried out for the other six metropolitan areas, but the results would not differ greatly from those for Kansas City, particularly regarding the degree of segregation caused by black preferences alone. The pattern of black preferences for fifty-fifty neighborhoods differs very little from one city to another.

At first glance it might seem surprising that black preferences alone can account for such a high degree of segregation, particularly when the vast majority of blacks prefer fifty-fifty neighborhoods. These two metropolitan areas are predominantly white, however; Atlanta households were 80 percent white in 1970, and Kansas City households were 83 percent white in 1980. Therefore, allocation of white households to meet black preferences creates a relatively small number of neighborhoods that are fifty-fifty, and a much larger number of neighborhoods remain nearly all white. Substantial racial imbalance is the inevitable mathematical result of black preferences for fifty-fifty neighborhoods in a region that is 80 percent white.

Interestingly, if black households were allocated to meet white preferences alone, almost perfect racial balance would be attained because average white

Table 3.4. Degree of Segregation Attributable to Black and White Preferences in Atlanta and Kansas City Areas

Metropolitan area	Index of dissimilarity		
	Actual	Simulation	Percent
Atlanta (1970)			
Black preference only	86	71	82
Black preference + white response	86	78	91
Kansas City (1980)			
Black preference only	80	61	76
Black preference + white response	80	69	86

preferences just about match the average percent black in these metropolitan areas. While black responses indicate that they would not leave a neighborhood that became majority white, they are not likely to choose such neighborhoods in the first place.

In other words, black preferences for fifty-fifty neighborhoods explain as much housing segregation as white preferences. Blacks prefer neighborhoods that have higher black ratios than well-integrated neighborhoods would yield in most metropolitan areas. Moreover, those fifty-fifty neighborhoods are precisely the types of neighborhoods that many whites would leave, thereby further increasing racial imbalance. Blacks tend to avoid predominantly white neighborhoods, which would be the prevalent type of neighborhood in a metropolitan area that was fully racially balanced.

These results are consistent with the conceptual analysis of Schelling, who demonstrated mathematically that relatively small differences in preferences for differing racial compositions can lead to a fairly large degree of segregation over a large population.[47] The Schelling thesis was tested and verified by Clark with preference data from five of the cities discussed here.[48]

These data do not say that past discriminatory conduct or racial intolerance by whites has not influenced current black preferences; indeed, that is likely to be true, given the history of American race relations. The analysis presented here does not speak to the source of these preferences, only to the fact that they have definite consequences for housing segregation above and beyond overt and illegal acts of discrimination.

The preferences shown in Figures 3.3 and 3.4 can also explain a large portion of existing housing segregation, even though the surveys may overstate white (and possibly black) tolerance for integrated neighborhoods; that is, even if persons are less likely to choose integrated neighborhoods than the surveys suggest, their stated preferences would still give rise to a very high degree of segregation.

The Role of Discrimination in Housing Segregation

The third major category of potential causes of housing segregation is racially discriminatory actions or policies of public agencies or private persons. The legal basis for raising housing segregation as an issue in school desegregation litigation is the possibility that a neighborhood school policy builds on unconstitutional housing segregation caused by governmental discrimination. In most school cases where housing segregation has been at issue, the major task for social science experts has been to evaluate the role of governmental discrimination versus nondiscriminatory factors such as economics and personal preferences.

Official discrimination did play a role in early housing segregation. Prior to the *Brown* decision, official discrimination in housing was manifested in numerous public policies and practices, including racially restrictive zoning (mainly in the South), official segregation in public housing projects, racially restrictive covenants in deeds that were enforceable until the Supreme Court's

Shelley v. Kraemer decision in 1948, and discrimination in Federal Housing Authority financing and insurance practices.[49] These types of discriminatory policies and actions undoubtedly contributed to segregated housing during the first half of the twentieth century, a period when many public policies, especially in the South, embodied widespread and "acceptable" racial prejudice and discrimination towards blacks.

Unlike assignment of students to schools, however, housing decisions are not made by public agencies, but rather by private decisions of buyers, sellers, landlords, and tenants, with real estate agents frequently (but not always) involved in the transactions. Given Supreme Court decisions that have made official housing discrimination illegal for at least forty years, it has been increasingly difficult to attribute most housing segregation to official governmental actions. Accordingly, many social scientists who have testified in school desegregation cases have also emphasized private discrimination in housing transactions as a major source of housing segregation.[50]

Although private discrimination in the sale and rental of housing units is illegal under federal and state laws, the Supreme Court has never endorsed a legal doctrine that recognizes a role for private housing segregation in school cases. Nonetheless, the extent to which housing segregation is influenced by private discrimination may well be an important consideration when shaping public policies about school desegregation above and beyond judicial decisions.

Assessing the role of racial discrimination in housing segregation has presented social scientists with two difficult assessment problems. The first is measuring the existence of discrimination in housing searches or decisions, and the second is determining the effect of this discrimination on the degree of housing segregation. The distinction between these two steps has not always been appreciated in social science studies, but there is nevertheless a critical difference between them.

The existence of discrimination, perhaps the less difficult of the two problems, has been assessed in audit studies, in which pairs of black and white "testers" visit real estate agents or apartment buildings and inquire about home or apartment availability. The testers are matched on various personal and economic characteristics, and each member of the pair visits a landlord or real estate agent at two different but proximate times, and judgments are made about whether the testers received equal treatment in terms of housing unit availability, number of units shown, and so forth. The most comprehensive audit studies have been sponsored by HUD. The largest, which was conducted in 1977, performed more than 3,000 audits in forty metropolitan areas throughout the United States.[51] A somewhat smaller replication of this study was carried out in 1989 (about 2,000 audits).[52]

Summaries of the findings from these two audit studies are shown in Table 3.5. In some cases treatment was judged equal, but in most cases either whites or blacks were judged to receive more or less favorable treatment, with whites having a higher rate of favorable treatment. Because differential treatment can arise from any number of idiosyncratic reasons unrelated to the race of a tester,

Table 3.5. Estimated Levels of Racial Discrimination in Housing Searches, HUD Audits, 1977 and 1989

Type	Equal treatment	Black favored	White favored	Discrimination against Blacks (net difference)
1979 Audit				
Rentals	31%	21%	48%	27%
Sales	37%	24%	39%	15%
1989 Audit				
Rentals	41%	20%	39%	19%
Sales	47%	18%	36%	18%

Sources: John F. Kain, "Housing Market Discrimination and Black Suburbanization in the 1980s," and M. Turner, R. Struyk, and J. Yinger, *Housing Discrimination Study: Synthesis*, table A-1. Based on audit studies by the U.S. Department of Housing and Urban Development.

the net difference in rates of favorable treatment is generally viewed as the proper measure of racial discrimination.

Racial discrimination against black home seekers clearly existed in both national assessments. The rates of discrimination in home sales are quite similar for the two studies, with a net discrimination rate against blacks of 15 percent in 1979 and 18 percent in 1989. The probability of racial discrimination against blacks in rentals, however, has fallen by 8 points over this ten-year period, with a rate of 27 percent in 1979 and 19 percent in 1989. Although the explanation for this decline in rentals is not certain, it may reflect stronger enforcement of antidiscrimination laws in large apartment complexes. Despite some variation in these rates of discrimination in different regions of the country, substantial discrimination probabilities have been documented in virtually all parts of the nation.

The existence of discrimination reported in Table 3.5 cannot be translated directly into a quantitative measure of the degree of housing segregation arising from discrimination for at least two reasons. First, audit pairs are matched on economic and social characteristics, when in reality the average black housing seeker has fewer economic resources and hence more restricted housing choices. Second, and more important, audit teams visit housing sources *randomly*, whereas in reality both blacks and whites make intentional choices of communities, real estate agents, or apartment buildings which already have particular racial compositions. The probability of experiencing racial discrimination is undoubtedly lower when a black person visits a predominantly black apartment building versus an all-white apartment building. In other words, audit studies assess the *potential* degree of segregation arising from discrimination in the hypothetical situation in which economically equal blacks and whites choose housing randomly, but they do not necessarily assess the actual degree of segregation arising from discrimination as encountered in real housing searches.

Another approach for determining the degree of housing segregation caused by discrimination is to ask blacks and whites directly about housing discrimination they have actually experienced. In most of the housing surveys conducted in connection with metropolitan desegregation cases, respondents were asked, "In your opinion, have you ever been denied a house or apartment in the [specified] area because of your race?"[53] For those saying yes, a follow-up question asked who was responsible, and respondents could choose from a list including real estate agents, landlords, lenders, and so forth. This question was asked in the Milwaukee, Little Rock, Los Angeles, Nash County, and Hartford housing surveys conducted by the authors and in another housing survey conducted by William Sampson for the St. Louis metropolitan case.

The rates of self-reported discrimination in these cities are shown in Table 3.6. The rates of reported housing discrimination for blacks range from a low of 5 percent in Nash County, North Carolina, to a high of 16 percent in Milwaukee. Excluding Nash County, whose rate is markedly lower than the rates in the larger and more urbanized areas, the average rate of self-reported discrimination for blacks in the other five metropolitan areas is about 13 percent.

Interestingly, the rate of self-reported discrimination for Hispanics is quite low in Los Angeles (4 percent) and much higher in Hartford (18 percent), the only two areas with sizeable Hispanic populations. The reason for this difference is not immediately clear because recent studies find similar levels of housing segregation for Hispanics in the two metropolitan areas.[54] One might speculate about several possible explanations, including national origins (Los Angeles Hispanics are mostly Mexican American and Hartford Hispanics are mostly Puerto Rican), familiarity (Los Angeles has a longer history of Hispanic residents), or simply greater tolerance of the white population in Los Angeles (their rate of black discrimination is also slightly lower).

The leading source of discrimination reported by blacks and Hispanics is landlords, who account for about half of all reports. The second leading source is real estate agents, who account for about a third of all reports. Lending agencies and government agencies are cited by no more than 1 percent of blacks in these cities. If all government or government-regulated agencies (including lenders and real estate agents) are combined as sources of "official" or governmental discrimination for the purpose of a school desegregation case, these surveys suggest that no more than 4 percent of blacks in any of these cities believe they have experienced government-sanctioned discrimination in housing. Most of the reports of perceived discrimination arise from private actions by landlords or sellers.

Although the rates of self-reported discrimination in these five cities are lower than the rate of discrimination found in national audit studies, the results are not necessarily inconsistent. In fact, if the rates in Table 3.5 are weighted for the proportion of black renters and homeowners, and then averaged for the two years, the self-report rate of discrimination is only about seven points lower than the audit study rates.[55] There are substantive reasons why the two mea-

Table 3.6. Levels of Self-Reported Housing Discrimination in Six Metropolitan Areas

City		Blacks	Hispanics	Whites
Milwaukee		16%		1%
Source:	Landlord	11%		1%
	Realtor	2%		*a
	Others[b]	3%		*
Little Rock		10%		1%
Source:	Landlord	4%		*
	Realtor	3%		0
	Others	3%		1%
St. Louis		10%		*
Source:	Landlord	3%		0
	Realtor	3%		*
	Others	4%		*
Los Angeles		12%	4%	3%
Source:	Landlord	7%	2%	2%
	Realtor	2%	*	*
	Others	4%	2%	*
Nash County, NC		5%		1%
Source:	Landlord	2%		1%
	Realtor	2%		0
	Others	3%		*
Hartford		15%	18%	2%
Source:	Landlord	10%	10%	1%
	Realtor	3%	3%	*
	Others	2%	5%	1%

[a] Asterisks indicate less than 1 percent.

[b] Includes sellers, banks, lending agencies, government agencies, and multiple choices. In no city did government and lending agencies combined exceed 1 percent.

sures might differ. As noted earlier, audit teams visit real estate agents or landlords at random, while actual housing searches reflect the preferences of the seekers. Assuming that most blacks prefer neighborhoods with substantial proportions of their own race, and that the probability of discrimination in such areas is lower, then blacks are less likely to experience discrimination than they would if they selected housing areas at random. In other words, the potential level of racial discrimination in housing can be higher than what is actually experienced.

The fact that discrimination is documented in both audit studies and surveys raises again the question of whether and how much black preferences—especially avoidance of majority-white neighborhoods—might be influenced by anticipation of housing discrimination or other forms of racial hostility. Although a precise answer to this question is difficult to find, that possibility cannot be dismissed. From a legal standpoint, however, the underlying causes of racial preferences are not relevant to a determination of constitutional violations. Conscious decisions by blacks to choose or avoid certain kinds of neighborhoods, if arrived at freely and without constraints, would not be considered governmental discrimination under current legal doctrines.

The survey studies suggest that in recent times relatively small proportions of blacks have experienced housing discrimination, and where discrimination does occur, less than half of the incidents can be attributed to public or governmental actions. The relatively small role played by discrimination is consistent with other evidence that a combination of existing preferences and economic levels can explain a high degree of current housing segregation, with preferences more important than economics.

The Relation between School and Housing Segregation

Given the substantial level of housing segregation in larger cities and metropolitan areas, clearly neighborhood school policies and geographic boundaries between school districts generate segregated schools or segregated school systems simply by reflecting the underlying housing patterns. Another major housing issue focuses on the specific causal relationship between school and housing segregation and the direction of causation.

Some social scientists have suggested that the causal process operates not only from housing to schools but also from schools to housing; that is, school segregation or desegregation can have independent influences on housing patterns, either countering or reinforcing existing housing patterns. The social scientists who advance this reverse causal process usually make two separate but related arguments.[56] The first argument is that a neighborhood school plan with predominantly white or minority schools might reinforce housing segregation by providing visible signals that designate some neighborhoods as minority and some as white.[57] In effect, so the argument goes, segregated schools can act as a beacon to alert newcomers to segregated neighborhoods. Given an initial state of segregated housing, which is reflected in segregated neighborhood schools, individual schools can be used by housing seekers to help identify both segregated schools and segregated neighborhoods. Because most white parents do not want to send their children to a predominantly black school, the argument continues, school segregation leads white families to choose white neighborhoods so that their schools are also predominantly white.

The second argument postulates the converse process: School districts with desegregated schools can contribute to a reduction in housing segregation by assuring families that schools will be racially mixed regardless of residence, thereby allowing factors other than a school's racial composition to determine housing choices. Moreover, school desegregation plans might contribute even more directly to integrated housing choices by bringing black and white families into contact with people and neighborhoods they ordinarily would not see.[58] In particular, busing minority children from the inner city to predominantly white suburban neighborhoods could lead to increased minority housing choices in these areas. In its strongest form, this argument suggests that desegregated schools could lead to desegregated neighborhoods.

Although the research on these issues is limited, several studies, including those by Wolf, Rossell, and Clark, have challenged the causal hypothesis that school desegregation contributes to housing desegregation.[59] A growing body of data allows further tests of the relationship between school and housing segregation.

Quite aside from the objective evidence on these processes, the causal theory of the beacon effect—that segregated schools cause segregated neighborhoods—has several logical problems. If white families make segregated housing choices to assure predominantly white schools or to avoid predominantly black schools, it also reasonable to assume that these same families would desire predominantly white neighborhoods—precisely what the housing preference data indicate. A behavioral model in which white families reject a majority-black school but accept a majority-black neighborhood is hard to imagine. A more logical theory would be that both school and housing choices reflect the same underlying dynamic, avoidance of majority-black environments, and that the school beacon is not a true cause of the housing segregation.

Moreover, a segregated school is not the only available signal of a segregated neighborhood. If a school system has perfectly desegregated schools but neighborhoods remain segregated—which actually happens in many desegregated school districts—a white house seeker who wants to avoid a black neighborhood has many alternatives for identifying the neighborhood, including talking to people who know the area, asking real estate agents, or simply visiting the area in question.

The assertion that school desegregation can reduce housing segregation must be evaluated for two different groups of movers: those new to an area and those already living in an area. For the first group, an important consideration is the fact that most school desegregation plans take place in the context of segregated housing. Assuming that newcomers have a means of discovering neighborhood composition other than looking at schools, the existence of desegregated schools should not affect housing choices for white families who prefer predominantly white neighborhoods. Moreover, desegregated schools should not affect choices of black families who prefer fifty-fifty neighborhoods; not only are there very few such neighborhoods, but they get the perceived benefits from desegregated schools even if they choose a segregated neighborhood.

For those who live in an urban area undergoing school desegregation, most social scientists have focused on the potential effects on upwardly mobile minority families: Desegregation exposes inner-city students and families to white neighborhoods and acquaintances, thereby promoting housing choices in those areas when these families decide to move. At least one case study supports this thesis.[60] This argument is not as compelling for white families with children, few of whom are likely to move into an inner-city minority neighborhood regardless of desegregation. Indeed, any positive effects on housing choices for whites are likely overwhelmed by the negative effects of the white flight that accompanies comprehensive desegregation plans, particularly if the plan creates large numbers of majority-black schools (see chapter 4).

Clark's detailed case study in Oklahoma City also raises questions about the mechanism behind the housing choice thesis for black families in a desegregation program. He found that of nearly 2,500 black families with children bused to majority-white schools, over a three-year period only 12 moved into a school zone to which they had been previously bused.[61] Black moves away from inner-city neighborhoods generally had destinations in inner-ring suburban areas (with existing black populations); they followed the normal pattern of black out-migration that has been documented in most larger urban areas.[62]

Although housing segregation may decline in some central cities during a school desegregation program, it is unclear whether it is due to integrative housing choices or to a redistribution of black households into areas formerly occupied by whites. The process of white flight and residential transition can be greatly accelerated if the desegregation plan involves comprehensive mandatory busing, especially if whites are bused into formerly black schools.

Another way to address the question of whether school conditions cause housing choices or vice versa is to consider survey results on the major reasons people give for selecting their current neighborhood. In the surveys conducted in seven of the cities undergoing metropolitan desegregation lawsuits, residents were asked their main reason for choosing their current neighborhood. Most of these questions were open-ended, so that persons could state in their own words why they chose their current neighborhood. Responses were combined into five general categories: neighborhood features, cost/and affordability, location or convenience characteristics, quality of schools or being close to schools, and various people characteristics (including race or socioeconomic characteristics).

Table 3.7 shows the percentage of respondents in these metropolitan areas that cited either the quality of schools or some other school factor as their main reason for choosing their current neighborhood. In these cities, the surveys make clear that school quality or school location were not among the most important reasons people cite for choosing their current neighborhood, and

Table 3.7. Percent Citing Schools as Most Important Reason for Choosing Current Neighborhood

Metro area	White	Black
Omaha (1978)	2	2
Kansas City (1982)	11	6
Cincinnati (1983)	17	10
Little Rock (1984)	16	8
Milwaukee (1986)	6	9
Nash County (1990)	8	2
Hartford (1991)	21	6

indeed schools ranked only fourth or fifth in importance compared to other major categories of reasons.

More important reasons for selecting current neighborhoods in these cities included economic reasons such as cost or quality of homes; neighborhood qualities such as space, quiet, and safety; and convenience or location factors such distance from work, from shopping, or from friends and relatives. The survey results clearly show that school characteristics are less important than economic or other preference factors in selecting a place to live. The survey results are consistent with the opposite theory, that people select a neighborhood on a variety of economic and preference factors, of which school quality is one consideration but less important than many others.

The major evidence supporting the thesis that school desegregation influences housing desegregation has been assembled in two studies by Pearce and others.[63] In the first study, seven pairs of cities were selected and matched on various criteria, with one city having a metropolitan desegregation plan and the other city not having one. She concluded that cities with metropolitan desegregation plans reduced housing segregation in the metropolitan area between 1960 and 1970 more than the matched cities without such plans (although most had intradistrict desegregation plans). This study has a number of methodological limitations, which have been thoroughly discussed by Rossell.[64]

A second study by Pearce and Crain expanded the number of cities and compared desegregation of schools and housing between 1970 and 1980, the decade that saw the greatest number of school desegregation plans implemented. Changes in both housing and school segregation, as measured by the index of dissimilarity, were assessed for the twenty-five largest central cities with black populations above 100,000 in 1980. They found a substantial correlation between reduction in housing segregation in the central city and a reduction in school segregation, which was interpreted as supporting the theory that school desegregation promotes housing desegregation.[65] The overall changes in housing segregation were quite small, however, in comparison to changes in school segregation. The authors observed that cities with smaller changes in school desegregation experienced a small reduction in housing segregation (2.4 points), while those with larger changes in school desegregation experienced a somewhat larger reduction in housing segregation (8.5 points). Most of the cities in the latter group had changes in school desegregation of more than 20 points, however, with an average of about 33 points.

Although the second study has more cities, it still has several technical problems that limit generalizability. The 1980 index of dissimilarity was computed for blacks versus nonblacks, which can change as a result of increasing Hispanic and Asian populations, which affect such cities as Los Angeles, Houston, Dallas, and Jacksonville (see Table 3.1). More important, the segregation index was computed for central cities and neglects the possible negative effects on city-suburban segregation caused by white flight as a result of a desegregation plan.

The potential impact of these methodological problems can be illustrated with a simple replication of the second Pearce study using data from Table 3.1. The major differences between this analysis and the Pearce analysis are that only cities with predominantly black minority populations are included, the index of dissimilarity is computed for counties in 1980 and 1990 rather than central cities, and changes in desegregation are assessed over a longer time period. Thirteen of the fourteen cities/and counties in Table 3.1 that have predominantly black minority populations were used for the analysis.[66] Changes in housing segregation are measured from 1970 to 1990, while changes in school segregation are measured from 1968 (before most comprehensive desegregation plans were implemented) to 1989.

These data show only a very small correlation between reduced housing segregation and school desegregation, and the overall change in housing segregation is smaller than changes in school desegregation. For all thirteen cities, the average housing segregation index was 85, 82, and 80 for 1970, 1980, and 1990, respectively, while school segregation was 80 in 1968, 55 in 1985, and 55 in 1980 (most school desegregation effects having taken place in the 1970s). Thus school desegregation declined significantly in these cities, but residential desegregation remains high within their respective counties.

Figure 3.6 plots the relationship between declines in housing and school desegregation, as measured by the dissimilarity index. Seven of the cities experienced substantial school desegregation between 1968 and 1990, averaging about − 41 points, but these same cities averaged only about a − 8 point reduction in housing segregation. The remaining six school systems experienced very slight school desegregation over this period, averaging about − 8 points, while

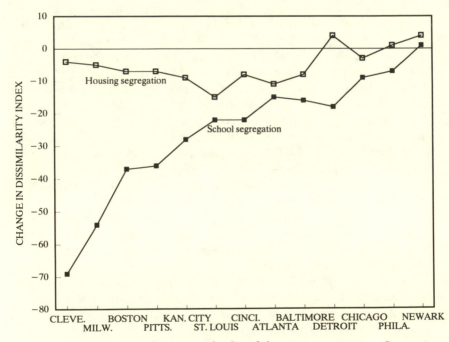

Figure 3.6. Relationship between school and housing segregation: Comparison of change in racial imbalance for schools and housing in thirteen cities, 1970–1990.

housing segregation declined by -2 points. Although the cities with more school desegregation experienced slightly greater reductions in housing segregation (as found in the second Pearce study), the housing changes are only one-fifth the size of the school changes.

One potential problem with the data in Figure 3.6 is that the 1970 index is based on central cities and the 1980 and 1990 indices are based on counties. However, all of the cities except Newark have index values over 80 in 1970, so it is unlikely that county index values (which are not available for 1970) are much higher.[67] Quite aside from changes in index values, the seven cities with substantial school segregation between 1970 and 1990 have an average school segregation index of only 38 but their housing index is 77. In other words, housing remains highly segregated in these counties in spite of very substantial racial balance in central-city public schools.

The lack of a strong effect of school desegregation on housing segregation is best illustrated by the two cities that experienced the largest decline in school segregation levels in this sample. Cleveland implemented a comprehensive mandatory busing program in 1979, and Milwaukee implemented a comprehensive voluntary magnet plan in 1976 (with some mandatory reassignment of black students). Cleveland's racial imbalance fell from 87 to 22 points between 1968 to 1989, but its county housing segregation remains highly segregated with an index at 85 in 1990 (versus 89 in 1970). Milwaukee not only has a city school desegregation plan but also a voluntary interdistrict plan that involves most school districts in the county. School segregation in Milwaukee fell from 79 to 31 points over the twenty-year period, but its housing remains highly segregated with an index value of 79 (versus 84 in 1970).

All school districts in Figure 3.6 (and all but Tampa in Table 3.1) had white enrollments under 50 percent by 1990, a situation undoubtedly affected by desegregation or mandatory busing plans in some cases. Given white aversion to attending majority-black schools, and given the fact that desegregation plans in a predominantly minority district often create many majority-black schools and substantial white flight, the fact that housing segregation has not increased in these areas is perhaps noteworthy. Whatever the reasons for the small declines in housing segregation, there is little evidence that school desegregation has played an important role.

Housing and School Desegregation Policy

The strategy of using housing discrimination and residential segregation as the basis for constitutional violations in school desegregation cases appears to have largely failed. Although this failure results in part from legal doctrines that limit the liability of school districts for the actions of other agencies, it is also due in part to increased knowledge about the causes of housing segregation, especially the articulation of that knowledge by experts in court cases.

In the case of interdistrict school segregation, the use of housing discrimination as the primary trigger for metropolitan desegregation plans has been almost completely unsuccessful. At the lower court level, most of the earlier social science testimony and evidence placed the major blame for housing segregation on both public and private discrimination. In more recent cases, however, the research and testimony concerning economic and social forces that shape residential segregation has figured more prominently in lower court cases, none of which has been overturned by the Supreme Court. While social science evidence was not necessarily the deciding factor in any one of these cases, it certainly was important to the outcomes.

Although the evidence also shows that racial discrimination continues to play a role in housing segregation, it is probably less important than the role of personal preferences and economic differences. Moreover, most of the documented discrimination stems from actions of individual landlords and sellers, and there is no existing legal doctrine making school systems liable for these private or, at best, quasi-public actions. Given the state of desegregation law, it seems unlikely that any future federal court would be willing to reorganize and consolidate city and suburban school systems or order a large interdistrict busing program solely on the grounds of this type of housing discrimination.

The situation for intradistrict cases is somewhat more ambiguous. Since *Swann,* the courts have permitted consideration of school actions, such as school construction, which can contribute to school segregation through effects on housing segregation. If such findings are part of an original court decision, then a lower court must consider whether housing segregation is a "vestige" of the original discriminatory conduct before it can issue a unitary ruling. In such proceedings, social science evidence on the present causes of housing segregation is quite likely to continue to be relevant, as it was in the Oklahoma City case.

A consistent theme throughout most court decisions is that school districts should not be held responsible for school segregation that arises from residential choices or other demographic and economic factors over which schools exercise no control, a principle reiterated in *Pitts*. To the extent that school integration policies are ever able to overcome or at least ameliorate the difficult problem of housing segregation, the change is apt to be by legislative option and not by court order.

Some degree of uncertainty is justified by the fact that the Supreme Court has never issued a written majority opinion on the use of housing segregation in metropolitan cases or decided any intradistrict school desegregation solely on the basis of government-sponsored housing segregation. A majority would probably agree, however, with Justice Powell's words in a 1979 dissent that "there are unintegrated schools in every major urban area . . . [which] results primarily from familiar segregated housing patterns, which—in turn—are caused by social, economic, and demographic forces for which no school board is responsible."[68]

Although housing segregation cannot be ruled out in future litigation, it remains a concern for many school districts that use traditional geographic zoning methods to assign students to schools nearest their homes. Acknowledging the absence of a legal obligation does not change the fact that neighborhood or community school policies will leave schools segregated unless some other type of assignment method is adopted, either voluntary or mandatory, to overcome the effects of housing segregation. Residential segregation remains the one reason why many school boards and other education policy makers will continue to consider desegregation policies to improve racial balance, and the fact that it may be legal does not change the policy concerns.

4

The Effectiveness of
Desegregation Remedies

In the complex body of case law on school segregation and desegregation, there has been one enduring feature in an otherwise variable landscape. If a school board is held liable for intentionally segregating its schools, then a federal court is obliged to order remedies that "restore the victims of discriminatory conduct to the position they would have occupied in the absence of such conduct."[1] While legal scholars may disagree over the meaning of intentional segregation and social scientists may argue about the benefits of desegregation, no federal court since the 1971 *Swann* decision has failed to order some type of school desegregation remedy after finding de jure segregation.

What constitutes an acceptable remedy? Three distinct but interrelated questions have dominated legal and social science discussions about desegregation remedies. The first is the proper *scope* of a remedy, particularly the conditions that trigger a systemwide desegregation plan, such as mandatory busing, that affects all schools. The second concerns the *definition* of desegregation and the standards that should be applied to judge whether a school or a school system is desegregated. The third is the *effectiveness* of particular types of plans or techniques in eliminating the dual school system and its vestiges as found by a court. Without question, the central and most difficult issue in effectiveness is the attainment of desegregated student bodies, given an appropriate standard for defining a desegregated school.

All three of these areas have been subjected to vigorous debates over such concerns as the degree of court intervention in school operations, how desegregation should be measured, the problem of white flight, and the effectiveness of mandatory versus voluntary desegregation techniques. Although these issues are covered in a general way by a host of court doctrines and standards, laws, and regulations, there is much room for variations and disagreement on the specifics of desegregation remedies.

There are, of course, legitimate differences among affected parties and constituencies on the questions of scope, definitions, and the types of outcomes for evaluating the effectiveness of a given desegregation remedy. The broadest approach is to consider all aspects of school programs (and even larger commu-

154

nity issues), regardless of the specific legal issues involved, including both short-term and long-term educational outcomes such as academic achievement and years of schooling completed. The narrowest approach might be to consider only student and staff assignment policies for the attainment of racially balanced schools and faculties.

The approach taken here is guided primarily by the legal context of school desegregation cases and the obligations of a school system under the law in general or under a particular court order. School systems operating under a court-ordered desegregation remedy usually have a formal desegregation plan that establishes the steps that must be taken to satisfy legal requirements as well as criteria for effectiveness. Despite differences from one desegregation plan to another, depending on the particular constitutional violations found by a court, most cases have a common core of remedial components, the two most frequent (and most problematic) of which are establishing racially integrated student bodies and racially balanced staffs.

For school systems not under court orders, assuming they have no history of potential constitutional violations, the questions of desegregation objectives, definitions, and effectiveness are more or less left to the discretion of school boards. If a school board is considering the adoption of a desegregation plan for the first time, they may be guided by general legal considerations or by the experiences of other school districts, but they are generally free to decide on particular desegregation goals and to adopt their own criteria for evaluating success.

The fact that a school system is under a court order does not automatically resolve questions about appropriate and effective desegregation remedies. There is still considerable debate among legal experts regarding what constitutes "vestiges" of a prior dual school system, as that doctrine was refined by the Supreme Court in its 1991 *Dowell* decision.[2] Perhaps the most contentious legal issue in this regard is racial differences in various academic and behavioral outcomes such as achievement test scores, dropout rates, and disciplinary actions. Another contentious issue revolves around practices that can lead to racial imbalance of classes within schools, such as ability grouping, tracking, and gifted or special education classes. Some of these issues have already been addressed in chapter 2, but some further discussion is appropriate as they pertain to the scope of remedies.

There is at least general consensus that a desegregation remedy must create schools with racially desegregated students and staffs, but there is much less unanimity on the precise standards for defining a desegregated school. Over the years many different definitions and standards have developed in case law and have been applied by social science experts who design desegregation plans. Obviously, any evaluation of effectiveness depends heavily on the definitions of desegregation and how it is measured, which must be addressed before the matter of effectiveness.

Beyond definitions, the first question under the general rubric of effectiveness is, simply, how much desegregation has taken place since the comprehensive desegregation mandates of *Green* and *Swann*? The answer is complicated by the changing demographic and racial composition of the nation as well as by the specific measures of desegregation used to assess trends. A second and closely related question concerns the impact of desegregation on white flight, or white enrollment losses that can be attributed to a desegregation plan, particularly plans that involve extensive mandatory busing. Given a sufficient degree of white flight, the effectiveness of a desegregation plan can be impaired by reducing the number of white students available to integrate minority students, even to the point of resegregating an entire school system.

A third question is the effectiveness of different types of desegregation plans for attaining integrated student bodies, especially the effectiveness of voluntary versus mandatory desegregation plans. For many years, up to at least the mid-1980s, courts generally assumed that mandatory plans are the only effective way to achieve "maximum feasible desegregation." In more recent years a number of social scientists have argued that, because of white flight and resegregation, mandatory plans are less effective over the long run than comprehensive voluntary programs.[3] Most of the social science debate here revolves around the extent to which white flight arises from ordinary demographic forces, the process of desegregation itself, or the specific techniques of a plan, particularly the mandatory busing of white students to predominantly minority schools.

Finally, the research on white flight and effectiveness is usually based on an analysis of school enrollments and a comparison of trends among school systems with different types of plans. This purely statistical approach ignores the most important causal link between a desegregation plan and changes in school enrollment, which are the opinions, attitudes, and behaviors of the principal actors in the desegregation process—parents and students. The relationship between plans and enrollment trends is ultimately determined by the responses to a desegregation program by parents, who must decide whether to support it, oppose it, participate, or withdraw. Lack of community and parental support for a desegregation plan can lead to community controversy, loss of public support for school funding, and, most important, loss of white and middle-class students, which can lead to long-term enrollment instability and resegregation. An understanding of community and parental opinions about desegregation and its techniques is therefore necessary for judging the ultimate success of any desegregation plan.

The Scope of Remedies

The scope of desegregation remedies has two major aspects. One is whether a remedy applies to an entire school system or only some portion of the system, such as one or more schools. The second aspect deals with the various facets or components of a remedy, that is, the types of school programs and policies covered by a desegregation plan.

The first aspect of scope is fairly well settled as far as the federal courts are concerned. For southern intradistrict cases, the existence of state segregation laws guaranteed that liabilities and remedies were systemwide. For northern intradistrict cases, the 1973 *Keyes* decision for Denver established the principle that if a constitutional violation affects a significant number of schools, then the whole system is considered de jure unless a school board can prove that other segregation was not government induced. As Justice Rehnquist forecast in the 1973 *Keyes* decision, this difficult burden of proof has generally not been met by northern school boards. Thus, systemwide liability has been found in nearly all northern intradistrict cases, generating desegregation remedies that cover all schools in a system.

For the less frequent cases of interdistrict violations, there have been more variations in liabilities and remedies; in only a few instances have desegregation orders applied to all schools in the affected systems. In the majority of metropolitan cases, as discussed in chapter 2, liability has not been found for suburban districts and thus mandatory remedies have been confined to central city districts, although in some instances voluntary interdistrict transfers may be part of a desegregation plan. In several metropolitan cases, most notably St. Louis and Kansas City, Missouri, the state was found liable and has been providing substantial financial support for desegregation efforts. One of the few cases where a comprehensive metropolitan remedy was imposed is Wilmington, Delaware. City and suburban (New Castle County) school districts were merged into one large metropolitan district, although it was later divided into four districts, each with a portion of the former city district.

Not all remedies are imposed by courts. During the 1970s, many school desegregation remedies were imposed by the Office of Civil Rights (OCR) in the Department of Housing, Education, and Welfare (but now in the Department of Education) for violations of the Civil Rights Act of 1964. In more recent years, OCR has not been as active, and remedies are not as extensive. They usually involve eliminating or modifying the offending policy rather than adopting a comprehensive desegregation plan.

School boards and some legal experts often assume that all components of a desegregation plan were established in the *Green* decision, which had described the "facets of school operations" that can be tainted by racial discrimination. These became the six well-known *Green* factors consisting of student assignment, assignment of faculty and staff, facilities, transportation, and extracurricular activities.[4] Technically speaking, however, lower courts have considerable latitude in their evaluation of discriminatory conduct. They can find fewer violations than these six areas, or, more likely, they may find discriminatory conduct in more than these six areas. Indeed, lower courts have found discriminatory practices affecting schools in the areas of housing, school curriculum and programs, and the professional qualifications of teachers.[5]

A more recent, more contentious set of scope topics has emerged in a number of school cases that are seeking unitary status. Plaintiffs have raised such issues as differences in academic achievement between white and minority students, differences in rates of disciplinary actions, and resegregation of students within classrooms through such practices as ability grouping or tracking and separate classes for gifted and special education students. These conditions or practices are often alleged to be vestiges of the prior dual school system and thus subject to remedy. Such possibilities have been raised by plaintiffs in unitary status proceedings affecting such diverse school districts as Darlington, South Carolina; San Jose, California; Topeka, Kansas; Yonkers, New York; and Wilmington, Delaware. In most of these cases, the original district court decisions did not identify such conditions as specific constitutional violations.

Whether the federal courts will accept these efforts to broaden the scope of desegregation remedies is not yet clear. In the Yonkers case, a district court has, for the first time, declared that the academic achievement gap between white and minority students is a manifestation of vestiges of a former dual school system and may require programmatic remedies provided by the state of New York.[6] It remains to be seen whether these or other "extra-*Green*" factors will stand up to the scrutiny of higher courts, particularly if a district court did not make a liability finding with respect to these conditions in its original decision.

Desegregation Definitions

Without question, the most critical definition in a school desegregation case is what constitutes a desegregated student body at each school because that definition ultimately determines the number of students who have to change schools (either voluntarily or by reassignment) in order to meet the objectives of a desegregation plan. The second most important definition is that describing desegregated faculty and administrators, which also implies possible mandatory movement of people.

For a better understanding of the types of desegregation methods and the ways effectiveness is evaluated, some other definitions are also appropriate here. Definitions for some of the major desegregation techniques are offered; they form the basis for a subsequent discussion of the differing types of desegregation plans utilized throughout the country. In addition, definitions are needed for several standardized measures of desegregation used by social scientists to evaluate the effectiveness of desegregation plans.

Desegregated Students

As reviewed in chapter 1, the legal definition of school desegregation has undergone significant change over the years since *Brown*. Affected parties once believed—with support from lower courts—that "de-"segregation should merely reverse illegal segregation, which would mean abolition of laws or practices compelling segregation. This early concept was implemented either by assigning students to newly drawn geographic attendance zones (e.g., neighborhood schools) or by means of "freedom of choice," whereby parents could freely choose any school for their children without regard to race or racial composition. Sometimes freedom of choice was combined with geographic zoning. The important feature of these early concepts is that schools were not required to have particular racial compositions in order to attain desegregation.

These early definitions of desegregation and their associated techniques did not meet constitutional requirements, however, when residential patterns generated racially identifiable schools or when southern systems used freedom of choice in ways that intentionally perpetuated the dual school system. The *Green* decision made clear that any desegregation plan for curing illegal segregation had to deal with the racial composition of schools. Two years later the *Swann* decision set forth specific guidelines for defining a desegregated school.

The most common definition of school desegregation after *Swann* was based on the concept of *racial balance*. A school is considered racially balanced if its racial composition matches that for the school system as a whole (for a given grade level) within some allowable percentage deviation. The racial balance definition approved in *Swann* (for the Charlotte–Mecklenburg system) called for a school's racial composition to differ by no more than plus or minus 10 percentage points from the system average; that is, if the school system was 30 percent black at the elementary level, then an elementary school would be considered desegregated—or racially balanced—if its composition was 20–40 percent black.

Most racial balance plans approved during the 1970s used relatively narrow bands for defining racial balance, although there were some exceptions. For example, both Boston and Norfolk used a plus or minus 10 percentage-point variance, but the courts in Denver and Columbus, Ohio, permitted somewhat greater variances of plus or minus 15 percentage points. One of the broader definitions of racial balance occurred in a federal case in South Carolina, which defined desegregation with a variance of plus or minus 20 percentage points.[7] That broader definition became somewhat more common in later years, being approved for new desegregation plans in Savannah, San Jose, and Yonkers during the late 1980s.

Not all courts or federal agencies have used racial balance as the basis of defining a desegregated school. A major problem with the racial balance concept occurs in predominantly minority school systems, in which a racial balance rule can classify a predominantly black school (e.g., 90 percent) as desegregated. Although the concept of desegregation could be narrowed to mean *only* racial balance, such an approach would be inconsistent with both legal doctrines and social science traditions, in that the essence of student desegregation involves the possibility of meaningful interracial contact. Indeed, in 1967 the U.S. Commission on Civil Rights defined any school more than 50 percent black as segregated.[8]

In several cases involving majority-black school districts, courts have resolved this dilemma by adopting an *absolute* standard of desegregation. For example, the St. Louis and Detroit districts, which were about 75 percent black when their first desegregation plans were implemented, a desegregated school was defined as one with a fifty-fifty racial composition. After creating as many fifty-fifty schools as possible, these desegregation plans of necessity left the remaining schools predominantly black. One of the more complex absolute definitions was adopted by a federal court in the Milwaukee case, which ordered a desegregation plan requiring that two-thirds of the schools be 25–50 percent black, one-sixth 20–65 percent black, and the remaining one-sixth 15–75 percent black.[9]

Given the considerable range of definitions, a 1992 national survey of desegregation plans by the U.S. Department of Education offers information on the frequency of various definitions for a desegregated school.[10] About 55 percent of districts with current desegregation plans use racial balance for defining desegregated school enrollments, another 12 percent used an absolute (or fixed-percentage) standard, and 33 percent have no precise numeric definition of a desegregated school.

For those districts using numeric standards of some type, the range and variability of desegregation definitions are noteworthy. The frequency of permissible variances is shown in the following list (a 40-point variance would correspond to a plus or minus 20 percentage-point standard or a fixed range from 10 to 50 percent):

Variance allowed	*Percent of districts*
Over 40 percentage points	10 percent
40 percentage points	28 percent
30 percentage points	24 percent
20 percentage points	12 percent
10 percentage points	9 percent
No variance	18 percent

Thus nearly 40 percent of school systems with quantitative standards for desegregation have an allowable variance of 40 percentage points or greater, and 60 percent have an allowable variance of 30 points or less.

The Supreme Court has often reiterated its statements in *Swann* that the constitution does not require a particular degree of racial balance in school enrollments and that racial balance of schools is only a starting point in devising a remedy to dismantle a dual school systems. The reality is that, twenty years after *Swann*, student racial balance remains the dominant guiding principle for defining a desegregated school.

Desegregated Faculties

Racial balance is also the principal standard for defining desegregated faculties. The legal definition of faculty desegregation was established in *Singleton*, a 1970 appellate decision affecting Jackson, Mississippi.[11] The *Singleton* rule holds that racial composition of the faculty in each school must be "substantially the same" as the composition of the faculty as a whole. The court opinion offered no quantitative standard or variation for being "substantially the same," but lower courts have adopted numerous differing standards for defining a desegregated faculty.

Faculty racial balance requirements and variances have generally become more flexible over the years since the *Singleton* decision. Variances of plus or minus 2.5 or 5 percentage points were not unknown during the 1970s, but during the 1980s courts have increasingly approved variances of plus or minus 10 or 15 percentage points as the standard for faculty desegregation. One reason for the increasing flexibility is the difficulty of maintaining a narrow racial balance when many teaching specialties (e.g., math and science, special education, bilingual) have racial and ethnic distributions which are disproportionate to the total faculty in a district, or, indeed to the available pool of teachers within a region of the country.

Desegregation Techniques

Like the many definitions of student desegregation, there are many techniques for attaining desegregation. There is also an important linkage between definitions and techniques, mainly because the narrowest racial balance requirements usually require more rigorous methods of student assignment. This raises the most important distinguishing characteristic of a desegregation technique, and its most controversial, which is whether it involves mandatory or voluntary assignment of students to schools.

There has been some controversy over the use of terms like *forced* or *mandatory* busing, and some social scientists and educators have been reluctant to use these terms when describing a desegregation plan. Actually, mandatory busing does not correspond to a particular desegregation technique; it was a label used by opponents of desegregation plans that replaced neighborhood school policies with cross-district busing. Critics of the term *mandatory* point out, with some justification, that it is emotionally loaded and not very precise. Neighborhood schools are a form of mandatory student assignment, and busing for reasons of distance or safety is common and noncontroversial in most school districts.

Mandatory busing became a convenient label for desegregation plans that changed the basis and purpose of school assignment and busing. Mandatory busing was coined to describe plans in which the purpose of busing was to attain racial balance rather that to overcome conditions of geography or distance; in the eyes of the average parent, the latter was a legitimate purpose of busing but the former was not. Moreover, although a neighborhood school policy is a form of mandatory assignment, it is revocable for middle-class parents who can afford to move. If middle-class parents come to dislike their neighborhood school, they can move to another neighborhood. When the basis of student assignment changes from geography to race, however, mobile parents lose their ability to choose public schools unless they move out of the school district altogether.

Quite aside from the labeling issue, there are good reasons for distinguishing between mandatory and voluntary desegregation techniques. They not only present differing logistical and cost considerations but also generate different responses in terms of community support and community responses, such as white flight. Most important, a high degree of racial balance (e.g., plus or minus 10 percent) is usually not possible without mandatory student assignment.

Turning to a description of specific techniques, several different types of mandatory techniques have been used in desegregation plans. The first mandatory technique is *contiguous rezoning* of attendance areas, either for some or all schools. This technique is used to some extent in most desegregation plans, and it may be the only technique necessary in smaller school systems. The rezoning technique consists simply of redrawing contiguous geographic attendance boundaries (often in concert with school closings or building new schools) to improve or maximize racial balance. A rezoning plan resembles an ordinary neighborhood or community school plan, except the attendance zones are drawn with both geography and racial balance in mind. Rezoning usually involve some reassignment of students from one school zone to another, but it can be less controversial than other forms of mandatory reassignment (unless extreme gerrymandering occurs) because fewer students have to be moved, and the moves are confined to a more limited geographic radius. Obviously, for larger school systems with substantial residential segregation, a rezoning plan by itself may not be able to attain the necessary degree of racial balance without the addition of other techniques.

Most mandatory busing plans, especially those in larger school districts, have *noncontiguous* attendance zones (i.e., two or more nonadjacent zones per school) and considerably more student movement and busing. There are two major types of noncontiguous zoning plans. The technique of *pairing/clustering* combines two or three schools of differing racial compositions, reorganizes grade structures so that only one school in the pair or cluster serves a particular grade level, and requires all students in the pair or cluster to attend that school for those grade levels. For example, a black kindergarten to sixth-grade (K–6) school and a white K–6 school in different parts of a school district can be combined into a pair, and all students from both schools would attend one school for grades K–3 and the other school for grades 4–6. Students attend their former neighborhood school for half the elementary years and are bused to another school for the other half. Of necessity a pair/cluster plan involves *two-way busing*, which means that both minority and white students travel to desegregated schools. A closely related approach is the *grade center* concept, in which certain schools are designated as centers for certain grades and all students in those grades are assigned to the centers in a racially balanced fashion.

The other noncontiguous mandatory technique is *satellite zoning* (sometimes called *pocket* or *island* zones), In which a geographic area with one racial mix is added to a nonadjacent school zone with a differing mix. A satellite zone can involve two-way busing, but it is also often used as a technique for *one-way busing*, which means attaching minority satellite zones to majority white schools. This technique has sometimes been used for a small minority population, such as the 1965 plan of Riverside, California; predominantly minority schools were closed, and minority students were zoned to white schools.

The essential difference between voluntary and mandatory techniques is that the first relies on choice and incentives and the second relies on mandatory reassignments. Of the two major voluntary techniques, the technique of *voluntary transfers* is the most straightforward. Often called a "majority-to-minority" program (or M-to-M for short), this techniques allows any student to transfer between regular schools if the transfer improves the racial balance of both the sending and receiving schools. For example, in a fifty-fifty district, a black student could transfer from a majority-black school to a majority-white school. The effectiveness of a voluntary transfer program is enhanced if free transportation is provided for transfers beyond normal walking distances; most court-ordered plans require subsidized transportation.

The other major voluntary technique is a *magnet school*, which offers a specialized, unique curriculum not available in regular schools. Examples of some of the more popular magnet program themes include computer science, performing and visual arts, math and science, back-to-basics, and honors for above-average students. In a desegregation plan, magnet programs are often placed in schools that would not otherwise attract an integrated student body. For example, magnet programs can be placed in predominantly black schools in the inner city to attract middle-class white students from outlying or suburban areas. Although magnet schools are usually the principal component of a comprehensive voluntary desegregation program, they can also be used as part of a mandatory plan to reduce loss of whites assigned to predominantly minority schools. Magnet schools received a substantial boost from a federal program, the Magnet School Assistant Program (MSAP), which provides two-year grants to school districts that are starting magnet schools as part of a desegregation program.[12]

Finally, a more recent type of desegregation technique is called *controlled choice*, which is a mixture of both choice and mandatory techniques.[13] In a pure controlled choice plan, all attendance zones are abolished, and parents are asked to list their choice of schools in order of preference. The school administration then assigns students to schools according the multiple criteria of choice, capacity, and racial balance requirements.

Although the controlled choice assignment process is designed to give as many first choices as possible, racial balance requirements mean that not all parents can receive their first or second choices, and many students are mandatorily reassigned to schools their parents did not choose, simply to attain racial balance. In this respect, some controlled choice plans can have a considerable degree of mandatory busing away from neighborhood schools. Most controlled choice programs also use magnet schools to attract white parents to schools in minority areas.

There are also variations on the theme of controlled choice, some of which might be called "limited" controlled choice plans. One example of limited controlled choice is a plan that maintains neighborhood schools unless a school fails to meet racial balance requirements, in which case any new students who move into that neighborhood or who start kindergarten can enroll in that school only if they improve (or do not adversely affect) its racial balance. For example, if a school is racially imbalanced in minority enrollment, then any new minority student would have to choose another school that meets racial balance requirements (which would normally mean a majority white school). In effect, racially imbalanced schools are "capped" for students of the race causing the imbalance.

Measures of Desegregation

Another challenge in assessing the effectiveness of desegregation plans is the problem of measurement. Just as a desegregated school has many different definitions, there are also many quantitative approaches for its measurement. The most straightforward approach, of course, is to simply count the number of schools that meet a particular definition, or the number of students enrolled in those schools, expressed as a percentage of the total population. While this method may be appropriate for a case study or for evaluation of a court order, it is not a standardized measure because it depends on a particular definition of desegregation. Therefore, this simple method cannot be used to compare the degree of desegregation from one district to another or to assess national trends in desegregation.

Fortunately, there exist several standardized statistical measures that are used by social scientists for assessing the extent of segregation or desegregation, and these measures can be used for a single school district or groups of school districts. Each summary measure also corresponds to a particular definition of desegregation, so that it may measure one definition of desegregation quite well but not necessarily other definitions. A brief description of these measures is necessary before examining the effectiveness of desegregation remedies.

One of the earliest standardized measures of segregation, the *index of dissimilarity*, was introduced in chapter 3. This index corresponds to the definition of segregation as racial imbalance (or desegregation as racial balance): The lower the value, the more each school matches the racial composition of the system as a whole, attaining a value of 0 when all schools in a system have exactly the same racial composition (perfect racial balance). Its highest value of 100 is attained when every school is either all white or all black (or minority), which means perfect segregation. Intermediate values represent the percentage of whites plus the percentage of blacks that must be moved in order to attain perfect racial balance.[14]

One important characteristic and limitation of the dissimilarity index is that it does not depend on the total percentage of whites in a district; that is, a value of 50 always has the same meaning regardless of the proportion of blacks and whites in the system. This feature is a limitation for two reasons: It cannot measure the degree of interracial contact in districts that have relatively high or low percentages of minority students, and it discounts or ignores the degree of white loss caused by a desegregation plan. A district that is 90 percent black can have a low dissimilarity index—and hence high racial balance—even if every school in the system is predominantly black.

Another standardized measure of segregation or desegregation is called the absolute *index of exposure*. This index measures the degree of interracial exposure (or potential contact) across all schools in a district. For a given minority group, the index is the average percent white in schools attended by the typical black or Hispanic student.[15] The upper limit of the exposure index for a minority group is the percentage of whites in a school system, which is attained when all schools have the same racial composition, and its lower limit is zero, when there are no white students in schools attended by minority students. Because the upper limit of the index depends on the percentage of whites in a system, comparing school districts with differing racial compositions requires showing the percentage white enrollment. This index not only has the advantage of reflecting the absolute degree of exposure between whites and minority groups but also reflects the loss of white enrollment that might be caused by a desegregation plan. The index is especially useful when tracing the desegregation of a school district over time.

Several other standardized indices are used in studies of desegregation effectiveness. Among the most straightforward is the percentage of various racial groups who attend schools with a specified racial composition, which can correspond to a particular definition of segregated or desegregated schools. For example, a segregated school can be defined as one with more than 50 percent minority students, or perhaps more than 80 or 90 percent, and the index would then be the percent of students (by race) in such schools. When such a measure is computed for relatively high concentrations of a minority group, it is frequently called an *index of racial isolation.*

Finally, one can compute an index that correspond to a particular definition of racial balance. Such an index is simply the percentage of students (black, white, etc.) who attend schools whose racial composition falls within some specified range of the system ratio. For example, one could compute the percentage of students (by race) who attend schools that are within plus or minus 20 percentage points (or 15 points) of the total percent minority in a school system.

Because each of these standardized indices measures a different definition of desegregation, a comprehensive assessment of effectiveness should rely on more than one measure. In particular, evaluations that rely only on the index of dissimilarity can give misleading results about effectiveness, because this index disregards the loss of white students that may be caused by a desegregation plan. While the dissimilarity index does summarize the degree of racial balance, it fails to represent the actual levels of interracial exposure. In this chapter, assessments of desegregation utilize both the dissimilarity and the exposure indices.

National Trends in School Desegregation

Given the vast judicial and legislative efforts to promote school desegregation in this nation, the first logical question about effectiveness should be how much desegregation has actually occurred. How many school districts have desegregation plans, what kinds of plans do they use, and what has been their impact on actual levels of desegregation, as measured by summary indices? Because the desegregation movement has been national in scope, these questions can be appropriately answered on a national scale.

The primary data for this section are derived from a national study of magnet schools and desegregation conducted by the American Institutes for Research (AIR) for the U.S. Department of Education in 1992.[16] This study is based on a national probability sample of 600 school districts, drawn to represent approximately 6,400 U.S. public school systems with more than one school for at least one grade level.[17] Information about desegregation plans was obtained from a school district questionnaire and official documents (written plans, court opinions) if necessary. Enrollment data were derived from several sources: the Office of Civil Rights (OCR) surveys of enrollment by race, the Common Core of

Data maintained by the National Center of Educational Statistics, and individual school districts, if the national files had missing data.

Prevalence of Desegregation Plans and Techniques

The prevalence of desegregation plans and the use of various desegregation
techniques can be estimated with data from the AIR study. Information about
whether a school district had a formal desegregation plan was obtained from 514
school districts, representing about 84 percent of the universe of districts and 86
percent of the universe of students.

Table 4.1 shows the percentage of districts that have a current desegregation
plan, that formerly had a desegregation plan, or that never had a formal desegregation plan as of the 1991–1992 school year, classified by the size of the school
district. Considering the total population of school systems in the nation, only 13
percent have a formal desegregation plan as of 1991, and another 5 percent
formerly had a desegregation plan.[18] This relatively low rate is influenced by the
large number of small school districts with enrollments under 5,000, in which
the prevalence of desegregation plans is only 7 percent.

In contrast, 70 percent of very large school districts (enrollment over 27,000)
have present or former desegregation plans, and the rate of present or former
plans is nearly 40 percent in large school districts (enrollments of 10,000–
27,000). Although larger school districts account for only about 10 percent of all
schools, they account for more than half of total enrollment and, most important, about three-fourths of black and Hispanic enrollment (6.8 million out of 9.1
million). Because larger districts have both higher proportions of minority students and higher rates of desegregation plans, about half the total black and
Hispanic student population is in larger school districts with present or former
desegregation plans.

Equally noteworthy, about 32 percent of all medium-sized and larger school
districts are subject to a *current* desegregation plan; only about 8 percent have
terminated a desegregation plan. Of the 40 percent of school districts that

Table 4.1. Prevalence of Formal Desegregation Plans[a]

	Size of School District				
	Small (< 5,000)	Medium (5,000–10,000)	Large (10,000–27,000)	Very large (> 27,000)	All districts
Current plan	7	25	34	60	13
Former plan	4	9	5	10	5
Never a plan	90	66	62	30	83
(Districts)[a]	(4,012)	(770)	(421)	(145)	5,348
Students (millions)					
Total N	8.9	5.4	6.6	9.3	30.2
Black + Hispanic	1.1	1.2	2.0	4.8	9.1
Percent	12	22	30	52	30

[a]Weighted to represent the universe of districts.

adopted or were ordered to adopt a desegregation plan since 1968, only about one-fifth terminated those plans by 1992. Contrary to some popular impressions, a significant proportion of medium-sized and larger school districts continue to maintain formal desegregation policies, many of which were ordered during the 1970s.

Small school districts have an average black and Hispanic enrollment of just over 10 percent of total enrollment, which means that most small school systems are predominantly white. Moreover, most small school districts are likely to have at most one high school, one middle school or junior high, and three or four elementary schools, and therefore desegregation can be usually be accomplished with conventional zoning methods as opposed to the more controversial busing techniques employed in larger school districts. Clearly, desegregation is not a significant issue in small school districts that are predominantly white. For this reason, most of the analysis of effectiveness presented in later sections is based on larger school systems.

Turning next to desegregation techniques, the AIR study found that most desegregation plans use a mixture or combination of the various desegregation techniques defined earlier, particularly in larger school districts. Many mandatory plans rely on both mandatory techniques, such as pairing and clustering, and magnet schools. Most voluntary plans use both magnet schools and M-to-M transfer programs, and they frequently employ contiguous (geographic) rezoning techniques to improve racial balance. Most controlled choice plans also use magnet schools to encourage parental choice of nonneighborhood schools.

The AIR study defined five general types of desegregation plans. Table 4.2 shows the definitions of these plan types and the proportion of districts with each type of plan, for medium-sized and larger school districts with current plans.[19] As of 1992, the majority of medium-sized or larger school systems with desegregation plans in the AIR sample utilize mandatory techniques of some sort. The modal category (37 percent) is mandatory other, which means some type of mandatory reassignment without magnet schools. Another 27 percent use mandatory magnet plans involving pairing or noncontiguous zoning in combination with magnet schools, and 6 percent use controlled choice.

The size of the school district has a significant impact on the type of mandatory plan. Mandatory other is most common in medium-sized districts (53 percent), where size permits many districts to desegregate by using only contiguous rezoning (particularly at the secondary school level). In contrast, almost half (47 percent) of very large school districts use mandatory magnet plans involving some form of noncontiguous zoning, or "mandatory busing." Altogether more than two hundred medium-sized and larger school districts still maintain mandatory desegregation techniques of some type.

The AIR study also shows that voluntary desegregation plans have become more commonplace in recent years. By 1991 30 percent of the districts employed voluntary desegregation plans, most of which use magnet schools (and possibly some contiguous rezoning) to accomplish desegregation. Voluntary magnet programs are somewhat more common in larger than in medium-sized

Table 4.2. Prevalence of Current Desegregation Methods[a]

| | Size of School District | | | |
Plan type	Medium (5,000–10,000)	Large (10,000–27,000)	Very large (> 27,000)	All districts
Voluntary M-to-M (can include contiguous rezoning but not magnets)	12	5	6	8
Voluntary magnet (can include M-to-M or contiguous rezoning)	18	23	29	22
Mandatory magnet (pairing/clustering or satellite zones with magnets)	14	29	47	27
Mandatory other (any type of rezoning but no voluntary techniques)	53	35	13	37
Controlled choice (all have magnets)	5	8	5	6
(Districts, weighted)	(131)	(96)	(79)	(306)
(Districts, unweighted)	(44)	(60)	(79)	(183)

[a] Weighted to represent the universe of districts.

school districts. Although not shown in Table 4.2, more than one-third of school districts with current voluntary plans at one time operated mandatory desegregation plans. Thus only about 20 percent of medium-sized and larger districts with current desegregation plans began their desegregation policies with voluntary techniques.

The growing importance of magnet schools is also apparent in Table 4.2. About 55 percent of school districts with desegregation plans use magnet schools to some degree, in combination with other mandatory or voluntary techniques. Magnet schools are especially commonplace in very large districts, where about 80 percent of districts have magnet schools as part of their desegregation plans. Thus a high proportion of students in districts with desegregation plans have at least some access to voluntary magnet plans.

The widespread use of mandatory pairing/clustering techniques during the 1970s can be illustrated by naming some of the larger or more celebrated school districts that adopted plans using pairing/clustering. Mandatory pairing and clustering (or grade centers) were used in Little Rock, Los Angeles, Pasadena, San Francisco, Denver, Savannah–Chatham County, Jefferson County (Kentucky), Prince Georges County (Maryland), Detroit, Pontiac (Michigan), Omaha, Charlotte–Mecklenburg County, Cleveland, Columbus, Dayton, Oklahoma City, Greenville County (South Carolina), Memphis, Nashville, Dallas, Norfolk, and Seattle. All but one of these plans, Seattle, were ordered by a federal or state court in connection with desegregation litigation. Seattle is the only large city to adopt a major mandatory busing program without being pressured or ordered to do so by a federal agency or court.

Major desegregation plans that relied mainly on combinations of noncontiguous or satellite zoning include Jefferson County (Alabama), Mobile, Riverside (California), Wilmington–New Castle County, Columbus–Muscogee County (Georgia), Baton Rouge, Boston, Pittsburgh, and Roanoke (Virginia). Many smaller districts, mostly in the South, were able to desegregate by means of contiguous rezoning plans alone or in combination with selective school closings. One of the better known districts that adopted a rezoning-only plan is Topeka, Kansas, a district involved in the original *Brown* decision.

The list of larger school districts that were able to desegregate initially with comprehensive voluntary plans is much smaller, but the list grows longer if districts that converted from mandatory to voluntary plans are added. Districts with original comprehensive voluntary plans (in many cases coupled with rezoning) include Long Beach (California), San Diego, San Bernardino, DeKalb County (Georgia), Worcester (Massachusetts), Buffalo, Cincinnati, Tacoma, and Milwaukee. Districts that were allowed to end mandatory plans and return to neighborhood schools with voluntary options (in some cases because of a unitary declaration by a federal court) include Austin, Los Angeles, Norfolk, Oklahoma City, and Savannah.

Districts that began initially with some variant of a controlled choice program include Glendale, California; Cambridge, Massachusetts; Montclair, New Jersey; San Jose, California; and Yonkers, New York. Districts that have converted from a regular mandatory plan to controlled choice include Boston and Seattle. Little Rock also adopted a controlled choice plan but later abandoned it and returned to neighborhood schools with voluntary options.

More voluntary or controlled choice plans were ordered by the courts during the 1980s than traditional mandatory busing plans (with noncontiguous zoning). One reason is that most larger school districts have already gone through the litigation process and are therefore engaged in or have completed some type of desegregation remedy. Another reason is the growing evidence, reviewed in subsequent sections, that comprehensive voluntary plans with magnet schools can be as effective as mandatory plans, particularly when the racial balance standards allow a variance of plus or minus 20 percentage points. Finally, given a court definition that calls for relatively narrow racial balance requirements, controlled choice would be recommended by many experts because it does allow for some degree of choice.

Trends in Desegregation Measures

How effective have these plans been in desegregating students? Given the prevalence of desegregation plans shown in Table 4.2, particularly in larger school districts, there should be some demonstrable impact on the level of desegregation for the country as a whole. Desegregation trends will be evaluated using the index of dissimilarity (racial imbalance) and the index of interracial exposure, as described earlier. Moreover, this analysis will be confined to school districts with more than 10,000 students. Not only do these districts contain three-fourths of all black and Hispanic students but also they are the districts where desegregation plans are most likely to occur.

Because the level of attainable desegregation depends on the mix of white and minority pupils, this discussion begins with the national trends in racial composition of the public schools. Figure 4.1 shows the percentage of white, black, and Hispanic students between 1968 and 1989 in larger school systems. During the twenty-year period since the start of affirmative desegregation policies, the percentage of white public school students in larger school systems has fallen markedly, from 73 to 52 percent of the total enrollment in these systems. There has been a modest increase in the percent of black students, from 19 to 25 percent, but the largest increase has occurred for Hispanic students, whose proportion has grown from 6 to 17 percent. Asian students, not shown in the graph, increased from less than a percent to about 4.5 percent.

Clearly, the opportunities for meaningful desegregation in larger public school districts are increasingly affected and limited by changing demographics and the declining proportion of white students. The extent to which these population trends are themselves affected by desegregation policies is taken up in a later section.

Turning next to trends in school desegregation, Figure 4.2 shows the national

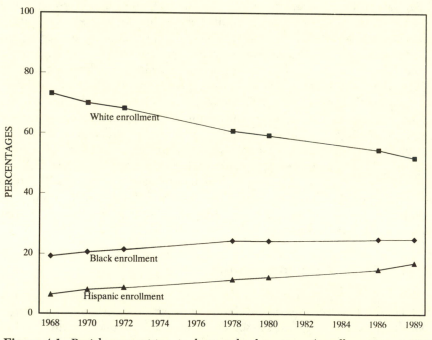

Figure 4.1. Racial composition in large school systems (enrollment over 10,000). *Source:* National Survey for U.S. Department of Education (see Steel et al., *Magnet Schools and Issues of Desegregation, Quality, and Choice*).

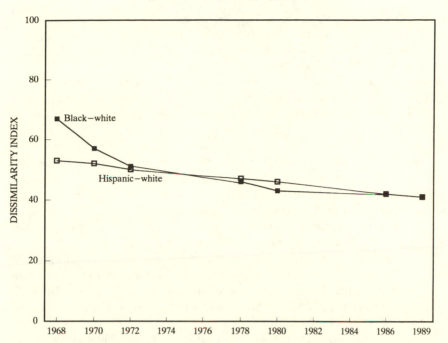

Figure 4.2. Racial imbalance in large school systems (enrollment over 10,000). *Source:* National Survey for the U.S. Department of Education.

trends in racial imbalance for blacks and Hispanics, each relative to whites, in larger public school systems using the index of dissimilarity. In 1968 there was a considerable degree of black-white imbalance in larger school systems, with an average dissimilarity index of 67. The index dropped sharply to 51 over the next four years, but after 1972 the index declined more gradually, falling to 43 by 1980. Black-white imbalance changed very little after 1980, remaining somewhat above 40 points since that time. These trends demonstrate that desegregation was effective in reducing racial imbalance, but the effects occurred primarily during the early 1970s, when the federal courts began enforcing the *Green* and *Swann* mandates.

Figure 4.2 shows that Hispanic-white imbalance was not as severe as black-white imbalance in 1968, primarily because of their small numbers in most school districts. The index fell from 53 to 42 between 1968 and 1972. After 1972 the trend for Hispanic-white imbalance resembles that for blacks, with most of the declines taking place by 1980. During the late 1980s Hispanic-white imbalance has been at about the same level as black-white imbalance, with a dissimilarity index averaging just above 40. Given a school system that is approximately half white and half minority, a dissimilarity index of 40 means that approximately 20 percent of white and 20 percent of minority students would have to be moved to attain perfect racial balance.

While the dissimilarity index reveals considerable improvement in racial balance, this index does not take into account the considerable loss of white enrollment shown in Figure 4.1. This limitation is remedied in Figure 4.3, which charts the national trends in black and Hispanic exposure to white students in larger public school systems. The index is the average percent white in schools attended by black or Hispanic students.

At the beginning of the period, the exposure index shows considerable segregation of black students. In larger school systems, the average black student attended schools that averaged only 43 percent white, even though all schools averaged 73 percent white at that time (see Figure 4.1). As a result of desegregation efforts, the exposure of black to white students climbed to 54 percent by 1972 (when schools were 68 percent white). The black-white exposure index did not get any higher, however, not only because desegregation efforts diminished after 1972 but also because white enrollment was declining. By 1989 the exposure index had fallen to 47, only 4 points above where it began in 1968. Since white enrollment had fallen to 52 percent by this time, however, the upper limit of the exposure index was also much lower in 1989 than in 1968.

In other words, school desegregation efforts initially improved black-white exposure in larger public school districts, but after several years exposure began declining, in large part because of falling white enrollments. Again, this raises the important question of whether the desegregation activities themselves contributed to these white population declines.

The trend for Hispanic exposure to whites differs considerably from the trend for blacks, especially during the early years. In 1968 the average Hispanic

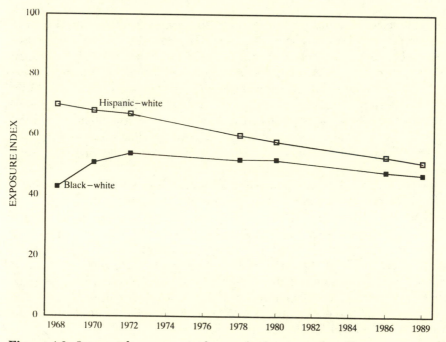

Figure 4.3. Interracial exposure in large school systems (enrollment over 10,000). *Source:* National Survey for the U.S. Department of Education.

student in larger school systems attended schools that averaged 70 percent white, only 3 points below its maximum possible value. Over the next twenty years Hispanic-white exposure declined considerably to only 51 percent by 1989—just 4 points higher than black-white exposure. However, this trend exactly parallels the decline in the overall percent white, as shown in Figure 4.1. In fact, in most years for which data are available, the Hispanic-white exposure index is just 1 or 2 points below the upper limit of the index, as determined by the overall percent white. Thus the declining exposure index for Hispanic students in larger school systems is attributable more to declining white enrollments than to racial isolation within these systems.

How do these results compare to other studies of desegregation trends? There are very few published studies of national school desegregation trends, and the only studies covering a comparable time period are two by Orfield and others conducted for the National School Boards Association in 1989 and 1992.[20] These studies are based only on the OCR enrollment surveys, which utilize various sampling plans after 1974 and include all school districts with desegregation plans. Because of the sampling procedures employed by the OCR surveys, the school districts surveyed in a given year do not necessarily constitute a national representative sample, particularly because they over represent districts with plans. Also, the Orfield studies compute exposure indices for only five years (1970, 1980, 1984, 1986, and 1988), and they do not present data on the overall trend in percent white enrollment, which is the upper limit of the exposure index.

In spite of data differences, many of the trends analyzed in the Orfield studies are consistent with Figures 4.2 and 4.3, based on the AIR national survey. In general, the Orfield studies show that most school desegregation took place between 1968 and 1972, with only small improvements after that period. The studies also shows differing patterns of interracial exposure for black and Hispanic students, with blacks showing improvement since 1968 and Hispanics showing a steady decline between 1968 and 1988. One important difference is that the Orfield study shows Hispanics with a lower exposure to whites than blacks in 1988 (by about 4 points), while the data from the AIR national survey show that Hispanics have higher a exposure than blacks.[21] Finally, the Orfield studies show one interesting statistic not compiled in the AIR study: In 1968 nearly 80 percent of black students were in schools with more than 50 percent minority enrollment, which dropped to about 65 percent by 1972 and has changed very little since then.

Two of Orfield's conclusions about desegregation trends are not fully supported by the data from the AIR national survey. First, he concludes that there is little evidence for the resegregation of black students, mainly because the exposure index rises between 1970 and 1980 and then is relatively stable after that time. However, because Orfield computes the exposure index only for 1970 and 1980, his data do not show the gains in black-white exposure between 1968 and 1972 and the subsequent declines after the peak in 1972. According to Figure 4.3, about half the gain in black-white exposure between 1968 and 1972 was lost because of declining white enrollments between 1972 and 1986. This pattern is consistent with a resegregation process, although it cannot necessarily be attributed to resegregation itself without further analysis.

Second, Orfield concludes that Hispanic segregation is becoming a more serious problem than black segregation, in part because Hispanic-white exposure continues to decline while black-white exposure has leveled off. Aside from the fact that the AIR data shows Hispanic-white exposure somewhat higher than black-white exposure, the Orfield study did not include the trend for white enrollment. Although Hispanic-white exposure has declined substantially between 1968 and 1989, the main reason appears attributable to the overall decline in white enrollment rather than to a problem of within-district segregation.

Although the desegregation movement has clearly improved racial balance for both black and Hispanic students and has also improved the exposure of blacks to whites, the declining white enrollment in larger school districts is clearly limiting the possibility of further improvement. Indeed, if white enrollment losses continue, especially in larger systems that enroll most minority students, then both black and Hispanic exposure to white students can be expected to drop in future years regardless of the degree of racial balance within these systems, at least in the absence of extensive interdistrict desegregation policies.

Desegregation and White Flight

The national trends for the racial composition and the desegregation of public schools underscore the importance of the white flight problem. Although desegregation trends show improving racial balance and improved black-white exposure in larger school systems, declining white enrollments are reversing the gains for blacks realized in the 1970s and are causing declining levels of interracial exposure for both blacks and Hispanics. The extent to which desegregation itself or certain types of desegregation plans have contributed to these white enrollment losses is clearly a critical issue in desegregation policy.

After the educational and psychological effects of desegregation, the impact of desegregation on white flight is the second most popular topic studied by desegregation researchers. Its importance to desegregation policy is obvious: Effective and meaningful desegregation can exist only if there are sufficient numbers of all races (or ethnicities) to provide a meaningful degree of interracial contact. If white flight reaches a degree that removes most whites from a school system, then little meaningful desegregation can take place regardless of the degree of racial balance.

Legal Significance

As noted in chapter 1, the white flight issue played virtually no role in most federal court decisions during the 1970s. Its absence can be traced to several Supreme Court rulings, starting with the 1955 *Brown II* decision, which stated that community "disagreement" with desegregation was irrelevant in fashioning a desegregation remedy. The Supreme Court eventually took up the white flight issue explicitly in its 1972 *Scotland Neck* decision, when it held that white flight "cannot . . . be accepted as a reason for achieving anything less than complete uprooting of the dual public school system."[22]

Court rulings in the early 1970s made clear that white flight was viewed as a form of opposition to desegregation and, as such, simply another manifestation of the racial prejudice that had caused segregation in the first place. Whatever the reasons, during the 1970s most lower federal courts generally did not consider the white flight issue when evaluating desegregation plans, in spite of extensive demographic and social science evidence introduced in some cases.

A typical court response to white flight testimony occurred in Pasadena in 1974, where the district court dismissed the argument that white losses were caused by its mandatory busing plan. Another instance occurred in Dallas, where an appellate court overruled a lower court's approval of a more limited busing plan that had been defended on the grounds of white flight.[23] Ultimately, after further hearings, the more limited Dallas plan was approved by the appellate court in 1979. The Dallas appellate decisions were denied review by the Supreme Court, which prompted a dissent written by Justice Powell and joined by Justices Stewart and Rehnquist. The dissent stated that even though the limited busing plan had finally been approved, the problems of white flight and resegregation had not received enough attention by the high Court and that the Dallas case offered an opportunity to clarify the role of these issues in designing desegregation remedies.[24]

White flight began playing a more important role in the design of desegregation plans and in court decisions during the late 1970s. By this time a considerable number of studies of the white flight problem had been published, and greater consensus had emerged among researchers that white flight could undermine the effectiveness of a desegregation plan. Starting in 1977, social science evidence and testimony on white flight played a major role in the desegregation cases of San Diego, Los Angeles, Norfolk, Savannah, and Hattiesburg (Mississippi).

In the San Diego case, which came under California state court action, white flight testimony by this author and Christine Rossell in 1977 led to one of the first court-approved voluntary plans in the nation.[25] In Los Angeles, also a state case, extensive evidence and testimony about white flight by this author, Reynolds Farley, and others in 1979 were also accepted by the court, although not for the purpose of approving a voluntary plan. Instead, white flight estimates were incorporated into the plan so that more white students were bused in order to attain a specified level of racial balance, after taking into account white losses.[26]

In Norfolk, which had been declared unitary in 1975, William Clark and this author introduced white flight evidence and testimony in 1983 as part of the rationale for ending a mandatory busing plan. As noted in chapter 2, the district court opinion relied on this evidence in approving the school board's plan to return to neighborhood schools, and the decision was upheld on appeal.

In Hattiesburg, Mississippi, a district court approved a plan that left two predominantly black schools out of a plan, chiefly on the grounds of white flight testimony by Christine Rossell. Although the appellate court overturned this decision and ordered inclusion of the two schools in the plan, the higher court made it clear that white flight concerns are "legitimate when choosing among constitutionally permissible plans."[27] In other words, if one plan is shown to have less white flight than another and therefore is more effective in desegregating a school system, then the white flight argument is a legitimate consideration.

Studies of White Flight

Although the phenomenon of white flight has a long history in social science research, in 1975 it became a controversial issue in school desegregation policy when James S. Coleman and others published a comprehensive study of school segregation trends.[28] Studying racial enrollment trends in the sixty-seven largest central-city school districts between 1968 and 1973, Coleman and his colleagues concluded that desegregation was causing significant white flight in central cities and increasing the segregation between cities and their suburbs. Although Coleman found several demographic causes of white enrollment losses, particularly the percentage of blacks and the size of the district, he concluded that desegregation was accelerating white flight above and beyond that caused by other demographic processes.

The Coleman study was immediately criticized by several social scientists, most notably Farley, Rossell, and Pettigrew.[29] Using different data and statistical techniques, none of these critics found school desegregation to be a significant cause of white flight. To their credit, both Farley and Rossell continued to collect data and refine their statistical techniques, and both eventually published later studies that were more consistent with the original Coleman findings. The second Farley study, which analyzed the largest 125 school districts from 1968 to 1974 with a statistical model similar to Coleman's, found that the effects of desegregation on white flight were strongest in larger, central-city school districts with higher proportions of black students.[30]

The second Rossell study used a nonrandom national sample of 113 school districts and also used different statistical techniques than those employed by Coleman and Farley. Rossell concluded that school desegregation did cause significant white flight and that the effects were strongest in districts with higher percentages of black students and districts where large percentages of white students were reassigned to formerly black schools (e.g., two-way mandatory busing plans).[31] White flight was much lower in school districts that desegregated primarily by reassigning blacks to white schools (one-way busing).

Other national studies have come to similar conclusions about white flight, including a study of fifty-four court-ordered mandatory busing plans in larger school districts conducted by this author. In central-city school districts with higher percentages of black enrollment, I found mandatory busing to raise white loss rates by three to five times that due to underlying demographic processes.[32] Using U.S. Census and Vital Statistics data to calculate preexisting demographic trends, this study estimated that over a five-year period about half of the total white enrollment loss was due to the busing plans and the other half was due to normal demographic processes such as declining birth rates and net out-migration rates.

Another large national study of more than 1,200 school districts by Franklin Wilson also found significant white flight in desegregating districts.[33] Unlike the earlier studies by Rossell and me but in agreement with both Coleman and Farley, the Wilson study concluded that any type of school desegregation that increases interracial contact causes white flight, regardless of the type of plan— mandatory or voluntary. Wilson also concluded, unlike Coleman and Rossell, that the white flight effect was short term, limited primarily to the first year of busing. It should be noted that the majority of school districts in this study were relatively small.

A more recent study of the white flight problem by Welch and Light was commissioned by the U.S. Commission on Civil Rights. The study was based on a probability sample of 125 districts with enrollments over 15,000 and racial compositions between 10 and 90 percent black. The study collected enrollment and plan data from these districts covering the period from 1968 to 1984. This study also concluded that desegregation caused white flight and that the type of plan influenced the degree of white loss.[34]

A summary of the white flight results from this study is presented in Figure 4.4. The chart shows annual white loss rates before and after desegregation for

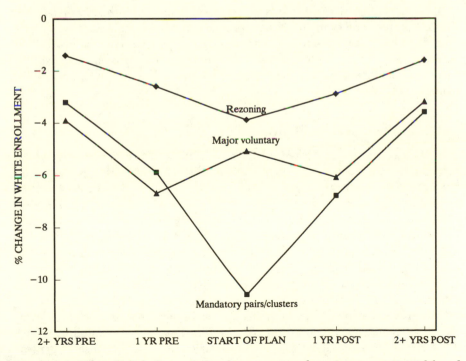

Figure 4.4. White flight before and after desegregation plans. *Source:* see F. Welch and A. Light, *New Evidence on School Segregation.*

seventy-nine school districts that desegregated after 1970 employing three different techniques: mandatory pairing/clustering, contiguous rezoning, and comprehensive voluntary methods (including magnet schools and M-to-M programs).[35] The mandatory techniques of pairing/clustering clearly led to the largest white flight (largest annual percentage of white loss), with the white loss rate at the start of busing three times greater than the loss rate two years before busing began.

White losses are also elevated in the year just before busing begins, which is "anticipatory" white flight. Although white flight is greatest when mandatory busing is actually implemented, some parents leave a school system (or fail to enter) in anticipation that busing is about to begin. This may be particularly true if private school resources are scarce and there is concern about getting into a private school while capacity exists.

Although the rate of white loss for voluntary busing plans is higher than for rezoning plans, even rezoning plans show an elevated rate of white loss during implementation. While rezoning is a type of mandatory reassignment plan, it maintains contiguous zones and therefore is closer to a neighborhood school policy than a pairing or clustering plan that utilizes noncontiguous zones. It is especially noteworthy that white flight in voluntary plans is higher the year *before* busing, when there may be doubt about what the plan entails, than when busing starts and parents realize that their children are not required to change schools.

Although the white flight rate is lower in voluntary plans than in mandatory plans, it is still significantly higher during the three-year implementation phase (one year before, during, and one year after) than it was two years before or after busing began. These white loss rates for voluntary plans, then, suggest that increased racial contact alone leads to some white enrollment losses, even if that contact takes place in formerly white schools.

Case Studies of White Flight

The studies reviewed to this point have dealt with white enrollment change for school systems as a whole. The problem with district-wide studies is that not all students and schools are affected by a mandatory plan; even in a pairing or clustering plan, many students remain at their current neighborhood school. If most white flight is caused by reassignment to minority schools, then a more precise estimate of white flight is attained by examining enrollment changes for individual schools. This information is also important for designing a plan and evaluating its effectiveness. Obviously, the degree of white flight affects the amount of desegregation or racial balance that can be attained in individual schools.

This problem is solved by examining the losses of whites assigned to individual minority schools, called *no-shows*. No-show rates are illustrated in Figure 4.5 for four school systems that adopted mandatory pairing/clustering plans during the 1970s. No-show rates are calculated by comparing the number of white students reassigned to predominantly minority schools with the number

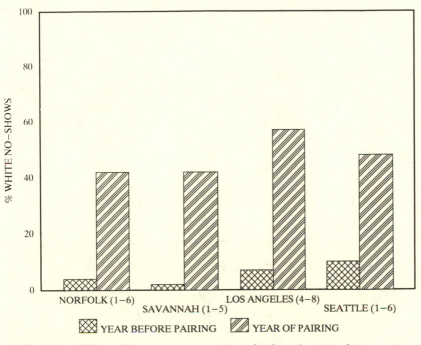

Figure 4.5. White no-show rates at minority schools in four mandatory pairing plans. (Numbers in parentheses are grades in the pairing plan.)

who actually attend those schools when busing starts. The no-show rates in these four pairing plans range from 42 to 57 percent, which means that about half of white students mandatorily reassigned to predominantly minority schools do not in fact show up at those schools the following year.

Not all of these white losses are due to the busing plan; ordinary demographic changes contribute to some white loss. In Figure 4.5 the white loss rates before busing are shown in the left-hand bars, labeled as "year before pairing." Assuming that all prebusing loss rates are due to demographic factors (rather than anticipatory white flight), then only a small portion of the no-show rate in these school systems is due to demographic changes. Note also that the highest no-show rate is for Los Angeles, which had the longest average busing distance of any of these plans (and perhaps longer than any other mandatory busing plan in the nation). *Average* one-way bus rides in the Los Angeles plan were fifty-five minutes, due to the long distances between predominantly white and predominantly minority neighborhoods. Finally, these no-show rates are similar to those calculated by Christine Rossell for the Boston and Baton Rouge mandatory busing plans, which were 45 percent and 56 percent, respectively.[36]

These no-show rates are quite consistent with the survey results presented later in Figure 4.15, which shows the percentage of whites who say they would "definitely" withdraw their children from the school system if reassigned to a predominantly minority school. The no-show rates are also consistent with the districtwide white loss rates shown in Fig. 4.4, once nonbused white students are taken into account. For each school pairing, for example, approximately half the white students remain in their neighborhood school at a given time, and schools that are already desegregated or nearly desegregated (often secondary schools) are often left unchanged or are subject to only minor zone adjustments. Therefore, a white no-show rate of 45–50 percent can translate into a district-wide loss of 10–15 percent, depending on the extent of white reassignment.

The consensus at this point is that school desegregation contributes to white flight and that the flight can be quite large for some school systems, especially those systems that are larger, have higher minority concentrations, and have suburban or private school systems that can serve as alternatives for those who flee a desegregation plan or for new residents who want to avoid one. There is less consensus about whether some types of desegregation plans create more white flight than others and about the long-term consequences of white flight on effectiveness.

Effectiveness of Alternative Desegregation Plans

The central question of effectiveness is whether certain types of desegregation plans are more effective than others in attaining stable, long-term desegregation. White flight plays a central role in answering this question because techniques that cause significant white flight also reduce minority exposure to white students and may well lead to resegregation, whereby a school system is transformed into a predominantly minority system. Even in the absence of resegregation, a plan that substantially increases white losses might produce less desegregation in the long run than a plan that causes lower white losses.

The debates about white flight and effectiveness have generally revolved around the effectiveness of comprehensive mandatory versus comprehensive voluntary desegregation plans. One school of thought maintains that mandatory techniques are most effective for student desegregation, which is generally defined as racial balance and measured by the index of dissimilarity. This school of thought, which dominated federal court decisions during the 1970s, puts less emphasis on the importance of interracial exposure and the role of white flight.

A second school of thought maintains that comprehensive voluntary plans (with magnet schools) are more effective than mandatory plans in limiting white flight and increasing interracial exposure and contact. This school of thought, best represented by the works of Rossell, generally defines and measures desegregation in terms of the exposure index, not only because it takes into account white enrollment losses but also because it reflects the actual exposure of black students to white students. Her writings are critical of a strict racial balance definition of desegregation (and its measurement in terms of the dissimilarity index), not only because racial balance ignores the level of white enrollment but also because attaining a high degree of racial balance maximizes the reassignment of whites to minority schools, thereby causing the most white flight.

A third school of thought represented by Coleman's original work on white flight, suggests that the main causal mechanism in white flight is interracial contact itself. Any method that increases interracial contact by the same degree, whether voluntary or mandatory, accelerates white flight and can promote resegregation between cities and suburbs or between public and private schools. According to this conception, a comprehensive voluntary plan that produces the same level of interracial contact as a mandatory plan should produce the same degree of white loss, and therefore in the long run the type of plan may not ultimately make a difference on either white flight or effectiveness.

Although some published empirical studies support one school or another, most of the existing studies are limited either in sample size or the duration of enrollment data. The new national data from the AIR study offer a unique opportunity to test these differing hypotheses about effectiveness with a large and representative sample of school systems over a twenty-one year period from 1968 to 1989.

Existing Studies

In contrast to the white flight issue, relatively few studies compare the effectiveness of alternative plans in general and mandatory versus voluntary plans in particular. Several of these studies are relatively dated, with enrollment data extending only to 1980 or so, and most are based on relatively small samples of school districts. Leaving these limitations aside, the most important published studies to date are those by Smylie, Orfield, and Rossell.

A 1983 study by Smylie is representative of studies that compare the effectiveness of alternative plans by using only the criterion of racial balance as measured by the index of dissimilarity.[37] The analysis was based on fifty-one school districts, most of which had student enrollments exceeding 30,000, and his most recent data for the purpose of evaluating trends were from 1978 or 1980. The study concluded that mandatory plans led to greater reductions in racial imbalance than voluntary plans and that there was no important difference in white flight according to the type of plan. The chief limitation of this study, aside from the sample size and the time interval, is that it did not examine the trends and patterns of interracial exposure.

Orfield has examined the effectiveness of alternative plans by using data from his reports on school desegregation trends for the National School Boards Association. In a 1988 study he compared 1984 exposure indices for twenty-four large-city school districts classified into the most and the least desegregated, identifying each as having either a voluntary or a mandatory desegregation plan.[38] The study concluded that cities with the highest level of desegregation were those that had adopted mandatory plans.

Orfield's 1992 trend study also conducted a limited analysis of white losses for thrity-two selected school districts, classified according various plan features.[39] Addressing the argument that mandatory plans fail because of white flight, the study concluded that the type of plan did not make much difference in the total white enrollment losses, as calculated between 1967 and 1988. With the exception of several countywide school systems, most systems experienced substantial white losses over this interval whether they used mandatory or voluntary magnet plans.

Aside from being limited to selected samples of school districts, neither of the Orfield studies presented trends or patterns in exposure indices over time or controlled for demographic differences between districts by means of appropriate statistical analyses.[40]

The most comprehensive analysis of effectiveness among published studies to date was carried out by Rossell.[41] This study analyzed twenty mandatory and twenty voluntary magnet desegregation plans, matched generally on such characteristics as size, racial composition, and city-county status. The analysis covered several outcome measures and utilized statistical regression techniques to control for demographic differences among districts. The study's basic conclusions are as follows:

1. White enrollment loss was greater in mandatory plans with magnets than in voluntary magnet plans.
2. Mandatory plans produced greater interracial exposure (as measured by the exposure index) than voluntary magnet plans during the first several years of implementation, but the voluntary magnet plans produced greater exposure over the long run.
3. Mandatory plans produced greater racial balance for longer periods of time (as measured by the dissimilarity index), but voluntary magnet plans eventually caught up with mandatory plans and produced about the same level of racial balance.

In other words, the twenty mandatory plans produced more racial balance than voluntary plans for longer periods of time, and they led to greater interracial exposure over the short run. Over the longer run, however, after controlling for demographic characteristics, the higher rate of white losses caused by mandatory plans reduced their effectiveness, and voluntary plans ended up with as much racial balance and somewhat greater interracial exposure than mandatory plans.

Unlike the Smylie and Orfield studies, the Rossell study used regression analysis to control for demographic differences among school districts. Like the Smylie and Orfield studies, the sample size is relatively small, and it was not a probability sample drawn to represent the national population of desegregated school systems.

The AIR National Survey

The AIR national survey of magnet schools and desegregation plans allows the first test of desegregation effectiveness using a large, representative sample of school districts. Although the primary objective of the study was to describe the utilization and characteristics of magnet schools in desegregation plans, a secondary goal was to assess the impact of magnet schools on desegregation outcomes. The existence of detailed desegregation plan data allows a comparison of the effects of desegregation plans on long-term outcomes, including racial composition, racial balance, and interracial exposure.[42]

Again the analysis here is confined to those school systems enrolling 10,000 or more students. Aside from enrolling three-fourths of all minority students in the nation, these systems exhibit the greatest the variety of desegregation techniques. The reason for variety of plans lies in the number of schools. School districts with more than 10,000 students usually have at least five secondary schools and ten elementary schools. The larger the number of schools, the greater the logistical challenge for increasing desegregation and racial balance at all grade levels. Desegregation plans in larger school systems inevitably require a considerable degree of "busing," either the mandatory forms associated with noncontiguous attendance zones or the voluntary forms associated with magnet schools and M-to-M transfer programs.

Plans versus No Plans. The first task is to examine the impact of having a formal desegregation plan versus no formal plan. In general, the AIR study confirmed that districts with desegregation plans show greater changes in desegregation levels than districts without formal plans, although the changes are not as large as some might expect.

Figure 4.6 shows the trends in black-white imbalance for approximately three hundred larger school systems with and without formal desegregation plans.[43] Districts with formal plans show a sharp reduction in black-white imbalance between 1968 and 1972. The average index of dissimilarity fell from 69 to 45 during these years, confirming this period as the high point of desegregation activity. Subsequently, the index falls more slowly until it reaches 37 in 1980, but racial imbalance changes very little after 1980.

School systems without formal desegregation plans were not as imbalanced in 1968, showing an average dissimilarity index of 55. Surprisingly, these systems also show a substantial decline in racial imbalance between 1968 and 1972, albeit not as sharply as systems with plans, and their average index fell to 38 by 1980. Further examination of this trend within region reveals that most of these early declines occurred in the South, and many are districts that dismantled their dual school systems following the Supreme Court's *Green* decision without a formal plan (e.g., closing black schools, drawing regular geographic zones, and so forth). It is noteworthy that throughout the 1980s there was virtually no difference in racial balance between plan and nonplan districts, indicating that substantial desegregation can occur in school districts without formal desegregation plans.

The trends for Hispanic-white imbalance (not shown) resemble those for black students. Systems with formal plans show a reduction in dissimilarity from 56 to 40, while systems without plans show a reduction from 47 to 35. Hispanics are less imbalanced in systems without plans, both at the beginning and at the end of the period, but systems with formal plans reduced the index by 16 points, compared to only 12 points for those without formal plans.

The impact of desegregation plans on interracial exposure shows somewhat

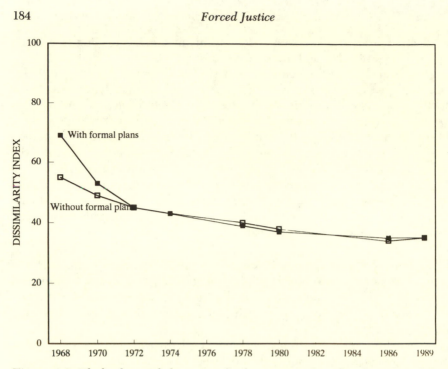

Figure 4.6. Black-white imbalance in school systems with and without formal deseg-regation plans (enrollment over 10,000). *Source:* National Survey of the U.S. Department of Education.

different patterns of results. Figure 4.7 compares the trends in black-white exposure for larger districts with and without formal desegregation plans. Like the results for racial imbalance, districts with plans show a substantial improvement in black exposure to whites between 1968 and 1972, with the percent white in the typical black student's school increasing from 36 to 53 percent in just four years. Exposure remained relatively stable for districts with plans until 1980, when it began a gradual decline to 49 in 1989. Again, districts without formal plans show a slight increase from 73 to 76 during the first four years (mostly attributable to southern districts), and they, too, show a gradual decline to 65 by 1989. Although districts without plans have higher exposure levels in 1989, they also started out with higher levels; districts with plans had a net increase in exposure of 13 points whereas districts without plans had a net loss of 8 points over the entire period.

The declines in exposure after 1980 are due largely to declines in percentage white for both groups. From 1968 to 1989, districts with plans fell from 72 percent to 53 white, and districts without plans fell from 83 percent to 69 percent white. These patterns suggest that the main reason for declining exposure in both groups is the reduction of percentage white after 1980, which is the upper limit for the exposure index. In 1989 the exposure index is only 4 points below its maximum value for districts with plans as compared to 5 points for districts without plans.

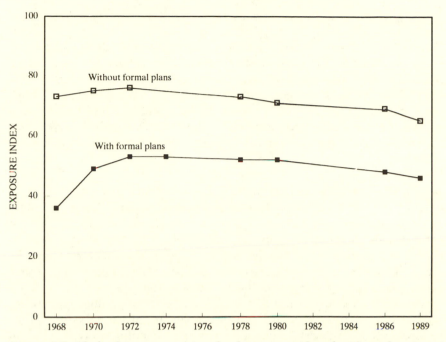

Figure 4.7. Black-white exposure in school systems with and without desegregation plans (enrollment over 10,000). *Source:* National Survey for the U.S. Department of Education.

Hispanic-white exposure has also declined in districts with plans, but the index is only slightly below the percent white, indicating that Hispanics have experienced high exposure relative to the available white population. Like black-white exposure, Hispanic-white exposure was higher in districts without plans than in districts with plans. In 1968, the exposure index for Hispanics was 73 and 82 for districts with and without plans respectively, a difference of 7 points; by 1989 the exposure index is 53 and 66, respectively, a difference of 13 points. Like black students, then, the exposure of Hispanics to whites in 1989 is more favorable in districts without plans than districts with plans, but this is attributed to the fact that the nonplan districts have a higher white percentage than the plan districts. Exposure is also higher for Hispanics than blacks in districts with plans, thereby indicating that desegregation has been somewhat more effective for Hispanic students than black students.

The overall conclusion is that districts with formal desegregation plans produce greater desegregation than districts without plans. Districts without plans did show some improvements in desegregation during the early years, and they actually have higher levels of interracial exposure by 1989—but mainly because they began with a higher white enrollment in 1968. The results also show that districts with formal plans experienced a greater decline in the percentage of white enrollment, and therefore the price of improved desegregation may have been increased white enrollment losses. An accelerated decline in the percentage white in a district obviously restricts future gains in interracial exposure.

The white flight result is confirmed by a more rigorous statistical analysis of the AIR data, controlling for various school district characteristics.[44] A multiple regression analysis was carried out using the percentage change in white enrollment (1968 to 1989) as a dependent variable and a series of school district demographic and socioeconomic factors as independent variables.[45] After controlling for school district characteristics, school districts with desegregation plans experienced a significantly greater decline in white enrollment than non-plan districts.

Type of plan. The most important issue in the effectiveness debate is whether mandatory plans produce more desegregation than voluntary plans. For this analysis, larger districts with current plans are classified as mandatory if they ever had a mandatory desegregation plan during the study period, and they are classified as voluntary only if they have always operated a voluntary plan.[46] In addition, because of the important regional variations, the results are presented separately for southern and nonsouthern school systems. In general, the AIR survey shows that mandatory plans in larger school systems produced somewhat greater (and more rapid) racial balance than voluntary plans in the South (but not elsewhere); there is virtually no difference between the two types of plans regarding the current level of interracial exposure in either region.

Figure 4.8 compares the black-white dissimilarity index for 136 larger school systems with voluntary or mandatory desegregation plans.[47] For southern districts with mandatory plans, racial imbalance dropped rapidly between 1968 and 1972, with little change after that time. Southern districts with voluntary plans also show declines in racial imbalance, but not nearly to the degree shown by mandatory plans.[48] The pattern for nonsouthern districts is quite different. The improvement in racial balance for both types of plans is more gradual, reflecting the later start of desegregation efforts outside the South. Most important, non-southern districts show less difference between the two types of plans, although in all years racial imbalance is slightly lower in mandatory than in voluntary plans.

Figure 4.9 compares the trends in black-white exposure for both types of plans. Again, the patterns are quite different by region. Both types of plans led to very rapid improvements in exposure in southern districts, although mandatory plans attained higher levels of exposure during the 1970s. By 1989, however, both types of plans show similar levels of interracial exposure. Northern districts show more gradual patterns of change, with maximum exposure attained around 1980 followed by declines until 1989. Unlike southern districts, voluntary plans in nonsouthern districts produce somewhat higher levels of exposure than mandatory plans, although by 1989 the exposure index is virtually identical for the two types of plans.

The similar results for the two types of plans in nonsouthern districts are not influenced by the percentage white enrollment, which was about the same for the two types of plans at the beginning of the period (73 percent) and at the end

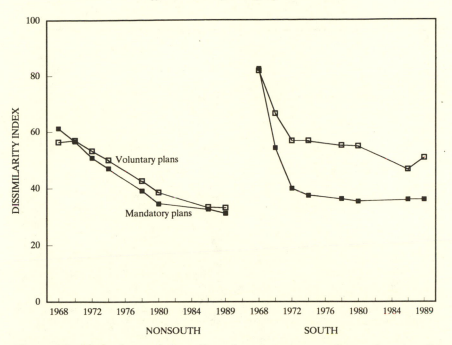

Figure 4.8. Black-white imbalance for voluntary versus mandatory plans (enrollment over 10,000). *Source:* National Survey for the U.S. Department of Education.

(50 percent). For both types of plans, the difference between actual exposure and its maximum possible value (the percent white) is only about 5 or 6 points in nonsouthern districts. The gap between actual exposure and the percent white is greater for southern districts, about 13 points, suggesting that desegregation has been somewhat less effective in the South in terms of interracial exposure (relative to its maximum value).

The trends for Hispanic-white imbalance and exposure also show few differences between voluntary and mandatory plans, particularly outside the South where the majority of Hispanic students are found. In nonsouthern districts, the white exposure index for Hispanics is 46 for both types of plans, and the dissimilarity index is 36 in voluntary plan districts compared to 34 for mandatory plan districts. Thus both types of plans are equally effective in desegregating Hispanic populations.

The trends shown in Figures 4.8 and 4.9 are primarily descriptive and do not take into account demographic and other differences between school districts. Using multiple regression techniques to control for these district characteristics, the effectiveness of voluntary versus mandatory plans was tested against districts without desegregation plans.[49] Using the exposure index as the criterion, voluntary and mandatory plans both produced significantly higher exposure levels than districts without plans, once school district demographic and socioeconomic differences were taken into account. However, the differences in effectiveness between mandatory and voluntary plans were small; generally,

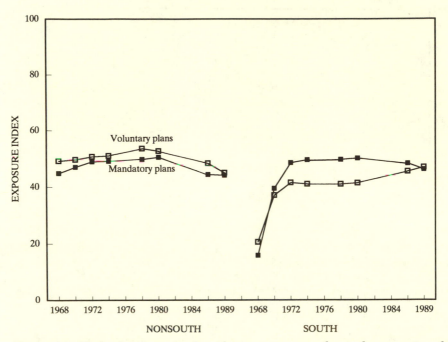

Figure 4.9. Black-white exposure for voluntary versus mandatory desegregation plans (enrollment over 10,000). *Source:* National Survey for the U.S. Department of Education.

voluntary plans were somewhat more effective than mandatory plans in raising black exposure to whites. Regarding the change in percent white, the regression analysis also demonstrated that mandatory plans are associated with greater losses in white enrollment than voluntary plans.

The regression results confirm the suggestion in the descriptive trends presented in Figures 4.6 to 4.9. Desegregation plans are effective in reducing racial imbalance and increasing interracial exposure when compared to districts without plans, but desegregation plans are also associated with greater changes in racial composition, reducing the percent white to only about 50 percent in school systems with enrollments over 10,000. Then again, although mandatory plans generate somewhat more racial balance than voluntary plans, voluntary plans appear to be somewhat more effective in raising interracial exposure. Unfortunately, both types of plans accelerate declines in the percentage of white enrollment, although the losses are significantly greater for mandatory plans once school district characteristics are taken into account.

Case Studies

Although the AIR national survey has the advantage of a large and representative sample of school districts, the very size of such a study also has its disadvantages. The major problem in this regard is determining certain detailed plan information that might affect long-term effectiveness. The AIR survey established the use of specific desegregation techniques, such as magnet schools or noncontiguous zoning, but it could not obtain detailed information on how many schools and how many students are affected by all components of a desegregation plan, particularly for mandatory techniques. This problem was compounded by school districts that made significant changes to their desegregation plan, sometimes adopting entirely new plans affecting different numbers of schools and students.

For this reason case studies remain useful for exploring variations in the effectiveness of different types of desegregation plans, particularly variations within the broad typology of mandatory and voluntary plans, as well as variations over time for districts that have implemented more than one type of desegregation plan. The case study approach can be used to evaluate the effects of adoption and the timing of specific techniques that can in turn be used to interpret trends and patterns in various desegregation outcomes.

The case study approach is illustrated here by considering results from eight desegregation plans in larger school districts that I have been tracking for the past twenty years or so. The cases consist of four comprehensive mandatory plans for Boston, Denver, Norfolk, and Savannah and four major voluntary plans for Buffalo, Cincinnati, Milwaukee, and San Diego. All districts were highly segregated in 1968, in terms of both imbalance and exposure, and all were majority white at this time, ranging from 57 percent white for Cincinnati and Norfolk to 76 percent white for San Diego. All of these plans were adopted sometime during the 1970s, and extensive information has been compiled for plan details, timing, and desegregation outcomes.[50]

Two of the mandatory cases, Boston and Denver, implemented comprehensive, court-ordered mandatory plans during the mid-1970s and maintained mandatory plans until at least 1990; Denver used pairing/clustering and Boston used noncontiguous zoning. Both Norfolk and Savannah implemented comprehensive, court-ordered pairing/clustering plans in 1970 and 1971 and maintained them for more than ten years. Norfolk was declared unitary in 1975, and it ultimately ended mandatory pairing of elementary schools in 1986, returning to neighborhood schools with a majority-to-minority transfer program as the only desegregation option for that grade level. Secondary schools remained desegregated by means of satellite zones. Savannah also ended its mandatory program, but because it had not been declared unitary, it replaced the mandatory plan with a comprehensive, voluntary magnet plan (with some contiguous rezoning) starting in 1987. The goal of that plan was to desegregate all schools to within a plus or minus 20 percent deviation by 1990.

Both Cincinnati and San Diego have operated court-approved voluntary magnet plans from the outset, beginning in 1973 and 1977, respectively. Both programs expanded in various ways, especially by adding more magnet schools over the next ten years. Milwaukee adopted a comprehensive voluntary magnet plan starting in 1976, which converted a number of formerly black schools into magnet schools, requiring black students to choose between the magnet program or the M-to-M program (meaning a transfer to another school). Buffalo implemented a comprehensive voluntary M-to-M program in 1977 with some rezoning and added magnet schools in 1980. In 1981 the court ordered a limited number of pairings involving magnet schools at the elementary level.

Both Norfolk and Savannah attained a very high degree of racial balance by 1972; Boston and Denver attained substantial balance by 1976 after their plans went through several stages (including court appeals in the case of Denver). During the late 1970s racial imbalance began increasing somewhat in all four districts, with a substantial increase for Norfolk in 1986, when it ended elementary pairing. The four voluntary plans experienced incremental but steady reductions in racial imbalance between 1968 and 1986, revealing the more gradual effects of voluntary techniques. By 1988 the four mandatory plans had dissimilarity indices ranging from 31 (Norfolk) to 43 (Denver); the four voluntary plans had indices ranging from 29 (Milwaukee) to 44 (San Diego). In spite of substantial plan differences and plan changes, over the long run there were no clear differences in racial balance between the four mandatory plans and the four voluntary plans.

The trends for black-white exposure and for percentage white enrollment for the mandatory plans are shown in Figure 4.10. The patterns for the exposure index are quite similar for all four districts between 1968 and 1980, excepting Boston's decline in exposure between 1968 and 1972 (prior to court-ordered busing). The exposure indices climbed rapidly with the onset of busing, closely approaching the districtwide percent white in each case. However, the percent white declined markedly at the time of implementation; even though each district was majority white in 1968, no district attained an exposure index at or above 50 even in the first year of desegregation. Moreover, the exposure index dropped steadily in all four districts as the percent white continued to decline, falling to between 32 to 35 for all but Boston. Because of an extraordinary degree of white flight, Boston's exposure index fell to a remarkably low 20 points, which is even lower than its exposure levels during the predesegregation years.

Interestingly, the decline in total percent white stopped in the mid-1980s for both Savannah and Norfolk, the only two districts to end mandatory pairing at the elementary level. For at least two or three years following the end of pairing, both districts experienced an increase in white enrollment in the elementary grades. The falling percent white in Boston and Denver, which maintained some form of mandatory plan throughout this period, showed no sign of ending through 1990.

The changes in exposure for Savannah and Norfolk after ending mandatory busing for elementary grades are noteworthy. Norfolk returned to neighborhood schools without magnet programs, and because some schools became nearly all black, the exposure index declined. Savannah, which also returned to neighborhood schools but with magnet programs at predominantly black schools, produced an increase in exposure to 35 points by 1990 (not shown in Figure 4.10).

The trends in black-white exposure for the four voluntary plans are shown in Figure 4.11. Again, the pattern of improvement in exposure is generally more

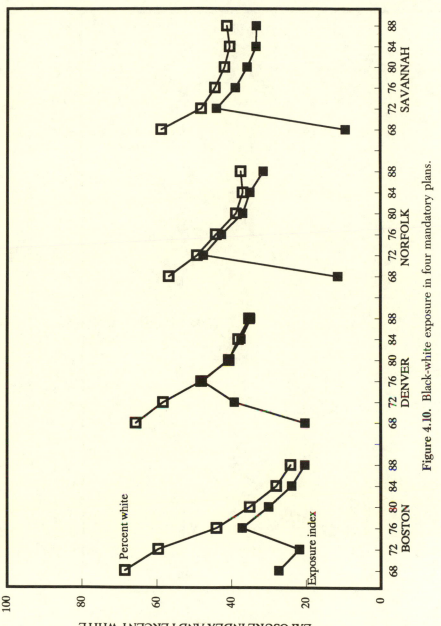

Figure 4.10. Black-white exposure in four mandatory plans.

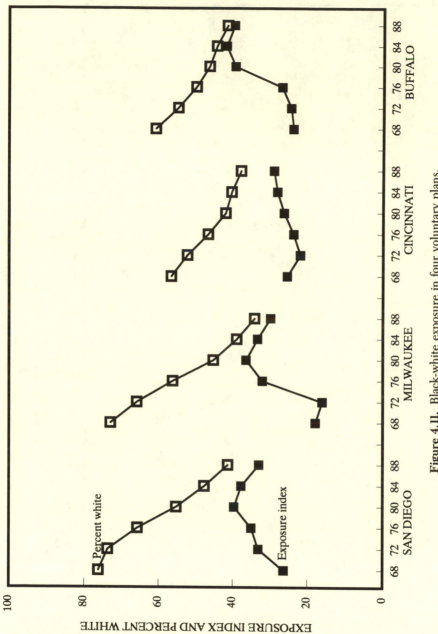

Figure 4.11. Black-white exposure in four voluntary plans.

gradual for the voluntary plans, especially San Diego and Cincinnati, which did very little rezoning. In all districts but Cincinnati, however, exposure began declining during the 1980s because of continuing declines in percent white enrollment. Cincinnati is the only case study here that shows a pattern of increasing levels of black-white exposure, although its value of 29 in 1988 is the lowest of the four districts. Although Buffalo has the highest rate of black-white exposure of all eight districts, there is no clear evidence among these cases that voluntary plans have led to higher interracial exposure than mandatory plans.

The reason, made abundantly clear in Figure 4.11, is that the total percentage of white enrollment declined as much in the voluntary plans as in the mandatory plans. The most striking fact, apparent in both Figures 4.10 and 4.11, is that all districts, regardless of the type of plan, have experienced very substantial declines in the percentage of white enrollment. Whereas Boston shows the largest decline (44 points), the next two largest declines occurred for San Diego and Milwaukee (35 and 39, respectively), both of which operate predominantly voluntary plans.

Undoubtedly, unique demographic and geographic characteristics, not systematically analyzed here, contribute to some of these variations. Savannah is a countywide school district, and San Diego (like all of southern California) is experiencing a massive in-migration of Hispanic families. Some of these districts, such as Boston and Milwaukee, are surrounded by a large number of predominantly white suburban school systems that may offer attractive alternatives to living in a central city. All of these factors and others contribute to the pattern of white decline in these districts.

Nevertheless, both mandatory and voluntary plans appear to contribute to the loss of white enrollment. Although natural demographic forces also contribute to these losses, white flight from desegregation appears to be a significant factor in all of these cases. The only two cases in which white enrollment losses appear to have slowed down are Savannah and Norfolk, both of which converted from a mandatory to a voluntary desegregation plan. To the extent that voluntary plans can reduce white flight and stem the transition to predominantly minority school systems, then, the process does not happen automatically, and other conditions must also be considered. Some of those conditions may well relate to community and parental attitudes, which are discussed in a subsequent section.

Although voluntary desegregation plans may not stop white enrollment losses, all the evidence reviewed here, including case studies and the national AIR study, supports the conclusion that mandatory plans are no more effective than comprehensive voluntary plans in producing long-term interracial exposure. This conclusion has important policy implications for courts and school systems that are evaluating alternative mandatory and voluntary plans as to their ultimate effectiveness; in particular, it rebuts the school of thought that mandatory plans are the most successful method for attaining desegregation.

The evidence reviewed here is also consistent with the early work on white flight by Coleman and his finding that any type of desegregation plan that substantially increases white and minority contact, whether mandatory or voluntary, can increase white enrollment losses.

Staff and Faculty Desegregation

Most desegregation plans implemented over the past twenty years include other components, the most common of which is a policy for racial balance of staff and faculty. The *Singleton* rule (described earlier), applied in most desegregation plans, calls for the faculty racial composition at each school to be within plus or minus 10 or 15 percentage points of the total system composition.

Faculty racial balance is maintained to some degree in all of the desegregation cases considered here, although it is not maintained with the same rigor in some cases that are no longer under court supervision, such as Norfolk and Cincinnati. Most faculties in larger school districts are majority white, and a predominantly black faculty would be highly unusual in any of these districts, even those not under active court supervision.

There has been somewhat less success in maintaining racial balance among principals. In most school districts with a sizeable black enrollment and black faculty, it has been more difficult to maintain a balanced racial mixture for school principals, and there is some tendency for majority-white schools to have white principals and for predominantly black schools to have black principals. Interestingly, in some communities it is harder to place a white principal at a black school than vice versa. The explanation usually offered by school administrators and board members is resistance on the part of black parents on the grounds that black "role models" are needed for their children. Although this reasoning has generally been rejected by the courts whenever it has been raised, the practice is widespread except where a court order strictly forbids it.

School policies for faculty racial balance have generally been less controversial than those for student balance. They have been an issue in some districts with strong teacher unions because they can restrict teacher choices or other union prerogatives. In Boston, for example, the teachers' union recently appealed a court order that gave seniority advantages to black teachers in order to raise the percentage of black teachers in the system; the union eventually lost the appeal. Faculty balance can also create a staffing problem at some schools because racial balance guidelines are applied to the whole faculty rather than by specialty. In many school districts, black teachers are underrepresented in math and science; at some grade levels, meeting racial balance goals can conflict with maintaining adequate numbers of math and science teachers.

Aside from occasional administrative or union complaints, however, faculty racial balance policies have not generated the kind of disputes associated with mandatory student desegregation. These policies are among the few instances in American society where racial quotas have been accepted and institutionalized with little vocal protest from the community.

Community and Parent Views on School Desegregation

The studies and data reviewed in preceding sections document the quantitative results of desegregation plans on the racial composition of school systems and individual schools. To interpret the meaning of these statistical findings more fully, the individual actors whose behaviors ultimately determine the success of a desegregation plan should be considered. This approach leads to an evaluation of the attitudes of citizens and parents toward school desegregation in general and toward specific types of desegregation plans.

In assessing public views on school desegregation, attitudes about the general concept of school desegregation must be distinguished from opinions about specific desegregation techniques. As discussed in chapter 3, although white racial prejudice and opposition to housing integration have declined significantly since the *Brown* decision, there is still considerable reluctance by whites to living in neighborhoods that exceed 50 percent black or minority. The issue that divided white and nonwhite opinion on housing integration was not so much the principle of integration, but rather how housing desegregation was to be defined in terms of specific racial compositions. A similar distinction between principles and specific policies exists for attitudes toward school desegregation.

School Desegregation in General

Today there is virtually no support for racially separate schools, and the general principles of school integration and desegregation are strongly supported by the vast majority of white and minority citizens. For example, when asked whether black and white students should attend the same or separate schools, only about one-third of whites said "same schools" in 1942.[51] Those answering "same schools" rose to 50 percent by 1956, 75 percent by 1970, and 90 percent by 1980. According to several surveys done in individual cities in 1990, fewer than 5 percent of whites endorse the principle of racially separate schools.[52]

When the racial composition of an integrated school is specified, however, the opinions of black and white respondents begin to diverge, as they do in the area of housing integration. The vast majority of black parents are willing to send their children to schools with widely varying racial compositions, but white parents' acceptance of desegregated schools depends upon the specific racial composition. As the minority percentage in a school increases, white parents are less likely to say they would be willing to send their children to such a school.

The effect of racial composition on white support for desegregated schools is apparent in Figure 4.12, which uses Gallup Poll results to establish long-term national trends in white attitudes toward schools with differing racial compositions. The actual question asked in these national surveys is, "Would you, yourself, have any objection to sending your children to a school where [a few/half/more than half] of the children are black?" Between 1958 and 1983, the

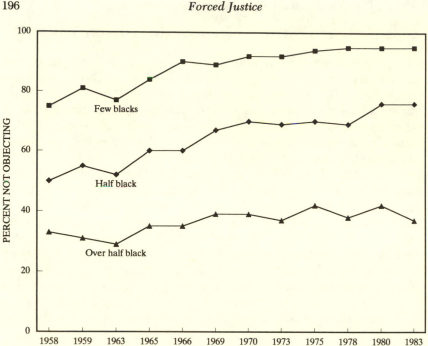

Figure 4.12. White acceptance of sending child to school with specified racial composition (national). *Source:* Gallup and NORC polls reported in Shuman et al., *Racial Attitudes in America*, Table 3.3.

percentage of whites not objecting to sending their children to a school with a few black children rose from 75 percent to 95 percent. Even more dramatic, the percentage not objecting to a school that was *half* black rose from 50 percent to 76 percent over the same time period. However, the percentage of whites not objecting to sending their children to a school that was more than half black has risen only from the low 30s to the high 30s, and there was virtually no change after 1969—during a time when major desegregation plans were being adopted in many school systems throughout the country.

These national survey results are highly consistent with surveys of parent attitudes that the author has conducted in a number of school systems as part of intensive case studies, some as recent as 1990. In six of these cities, white parents were asked if they would object to having their children attend schools with two racial or ethnic compositions: half white and half black or minority or one-third white and two-thirds black or minority.[53] The surveys were conducted in Los Angeles in 1977; Chicago in 1981; Norfolk in 1982; Worcester, Massachusetts, in 1989; DeKalb County, Georgia, in 1990; and Topeka in 1990. The minority group specified in the Chicago, Norfolk, DeKalb County, and Topeka surveys was black; the minority group specified in the Los Angeles and Worcester surveys included both black and Hispanic students.

The survey results for these six cities are shown in Figure 4.13 (note that the results are percent *objecting*, whereas Figure 4.12 shows percent *not objecting*).

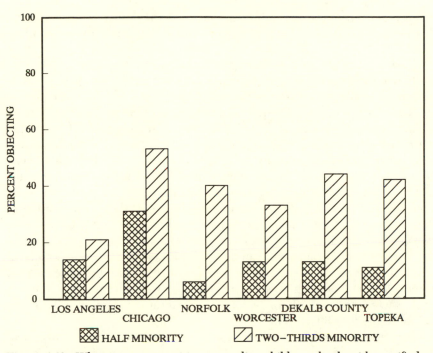

Figure 4.13. White parent opposition to sending child to schools with specified racial composition (case studies).

There is some variation from city to city, with Chicago showing the highest levels of objection to both mixes. With the exception of Chicago, only 6–14 percent of white parents in these cities object to sending their children to a 50 percent black or minority school, which indicates even greater acceptance of this particular racial composition than seen in the national surveys. Of course, the minority proportions in these larger school systems is considerably higher than that in the national population of school systems.

With the exception of Los Angeles and Worcester (where parents were asked about a combined black and Hispanic composition), however, 40–50 percent of white parents object to their children attending a school that is two-thirds black, which is consistent with the national surveys. In other words, the fact that the black populations are much higher in these school systems—comprising more than half the student populations in Chicago, Norfolk, and DeKalb County— does not diminish white reluctance to send children to a majority black school.

The national and local surveys reveal that almost all white parents support the principle of school integration and a large majority are willing to having their children attend a desegregated school with up to a fifty-fifty racial composition. Yet nearly half of white parents say they are not willing to send their children to a school in which they would be in a minority, or at least where a majority would be black. Indeed, many white parents would probably claim that a majority-black school is not a desegregated school by their definition, which receives considerable support from early definitions of segregated schools. Before the racial balance concept was favored by the courts, the U.S. Commission on Civil Rights defined a segregated school as one with more than 50 percent black students.

Why are most white parents willing to accept a fifty-fifty school but not a majority-black school? Some social scientists have suggested that, because most blacks accept minority status in a desegregated school, the unwillingness of whites to do the same is a reflection of racial prejudice. However, it is hard to argue that whites who accept a fifty-fifty school are racially prejudiced simply because they are unwilling to accept a higher minority ratio, especially when whites constitute the large majority not only in the nation as a whole but in most metropolitan areas as well. The reluctance of whites to accept minority status cannot be based on racial prejudice alone, as that concept has been traditionally defined, because racial prejudice should lead to rejection of *any* significant contact with members of another race. Rather, other factors must be at work.

No unequivocal evidence provides a definitive answer, but there are a number of possibilities. Perhaps the simplest explanation is that, in a society in which whites not only make up the majority population but also exert control over most institutional realms, minority status for whites represents a loss of control. This theory would help explain the significant change in attitudes for ratios above the fifty-fifty level.

Another possible explanation, which emerges from interviews I have had with parents in case studies, involves the perceived level of instruction in schools or classrooms that are predominantly black. Given the educational disadvantages of many black children, white middle-class parents are often concerned—rightly or wrongly—that instruction will be slowed down at the expense of their children. In other words, the problem with a majority-black school or classroom in the eyes of many middle-class parents is not race per se but the perceived influence it has on the instructional program. Indeed, a heightened pace of instruction is the same reason why many black parents are willing to send their childern away from their segregated neighborhood school to an integrated school across town, as is discussed here shortly.

An explanation based on educational quality would also predict that middle-class white parents would object to any classroom with a majority of low-achieving students regardless of race (such as high-poverty white students), but there are little data from national or local surveys on this precise point. Whatever the reasons for white reluctance to attend majority-black schools, these attitudes have been a major obstacle to the long-term effectiveness of a desegregation plan. Quite aside from the problems of desegregation plans that rely heavily on mandatory busing of students, any plan that creates a large proportion of majority-black (or predominantly minority) schools, whether by mandatory or voluntary means, can produce an intrinsically unstable enrollment due to white reluctance to attend such schools.

Desegregation Plans

In addition to differing on the racial composition of a school, black and white parents also differ on their attitudes and responses to specific desegregation techniques. There is overwhelming evidence, from both national and local surveys, that the most important factor in community support for a desegregation plan is whether it relies primarily on mandatory or voluntary methods.

Some of the evidence on this point is summarized in Figure 4.14, which shows national trends for the percentage of whites and nonwhites who oppose the use of busing "to achieve a better racial balance in schools," which has been asked in a consistent manner in various Gallup Polls over a twenty-year period. Between 1971 and 1982, when most mandatory desegregation plans were implemented, about three-fourths of white adults opposed the use of busing to improve racial balance, and there was no indication of any change in opposition. The 1991 Gallup Poll, however, shows a significant drop in white opposition to busing, although it is still opposed by an ample majority (62 percent). A similar drop in white opposition to busing was documented in the late 1980s in polls conducted by Louis Harris and Associates.[54]

Nonwhite and black support for busing for racial balance has always been greater than white support. In the Gallup Polls there is no clear trend for nonwhites, and the most recent survey records about 36 percent of blacks who oppose busing for racial balance. A majority of black parents support school busing for the purpose of improving racial balance.

Why white opposition to busing for racial balance decreased nationally after the late 1980s is not immediately clear. The controversy over busing has diminished at the national level in recent years, perhaps because there have been relatively few new cases of mandatory busing. In addition, the term *busing* may

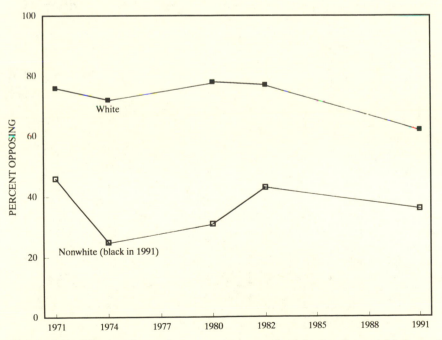

Figure 4.14. White and nonwhite opposition to school busing for racial balance (national). *Source:* Gallup polls.

have become somewhat more ambiguous during the 1980s with the increased
use of voluntary busing techniques such as magnet schools, which enjoy
widespread support (as discussed later in this chapter). It is also possible, of
course, that white parents are more accepting of all types of desegregation
plans, including mandatory busing.

This last explanation is not supported by the local surveys I have undertaken
in connection with case studies. In addition to the six school districts shown in
Figure 4.13, surveys in Yonkers (1986), Savannah (1986), and an earlier survey in
DeKalb County (1986) inquired about parents' views on various desegregation
options, including both mandatory and voluntary busing techniques. In these
local surveys the question on busing was worded somewhat differently than in
the national surveys, in most cases asking parents whether they supported or
opposed a "mandatory busing plan for improving school integration."[55]

The views of black and white parents on mandatory busing in these eight
school districts is shown in Figure 4.15. In spite of different question wordings,
different cities, and different time periods, white opposition to mandatory busing for school desegregation is substantial in all districts, and it is generally
stronger than in the national surveys. In all but one case (Norfolk), white
opposition to mandatory busing ranges from 70 to 88 percent, and the opposition remains strong even in the three surveys conducted during 1989 and 1990
(Worcester, DeKalb County, and Topeka).

Moreover, the two districts where opposition was somewhat weaker, Norfolk

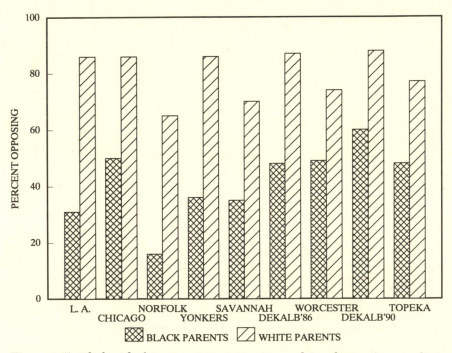

Figure 4.15. Black and white parent opposition to mandatory busing (case studies).

and Savannah, had maintained comprehensive mandatory busin[...]
riods exceeding ten years at the time of the surveys. Because[...]
districts had experienced considerable white flight during th[...]
their plans, it is reasonable to assume that many white paren[...]
mandatory busing had withdrawn from these school systems. In spite of wh[...]
flight, opposition to mandatory busing was still substantial in these two desegregated districts, even after the political controversy had waned and the policy
had become routine. Indeed, both of these districts eventually ended mandatory busing for elementary schools.

A sizeable fraction of black parents also oppose mandatory busing in many of
these school districts, and opposition is higher in most districts than in the
national surveys. Opposition to mandatory busing was particularly strong in
Chicago and in the three cities surveyed in 1989 and 1990, approaching or
exceeding 50 percent. These local surveys show no sign that black opposition to
busing is tapering off, and if anything it was stronger in the more recent surveys.
In this regard, the increase in black parent opposition to mandatory busing in
DeKalb County, from 48 percent in 1986 to 60 percent in 1990, is particularly
noteworthy.

In contrast to mandatory busing, support for voluntary desegregation techniques is strong among all groups, white and minority, in all communities that
have been surveyed. Open enrollment (majority-to-minority) policies are supported by large majorities of white, black, and Hispanic parents in the cities I
surveyed. Relatively few whites indicate they would transfer their children to a
majority-black school, given an open enrollment option, but appreciable numbers of black parents (15–20 percent on the average) say they would definitely
transfer to a regular majority-white school if free transportation was provided.
Importantly, neither black nor white parents in these surveys would object if
"considerable numbers" of opposite-race students were bused into their children's present school as part of a desegregation program.

Support is even stronger for voluntary magnet programs in these school
districts, and indeed this particular technique receives a strong endorsement
from more parents than any other technique for school desegregation. An illustration of the support for magnet schools is shown in Figure 4.16. In the five
cities where this question was asked, more than 70 percent of both white and
black families support magnet schools, and in the 1989 and 1990 surveys the
support exceeds 80 percent for both groups. In many school districts the support of both groups approaches or exceeds 90 percent. Hispanic parents also
strongly support magnet programs; in the two districts with sizeable Hispanic
populations, magnet programs were supported by 88 percent of Hispanic parents in Yonkers and 91 percent in Worcester.

Unlike open enrollment, moderate fractions of white parents indicate a
willingness to enroll their children in a desegregated magnet program, even if
that program is located in a predominantly minority school some distance away.
The willingness of white parents to enroll in magnet programs is sensitive to
distance, to the racial composition of the magnet program, and the racial composition of the school's neighborhood, and it also varies from one school system

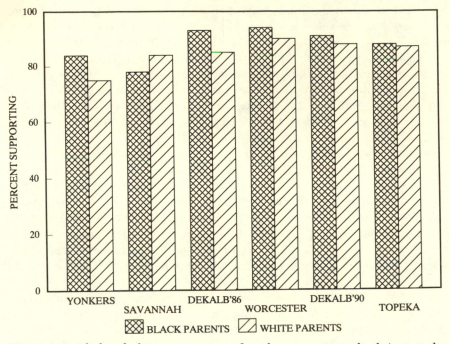

Figure 4.16. Black and white parent support for voluntary magnet schools (case studies).

to another. Specifying a magnet program whose black-white composition is maintained at fifty-fifty but is in a predominantly minority school located 30 to 45 minutes away by bus, the percent of white parents who say they would "definitely" enroll a child in the program ranges from 5 to 20 percent, with an average across districts of about 10 percent. Higher proportions of white parents, up to 30 percent, say they would enroll if the program is closer, located in a white neighborhood, or if the "probables" are also counted.

In contrast to the willingness to support and participate in magnet programs, not only do white parents oppose mandatory busing but also substantial numbers say they would leave a public school system if their children were reassigned to another school in a minority neighborhood as the result of a mandatory desegregation plan. The withdrawal from the system would occur by moving to another school district or by transferring to a private or parochial school (the latter being the most common choice).

The percentage of black and white parents who say they would "definitely" leave a school system if reassigned to a desegregated school from 30 to 45 minutes away (in a minority neighborhood for whites and in a white neighborhood for blacks) is shown in Figure 4.17 for eight local surveys. Although there is considerable variation in white parent responses, anywhere from 20 (Savannah) to more than 40 percent of white parents (Los Angeles, Chicago, and DeKalb County) say that they would *definitely* transfer to private schools or move away from the school system if their children were reassigned to another school in a

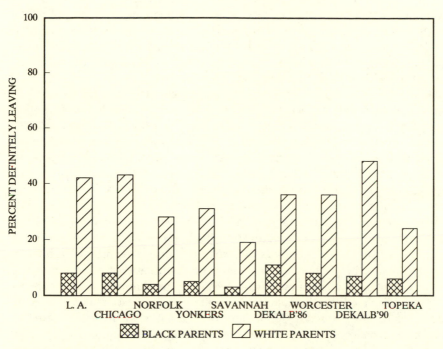

Figure 4.17. Black and white parents who would definitely leave school system if bused (case studies).

minority neighborhood as part of a desegregation program. The responses are sensitive to distance, with higher rates of white withdrawal for the longest bus rides. The percentage of whites who say they would definitely leave a school system if their children are bused is of the same order of magnitude as the no-show rates presented in Figure 4.5.

Although a significant number of black parents also oppose mandatory busing in these districts, very few indicate they would leave the public schools if their children were bused. In all but one case, fewer than 10 percent of black parents say they would definitely leave the system if this happened. Although the strength of opposition to mandatory busing may be less among black parents, other factors may contribute to a low rate of stated black withdrawal. Undoubtedly, limited financial resources would be a major barrier to black flight from the public schools.

Interpretation of Desegregation Attitudes

The attitude and opinion studies reviewed here show substantial and increasing white support for the concept of school integration in general, which includes willingness to send children to schools with up to one-half black or minority enrollments. The studies also show strong white parental support for various voluntary desegregation techniques such as magnet schools or majority-to-minority programs, and no significant opposition to increasing the minority enrollment in their children's current schools. A significant fraction of white parents would object to sending their children to predominantly minority schools, however, and a large majority remain strongly opposed to the technique of mandatory busing—or to any method that would reassign their child to a distant school in a black neighborhood.

Blacks not only strongly support the concept of school integration but also are more willing than whites to accept widely varying racial compositions of schools. Black parents are also more likely to support all types of desegregation methods, including mandatory busing, but they support voluntary programs more strongly than mandatory methods. Although a sizeable fraction of black parents would object to being reassigned to a distant desegregated school in a white neighborhood, relatively few say they would actually withdraw from the school system if that reassignment actually happened.

These patterns of attitudes are generally, but not entirely, consistent with the quantitative assessments of desegregation plans reviewed in earlier sections. For example, substantial numbers of black students participate in voluntary majority-to-minority programs, and magnet programs have attracted significant numbers of white students into schools located in predominantly black or minority neighborhoods, to the point that voluntary desegregation plans can be as effective as mandatory plans. Mandatory desegregation plans lead to greater white flight than voluntary plans, and, everything else being equal, systems with higher minority enrollments (and with more majority-black schools) have higher rates of white loss.

Nevertheless, the attitude studies here do not seem to imply the degree of white loss that actually occurs in voluntary plans, particularly in districts that are (or that become) predominantly black or minority. Whether these elevated white losses are due to the racial composition of school districts or schools (e.g., greater than 50 percent minority) or simply to increased black-white contact is not clear at this point. The former explanation would be consistent with attitude studies, but the latter would suggest that white attitudes toward desegregated schools are more positive than their behavior reflects.

Some social scientists have argued that support for the principle of racial integration is inconsistent with opposition to policies that implement such principles, including opposition to school busing (for racial balance) and affirmative action. Various theories have been formulated to explain the alleged inconsistency, including the notions of "superficial tolerance" and "symbolic racism." Others see no inconsistency in these differing attitudes, holding that support for school integration and opposition to *compulsory* integration are both consistent with American democratic values of freedom and egalitarianism. To what extent do these various theories apply to the patterns of attitudes and behaviors reviewed here?[56]

The superficial tolerance argument, best illustrated by the work of Jackman, holds that most Americans (and especially the better educated) endorse the general principles of integration and equal opportunity only for the sake of consistency with democratic values; they reject genuine attempts to implement those principles because of a greater commitment to the status quo, in which whites enjoy political dominance, greater socioeconomic status, and a minimum of contact with poor and minority populations.[57] In effect, whites oppose school busing, affirmative action, and other governmental actions to implement integration and equal opportunity because these policies threaten their advantaged positions.

The theory of symbolic racism, first articulated by Sears and others, puts opposition to busing into a broader context of evolving racial attitudes in which "old-fashioned" racism has given way to a new type of "symbolic" racism.[58] This theory of racism accepts the diminished role of traditional white prejudice and discrimination against blacks, such as beliefs in racial inferiority, support for segregation, and unequal treatment. They argue that, nevertheless, racism has not entirely gone away; it returns in a symbolic form that combines latent antiblack feelings (learned in childhood) with traditional American values embodied in the Protestant work ethic, which emphasize hard work, self-reliance, and delay of gratification.

Operationally, *symbolic racism* is defined as beliefs that blacks (or their leaders) are demanding too much or pushing too hard (or too fast) in their quest for civil rights and that blacks are receiving more special treatment than they deserve (from government, media, and others). As defined, symbolic racism has been shown to have independent effects on voting against black political candidates and on opposing such civil rights issues as school busing and affirmative action. Indeed, school busing and affirmative action can be seen as epitomes of symbolic racism, in which whites can oppose movement toward black equality by appealing to traditional American values against quotas and racial preferences.

Finally, Lipset and others contend that these attitudes are not inconsistent and that differences in support for principles versus policies arise from the weight given to equality on the one hand and individual freedom on the other.[59] They offer what might be called a "value" theory, which sees American democratic values as supporting both racial integration and equal opportunity, which in turn leads to policy positions in opposition to racial discrimination and in support of compensatory actions (especially to remedy past wrongs). Yet American democratic values also place heavy emphasis on individual freedom, and most Americans draw the line at compulsory policies such as mandatory busing and preferential treatment (or quotas) such as affirmative action because they have the potential to violate the freedom and opportunities of nonminorities. In short, the American value of equal opportunity stops short of guaranteeing equality of results.

None of these theories seems to provide a complete accounting for the attitude patterns reviewed in this section, but the value theory appears to offer a closer fit than the other two, particularly regarding support for voluntary versus mandatory desegregation methods. Looking first at attitudes only, a major problem with both the superficial tolerance and the symbolic racism theories is that they treat school busing (and implicitly the mandatory version) as synonymous with the entire process of school desegregation, failing to note the very different attitudes by both whites and blacks toward different types of desegregation methods.

If the underlying reason for opposing school busing is opposition to real change or to latent antiblack feelings, why would whites support a majority-to-minority policy that promises to turn a predominantly white school into one that is 50 percent black? Because whites are not reluctant to oppose mandatory busing or racial compositions exceeding 50 percent black, why would they voice support for voluntary magnet programs that cause major changes in the racial composition of schools? During the 1970s, one might have responded that only mandatory plans are effective, that whites know this, and that support for a voluntary plan was a "safe" response that kept the illusion of support for integration while maintaining the status quo. By at least the mid-1980s, however, there was ample information that some voluntary busing methods were quite effective for changing the racial composition of schools.

Equally significant, how do the superficial tolerance or symbolic racism theories explain the substantial fractions of blacks and Hispanics who also oppose mandatory busing techniques, with virtually no opposition expressed for voluntary techniques? It is hard to argue that minority opposition to mandatory desegregation methods is attributable to any type of latent antiminority feelings. Rather, other factors must be at work to explain why mandatory desegregation techniques are less favored by both white and minority parents. From this standpoint, the values theory advanced by Lipset seems to make the most compelling argument since by definition a mandatory busing plan clearly limits individual freedom and choice more than a voluntary one.

By contrast, the values theory does not automatically explain why the opposition to mandatory plans is so much stronger among whites than among blacks. Because there is no basis for asserting that, everything else being equal, whites value individual freedom more than blacks, something of greater value to blacks than to whites must compensate for the possible loss of freedom. One might reasonably presume greater black commitment to the *concept* of desegregated schools since desegregation is the designated remedy for the aggrieved party, but there is more.

First, because of economic constraints, many black families do not believe they have the same freedom enjoyed by most middle-class families in choosing a neighborhood and an associated school, so the perceived loss of freedom resulting from a mandatory plan may be less than that perceived by whites.[60] Second, and more important, school desegregation is much more than an abstract concept to most parents, especially those in districts designing a plan; it means decisions about attending real schools and the perceived costs or benefits of attending those schools. The critical question is how a desegregated school is actually viewed by black and white parents, a topic not usually addressed by the various cognitive and value theories previously mentioned.[61]

This question was addressed in part in a 1993 East Baton Rouge survey (reported in chapter 2) and the 1977 Los Angeles survey. In East Baton Rouge, only 28 percent of white parents said racial balance was important for the success of students in school, compared with 61 percent of black parents. In Los Angeles, most white parents believed that desegregation would neither benefit education nor improve race relations, and at the same time it would lead to more discipline problems and heightened racial tensions. Most black parents believed that desegregation would enhance the education of minority (but not white) students and would reduce racial prejudice.

Further, several local surveys asked about the reasons for opposing mandatory busing. White parents give a large number of specific reasons, most of which involve some type of personal sacrifice or inconvenience: lack of improved education, loss of choice, distance, lost time, safety, lost friends, and cost. Interestingly, the most common reason for blacks parents who opposed mandatory busing was lack of improved education. Thus mandatory busing means much more to parents than simply fulfilling the goal of integrated schools, and it also means more than simply a limitation on personal freedom. It represents a whole complex of perceived advantages and disadvantages, not only in the abstract but also in comparison to parents' perceptions of their children's current school.

Thus, one set of "rational" reasons for different attitudes toward mandatory busing by blacks and whites is different conclusions about its potential harms and benefits. Although one might argue that racial prejudice shapes white views of the harms and benefits of desegregation in the first place, the evidence presented in chapter 2 offers a legitimate and unprejudiced basis for believing that desegregation lacks benefits for white children. Even the most optimistic reviewers of desegregation benefits agree that there are no demonstrable effects on white achievement. While persons who are racially prejudiced would undoubtedly perceive greater harms arising from desegregation, unprejudiced white persons can oppose some forms of desegregation based on a legitimate viewpoint that the costs outweigh the benefits.

One study that attempted to sort out the effects of traditional prejudice, symbolic racism, and perceived costs and benefits was by McClendon.[62] In a survey of white adults in Akron, he employed a structural equation model to find that expected costs (safety, education, race relations) were strongly related to opposition to both two-way and one-way busing. Neither traditional prejudice nor symbolic racism had *direct* effects on busing attitudes, although they did have direct effects on perceived costs and hence indirect effects on busing attitudes. This correlational study did not attempt to estimate the proportion of whites opposed to busing who felt that way because of costs and not because of racial prejudice.

These survey results offer strong support for a personal cost-benefit model of community support for school desegregation techniques.[63] Most white parents see mandatory busing as entailing significant personal costs or inconvenience and at the same time offering few benefits for their children. Many black parents, by contrast, believe mandatory busing will produce significant educational and social benefits for their children, thereby justifying some personal costs and sacrifices. Given these contrasting beliefs and perceptions, then, it is not surprising that white parents are more strongly opposed to mandatory busing than most black parents.

This is not to say that none of the opposition to mandatory busing is racially motivated. White support for the principle of school desegregation is strong, but it is not universal. In the local surveys, a small but nontrivial minority of white parents object to fifty-fifty schools (usually 10–15 percent, depending on the district), and about the same proportion oppose voluntary busing of minority children into their current school. Given some degree of hiding true feelings about attending desegregated schools, old-fashioned racism might be applied to 20–25 percent of white respondents in these surveys who would object to attending any school with more than a token number of black students.

What about whites who sincerely support desegregated schools up to fifty-fifty ratios, but who object to ratios over fifty-fifty? It is possible to define racism to apply to such attitudes, but it would be a very different form of racism than that implied by traditional definitions. Whites who support and willingly send their children to schools that are half white and half minority—but who would avoid a predominantly minority school—may well be concerned about loss of control, being in minority status, or lower standards of instruction (due to achievement differences). Whether or not these concerns are based on valid information, it is hard to justify portraying this white parent as an example of classical racial bigotry.

Desegregation and Resegregation

The results of desegregation remedies yield a mixed picture at best. On one hand, desegregation policies, especially those initiated by court actions, have had a significant impact on the distribution of students among the public schools, and there is more racial balance and more interracial exposure than there would have been without any court interventions. On the other hand, the level of desegregation never reached the degree envisioned by many desegregation advocates, and it is now declining, according to one important indicator. Given the enrollment trends in larger public school systems, it is unlikely to improve by any significant degree in the near future and is more likely to get worse, given the current state of desegregation law. Moreover, even the moderate headway in desegregation during the 1970s has not been without some serious costs.

If school desegregation is defined as racial balance, then the desegregation era has had considerable impact on the segregation of black students. Desegregation has brought more uniformity to the racial composition of individual schools, and in larger school districts racial imbalance has been reduced significantly. In districts that have formal desegregation plans, racial imbalance has been reduced by nearly half, according to the index of dissimilarity, most of this occurring by 1980. Moreover, desegregation plans have led to a reduction in the percent of black students in predominantly minority schools.

A less optimistic picture emerges, however, when other desegregation measures are considered. According to a traditional definition of segregation, in which a segregated school has a majority of nonwhite students, the impact of desegregation is considerably diminished. The percentage of black students in majority nonwhite schools has fallen by only 14 points, from 77 to 63, which means that most black students still attend segregated schools by this definition.

More important, less progress has been made on the important criterion of interracial exposure. In larger school systems, where most minority students attend school, the average percentage of whites in schools attended by black students increased by 11 points between 1968 and 1972, but it then decreased by 7 points between 1972 and 1989, ending the period at 47—just 4 points higher than where it started. Thus the average black student still sits in classrooms that are majority nonwhite. The interracial exposure between whites and Hispanics in larger school systems has actually decreased during the entire period, but Hispanic-white exposure has always been high relative to white enrollment, and Hispanics enjoy somewhat higher exposure rates than black students.

The reason for the meager improvement in black exposure and for the decrease in Hispanic exposure is the very significant loss of white enrollment in larger school districts. As desegregation plans have improved the racial distribution of students, the simultaneous declines in white enrollments have reduced the potential for interracial contact. Some of this loss is due to demographic forces that would have occurred in the absence of the desegregation movement; indeed, cities like New York, Chicago, and Philadelphia have had very little change in racial balance but have nonetheless lost substantial white enrollment. Still, desegregation in both its mandatory and voluntary forms has accelerated the loss of whites, although the effects are larger for mandatory plans.

Because of the white flight problem, mandatory busing plans have been no more successful than voluntary plans in attaining long-term racial balance or contact, even though "on paper" they would appear to be so. The racial balance and interracial exposure that a mandatory plan could produce in theory—if everyone stayed in the system and went to their assigned school—are undermined by the white flight and demographic changes set in motion by reassigning children to schools they would not otherwise choose.

Survey studies of parental views of desegregation and responses to desegregation plans explain much of the white flight problem. Most white parents—and some minority parents—are opposed to mandatory busing for the simple reason that it entails personal costs without commensurate benefits. Minority parents, particularly black parents, are more supportive of mandatory busing because the personal cost is justified by its perceived educational and social benefits. Given these various viewpoints, often strongly held, the onset of a mandatory busing program is usually accompanied by significant white flight. White losses can take the form of transfers to private schools, moves to an adjacent school system, or failure to replace white families who move for nonbusing reasons.

The surveys also show that voluntary desegregation programs, such as magnet programs or general school choice options, are endorsed by parents of all races. The support for voluntary desegregation methods in these special studies might be seen as the synthesis of two independent ideological strains documented by many national surveys: Most parents support the goal of school desegregation, but most also support the concept of school choice. Given a conflict between the two objectives, most white parents come down on the side of choice, but most minority parents—many of whom cannot exercise school choice—come down on the side of desegregation.

Although mandatory busing plans may produce more white flight in the short run, voluntary desegregation plans do not appear to solve the white loss problem. Over the past twenty years, most larger school systems with voluntary plans have continued to lose white students and generally end up resembling systems with mandatory plans: similar levels of interracial exposure *and* a predominantly minority enrollment. Obviously, demographic factors are also at work in these cities, but one cannot eliminate the possibility that voluntary desegregation plans have also contributed to this resegregation process.

The survey studies offer at least one explanation of how voluntary plans can lead to slower but nonetheless significant long-term white flight. While most white parents endorse school desegregation and support voluntary desegregation methods, they make clear distinctions between the racial compositions they are willing to accept in a desegregated school. A significant fraction of white parents object to sending their children to a school that is majority black, and a much smaller fraction objects to a fifty-fifty balance. All larger school districts experience some demographic changes that lower their percentage of white enrollment and move them closer to fifty-fifty or to majority black enrollments, and this white loss may be accelerated to some extent by the white flight of persons who object to any type of desegregation.

As voluntary plans then strive to attain racial mixes in schools that approximate the school system composition, it is increasingly likely that more formerly white schools reach and exceed racial compositions unacceptable to many white parents. When these parents leave, white enrollment falls even more, thereby changing the racial balance standard, which leads to more voluntary busing and increased minority concentrations in formerly white schools. This process can become a vicious circle of white loss, changed standards, increased voluntary busing, and more schools with majority nonwhite enrollments.

Although the final answer is not in on the resegregation question, the original Coleman thesis—that extensive desegregation of any type leads to white flight and increasing segregation between central cities and their suburbs—may well be correct. If so, to achieve both increased desegregation and enrollment stability in the future will be a great challenge.

In the meantime, a fair question is whether the enormous controversy and disruption caused by the more intrusive mandatory desegregation plans are worth the very modest gains in interracial exposure actually realized. This question becomes all the more important when coupled with the limited educational and social benefits of desegregation, as documented in chapter 2. This inquiry now turns to these broader implications of desegregation policy.

5

The Future of Desegregation and Choice

Like most issues stimulated by the civil rights movement over the past four decades, the tangled web of policy questions associated with school desegregation defies easy resolution. The debate over desegregation policy has touched upon many aspects and levels of human society, including values, law, education, and social theory; therefore, arriving a succinct set of policy conclusions, especially one accompanied by substantial consensus, is unrealistic. The debate cannot and should not be reduced simply to a matter of law, to ideological differences, or to disagreements over social science theories. Any attempt to oversimplify the desegregation issue does injustice to those with the greatest stake in its outcome, namely, the students, parents, and educators who reap its rewards and shoulder its costs.

Adding to this complexity is the fact that desegregation issues have shifted so much over time that the important policy questions differ from one decade to the next. During the 1950s, the legal and value debate was over compulsory segregation, and social theorists debated whether separate schools were harmful or beneficial for children. During the 1970s, the legal and value debate shifted to compulsory desegregation and whether the benefits of mandatory busing justified its deep divisiveness and its unintended consequences.

During the 1990s the debate has shifted once again, this time in several directions. The federal courts struggle with the conditions under which to grant unitary status (and dismissal) to school districts with court-ordered desegregation plans. Surprisingly, considering the great controversy in the 1970s, school boards in the 1990s debate whether to seek unitary status or, if not under court order, to adopt desegregation plans on their own. Civil rights groups are back in court, not only to oppose unitary status but also to demand even broader remedies than those granted during the 1970s. They have requested metropolitan remedies between cities and suburbs, and they have petitioned for racial parity in classrooms, discipline rates, and even academic achievement.

Ironically, some of these latest court challenges have come full circle, invoking the psychological harm thesis of *Brown* that most legal scholars dismissed as irrelevant to the law. These new petitions reassert that racial differences in academic achievement or in disciplinary problems are vestiges of the original dual school system—gone now for over twenty years in most school systems—and must be remedied by further court relief.

Finally, before mandatory busing has been put to rest, a new movement has arisen to give parents greater choice in selecting schools, both within and between school districts, and between public and private schools using state-financed vouchers. The choice movement has no direct relationship to the desegregation movement, but it has definite implications for desegregation policy. Both movements have the same end, which is to improve the quality of American education, but they see different problems in education, and they clash in their methods for fixing those problems.

Apart from legal considerations, the desegregation movement sees the main problem as low achievement by minorities and the poor, which is caused by a combination of racial isolation and inadequate resources and which can be solved only by increasing racial balance first and allocating more resources second. The choice movement sees American education as suffering from a decline in standards, stagnation in learning, and insular bureaucracies that spend too much money for too little gain; their solution is to increase choice, especially between public and private schools, in which free market competition will weaken bureaucratic control and revitalize public school systems. They clash in methods because maximizing choice generally means ignoring race and abandoning traditional school assignment policies, while maximizing racial balance means restricting choices.

The implication of the choice movement is but one facet of the ongoing debate over desegregation policies. Many other facets affect the future of desegregation and choice. What should be the priority of desegregation goals in relation to other school goals? How much desegregation is necessary or desirable? What are the legal mandates and requirements for initiating or terminating a desegregation plan? What type of desegregation plan is most effective? What should the relationship be, if any, between desegregation and schools of choice? Are they completely incompatible, or might there be a common ground that takes advantage of their most desirable features? These sorts of questions are asked and debated in many different forums. They are debated by educators and parents in many school districts, with or without desegregation plans; by the courts, where desegregation litigation is ongoing; by state governments, where school choice legislation is pending; and by social scientists, who still disagree about the relative costs and benefits of desegregation and choice policies.

No two experts in desegregation policy or law have the same answers to these questions; arriving at a consensus is hampered by differing interpretations of the law and the relevant social science evidence. Nonetheless, clarifications in the law coupled with improved knowledge about desegregation and its effects offer hope for a more reasoned and practical basis for school desegregation and choice polices. Drawing on the legal principles, social science research, and case materials discussed in earlier chapters, this chapter attempts to answer some of these questions in light of this knowledge and experience.

The questions and answers about desegregation policy depend on whether a school district is under a court order or government mandate of some type. For this reason, the discussion of current legal and educational issues is organized according to school systems with and without government-mandated deseg-regation plans. A separate section takes up the implications of school choice for the desegregation movement.

Debates over desegregation policy are all too often dominated by ideological passions or purely legal theories that sometimes obscure the most critical issue for all parties, namely, how to provide, maintain, and enhance high-quality education for all members of society. Any law, court decision, or policy on school desegregation ultimately is judged by its contribution to or interference with this priority. The concluding section looks at the future of desegregation and choice policy to suggest ways in which they can best serve the broader goals of high-quality education.

Systems with Desegregation Plans

The national survey data presented in chapter 4 indicated that many hundreds of school systems maintain formal desegregation plans, and the likelihood of having a plan is quite high in larger districts with appreciable fractions of minority students. For school systems that currently have formal desegregation plans, the national survey indicated that about half were mandated by court orders or other governmental agencies.

For most school systems with current government-mandated desegregation plans, the educational and social benefits of school desegregation are generally subservient to the issues of student and faculty assignment and to the allocation of school resources. Under current federal law, a desegregation plan must remedy unconstitutional segregation, and the primary legal question is whether a desegregation plan is effective in eliminating segregation and its vestiges. For most courts, this usually means a plan that rectifies the so-called *Green* factors: racially balancing schools and staff, equalizing resources, and eliminating dis-crimination in other areas such as transportation and extracurricular activities. In some cases, specific curriculum changes or improvements are ordered, but until recently equality in educational outcomes has not been an issue.

Several important policy questions face school systems under a court order. Perhaps the most important concerns the issue of unitary status. When and under what conditions should a district seek a declaration of unitary status, which means it has fully satisfied a valid court-ordered remedy and can be freed from court supervision? A second question arises for those districts that decide, for any reason, not to seek unitary status. Can a desegregation plan be changed, particularly if it is no longer providing effective desegregation or otherwise not meeting educational needs? Finally, a number of school systems are facing new challenges by plaintiffs who are demanding further remedies in student assign-ment, classroom racial balance, academic programs, and even reduction of the achievement gap between white and minority students.

The Question of Unitary Status

A decision to seek unitary status is not automatic for most school boards, even after many years of being under a court order. Being free from federal court supervision would seem to have little or no down side, being somewhat analogous to a person being freed from prison. Given the politics of school desegregation, however, being under a court order has certain advantages, and for some school boards the advantages of staying under court supervision outweigh the advantages of being unitary. I have consulted with a number of school systems that have chosen not to seek unitary status, even after long-term compliance with a desegregation plan.[1]

The advantages of unitary status are obvious to some school boards. Until a court-supervised school system is declared unitary, a school board is usually obliged to obtain approval from the plaintiffs (typically the NAACP or the Department of Justice) and from the court for any policy or action that affects any aspect of a desegregation plan. These actions can include such common decisions as opening new schools, closing old ones, changing attendance zones, adding magnet programs, changing student transfer or teacher assignment policies, or even modifying the curriculum. In some cases, obtaining court approval is routine, but if a change is opposed by plaintiffs, the decision cannot be implemented without the delays and costs of a court hearing and the risk that it will not be approved. Many school boards and school administrators object to the loss of authority and the inefficiency of having to go to court to resolve such commonplace policy decisions.

If declared unitary, a former dual school system is like any other school system, and no school policy or action can be successfully challenged in court without proving segregative effects and discriminatory purpose on the part of the school board. This includes changing or abandoning a court-ordered desegregation plan, if the purpose in doing so can be defended on legitimate education or desegregation grounds. Indeed, changing or discarding a desegregation plan may be one of the main reasons for seeking unitary status.

For these reasons, many school systems have sought or are seeking unitary status, and this activity increased after the important Supreme Court decisions in *Dowell* (Oklahoma City) and *Pitts* (DeKalb County). A number of school systems have been granted unitary status, including Norfolk, Virgina; Austin and Dallas, Texas; Oklahoma City; DeKalb County, Columbus–Muskogee County, and Savannah–Chatham County, Georgia; and Columbus, Ohio. Some districts (e.g., Wilmington–New Castle County, Delaware; St. Louis) have petitioned for unitary status but the cases have not yet been decided, and other districts (Denver; Jacksonville–Duval County, Florida; Topeka, Kansas) had their petitions denied. Denver is maintaining its original desegregation plan, and both Duval County and Topeka had to adopt new or modified desegregation plans to improve desegregation.

The advantage of remaining under court supervision may be less obvious to the outside observer. It is not simply the desire to maintain a desegregation plan, which can be done by a school board without a court order. In some cases, school boards want to maintain strong desegregation policies, including mandatory busing, which are controversial in most communities. By remaining under court supervision, a school board can be protected from community activists who want to stop the plan, on the grounds that the plan is required by the court and the board has no discretion over it. In other cases, legal counsel may advise a school board that the district court is unlikely to grant unitary status, for a variety of reasons, and that the best course is continued compliance with a desegregation plan.

Another advantage of remaining under a court order, in the eyes of some school board members and administrators, is to maintain various staffing policies that might be difficult to enforce in the absence of court supervision, especially the *Singleton* rule, which requires racially balanced staff at each school. In some school systems there are strong pressures from the community—often from black leadership—to adopt the "role model" approach for staff assignment, in which teachers and principals are assigned disproportionately to match the predominant race of a school. In such cases the court order can be invoked to justify maintenance of the *Singleton* rule for racially balanced staffs.

An increasingly common reason for not seeking unitary status has to do with funding issues. There are many state and federal programs now that offer financial assistance to school systems with desegregation plans, and in some cases the funding requires or gives priority to school systems under court orders. Loss of court supervision might mean a loss of desegregation funds, such as magnet school support, thereby restricting the type and scope of a desegregation program.

Many federal district judges are willing to accept a status quo approach, leaving it up to the parties to seek unitary status or further relief. Others have been unwilling to grant unitary status, even after a desegregation plan has been in effect for more than ten years. In view of the new Supreme Court decisions on unitary status, continued supervision seems contrary to the spirit of the law if it is primarily for purposes unrelated to the original remedial order, such as obtaining more funds or making it easier to maintain unpopular policies. Whether federal courts will encourage unitary hearings even when plaintiffs or defendants are happy with the status quo remains to be seen.

Obtaining Unitary Status

A unitary status hearing is normally requested by a school board. At the hearing, the board must prove several things, according to the most recent Supreme Court opinions: that it has implemented a desegregation plan in good faith, that the plan was effective in eliminating all vestiges of segregation insofar as "practicable," and that no new constitutional violations have taken place.

Unless a lower court orders otherwise, there is no required length of time that a plan be maintained, although a minimum of three years is a good rule of thumb. More important, a school district is not responsible for overcoming racial imbalance due strictly to demographic and other external forces once a plan has been implemented. The critical consideration is whether the plan was effective in eliminating those conditions arising from the prior dual school system, such as designated one-race schools, unequal resources, imbalanced faculty, and so forth.

Determining good faith compliance may be the easiest of the three requirements. It generally means that the school board and administration implemented the original plan promptly and with full school board support, with no attempts to undermine the plan, and with no major changes to the plan unless approved by the court.

Evaluating the vestiges of a former dual school system is the most complex of the three criteria, and here plaintiffs and school boards are most likely to disagree. The vestiges have to be evaluated with regard to each of the so-called *Green* factors: student assignment, faculty and staff assignment, extracurricular activities, equality of facilities and programs, and equal burdens in transportation. Some court orders include remedial provisions in areas other than the six *Green* factors, and of course these aspects of a plan must also be evaluated. Generally speaking, the first three factors generate the most disagreement about vestiges, with student assignment the most contentious. One of the most important clarifications of Supreme Court decisions in *Pitts* is that a school system can be declared unitary with respect to one of the *Green* factors, such as student assignment, but not in others, so that court supervision can be lifted one factor at a time.

Although there is no accepted set of rules for determining vestiges, several conditions may well be considered vestiges by a federal court: (1) former black or white segregated schools that never had significant attendance by the opposite race, unless justified by geographic location, demographic changes, or other objective factors; (2) a tendency for schools with a majority of one race to have the same-race principal over long periods of time; (3) a school faculty racial composition that consistently deviates by more than 10 or 15 percentage points from the total faculty composition; and (4) deficient school programs or resources (such as lower per-pupil expenditures or larger class sizes) in predominantly minority schools.

If a formerly black or white school attained some reasonable degree of racial balance at some point in time, however, and the school later became racially identifiable (with either the same or a different race), such a school would not necessarily be a vestige. The question then becomes whether the racial change was due to school board actions or to demographic factors. If the racial change can be attributed to demographic shifts, then the Supreme Court rules in *Pitts* indicate that it should not be considered a vestige. It is often necessary to conduct analyses of demographic changes and the effects of school boundary changes in order to arrive at a defensible conclusion.

It is increasingly likely that plaintiffs will raise additional conditions as vestiges of the former dual school system, including racial imbalance in classrooms, unequal representation in gifted and talented or special education programs, racial differences in rates of disciplinary actions, and even racial differences in academic outcomes such as dropout rates and achievement test scores. One or more of these issues have been raised by plaintiffs in unitary or new remedial proceedings in San Jose, California; Topeka, Kansas; Wilmington–New Castle County, Delaware; and Yonkers, New York. The original remedial orders rarely include provisions dealing with these issues, other than occasional reporting requirements in which such differences may be illustrated.

How these new vestige issues will be resolved in future litigation is not immediately clear. In some cases, school boards have agreed to consent decrees in lieu of a unitary hearing, in which they have agreed to continue a desegregation plan for a limited period of time and to take additional steps to deal with one or more of these extra-*Green* conditions.[2] Relatively few court decisions have held a school system responsible for eliminating these disparities, but one notable exception is a 1993 decision in the Yonkers case. The federal district court in Yonkers may well be the first court in the nation to declare that unequal achievement test scores reflect vestiges of the prior segregated school system.[3]

Changing a Desegregation Plan

For school systems that cannot or do not want to be declared unitary, a common question is whether a desegregation plan can or should be changed. Sometimes this issue is raised by plaintiffs who are seeking further relief, and in other cases it is raised by a school board that is dissatisfied with a particular type of desegregation plan. In larger school systems that have implemented a mandatory busing plan that remains controversial and that has caused significant white flight, the question may come up because the original plan is no longer providing effective desegregation.

In some cases, a school system might want to change the definition of desegregation. In earlier years, some very narrow definitions of racial balance were approved by a court, including plus or minus 5 or 10 percentage points from the system average, which proved very hard to maintain without repeated changes of school attendance boundaries. More recently, federal courts have approved racial balance ranges with plus or minus 20-point deviations, definitions that offer far greater flexibility and fewer disruptions in student assignment. The basis for a broader definition of desegregation is found in Supreme Court doctrine, where there is no requirement to maintain a narrow racial balance standard "in perpetuity."

A more common motivation for changing a desegregation plan is to convert a mandatory busing plan to a voluntary plan with magnet schools. To change from a mandatory to a voluntary plan while under a court order, a school system has to show that a voluntary plan will be at least as effective as the mandatory plan, which usually means conducting analyses of white flight, conducting surveys to estimate the rates of future participation in various types of desegregation plans, and using this information to compare the effectiveness of alternative plans. Such surveys and analyses have now been carried out in a number of school systems, as described in chapter 4. Given the national findings concerning the effectiveness of mandatory versus voluntary programs, it should be possible to convince a court that a comprehensive voluntary plan is at least as effective as a mandatory plan in producing long-term desegregation.

A good example of a conversion from a mandatory pairing plan to a voluntary magnet plan occurred in the Savannah school system, which enrolls about 35,000 students and is about 60 percent minority. The new plan, which was approved by a district court in 1988 and upheld by the Eleventh Circuit Court of Appeals, defined a desegregated school as one meeting a plus or minus 20 percent variance for racial balance. New attendance zones were drawn on a contiguous, geographic (or neighborhood) basis, and two new schools were constructed in predominantly black areas of the city. Surveys showed that most schools remaining predominantly black after rezoning could be desegregated with magnet programs, and most predominantly white schools could be desegregated with a majority-to-minority transfer program. After five years of compliance, the plan met most of its objectives, and a petition for unitary status was filed in 1993. After the new voluntary plan had been in operation for two years, the first large school bond measure was passed by the electorate after many years of bond issue failures. Savannah was granted unitary status by the district court in 1994.

Many other school systems have changed desegregation plans or are in the process of seeking a change, including East Baton Rouge Parish, Louisiana; Darlington County, South Carolina; Polk County, Florida; Charlotte–Mecklenburg, North Carolina; Boston; and Seattle. In most of these cases, the changes are designed to have more neighborhood schools and to increase school choice, particularly by the use of magnet programs. Some of these systems, such as Boston and Seattle, have changed from mandatory busing plans to controlled choice plans. Although controlled choice plans do increase choice for many parents, they still maintain mandatory school reassignment for some parents in order to meet racial balance goals and can still cause white and middle-class flight. Unfortunately, by the time Boston and Seattle adopted controlled choice plans, they had already lost a significant fraction of their white enrollment, and the controlled choice plans have had little impact on improving desegregation in those cities.

Systems without Desegregation Plans

As shown in chapter 4, most of the approximately 15,000 public school systems in the United States do not have formal desegregation plans. The most important reasons are size and racial composition. Of the approximately 13,500 systems with enrollments under 5,000, most have only one or two schools at each grade level, and the issue of desegregation or racial balance between schools simply does not arise. Likewise, the issue of desegregation is not problematic in many thousands of school systems that are predominantly of one race, being over 90 percent white, black, or Hispanic. Even in school systems with more than 5,000 students, about 60 percent have never had a formal desegregation plan.

For those districts without desegregation plans or with plans not required by a court or governmental agency, the desegregation policy issues are different but no less difficult. Generally, three categories of desegregation policy questions arise and are debated by school boards and other interested parties. What types of school policies or actions can trigger a government-ordered desegregation plan? Assuming no legal obligation, what are the benefits and costs of having a desegregation plan? If a school board wants a plan, what kind of plan is most effective?

The Issue of Liability

Given the complex history and current status of desegregation law, a detailed forecast of those policies and actions that can violate the Constitution or various federal and state civil rights laws is impossible to offer. However, some guidelines follow about those conditions that, under current federal law, might lead to a violation of the Fourteenth Amendment or the federal Civil Rights Act.

According to current constitutional law in school desegregation cases, a violation of the federal Fourteenth Amendment occurs whenever a school policy or action (1) has a significant segregative effect and (2) is designed with a racially discriminatory motive—to racially segregate one or more aspects of a school system—rather than a legitimate educational purpose. Additionally, Title VI of the Civil Rights Act of 1964 prohibits any type of racial discrimination in a school system that receives federal funds, and later amendments require that any rules promulgated under Title VI must be applied uniformly to schools regardless of the cause of segregation (de jure or de facto).

How do these general principles translate into specific conditions that violate the Constitution or the Civil Rights Act? It is relatively easy to determine segregative effects, usually defined as racial imbalance in school enrollment or in faculty assignments or unequal resources at schools with differing racial compositions. Proving that these imbalances or inequalities were created for discriminatory or segregative purposes is much harder. Some of the specific policies or actions that are likely to attract scrutiny and that have often led either to constitutional violations or to formal allegations under the Civil Rights Act are as follows:

1. Opening new schools or changing school attendance boundaries that significantly increase racial imbalance, even though feasible alternatives exist that would either lessen imbalance or have no adverse effect
2. Permissive transfer policies that increase racial imbalance by allowing student transfers from one school to another without regard to racial impact (e.g., freedom of choice)
3. Assignment of faculty at individual schools so that racial imbalance is substantially greater than plus or minus ten or fifteen percent from the faculty total or consistent assignment of principals whose race matches the predominant race in a school

4. Consistently unequal distribution of resources or programs (expenditures, class sizes, and curriculum) among schools of differing racial compositions

This list is not necessarily exhaustive, and none of these conditions automatically signifies a violation of the law. They are simply the kinds of conditions that are most likely to bring federal lawsuits or investigations by the Office of Civil Rights (OCR) and that would trigger an obligation by the school system to offer educational or other reasonable rationales for such policies or practices.

According to current Supreme Court doctrines and regulations for enforcing Title VI of the Civil Rights Act, one of the conditions that should *not* trigger a federal lawsuit or an OCR investigation is the mere existence of racially imbalanced enrollments. If racial imbalance arises from demographic forces or housing patterns, absent clear influence by school board policies or actions, then a school board is not obligated to eliminate the imbalance under federal law. Complaints may be initiated, but a school board should prevail unless the challenger can prove that the racial imbalance is the direct product of school board policies or actions, excluding the maintenance of a neighborhood school policy.

A new movement has generated substantial controversy in some predominantly minority school systems, such as Baltimore, Detroit, and Milwaukee, about school programs designed to serve black males only; various educational benefits not available in regular programs are claimed. Although most courts might see a legitimate educational purpose for a program that stresses particular racial or cultural content, such programs are unlikely to pass current constitutional muster if they actually exclude female and white students. The only way a black-only program might meet the "compelling government interest" standard for justifying racial classifications is to present very convincing evidence showing that the presence of females or white males is deleterious to black male achievement.[4] These proposals and programs, however, are too recent to have generated definitive federal court decisions.

In addition to federal laws, a number of states have laws dealing with racial balance or racial isolation, some of which call for specific racial balance policies (regardless of the causes of imbalance); some states make various types of funds contingent upon a racial balance plan. States with such laws include Connecticut, Massachusetts, Michigan, and Washington. California had such a law until 1991, when it expired because of a sunset provision. Nonetheless, California still spends more money than any other state in support of local desegregation plans, about $470 million in 1990–1991, and even though there is no longer a law, the state still maintains a desegregation budget.

Should a Desegregation Plan Be Adopted?

Assuming that a school system is not under a current government mandate for desegregation and that it has done nothing to cause racial imbalance in its schools, then the question of whether to adopt a specific desegregation plan is no different than any other type of educational policy question. A school board should consider the advantages and disadvantages of adopting a desegregation plan or, more specifically, compare its benefits to its costs and then make decisions about whether to have a desegregation plan and what type of plan to adopt. Clearly, the decision to adopt a desegregation plan usually depends on the type of plan adopted, because the type of plan influences budget costs and, more important, community support or opposition.

School board and community debates over whether to adopt a desegregation plan usually center around some version of the harm and benefit thesis as discussed in chapter 2. Because many educators, civil rights groups, and social scientists endorse this thesis, usually some school board members support a desegregation policy because of its presumed benefits. Other board members may be more skeptical about the harm and benefit thesis but support a plan nonetheless because of political pressures or the fear of being accused of opposing minority interests. School board members who oppose desegregation plans—and particularly a mandatory busing plan—are usually skeptical about its benefits and believe that any benefits are outweighed by its costs. Costs include both monetary and nonmonetary considerations, such as community controversy or the loss of middle-class or white enrollment. Obviously, the degree to which a school board member wants a desegregation plan depends on the perceived trade-off between its benefits and its costs.

The evidence on the educational benefits of school desegregation, as reviewed in chapter 2, is mixed at best; few studies that show consistent, across-the-board educational and social benefits for most minority students attending desegregated schools. A number of studies show educational benefits for *some* minority students (usually not white students), particularly those who volunteer for a desegregation program and who remain in it for a number of years. Even these benefits are not unique to desegregated schools, and many minority students can attain equally successful educational outcomes while attending segregated schools.

Given the modest and variable educational benefits attributable to desegregated schools, the issue of costs would appear to deserve more attention by school boards than it often receives. In view of the serious budgetary constraints faced by most states and school boards today, careful assessment must be made of all discretionary educational programs as to their potential contribution to learning and educational attainment. Desegregation programs can be costly, usually in terms of transportation costs and the provision of magnet schools. Annual desegregation costs on the order of $1,000 per desegregated student are not unusual, particularly when a plan includes magnet schools, which is substantial considering that the national average cost of public schooling is about $4,500 per student. This amount of money per student is considerable in the absence of clear educational benefits.

Nonmonetary costs arise in the form of public opposition or controversy and the loss of middle-class or white families, depending on the type of plan implemented. Public opposition and controversy can lead to disruption of the learning process, reduced parental involvement, and lack of community support, all of which can have deleterious effects on the education process. Public opposition to a desegregation plan can also have adverse financial impacts, particularly when a school bond is voted down by an electorate upset with desegregation policies.

If the public opposition is strong enough, a desegregation plan can lead to substantial white and middle-class flight, especially in urban school systems, which often exacerbates preexisting demographic trends. White flight makes it even harder to attain racial balance goals; indeed, in some cases it has led to predominantly minority school systems. White flight can occur in voluntary plans as well as mandatory busing plans, however, so this problem is not necessarily eliminated by adopting a voluntary desegregation plan.

A discussion of benefits and costs is routine for most educational policy debates. Unfortunately, the ideological commitments of some advocacy groups has tended to discourage a dispassionate assessment of desegregation policy; those who question the benefits of desegregation are often accused of harboring racist attitudes or, at best, as serving the interests of racism. In this type of climate, many school board members who are skeptical of the benefit thesis or who are concerned about budget costs may not express their concerns.

Choosing a Desegregation Plan

Assuming that a school board wants a desegregation plan, one way to maximize the benefits and minimize the costs is to take advantage of the evidence on the harm and benefit thesis and on the effectiveness of different types of desegregation programs. This body of knowledge and experience, taken as a whole, suggests some reasonable approaches to desegregation plans that may well satisfy both proponents and skeptics of school desegregation policies.

The approach taken here proceeds on certain conclusions derived from my research and experience in connection with actual desegregation plans. These premises can be expressed as a set of design principles for a desegregation plan.

Type of plan. To the extent that desegregated schools have significant educational benefits, the benefits have been documented primarily for voluntary programs in which parents or students can choose between a neighborhood (geographic) school or a specific desegregated school program; they can choose to return to their neighborhood school if they are not satisfied with the desegregation program for whatever reason.

Racial Composition. No specific school racial composition has been shown to produce the greatest educational benefit, although an earlier social theory suggested that there be at least 50 percent white or middle-class students in a given school. Aside from educational benefits, a school whose racial composition exceeds 50 percent minority tends to be unstable and can generate white and middle-class flight from or avoidance of that school.

Mandatory busing. Whatever the educational benefits of desegregation, mandatory busing to nonneighborhood schools (whether from pairing, noncontiguous zoning, or controlled choice) is highly controversial and often contributes to loss of white or middle-class populations. Moreover, mandatory busing plans over the long run have proven no more effective than comprehensive voluntary plans in promoting interracial contact.

Rezoning. Changes to regular geographic-based attendance zones, whether arising from capacity needs, the opening of new schools, or the closing of old schools, are normal operating procedures for all school systems and, where possible, should be designed in a way that promotes racial balance. Geographic rezoning to increase racial balance is the most cost-effective desegregation technique, although it can also be controversial because it always produces some mandatory reassignments.

Majority-to-minority transfers. Other than some type of mandatory assignment, the most cost-effective voluntary method for improving racial balance at predominantly white schools is the majority-to-minority program, which encourages students to transfer from a school where their race is a majority to a school where their race is a minority. Providing transportation makes this program more effective (at a higher cost) and is required in most court-ordered plans, but where not mandated it becomes a school board decision based on available resources. One way to minimize cost here is to subsidize transportation only for transfers to schools that need M-to-M transfers to attain desegregation.

Magnet schools. Other than mandatory assignment, the only effective way to attract sizable numbers of white students to predominantly minority schools is to install magnet programs that offer specialized curriculum or instructional styles not available in regular neighborhood schools. Ideally, a magnet school should be dedicated so that all students attend the magnet school on a voluntary basis; no students would be assigned. If capacity limitations prevent this, then it should be a program-within-a-school. In both cases, racial balance in magnet schools or classes should be maintained at no less than 50 percent white to minimize white avoidance. Subsidized transportation is usually required to maximize participation rates. Magnet schools are generally more costly than regular schools because of special faculty, equipment, and supplies.

These guidelines can be used to design a desegregation plan that improves racial balance and provides increased desegregation opportunities with a minimum of adverse consequences. The only limitation is the scope of a plan and its cost. Generally speaking, the most costly aspect of a voluntary desegregation plan is magnet schools, and available resources may limit the number of magnet schools unless funds can be attained from state or federal programs. Several states fund magnet programs, and a fairly large federal program, the Magnet School Assistance Program (MSAP), supports magnet schools in about sixty school systems.

In the absence of a legal mandate, a rigid definition of racial balance for all schools does not have to be adopted; the goal of a desegregation plan can be as simple as "improving" racial balance where possible, subject to available resources. Also, all schools in a district do not have to be part of a plan; a desegregation plan can be targeted for a smaller number of schools in which desegregation might be most beneficial and feasible.

There might be some argument against limiting magnet programs to certain schools on the grounds that not all students have access to a specialized program. Survey studies show, however, that most parents strongly support the magnet concept, but fewer than half want to leave their current neighborhood school to attend a magnet. A magnet program needs to be designed around a realistic estimate of magnet demand, a lesson learned too late in Kansas City, where almost all schools were converted to magnets at a great cost to the state of Missouri. Most of these magnet schools are failing to attract an integrated student body, simply because the number of schools far exceeds the demand of white students.

If a definition of racial balance is adopted, it should be as broad as possible, such as plus or minus 20 or 25 percentage points from the overall racial composition. Some schools might be excluded from a racial balance goal for reasons of distance or geography. In other cases, an absolute definition might be more appropriate, such as a minimum or a maximum percentage of minority students in each school. The point is to make the desegregation goals as flexible as possible in order to minimize the disruption and controversy associated with trying to maintain narrow and rigid numerical quotas in every school. If a desegregation plan is being developed in connection with a court or government agency mandate, it is important to emphasize that many federal courts have approved a plus or minus 20 percent range, although in most court-ordered plans this standard must be applied to all schools in the system unless a very strong case can be made for excluding individual schools.

A good example of a desegregation plan adopted voluntarily by a school board occurred in 1991 in Knox County, Tennessee, serving an enrollment about 50,000 of which 13 percent are black. In spite of the relatively low minority enrollment, most minority students were concentrated in predominantly black schools in the city of Knoxville, which formerly had a separate school system. The county school board wanted a desegregation program primarily to improve educational opportunities for inner city children. The county district adopted a desegregation standard of 20 percentage points above the districtwide percent black; there is no lower limit because of the low overall percentage of black students. The proposed plan desegregated most inner city schools and closer-in county schools by a closing a number of small, imbalanced facilities; building several new schools; rezoning to improve desegregation using contiguous boundary lines; and adopting an M-to-M program and several magnet programs in inner-city schools.

Another example of the voluntary adoption of a desegregation plan occurred in Wausau, Wisconsin, a smaller school district whose minority population is predominantly Southeast Asian, most of whom were living below the poverty line. Faced with several predominantly minority schools in the downtown section and two new schools opening in the less populated outskirts, the school board adopted a policy of socioeconomic balance, which would have the effect of balancing the minority enrollment as well. The initial plan was based on mandatory reassignment, and the ensuing controversy led to a recall election and the replacement of all but one former board member. The new board modified the plan by allowing any reassigned student to opt for their original school, which defused the controversy and allowed the rest of the plan to go forward.

Interdistrict Plans

These design principles can be applied to an interdistrict plan as well as an intradistrict plan. In an interdistrict plan, usually involving a central city and its suburbs, a voluntary transfer (M-to-M) plan generally attracts minority students to predominantly white suburban schools, such as the METCO program in Boston and Project Concern in Hartford and New Haven, Connecticut. Voluntary programs have also led to thousands of minority transfers to suburban schools in Milwaukee and St. Louis.

If funds are available from the state, magnet schools can also be placed in the central city district to attract suburban whites. Central city magnet schools have attracted about 1,000 white suburban students in Milwaukee and 1,200 in Kansas City. A special survey in Kansas City suggested that this number might go higher, but under no circumstance would there be enough suburban white student demand to desegregate all of the city magnet schools. In some cities, such as Kansas City, magnet programs are permitted to have a racial composition exceeding 50 percent minority, usually because of minority student demand. Survey studies show, however, that such a policy could be self-defeating by reducing white enrollment from what it might be if the maximum ratio was held to fifty-fifty.

Although voluntary desegregation plans are usually not controversial, the biggest obstacle in recent years has become the issue of funding. With many states facing significant budget shortages and deficits, education funding is in fierce competition with other state priorities, and simply maintaining level funding (as opposed to takings cuts) can be considered a victory. In this climate, obtaining or maintaining funds for a desegregation program without clear and concrete educational advantages can be very difficult. The prospects for state funding are not helped by federal court orders such as those in Missouri, which have required the state to spend over three billion dollars for desegregation and other remedial programs in Kansas City and St. Louis. Some states are justifiably worried that, if they volunteer to fund some type of desegregation program, a court may later force them to spend much more than they had planned.

Desegregation and Choice

Both the desegregation and the choice movements focus on the allocation of students to schools, and both have been controversial, albeit regarding different issues. The controversy in desegregation policy is the requirement for school racial balance, which usually restricts choice of schools, particularly in mandatory busing plans. The main controversy in choice policy is state-funded vouchers for private and parochial schools, which critics contend will promote white or middle class transfers to private schools, leaving the public schools to serve an increasingly minority and impoverished population. Choice supporters usually oppose desegregation policies and vice versa; the former place greater weight on the value of freedom of choice, whereas the latter place greater weight on the value of racial and economic balance.

Although why these movements clash is clear, a more important question for policy makers is whether they share any common ground on which strategies might be devised that draw on some of the better and more popular aspects of each movement. In this regard, voluntary desegregation plans bear close scrutiny because they do embody some of the same principles underlying the school choice movement.

The Choice Movement

The school choice movement is relatively recent (at least compared to desegregation policies), with substantial support coming from the Reagan and Bush administrations and from many state governments. A number of states have passed school choice legislation, the major purpose of which is to increase the opportunities for school choice either within a single school system or between separate school systems. Most existing school choice statutes apply only to public schools, but at least one state (Wisconson) has adopted an experimental voucher program for private schools. In many other states, general choice legislation is pending or the subject of initiative drives, including vouchers for private and parochial schools.

Interdistrict public school choice policies have been adopted in Arkansas, Iowa, Massachusetts, Minnesota, Nebraska, and Ohio. The only publicly funded private school voucher policy is a small experimental program adopted by the state of Wisconsin for the city of Milwaukee, where minority students are offered vouchers to attend nonsectarian schools. Legislative or initiative proposals for full voucher programs have been undertaken in such states as California, Colorado, Florida, Georgia, Illinois, Michigan, and Oregon. This movement has a great deal of popular support; a recent Gallup poll shows that 70 percent of all adults support a voucher program that would include private and parochial schools, which rises to an astonishing 86 percent for blacks and 84 percent for Hispanics.[5] By contrast, none of the voucher initiatives for private schools has survived the ballot box; they have been defeated soundly in Oregon in 1991 and in California in 1993.

A general school choice policy, without restrictions, can have adverse effects on racial balance, although not necessarily intentional. If a choice policy is supported by state funds as opposed to private funds, then constitutional and civil rights laws will probably apply to its potential racial impacts. Recognizing this fact, most existing choice statutes prohibit school choice that adversely affects the racial balance of schools or that is in a district subject to a court-ordered desegregation plan. However, some state policies and many of the voucher proposals being pursued by initiative drives make no mention of racial impacts.

Since racially balanced schools are not required by the federal Constitution or by civil rights laws (assuming no violation of those laws), there is no legal reason why a general school choice policy has to promote desegregation. If a state choice policy has no restrictions relating to racial balance and the policy leads to significant adverse effects on the racial balance either within or between school systems, however, then the policy might be legally challenged on the grounds of federal constitutional or statutory violations.

The success of such a constitutional challenge would hinge on the purpose of the legislation. The challenger would have to prove that the policy has a discriminatory purpose and has no compelling government interest (e.g., educational value) to justify its effects on racial balance. Given current Supreme Court doctrine on school segregation, proving that school choice policies are discriminatory and have no legitimate educational value would probably be difficult, particularly if a significant number of minority students take advantage of a choice program. There is no intrinsic reason why the proof of discriminatory purpose should differ if the schools of choice were public or private, although the inclusion of parochial schools in a choice policy could raise other constitutional issues regarding separation of church and state.[6]

Although not by design, a general choice policy has at least one important communality with a voluntary desegregation policy. Both policies aim to increase choices among public schools, including choices within and between separate school systems. The main difference between them is that a desegregation policy has an additional objective of improving racial balance, so that it necessarily restricts choices that worsen racial balance.

Can this similarity between general choice policies and voluntary desegregation be used to fashion a common-ground policy that could appeal to supporters of both movements? Clearly, a compromise policy is not likely to win the support of those who believe that racial balance is so important that it justifies mandatory school busing, which is antithetical to the concept of expanded school choice, or appeal to those who believe that there should be no restrictions whatsoever on the choice of schools, even if it worsened segregation in the public schools. Yet a common-ground policy might appeal to a significant cross-section of the citizenry, given national polls showing that large majorities endorse the general concepts of both school choice and school integration.

A common-ground policy that increases school choice might improve support for school desegregation, which frequently loses public support when it is associated only with measures that reduce choice of schools, such as mandatory busing. Support for desegregation might be particularly enhanced if a common-ground policy includes both public and private schools, even parochial schools. A common-ground policy might improve support for more school choice if it prevents adverse effects on school segregation, especially if it improves the desegregation and choices of economically disadvantaged and minority students. General choice policies can lose support by ignoring the potential consequences of unrestricted choice for inner city schools. A common-ground policy that can appeal to supporters of both expanded school choice and improved desegregation might generate greater political support and thereby enhance its chance for adoption.

The most controversial issue in the choice movement is vouchers for private and parochial schools. Voucher proposals are strongly opposed by most teachers' unions and professional educators' associations on the grounds that they would reduce funding for public schools and leave only hard-to-teach students in the public school systems. From a desegregation standpoint, however, a private school voucher program may offer the only realistic desegregation for those minority students who now attend public schools in predominantly minority urban school systems, which includes most of the larger cities in the nation. There are very few opportunities for desegregation within these large city systems, and desegregated suburban public schools may be limited in availability and entail long travel times. This may well explain the strong black and Hispanic support of the voucher concept shown in the recent Gallup Poll.

Equity Choice: A Common-Ground Concept

Anyone who has had many years of experience in the field of school desegregation—attorney, jurist, educator, or social scientist—develops opinions about what works and what does not work. I hope these opinions are based on objective evidence and experience, but some value judgments cannot be helped, particularly on such basic values as the relative importance of equality on the one hand and individual freedom on the other. With this caveat in mind, the following is a modest proposal that combines some of the more popular goals and methods of the desegregation and choice movements. Because of these dual purposes, I call it an "equity choice" concept.

This equity choice concept generally assumes that none of the school systems involved is subject to a court-supervised desegregation plan. For systems under a court order, the proposed policy would have to be approved by the court, which might entail certain modifications to ensure that the specific desegregation objectives of the court order are adequately served.

First, in order to expand school choice, an equity choice policy should allow parents or students to choose any public or private school within a reasonably large geographic area surrounding their residence, independent of school system boundaries. Existing school assignment policies would apply to parents and students currently attending public schools who do not wish to change schools; presumably, if they are satisfied with their current public school, they would not utilize the choice policy. Obviously, a private school might choose not to participate in a state-sponsored choice policy.

Second, existing state and local school funds would follow transferring students in the form of vouchers or transfer payments; local funds would be calculated as marginal costs, so that a sending district would only lose those funds actually spent on educating the transferring student. State funds that are currently allocated on a per capita basis would simply follow a student to the school of choice. If a receiving school's (or school system's) per-capita marginal costs were lower than the funds following a transferring student, the excess would go to a special state equity choice fund. If a receiving school's marginal costs were higher than the state and local sending district funds, then students below some specified income level could apply for a scholarship from this special choice fund, but students above this level would have to make up the difference in the form of a tuition payment to the receiving school (with the exception of magnet school students, as explained here later).

Third, a state would offer capital improvement funds to its central-city school systems to create a number of specialized magnet programs to be placed in schools serving disadvantaged populations. Their major purpose would be to attract private and suburban students to those schools. The operating costs would be born by the city, with higher per-capita costs being allowed for each magnet school. Middle-class students from private or suburban public schools who transfer to these urban magnet schools would also be eligible for tuition scholarships from the special equity choice fund.

Fourth, transferring students would be eligible for a transportation subsidy from the special equity choice fund only if their transfer improved the racial (or possibly economic) balance of the sending and receiving schools. Within this class of transfers, priority would be given to (1) students below some income level who are transferring from city to private or suburban public schools and (2) middle-class students who are transferring from private or suburban public schools to an urban magnet school.

Given current funding realities, this type of funding formula should add to the special fund whenever large-city public school students transfer to most private and parochial schools and even to nonaffluent suburban systems that have lower operating costs than large city systems.[7] The funding restrictions should also inhibit large-scale migration of middle-class students from urban public school systems to elite private schools or to affluent suburban systems; most of these schools have higher costs than the sending system, and therefore additional tuition payments would be required. At the same time, the special equity choice fund would provide funding for those poorer and minority families who perceive better educational opportunities in a private or suburban school.

Fifth, rather than requiring that transfers improve racial balance (as they would in a regular desegregation plan), an equity choice policy would require that receiving schools give priority to transfers that improve the racial balance of the receiving school, with the racial composition of the geographic region as a reference point. In this way, for example, central-city minority students applying to a predominantly white suburban school would be placed before white central-city applicants, and white applicants to magnet schools would be placed before minority applicants.[8] In addition, such desegregative transfers would also be eligible for additional funding support from the special equity choice funds if the receiving school has higher marginal costs than the sending school.

The funding provisions, incentives, and transfer priorities of this model policy should generally promote desegregation in a metropolitan area while expanding opportunities for choice. It should encourage some middle-class suburban and private school students to transfer to magnet programs in disadvantaged and predominantly minority urban schools, and these magnet programs would also represent significant educational enhancements for disadvantaged urban schools. The policy should also facilitate minority and low-income student transfers from urban systems to suburban and private schools by offering tuition and transportation subsidies. Indeed, this model policy embodies a number of elements that have enhanced both choice and desegregation in public schools in several metropolitan areas, including the interdistrict transfer policies in Boston, Milwaukee, Kansas City, and St. Louis. There is no reason, in principle, why the inclusion of private schools in such a policy would not improve the racial balance between public and private schools as well.

Not all private or parochial schools would be expected to participate in a state-sponsored choice policy, for the simple reason that acceptance of state funds would, sooner or later, lead to at least some state regulation and some loss of autonomy for the private schools. For example, in exchange for accepting state funds, private schools might have to comply with state and federal special education requirements, which would lead to increased costs and possibly other policy complications. It is entirely possible, however, that state choice plans would encourage expansion of private and parochial schools, thereby providing more transfer capacity.

This equity choice policy could be modified in various ways to satisfy federal desegregation requirements, if one or more school systems in a metropolitan area is under a court order. In fact, it might produce even greater desegregation if it replaces a central-city mandatory desegregation plan that has caused substantial white flight. Restoration of neighborhood schools, with or without voluntary magnet schools, has led to white enrollment gains in a number of school districts, including the Norfolk and Savannah systems.

To meet the requirements of a federal desegregation remedy, a metropolitan choice plan would need further constraints on transfers that affect racial balance. For example, an equity choice policy used as a court-approved desegregation plan could not allow transfers that increase racial imbalance between a sending and receiving school, with the metropolitan racial composition as a reference point. Without special circumstances, white students could not transfer from a majority nonwhite to a majority white school, and nonwhite students could not transfer from majority white to majority nonwhite schools.

This outline of an equity choice policy obviously leaves out many administrative and procedural details that would have to be ironed out before such a concept could be turned into a concrete program. Implementation would require an administrative structure of some type to monitor the transfer process, to set marginal cost rates for individual schools or school systems, to arbitrate transfer issues for individuals or between school systems, and to allocate equity choice funds. One of the more important features of an implementation plan would be to publicize and advertise transfer opportunities and magnet schools, especially for disadvantaged inner-city families who might lack informal networks to inform them of better school programs.

Most important, implementation of this equity choice policy would also require state funding commitments, including funding for urban magnet schools, administrative mechanisms, and other start-up costs. Because it is impossible to know in advance how many cost-saving transfers would take place, the equity choice fund would need initial funding and possibly permanent funding if cost-saving transfers are insufficient to provide necessary tuition or transportation subsidies for students below the poverty line.

In order to make a case for state or local funding for an equity choice policy or for any other type of desegregation or choice policy that requires public funds, the basic issue raised at the beginning of this chapter is important. The primary rationale for a state or a local school board to fund a desegregation or a choice policy, short of a court order, must ultimately be to enhance the quality of education.

Choice for What Purpose?

Although most American citizens support both desegregation and choice principles, including state vouchers for private schools, the public commitment to these two concepts is not strong enough to support any policy just because it expands choice or promotes desegregation. The 1993 defeat of the California choice initiative and the continued unpopularity of mandatory busing, which retains the power to recall elected school board members, underscore the conditional nature of this public support. If the public or an elected body is to be convinced that public funds should be used to increase school desegregation and choice, they must believe that funding will benefit educational quality while having no major adverse side effects.

In developing credible educational arguments for an equity choice policy, one must consider the evidence on the harm and benefit thesis, as presented in chapter 2, as well as other evidence on the effectiveness of general choice policies. Although credibility must start with a reasonable degree of consensus among experts who conduct studies in these fields, the arguments must also be persuasive to the general public and to the electorate, who will ultimately determine the fate of public funding for these policies.

Regarding desegregation, there is little evidence that changing a school's racial composition *alone*, while leaving the educational program unchanged, has any appreciable impact on the academic performance of minority students, and there is nearly unanimous consensus that it does not benefit white academic performance. Likewise, there is little evidence that increasing choice by itself, among schools that have few differences in educational programs, would have any impact on academic outcomes.

However, there is more evidence that desegregation can yield certain academic benefits if it is voluntary and allows transfers to schools with stronger academic programs, which could be true for transfers from high-poverty schools to middle-class schools or from regular schools to magnet schools. Likewise, if a general choice policy allows transfers from a mediocre urban public school to a better private or suburban public school, then educational benefits may also be realized.[9] In other words, whatever impacts they might have on the structure of a school system or on other outcomes, neither desegregation nor choice policies by themselves are likely to improve academic performance. If an equity choice increases *access* to better programs—more challenging, more interesting, more rigorous, and so forth—then academic benefits can be realized.

The conclusion that improved academic performance requires improved educational programs may seem to belabor the obvious, but perhaps only to readers who have not been exposed to the decades-old argument advanced by many supporters of school desegregation, in which racial balance alone is somehow supposed to correct educational deficiencies that may exist in predominantly minority schools. Those same kind of arguments are now being advanced by some supporters of general choice policies, who see market competition as a cure-all for the ills of many large urban school systems and who have no specific remedies for creating a better educational program for disadvantaged minority students. Neither racial balance nor market competition is a credible substitute for specific policies, such as magnet schools, that offer direct programmatic enhancements to disadvantaged urban schools.

The basic educational argument for an equity choice policy, then, is that it improves educational opportunities for individual students and families by increasing the *access* to better schools. With the exception of magnet programs placed in disadvantaged city schools, a choice policy by itself does not *create* better schools. An equity choice policy assumes that many good schools already exist within the private and public schools of a metropolitan area and that some additional good schools will be created by strategic placement of magnet programs. The purpose of the policy is to make good schools more accessible to a broader cross-section of parents and students who feel that their current school is not providing an adequate educational program. Another purpose of the policy is to structure priorities and incentives so that parental choices for better schools also contribute to desegregation.

The equity choice policy assumes that those parents who want better schools for their children will be motivated to find them and seek a transfer to them, with help from a solid publicity program. Indeed, this is happening today, as confirmed by the many thousands of parents who now participate in voluntary magnet schools or choice programs throughout the country, most in connection with voluntary desegregation programs. Of course, most parents probably will not want to change schools; surveys show that a majority of parents are satisfied with their current schools, public or private. Based on experience with existing voluntary desegregation programs, transfers of more than 10 percent of students as part of an equity choice policy would be unusual, and transfers that exceed 20 percent would be highly improbable.

Unlike the claims made for some desegregation and general choice proposals being advocated today, this equity choice policy does not claim to be a panacea for the many problems facing American education. It does promise a more realistic and politically more palatable policy for accomplishing many of the same goals of these separate desegregation or choice proposals, with a special emphasis on minority or disadvantaged families.

Affluent and middle-class families have always been able to exercise school choice to some extent if they wished to do so, either by paying for private schools or by moving to a community or neighborhood with good public schools. Only poor and working-class families cannot choose a better school for their children, if they happen to live in a neighborhood served by an inferior school and if they cannot afford to move or to pay private school tuition.

An equity choice policy that includes both private and suburban public schools may be the most hopeful approach for improving the desegregation and education of minority and low-income students who are now locked into ineffective inner-city schools. It proposes to equalize access to better schools, both public and private, so that minority and disadvantaged children can compete for better schools on an even footing with middle-class children. It aims to improve education and desegregation, not by simply changing racial balance or by allowing choice among similar schools, but by offering the opportunity to choose good schools to all parents who want better schools for their children.

Appendix: The NIE Study of Desegregation and Black Achievement

Data used in Tables 3.5 and 3.6 (Effect sizes in standard deviations)

Code/Grade	Reading Effect[a]	Math Effect[a]	Years	Number of Cases[b] Deseg.	Control	Armor Reading Effects
A2	0.75	0.49	2	34	34	0.89
B2	0.23	−0.02	1	25	32	0.34
B3	−0.04	0.59	1	11	28	0.17
C3	−0.01	−0.09	3	12	36	0.03
C3	Omitted		3	12	21	−0.55
DK	−0.41		1	17	23	−0.55
D1	−0.02		1	16	21	0.13
D2	0.30		1	25	23	−0.19
D3	−0.13		1	111	23	0.21
D4	0.33		1	13	24	0.10
D5	−0.31		1	13	21	−0.11
E6	0.04	−0.16	1	108	88	−0.01
F4	0.02	0.03	1	393	180	−0.03
F5	0.02	0.03	1	381	181	0.06
G2	0.00		1	64	50	0.00
G4	0.00		1	66	48	0.00
G6	0.00		1	70	65	0.00
H10	0.13	0.19	1	38	38	0.00
I1	0.22	0.18	2	20	140	0.54
I3	0.31	0.18	2	13	140	0.24
I4	−0.14	−0.17	2	10	147	0.19
J3	0.15	0.06	2	27	29	Omitted[c]
J4	0.58	−0.17	2	33	33	Omitted[c]
J5	0.76	−0.22	2	29	27	Omitted[c]
K9	0.07	−0.07	2	42	42	0.15
L4	−0.14	−0.15	2	810	1115	−0.16
M4	0.18	0.33	1	(86 Total)		0.27
N6	−0.05	0.10	3	124	150	−0.06
O4	0.61		1	24	24	0.75
O4	Omitted		1	12	12	0.00
P3	−0.15	0.04	2			Omitted
Q4	−0.30	0.43	3	20	21	−0.46
R3	0.11	0.07	1	90	17	−0.02
R5	−0.24	−0.53	1	61	29	−0.21
R9	0.21	0.24	1	124	25	0.08

Continued

Data used in Tables 3.5 and 3.6 (Effect sizes in standard deviations) (*Continued*)

Code/Grade	Reading Effect[a]	Math Effect[a]	Years	Number of Cases[b] Deseg.	Control	Armor Reading Effects
R11	−0.01	0.14	1	72	14	−0.25
S2	0.63	−0.16	1	12	15	0.53
Mean	0.106	0.054				0.063

[a] Effects from Miller for one-grade studies (A, C, E, H, K, L, M, N, O, P, Q, and S); Wortman for B, D, J, and R; and Stephan for F, G, and I.

[b] It should be noted that the studies with the largest sample sizes (e.g., over 50 in both treatment and control groups) generally have small effects.

[c] Some white students included in the desegregated group.

List of 19 core studies selected by the NIE panel

A. Anderson, Louis V., *The Effect of Desegregation on the Achievement and Personality Pattern of Negro Children*, unpublished doctoral dissertation. George Peabody College for Teachers, University Microfilms, No. 66-11237, 1966.

B. Beker, Jerome, *A Study of Integration in Racially Imbalanced Urban Public School*. Syracuse, New York: Syracuse University Youth Development Center, final report, May 1977.

C. Bowman, Orrin H., *Scholastic Development of Disadvantaged Negro Pupils: A Study of Pupils in Selected Segregated and Desegregated Elementary Classrooms*, unpublished doctoral dissertation. Buffalo: State University of New York, 1973.

D. Carrigan, Patricia M., *School Desegregation via Compulsory Pupil Transfer: Early Effects on Elementary School Children*. Ann Arbor, Mich.: Ann Arbor Public Schools, 1969.

E. Clark, El Nadel, *Analysis of the Difference between Pre- and Post-test Scores on Measures of Self-concept, Academic Aptitude, and Reading Achievement Earned by Sixth Grade Students Attending Segregated and Desegregated Schools*, unpublished doctoral dissertation Durham, N.C.: Duke University, 1971.

F. Evans, Charles L., *Short-term Desegregation Effects: The Academic Achievement of Bused Students, 1971-1972*, Fort Worth, Texas: Fort Worth Independent Schools District, 1973. ERIC No. ED 086 759.

G. Iwanicki, E.G., and R. K. Gable, *A Quasi-experimental Evaluation of the Effects of a Voluntary Urban/suburban Busing Program on Student Achievement*, paper presented at the annual meeting of the American Educational Research Association, Toronto, Canada, March 1978.

H. Klein, Robert S., *A Comparative Study of the Academic Achievement of Negro Tenth Grade High School Students Attending Segregated and Recently Integrated Schools in a Metropolitan Area in the South*, unpublished doctoral dissertation. University of South Carolina, 1967.

I. Laird, M. A., and G. Weeks, *The Effect of Busing on Achievement in Reading and Arithmetic in Three Philadelphia Schools*, Philadelphia, Penn.: The School District of Philadelphia, Division of Research, 1966.

J. Rentsch, George J., *Open Enrollment: An Appraisal,* unpublished doctoral dissertation. Buffalo: State University of New York, 1967.

K. Savage, L. W., *Arithmetic Achievement of Black Students Transferring from a Segregated Junior High School to an Integrated Junior High School,* unpublished masters thesis. Virginia State College, 1971.

L. Sheehan, Daniel S., "Black Achievement in a Desegregated School District, *Journal of Social Psychology* 107:185–192, 1979.

M. Slone, Irene W., *The Effects of One School Pairing on Pupil Achievement, Anxieties, and Attitudes,* unpublished doctoral dissertation. New York: New York University, 1968.

N. Smith, Lee Rand, *A Comparative Study of the Achievement of Negro Students Attending Segregated Junior High Schools and Negro Students Attending Desegregated Junior High Schools in the City of Tulsa,* unpublished doctoral dissertation. Tulsa: University of Tulsa, 1971.

O. Syracuse City School District, *Study of the Effects of Integration—Washington Irving and Host Pupils,* U.S. Commission on Civil Rights hearing in Rochester, New York, September 16–17, 1966.

P. Thompson, E. W., and U. Smidchens, *Longitudinal Effects of School Racial Ethnic Composition upon Student Achievement,* paper presented at the annual meeting of the American Educational Research Association, San Francisco, April 1979.

Q. Van Every, D. W., *Effects of Desegregation on Pupil School Groups of Sixth Graders in Terms of Achievement Levels and Attitudes Toward School,* unpublished doctoral dissertation, Wayne State University, 1969. University Microfilms No. 70-19074.

R. Walberg, Herbert J., *An Evaluation of an Urban-Suburban School Busing Program: Student Achievement and Perception of Class Learning Environments,* paper presented at the annual meeting of the American Educational Research Association, New York, N.Y., February 1971. ERIC No. ED 047 076 UD 011 284.

S. Zdep, Stanley M., "Educating Disadvantaged Urban Children in Suburban Schools: An Evaluation," *Journal of Applied Social Psychology,* 1, 1971. ERIC No. ED 053 186, TM 00716.

Notes

Notes to Chapter 1

1. *Brown v. Board of Education (Brown I)*, 347 U.S. 483 (1954).

2. *Green v. New Kent County*, 430 U.S. 391 (1968); *Swann v. Charlotte-Mecklenburg Board of Education*, 402 U.S. 11 (1971).

3. *Keyes v. School District No. 1, Denver*, 93 S. Ct. 2686 (1973). Although the Supreme Court also found a "dual" school system in a part of the Denver district, most of the remaining segregation (which corresponded to housing patterns) was assumed to be state caused unless the school district could prove otherwise.

4. *Milliken v. Bradley (Milliken I)*, 418 U.S. 717 (1974).

5. *Spangler v. Pasadena Board of Education*, 427 U.S. 424 (1976).

6. *Board of Education of Oklahoma City v. Dowell*, 111 S. Ct. 630 (1991).

7. In its decision in *Strauder v. West Virginia*, 100 U.S. 303 (1879), the Supreme Court struck down a law that prevented blacks from sitting on juries.

8. *Plessy v. Ferguson*, 163 U.S. 537 (1896).

9. Id. at 544.

10. *Sweatt v. Painter*, 339 U.S. 629 (1949); and *McLaurin v. Oklahoma State Regents*, 339 U.S. 637 (1949).

11. *McLaurin*, 339 U.S. at 641.

12. *Brown v. Board of Education*, 98 F. Supp. 797 (1951); *Briggs v. Elliott*, 103 F. Supp. 920 (1952); *Davis v. County School Board*, 103 F. Supp. 337 (1952); *Gebhart v. Belton*, 91 A.2d 137 Delaware (1952).

13. One exception was Kansas, which had state laws that permitted (but did not require) school districts to segregate the elementary grades. Ohio also had state laws that required racial segregation in the public schools, but they were repealed in the late 1800s by the Ohio state supreme court.

14. *United States v. Jefferson County Board of Education*, 372 F.2d 836 (1966).

15. "The Effects of Segregation and the Consequences of Desegregation: A Social Science Statement," *Minnesota Law Review*, 37:427–439 (1953), signed by thrity-two social scientists.

16. See, for example, Frank I. Goodman, "De Facto School Desegregation: A Constitutional and Empirical Analysis," *California Law Review*, 60:275–437 (1972); Mark G. Yudof, "School Desegregation: Legal Realism, Reasoned Elaboration, and Social Science Research in the Supreme Court," *Law and Contemporary Problems*, 42:57–109 (1978).

17. *Baltimore v. Dawson*, 350 U.S. 877 (1955) (beaches); *Holmes v. Atlanta*, 350 U.S.

879 (1955) (golf courses); *Gayle v. Browder*, 352 U.S. 903 (1956) (buses); *New Orleans Parks v. Detiege*, 358 U.S. 54 (1958) (parks).

18. *Brown I*, 347 U.S. at 494.

19. Id.

20. U.S. Commission on Civil Rights, *Racial Isolation in the Public Schools* (Washington, D.C.: U.S. Government Printing Office, 1967).

21. *Brown v. Board of Education* (*Brown II*), 349 U.S. 294 (1955).

22. Frank T. Read, "Judicial Evolution of the Law of School Integration since *Brown v. Board of Education*," *Law and Contemporary Problems*, 39:7–49 (1975).

23. *Brown II* at 299.

24. Equity principles generally include two parts: making whole, or restoring the position the victim would have had but for the violation, and balancing the interests of the victim with other legitimate interests (one of which was not opposition to desegregation by whites).

25. *Brown II* at 300.

26. *Briggs v. Elliott*, 132 F. Supp. at 777.

27. *United States v. Jefferson County*, 372 F.2d 836 (1966).

28. *Cooper v. Aaron*, 358 U.S. 1 (1958); *Watson v. Memphis*, 373 U.S. 526 (1963); *Calhoun v. Latimer*, 377 U.S. 263 (1965); *Rogers v. Paul*, 382 U.S. 198 (1965).

29. *Goss v. Knoxville*, 373 U.S. 683 (1963).

30. *Shuttlesworth v. Birmingham*, 358 U.S. 101 (1958).

31. *Green v. New Kent County*, 430 U.S. 391 (1968).

32. Id. at 437–442.

33. *Swann v. Charlotte-Mecklenburg*, 318 F. Supp. 786, 789 (1970).

34. Id. at 791.

35. Id. at 793. Although not cited here, justification for ignoring community opposition to a desegregation plan was provided in *Cooper v. Aaron*, 358 U.S. 1 (1958), which dealt with the desegregation of Little Rock, Arkansas.

36. *Swann v. Charlotte-Mecklenburg*, 431 F.2d 138, 142 (1970).

37. *Swann v. Charlotte-Mecklenburg*, 402 U.S. at 13.

38. Id. at 14.

39. Id. at 18–20.

40. Id. at 22–25.

41. Id. at 25–27.

42. Id. at 27–29.

43. Id. at 29–30.

44. Id. at 16.

45. Id. at 21.

46. Id. at 23.

47. Id. at 31–32.

48. Owen M. Fiss, "The Charlotte-Mecklenburg Case: Its Significance for Northern School Desegregation," *University of Chicago Law Review* 38:697–709 (1971).

49. *Spangler v. Pasadena*, 311 F. Supp. 501 (1970).

50. Id. at 521.

51. *Davis v. School District of Pontiac*, 309 F. Supp. 734 (1970); *Johnson v. San Francisco*, 339 F. Supp. 1315 (1971).

52. *Keyes v. Denver*, 313 F. Supp. 61 (1970).

53. Id. at 96.

54. *Keyes v. Denver*, 445 F.2d 990, 1004 (1971).

55. *Keyes v. Denver*, 93 S. Ct. 2686, 2697 (1973).

56. Id. at 2725.

57. *Milliken I*, 418 U.S. 717 (1974).

58. *Bradley v. Richmond, VA, School Board*, 338 F. Supp. 67 (1972).

59. *Bradley v. Richmond, VA, School Board*, 462 F.2d 1058 (1972).

60. *Bradley v. Milliken*, 338 F. Supp. 582 (1971).

61. *Bradley v. Milliken*, 484 F.2d 215, 250 (1973).

62. *Milliken I*, 418 U.S. at 753.

63. Id. at 721.

64. Id. at 745–746.

65. Id. at 780.

66. *Keyes v. Denver*, 93 S. Ct. at 2697 (emphasis in original).

67. In the *Keyes* decision, the Supreme Court endorsed a district court's conclusion that a school had been located "with conscious knowledge that it would be a segregated school" (93 S. Ct. at 2694; *Keyes v. Denver*, 303 F. Supp. 279, 285 (1969)); in a *Milliken I* footnote it apparently endorsed a "foreseeable consequence" standard employed by the district court in determining discriminatory intent on the part of the Detroit school board (418 U.S. at 738, fn 18).

68. *Oliver v. Michigan State Board of Education*, 508 F.2d 178, 182 (1974) (the case involved school segregation in Kalamazoo, Michigan).

69. *United States v. School District of Omaha*, 521 F.2d 530 (1975) (Eighth Circuit, now Tenth Circuit).

70. *Washington v. Davis*, 426 U.S. 229 (1976).

71. *Davis v. Washington*, 348 F. Supp. 15 (1972).

72. *Washington v. Davis*, 521 F.2d 956 (1975).

73. Basically, according to the Supreme Court's interpretation of Title VII at the time of *Washington v. Davis*, an employment practice with racially disparate effects (or impact) is illegal unless an employer can prove it is reasonably related to job or training performance. According to the watershed case in this field of law, *Griggs v. Duke Power Co.*, 401 U.S. 424 (1971), proof of discriminatory intent was not required to show a violation of Title VII.

74. *Washington v. Davis*, 426 U.S. at 239.

75. Id. at 240.

76. *Arlington Heights v. Metropolitan Housing Development Corp.*, 429 U.S. 252 (1977).

77. *School District of Omaha v. United States*, 53 L. Ed. 2d 1039 (1977).

78. *Dayton Board of Education v. Brinkman*, 433 U.S. 406 (1977) (*Dayton I*) and 443 U.S. 526 (1979) (*Dayton II*); *Columbus Board of Education v. Penick*, 443 U.S. 449 (1979).

79. *Dayton I* at 420.

80. James S. Coleman, Sara D. Kelley, and John A. Moore, *Trends in School Integration* (Washington, D.C.: Urban Institute, 1975).

81. *Brinkman v. Gilligan*, 583 F.2d. 243 (1978).

82. James R. Nearhood, "Foreseeable Racial Segregation: A Presumption of Unconstitutionality," *Nebraska Law Review* 55:144–160 (1975).

83. *Columbus v. Pennick*, 443 U.S. at 491.

84. See *Evans v. Buchanan*, 393 F. Supp. 428 (1975) (Delaware); *United States v. Board of School Commissioners of Indianapolis*, 419 F. Supp. 180 (1975) and 456 F. Supp. 183 (1978); and *Liddel v. Board of Education of St. Louis*, 491 F. Supp. 351 (1980), 667 F.2d 643 (1981), and 677 F.2d 626 (1982).

85. *Evans v. Buchanan*, 447 U.S. 916 (1980).

86. *Armour v. Nix*, No. 16708, Northern District of Georgia (1979), affirmed 446 U.S. 930 (1980); *Goldsboro v. Wayne County*, 745 F.2d 324 (1984) and *Jenkins v. Missouri*, No. 770420, Western District of Missouri (1984).

87. *Little Rock v. Pulaski County*, No. 85-1078, U.S. Court of Appeals, Eighth Circuit (1985).

88. For a general description of the San Diego plan, see David J. Armor, "White Flight and the Future of School Desegregation," in *School Desegregation*, ed. Walter Stephan and Joseph Feagin (New York: Plenum, 1980).

89. *Armstrong v. Board of School Directors*, 471 F. Supp. 800 (1979).

90. *United States v. Yonkers*, 635 F. Supp. 1538 (1986); *Diaz v. San Jose Unified School District*, 633 F. Supp. 808 (1985).

91. *Stell v. Savannah-Chatham County Board of Education*, 888 F.2d 82 (1989).

92. *Pasadena v. Spangler*, 49 L. Ed. 2d 599 (1976).

93. *Swann v. Charlotte-Mecklenburg*, 402 U.S. at 31–32.

94. *Spangler v. Pasadena*, 375 F. Supp. 1304 (1974).

95. Id. at 1310, fn 10.

96. *Spangler v. Pasadena*, 519 F.2d 430, 438 (1975).

97. *Pasadena v. Spangler*, 49 L. Ed. 2d at 608–609.

98. *Spangler v. Pasadena*, 611 F.2d 1239.

99. This author performed studies that supported the first two of these grounds: "An Evaluation of Norfolk Desegregation Plans," unpublished report to the Board of Education, December 1982. See also David J. Armor, "Response to Carr and Ziegler," *Sociology of Education*, 64: 134–139, 1991.

100. *Riddick v. School Board of Norfolk*, 627 F. Supp. 814 (1984).

101. *Riddick v. School Board of Norfolk*, 784 F.2d 521 (1986).

102. *United States v. Overton*, 834 F.2d 1179 (1987).

103. *Dowell v. Oklahoma City*, 338 F. Supp. 1256 (1972).

104. *Dowell v. Oklahoma City*, 606 F. Supp. 1548 (1985).

105. *Dowell v. Oklahoma City*, 677 F. Supp. 1503 (1987).

106. *Dowell v. Oklahoma City*, 795 F.2d 1516 (1986).

107. *Dowell v. Oklahoma City*, 890 F.2d 1483, 1488 (1989).

108. The majority opinion was delivered by Chief Justice Rehnquist, joined by Justices White, O'Conner, Scalia, and Kennedy; Justice Marshall wrote a dissenting opinion, joined by Justices Blackmun and Stevens; Justice Souter did not participate.

109. *Oklahoma City v. Dowell*, 111 S. Ct. 630 (1991).

110. *Milliken v. Bradley (Milliken II)*, 433 U.S. 267 (1977).

111. *Freeman v. Pitts*, 118 L. Ed. 2d 108 (1992).

112. *Pitts v. Freeman*, No.11946, Northern District of Georgia (1988).

113. *Pitts v. Freeman*, 887 F.2d 1438 (1989). Although the term *mandatory busing* was not used, the opinion did list pairing, clustering, and busing techniques, which are the key components of a mandatory busing plan (see chapter 4).

114. *Freeman v. Pitts*, 118 L. Ed. 2d at 136.

Notes to Chapter 2

1. Gunnar Myrdal, *An American Dilemma* (New York: Harper and Row, 1944); Kenneth Clark, *Prejudice and Your Child* (Boston: Beacon Press, 1955).

2. "The Effects of Segregation and the Consequences of Desegregation," *Minnesota Law Review*, 37:427–439 (1953).

3. U.S. Commission on Civil Rights, *Racial Isolation in the Public Schools* (Washington, D.C.: U.S. Government Printing Office, 1967).

4. "School Desegregation: A Social Science Statement," in brief of the NAACP et al., as amicus curiae in support of respondents, *Freeman v. Pitts,* U.S. Supreme Court on writ of certiorari to the U.S. Court of Appeals for the Eleventh Circuit, June 21, 1991.

5. Arnold Rose, *The Negro in America* (Boston: Beacon Press, 1956) 27–28 (a condensed version of *An American Dilemma*).

6. Kenneth and Mamie Clark, "The Development of Consciousness of Self and the Emergence of Racial Identity in Negro Children," *Journal of Social Psychology,* 10:591–599 (1939); and "Segregation as a Factor in the Racial Identification of Negro Pre-School Children," *Journal of Experimental Education,* 8:161–163 (1939).

7. Gordon W. Allport, *The Nature of Prejudice* (Cambridge, Mass.: Addison-Wesley, 1953); Morton Deutsch and Mary Evans Collins, *Interracial Housing* (Minneapolis: University of Minnesota Press, 1951); Samuel A. Stouffer et al., *The American Soldier* (Princeton, N.J.: Princeton University Press, 1949).

8. "The Effects of Segregation," 429–430.

9. "The Effects of Segregation," 437–438.

10. *Brown v. Board of Education,* 347 U.S. 483, 494 (1954).

11. "The Effects of Segregation," 428.

12. James S. Coleman, Ernest Q. Campbell, and others, *Equality of Educational Opportunity* (Washington, D.C.: U.S. Government Printing Office, 1966).

13. One of the largest reanalysis projects was carried out by the Harvard University seminar on the Coleman report, published as Frederick Mosteller and Daniel P. Moynihan, eds., *On Equality of Educational Opportunity* (New York: Random House, 1972).

14. U.S. Commission on Civil Rights, *Racial Isolation in the Public Schools* (Washington, D.C.: U.S. Government Printing Office, 1967).

15. U.S. Commission, *Racial Isolation,* 193.

16. U.S. Commission, *Racial Isolation,* 193.

17. David J. Armor, "The Evidence on Busing," *The Public Interest,* 28:90–126 (1972).

18. Harold B. Gerard and Norman Miller, *School Desegregation* (New York: Plenum, 1975).

19. Nancy St. John, *School Desegregation* (New York: Wiley, 1975).

20. James S. Coleman, Sara D. Kelley, and John A. Moore, *Trends in School Integration* (Washington, D.C.: Urban Institute, 1975).

21. Walter G. Stephan, "School Desegregation: An Evaluation of Predictions Made in *Brown v. Board of Education,*" *Psychological Bulletin,* 85:217–238 (1978).

22. Martin Patchen, *Black-White Contact in Schools* (West Lafayette, Ind.: Purdue University Press, 1982).

23. Christine H. Rossell, "Applied Social Research: What Does It Say about the Effectiveness of School Desegregation Plans," *Journal of Legal Studies,* 12:69–107 (1983); and "Estimating the Net Benefits of School Desegregation Reassignments," *Educational Evaluation and Policy Analysis,* 7:217–227 (1986).

24. Thomas Cook and others, *School Desegregation and Black Achievement* (Washington, D.C.: National Institute of Education, U.S. Department of Education, 1984).

25. Meyer Weinberg, *Minority Students: A Research Appraisal* (Washington, D.C.: National Institute of Education, 1977).

26. Robert Crain and Rita Mahard, "Desegregation and Black Achievement, a Review

of the Research," *Law and Contemporary Problems,* 42:17–58 (1978); and "The Effect of Research Methodology on Desegregation-Achievement Studies: A Meta Analysis," *American Journal Of Sociology,* 88:839–854 (1983).

27. For example, Jomills H. Braddock II and James M. McPartland, "Assessing School Desegregation Effects: New Directions in Research," in *Research in Sociology of Education and Socialization,* vol. 3, ed. A. C. Kerkhoff (Greenwich, Conn.: JAI Press, 1982); and "Social-psychological Processes that Perpetuate Racial Segregation," *Journal of Black Studies,* 19:267–289 (1989).

28. Robert E. Slavin, "When Does Cooperative Learning Increase Student Achievement?" *Psychological Bulletin,* 94:429–445 (1983).

29. Robert L. Crain and Jack Strauss, *School Desegregation and Black Occupational Attainment: Results from a Long-term Experiment* (Baltimore: Center for the Social Organization of Schools, Johns Hopkins University, 1986); Robert L. Crain, Jennifer A. Hawes, Randi L. Miler, and Janet R. Peichert, "Finding Niches: Desegregated Students Sixteen Years Later," (New York: Teachers College, Columbia University, 1989).

30. Gary Orfield, *Must We Bus? Segregated Schools and National Policy* (Washington, D.C.: The Brookings Institution, 1978); Willis D. Hawley and Mark A. Smylie, "The Contribution of School Desegregation to Academic Achievement and Racial Integration," in *Eliminating Racism,* ed. Phyllis A. Katz and Dalmas A. Taylor (New York: Plenum, 1988).

31. Willis D. Hawley, Mark Smylie, Robert L. Crain, Christine H. Rossell, R. Fernandez, Janet W. Schofield, and E. Trent, *Strategies for Effective Desegregation* (Lexington, Mass.: Lexington Books, 1983); Jomills H. Braddock II and James M. McPartland, "The Social and Academic Consequences of School Desegregation," *Equity and Choice,* February 1988: 5–73.

32. Janet W. Schofield, "School Desegregation and Intergroup Relations," *Review of Educational Research,* 17:335–412 (1991).

33. "School Desegregation: A Social Science Statement," in brief of the NAACP et al., as amicus curiae in support of respondents, *Freeman v. Pitts,* U.S. Supreme Court on writ of certiorari to the U.S. Court of Appeals for the Eleventh Circuit, June 21, 1991.

34. Id. at 14a.

35. Id. at 7a.

36. Id.

37. Id. at 14a.

38. Id.

39. Id. at 25a.

40. L. A. Bradley and G. W. Bradley, "The Academic Achievement of Black Students in Desegregated Schools: A Critical Review," *Review of Educational Research,* 47:399–449 (1977).

41. *Georgia State Conference of NAACP v. State of Georgia,* 775 F.2d 1403 (1985).

42. Cook et al., *School Desegregation.*

43. *Spangler v. Pasadena,* 311 F. Supp. 501, 533 (1970).

44. The first-grade test was administered in February, so that the students had been in the desegregation plan for only about one semester. A standard deviation is a measure of variation of individual scores around the average score, and many studies have documented a difference of one standard deviation between average black and white achievement scores. See, for example, Coleman and Campbell, *Equality of Educational Opportunity;* see also Ina V. S. Mullis, and others, *Trends in Academic Progress* (Washington, D.C.: U.S. Government Printing Office, 1991).

45. No controls for socioeconomic status were applied in this longitudinal analysis

consisting of the same students at each point in time. When different groups of students are compared over time, as in the usual trend study, it is prudent to control for socio-economic status, because changing SES levels could cause an apparent change in achievement scores or an apparent change in the black-white achievement gap. It is presumed here that the black-white gap is largely driven by SES differences. These issues will be taken up more fully in a later section on National Assessment results.

46. *Spangler v. Pasadena*, 375 F. Supp. 1304, 1308 (1974).

47. David J. Armor, "An Evaluation of Norfolk Desegregation Plans," report to the Norfolk Board of Education, December 1982.

48. Robert L. Green, "The Impact of Proposed Changes in the Desegregation Plan of the Public Schools of Norfolk, Virginia," report to the Norfolk Board of Education, March 29, 1982.

49. Crain and Mahard, "Desegregation and Black Achievement."

50. *Riddick v. School Board of Norfolk*, 627 F. Supp. at 821–822.

51. *Riddick v. School Board of Norfolk*, 784 F.2d 521 (1986); cert denied, 419 U.S. 938 (1986).

52. *United States v. Charleston County School District*, 738 F. Supp. 1513 (1990).

53. The control for poverty status still leaves considerable room for other SES effects, such as the educational status of parents. Although there is no way to be certain with these data, white students in predominantly black schools may come from families with lower levels of these unmeasured SES factors.

54. *Charleston County School District*, 738 F. Supp. at 1548.

55. *United States v. Charleston County School District* 960 F.2d 1227 (1992). The appellate court did vacate and remand one part of the lower court's decision on voluntary interdistrict transfers among the constituent districts, stating that desegregative inter-district transfers are not required but they cannot be denied just because their only purpose is desegregation.

56. In some recent federal court proceedings, plaintiffs have reintroduced the harm and benefit thesis by asserting that the minority-white achievement gap is a "vestige" of the former dual school system. For example, unitary status litigation or petitions have raised academic achievement issues in New Castle County (Wilmington), Delaware; San Jose, California; Dallas; and Savannah.

57. In 1989, the suburban district of Bloomfield had a minority enrollment of 70 percent (mostly black); the next highest suburban minority enrollments were Windsor at 30 percent and East Hartford at 20 percent. The minority enrollment has been increasing rapidly in several suburban districts; Windsor and East Hartford had 37 and 38 percent minority enrollments, respectively, as of 1992.

58. *Horton v. Meskill*, 172 Conn. 615 (1977); 376 A.2d 359, 372 (1977); *Horton v. Meskill*, 195 Conn. 24, 35 (1985).

59. Experts who testified about desegregation issues in general included Christine Rossell (for the state) and Gary Orfield, Charles Willie, William Trent, and Jomills Braddock II (for plaintiffs).

60. The socioeconomic factors were individual poverty levels (using participation in the federal free or reduced-price lunch program as the indicator) and several U.S. Census measures computed for all adults and for black adults only in each community, including percent with college degrees, average income, and percent of single-parent families.

61. As a sensitivity test, a regression analysis using only suburban black students was run to make sure that the relationships were not being dominated by the large number of

Hartford black students. The predicted reading score for Hartford blacks, based only on SES factors for suburban blacks, was 41.

62. The mean sixth-grade reading score is 43 for all black students and 57 for all white students, with a standard deviation of 13 points (all raw scores). Thus the black-white achievement gap for sixth-graders in the Hartford metropolitan area is about one standard deviation.

63. The school desegregation experts were David Armor, Robert Crain, Norman Miller, Walter Stephan, Herbert Walberg, and Paul Wortman, and the research methods specialist was Thomas Cook.

64. By adopting the requirement of a quasi experimental design with predesegregation measures, most panelists felt that controlling for socioeconomic status would not be necessary because those differences would be captured by differences in the pretest measure.

65. The effects shown in Figure 2.5 are taken from Miller for single-grade studies (twelve observations; he did not report estimates by grade in multiple-grade studies), Wortman as possible for multiple-grade studies (fifteen observations), and Stephan for multiple-grade studies not estimated by Wortman (eight observations). See the Appendix for more details.

66. Cook et al., *School Desegregation*, 17. Miller and Stephan eliminated study D because the segregated black students were in 50 percent black schools (compared to 5 percent for desegregated blacks) and study P because segregated blacks were in 42 percent black schools (compared to 5 percent for desegregated blacks); I eliminated study P on the same grounds and study R because whites were included with blacks in the desegregated group; Wortman used both in his analysis of thirty-one studies. The mean for all studies shown in Figure 2.5 is 0.11 and the median is 0.03.

67. Cook et al., *School Desegregation*, 40–41.

68. Ina V. S. Mullis and others, *Trends in Academic Progress* (Washington, D.C.: U.S. Government Printing Office, 1991). Most commercial test publishers change test forms and test content periodically, sometimes for security reasons and at other times to reflect changing curriculum content or standards.

69. Greg Anrig, "Test Scores on the Rise for Blacks," *The Trenton Sunday Star-Ledger*, May 27, 1984, p. 87; Nancy W. Burton and Lyle V. Jones, "Recent Trends in Achievement Levels of Black and White Youth," *Educational Researcher*, April 1982, pp. 10–17; G. D. Jaynes and R. M. Williams, eds., *Common Destiny* (Washington, D.C.: National Academy Press, 1989).

70. Gary Orfield, Franklin Monfort, and Melissa Aaron, *Status of School Desegregation: The Next Generation* (Washington, D.C.: National School Boards Association, 1992).

71. The number of cases would not permit a finer breakdown of racial composition. Given only two categories for racial composition, the majority-white, majority-nonwhite distinction corresponds to traditional definitions of a desegregated and segregated schools. Such a definition is also reasonable from a national perspective, given that the national school-age population is approximately 20 percent black.

72. Type of community is defined by school and U.S. Census measures and has four categories: Extreme Rural, Advantaged Urban, Disadvantaged Urban, and Other. Extreme Rural schools are those not in SMSAs; Advantaged Urban schools are in SMSAs and have high proportions of professional and managerial occupations; Disadvantaged Urban schools are in SMSAs and have high proportions of unemployed parents and welfare families. The schools in the disadvantaged category average 83, 55, 71, and 66

percent minority in 1978, 1982, 1986, and 1990, respectively. Thus they are both predominantly minority and high in poverty levels. Schools labeled Other are those in SMSAs, excluding disadvantaged and advantaged, and they average 82, 79, 77, and 80 percent white in 1978, 1982, 1986, and 1990, respectively.

73. Chapter 1 is the largest federal program for assisting disadvantaged students. Chapter 1 provides supplemental funds for remedial education in basic skills such as reading and math for schools with large proportions of poverty-level students, which generally means that many Chapter 1 schools have high concentrations of minority students.

74. There are other indicators of black socioeconomic well-being that appear to contradict the trends reported here, such as increases in illegitimate births, single-parent families, crime, and drug involvement. It must be emphasized, however, that the positive trends discussed here apply not to all black adults, but rather to those who have teenage children in school.

75. For example, blacks with parents who have post–high school educations score about 25 points higher than parents who have not graduated from high school (in both 1971 and 1990), but as shown in Figure 2.11 the proportion of black parents in this higher education category more than doubled during this period. The black achievement gains within educational categories average about 11 points, while 8 points of the gain can be attributed to the aggregate increase in parents' education.

76. Daniel Koretz, *Educational Achievement: Explanations and Implications of Recent Trends* (Washington, D.C.: Congressional Budget Office, 1987). For a more detailed discussion of the impact of compensatory education programs on black achievement, see David J. Armor, "Why Is Black Educational Achievement Rising?" *The Public Interest* 108:65–80 (Summer 1992).

77. J. E. Williams and J. K. Moreland, *Race, Color, and the Young Child* (Chapel Hill, N.C.: University of North Carolina Press, 1976).

78. Morris Rosenberg and Roberta G. Simmons, *Black and White Self-Esteem: The Urban School Child* (Washington, D.C.: American Sociological Association, 1971); Judith R. Porter and Robert E. Washington, "Black Identity and Self-Esteem," *Annual Review of Sociology*, 5:53–74 (1979).

79. St. John, *School Desegregation;* Walter B. Stephan, "The Effects of School Desegregation: An Evaluation 30 Years after *Brown,*" in *Advances in Applied Social Psychology*, ed. M. Saks and L. Saxe, (Hillsdale, N.J.: Erlbaum, 1986). The 1986 Stephan review is an update of his earlier review, Stephan, "School Desegregation," 1978.

80. Janet Ward Schofield, "School Desegregation and Intergroup Relations: A Review of the Literature," in *Review of Research in Education*, 17:335–412, ed. Gerald Grant (Washington, D.C.: American Educational Research Association, 1991).

81. Gerard and Miller, *School Desegregation;* Patchen, *Black-White Contact.*

82. In the original study, scores were presented separately for boys and girls, but they have been averaged here. See Gerard and Miller, *School Desegregation,* Table 10.2B.

83. Gerard and Miller, *School and Desegregation,* 237.

84. Patchen, *Black-White Contact,* Figure 7.4.

85. Patchen, *Black-White Contact,* 349.

86. St. John, *School Desegregation,* 85.

87. Stephan, "Effects," 187; Stuart W. Cook, "Social Science and School Desegregation: Did We Mislead the Supreme Court?" *Personality and Social Psychology Bulletin,* 5:420–437 (1979).

88. Stuart Cook, "Social Science"; Stephan, "Effects"; Robert E. Slavin, "Cooperative

Learning: Applying Contact Theory in Desegregated Schools," *Journal of Social Issues*, 41:45–62 (1985).

89. Anne Robinson, "Cooperative Learning and the Academically Talented Student" in *Cooperative Learning Series* (Storrs, Conn: National Research Center on the Gifted and Talented, University of Connecticut, 1991).

90. Armor, "Evidence on Busing"; Jomills H. Braddock II, "The Perpetuation of Segregation across Levels of Education," *Sociology of Education*, 53:178–186 (1980); Jomills H. Braddock II and James M. McPartland, "Assessing School Desegregation Effects," in *Research in Sociology of Education and Socialization*, vol. 3, ed. Ronald Corwin (Greenwich, Conn: JAI, 1982).

91. Robert L. Crain and Jack Strauss, *School Desegregation and Black Occupational Attainments* (Baltimore: Center of Social Organization of Schools, The Johns Hopkins University, 1985); Jomills H. Braddock II and James M. McPartland, "Social-Psychological Processes That Perpetuate Racial Segregation," *Journal of Black Studies*, 19:267–289 (1989).

92. Braddock and McPartland, "Assessing School Desegregation Effects," find in a national longitudinal study that attending desegregated K-12 schools is positively but not significantly related to years of college completed, but it is significantly related to years of college completed for those attending desegregated colleges. Crain et al., *Finding Niches*, find that attending desegregated schools is related to total years of schooling completed, and the effects are slightly stronger for males than females.

93. Figure 2.14 is adapted from Crain et al., *Finding Niches*, Table 2 (first and third bars) and Table B.1 (second and fourth bars). The original tables showed results separately for males and females, but they are combined here because the gender differences were not statistically significant.

94. In the follow-up survey, students were asked their reasons for withdrawing. The major reasons given, in order of frequency, are family moved, wanted to be with friends/relatives in city, racial problems/tensions at PC school, didn't like teachers/students at school, discrimination, expelled or suspended, didn't like PC school.

Notes to Chapter 3

1. Eleanor P. Wolf, "Northern School Desegregation and Residential Choice," *The Supreme Court Review*, 63:63–85 (1977); Robert Allan Sedler, "Metropolitan Desegregation in the Wake of Milliken: On Losing Big Battles and Winning Small Wars," *Washington University Law Quarterly*, 1975:535–620.

2. *Swann v. Charlotte-Mecklenburg Board of Education*, 402 U.S. 1 (1971). The Pasadena case was perhaps the best example of a lower court finding that neighborhood schools were unconstitutional because of housing segregation (*Spangler v. Pasadena*, 311 F. Supp. 501 (1970)).

3. See the dissent by Justice Stewart in *Milliken v. Bradley*, 418 U.S. 717 (1974).

4. *Armour v. Nix*, No. 16708, Northern District of Georgia (1979).

5. *Board of Education of Oklahoma City v. Dowell*, 111 S. Ct. 630 (1991); *Freeman v. Pitts*, 112 S. Ct. 1430 (1992).

6. *Dowell v. Board of Education of Oklahoma City*, 244 F. Supp. 971 (1965); *Spangler v. Pasadena Board of Education*, 311 F. Supp. 501 (1970); and *Swann v. Charlotte-Mecklenburg Board of Education*, 318 F. Supp. 786 (1971).

7. *Swann*, 402 U.S. at 20–21.

8. *Wright v. City of Emporia*, 407 U.S. 451 (1972); *United States v. Scotland Neck Board of Education*, 407 U.S. 484 (1972).

9. *Bradley v. Richmond, VA School Board*, 338 F. Supp. 67, 89–92, (1972).

10. *Bradley v. Richmond, VA School Board*, 462 F.2d 1058, 1066, (1972).

11. Karl E. Taeuber, "Demographic Perspectives on Housing and School Segregation, *Wayne Law Review*, 21:833–850 (1975).

12. *Bradley v. Milliken*, 338 F. Supp. 582, 587 (1971).

13. *Bradley v. Milliken*, 484 F.2d 215, 244 (1973).

14. Id. at 242.

15. *Milliken v. Bradley*, 418 U.S. 728.

16. Id. at 755. Housing discrimination was one of three types of potential interdistrict violations discussed in the dissent.

17. Sedler, "Metropolitan Desegregation"; William Taylor, "The Supreme Court and Urban Reality: A Tactical Analysis of Milliken v. Bradley," *Wayne Law Review*, 21:751–778 (1975); Robert R. Harding, "Housing Discrimination as a Basis for Interdistrict School Desegregation Remedies," *The Yale Law Journal*, 93:340–361 (1983).

18. *United States v. Board of School Commissioners of Indianapolis*, 456 F. Supp. 183 (1978).

19. *Evans v. Buchanan*, 393 F. Supp. 428 (1975).

20. 447 U.S. 916 (1980). This is the only case in which a federal court ordered the consolidation of a central city school district with surrounding suburbs. Interestingly, during the mid-1980s the district court approved a reorganization into four separate school systems, each of which included a part of the former Wilmington system. In effect, the Wilmington school system was broken up and parceled out among four much larger suburban school districts.

21. *Armour v. Nix*, No. 16708 at 28.

22. Id. at 19–21.

23. *Jenkins v. State of Missouri*, U.S. District Court for the Western District of Missouri, No. 77–0420-CV-W-4, June 5, 1984 at 42.

24. *United States v. Yonkers*, 624 F. Supp. 1276 (1985); also see the discussion of remedy in chapter 4.

25. *Dowell v. Oklahoma City*, 111 S. Ct. 630 (1991).

26. *Freeman v. Pitts*, 118 L. Ed. 2d 108, 137 (1992).

27. For representative views of this school see Taeuber, "Demographic Perspectives"; Yale Rabin, "The Roots of Segregation in the Eighties: The Role of Local Government Actions" and John F. Kain, "Housing Market Discrimination and Black Suburbanization in the 1980s," in *Divided Neighborhoods*, vol. 32 of *Urban Affairs Annual Reviews*, ed. Gary A. Tobin (Newbury Park, Calif.: Sage Publications, 1987).

28. For proponents of this view, see Anthony Pascal, *The Economics of Housing Segregation* (Santa Monica, Calif.: The Rand Corporation, 1967), 177–178; William A. V. Clark, "Residential Segregation in American Cities: A Review and Interpretation," *Population Research and Policy Review*, 5:95–127 (1986); and David J. Armor, "School Busing: A Time for Change," in *Eliminating Racism*, ed. P. A. Katz and D. A. Taylor (New York: Plenum, 1988).

29. There are now two large-scale national audit studies sponsored by HUD. The first was done in 1977. See R. E. Wienk, C. E. Reid, J. C. Simonson, and F. C. Eggers, *Measuring Discrimination in American Housing Markets* (Washington, D.C.: Department of Housing and Urban Development, 1979). The second was conducted in 1989; see M. Turner, R. Struyk, and J. Yinger, *Housing Discrimination Study: Synthesis* (Washington, D.C.: Urban Institute Press, 1991).

30. The index of dissimilarity has been criticized as a measure of housing segregation within central cities because it measures only racial imbalance and ignores the loss of white population (e.g., white flight caused by a desegregation plan). See Christine H. Rossell, "Does School Desegregation Policy Stimulate Residential Integration? A Critique of the Research," *Urban Education,* 21:403–420 (1987). Unfortunately, the dissimilarity index is the only measure available for long-term trends. The problem may be less serious when the statistic is computed for counties, as for 1980 and 1990 in Table 3.1; nearby suburban populations are included. It should also be noted that the index values in the table are based on block, not tract, data.

31. One of the most comprehensive treatments of changes in racial attitudes is H. Schuman, C. Sheeh, and L. Bobo, *Racial Attitudes in America* (Cambridge, Mass.: Harvard University Press, 1985).

32. Karl and Alma Taeuber, *Negroes in Cities* (New York: Atheneum, 1965).

33. Reynolds Farley, "Population Trends and School Segregation in the Detroit Metropolitan Area," *Wayne Law Review,* 21:867–902 (1975).

34. Kain, "Housing Market."

35. From exhibits prepared by Anthony Pascal in *Armour v. Nix* (1979) and *Jenkins v. Missouri* (1982).

36. The simulation presented here moved blacks from the city to the suburbs but did not move whites from suburban tracts into the city.

37. Taeuber, "Demographic Perspectives"; Joe Darden, "Choosing Neighbors and Neighborhoods: The Role of Race in Housing Preference," in *Divided Neighborhoods,* ed. Gary A. Tobin.

38. Taeuber, "Demographic Perspectives"; Kain, "Housing Market."

39. R. Farley, H. Schuman, S. Bianchi, D. Colasanto, and S. Hatchett, "Chocolate City, Vanilla Suburbs: Will the Trend toward Racially Separate Communities Continue?" *Social Science Research,* 7:319–344 (1978).

40. Schuman et al., *Racial Attitudes.*

41. This survey was reported in the *New York Times* on February 26, 1978.

42. Farley et al., "Chocolate City."

43. Id. at 32.

44. The cities are Omaha, Nebraska, 1978; Kansas City, Missouri, 1982; Cincinnati, Ohio, 1983; Little Rock, Arkansas, 1984; Milwaukee, Wisconsin, 1986; Los Angeles, California, 1987; Nash County, North Carolina, 1990; and Hartford, Connecticut, 1991. Some of these results have been reported in Armor, "School Busing"; William A. V. Clark, "Residential Segregation in American Cities," *Population Research and Policy Review,* 5:95–127 (1985); and William A. V. Clark, "Residential Preferences and Neighborhood Racial Segregation: A Test of the Schelling Segregation Model," *Demography,* 28:1–19 (1991).

45. Respondents who answered "don't know" or "makes no difference" are excluded from the averages; in most surveys these responses represented less than 20 percent of the samples.

46. Exhibits prepared by David J. Armor for *Armour v. Nix* (1979) and *Jenkins v. Missouri* (1984).

47. Thomas Schelling, "Dynamic Models of Segregation," *Journal of Mathematical Sociology,* 1:143–186 (1971).

48. Clark, "Residential Preferences."

49. *Shelley v. Kraemer,* 334 U.S. 1 (1948); Arnold R. Hirsch, "The Causes of Residential Segregation: A Historical Perspective," *Issues in Housing Discrimination,* Hearings of the U.S. Commission on Civil Rights, Washington, D.C., November 1985.

50. E.g., see Taeuber, "Demographic Perspectives."

51. Wienk et al., *Measuring Discrimination*. The data summarized in Table 3.5 was taken from Kain, "Housing Market."

52. Turner et al., *Housing Discrimination*.

53. This question was designed by William Sampson of Northwestern University and was first asked in the Milwaukee housing survey.

54. R. J. Harrison and D. H. Weinberg, *Racial and Ethnic Residential Segregation in 1990*, (Washington, D.C.: U.S. Bureau of the Census, April 1992).

55. The audit studies reported rates of discrimination separately for rental and sale units; because about 40 percent of blacks are buyers and 60 percent are renters in metropolitan areas, the probability of experiencing discrimination across both types of housing reported in Table 3.5 would be about 22 percent in 1979 and 19 percent in 1989, or an average of 20.5 percent. Of course, the self-report rate is based on a nonrandom sample of only five metropolitan areas.

56. See Taeuber, "Demographic Perspectives"; Diana Pearce, "Deciphering the Dynamics of Segregation: The Role of Schools in the Housing Choice Process," *Urban Review*, 13:85–101 (1981); Diana Pearce, Robert Crain, and Reynolds Farley, *Lessons Not Lost: The Effect of School Desegregation on the Rate of Residential Desegregation in Large Central Cities* (Washington, D.C.: Center for National Policy Review, 1984).

57. See Taeuber, "Demographic Perspectives"; and Wolf, "Northern School."

58. For the argument that school desegregation reduces housing segregation, see Pearce, "Deciphering"; and Pearce et al., *Lessons Not Lost*.

59. Wolf, "Northern School"; Christine H. Rossell, "Does School Desegregation Policy Stimulate Residential Integration? A Critique of the Research," *Urban Education*, 21:403–420 (1987); William A. V. Clark, "Does School Desegregation Policy Stimulate Residential Integration? Evidence from a Case Study," *Urban Education*, 23:51–67 (1988).

60. Kentucky Commission on Human Rights, *Housing and School Desegregation Increased by Section 8 Moves* (Louisville, 1980).

61. Clark, "Residential Preferences." About half of this group did not move during the interval of study, and among the thirty percent who moved within the Oklahoma City school district, the majority moved within predominantly black inner city neighborhoods.

62. Thomas A. Clark, "The Suburbanization Process and Residential Segregation," in *Divided Neighborhoods*, ed. Gary A. Tobin (1987).

63. Diana Pearce, *Breaking Down Barriers: New Evidence on the Impact of Metropolitan School Desegregation on Housing Patterns*, final report to the National Institute of Education (Washington, D.C.: Center for National Policy Review, November 1980); Pearce et al., *Lessons Not Lost*.

64. Rossell, "Does School Desegregation."

65. Pearce et al., *Lessons Not Lost*.

66. School data were not available for Washington, D.C. The cities with high Hispanic populations were excluded because the changes in the dissimilarity index for blacks versus nonblacks can reflect growing housing desegregation of blacks with other minorities rather than with whites.

67. The 1970 dissimilarity index has been computed for SMSAs of these cities, but they actually average about eight points lower than the values in Table 3.1, probably because they are based on tract data and the values in Table 3.1 are based on block data.

68. *Columbus Board of Education v. Pennick*, 443 U.S. 449, 480 (1979).

Notes to Chapter 4

1. *Milliken v. Bradley*, 418 U.S. 717, 746 (1974).

2. *Board of Education of Oklahoma City v. Dowell*, 111 S. Ct. 630 (1991).

3. See Christine Rossell, *The Carrot or the Stick for Desegregation Policy* (Philadelphia: Temple University Press, 1990); and David J. Armor, "White Flight and the Future of School Desegregation," in *School Desegregation*, ed. Walter G. Stephan and Joe R. Feagin (New York: Plenum, 1980).

4. *Green v. County School Board*, 391 U.S. 430, 431 (1968).

5. See chapter 3 for some of the housing cases; see *Bradley v. Milliken*, 433 U.S. 267 (1977) (*Milliken II*) for programmatic remedies; and see *Pitts v. Freeman*, No. 11946, Northern District of Georgia (1988) (affirmed in *Freeman v. Pitts*, 112 S. Ct. 1430) for violations and remedies regarding teacher experience.

6. *United States v. Yonkers*, 833 F. Supp. 214 (1993).

7. *Adams v. Weinberger*, 391 F. Supp. 269 (1975).

8. U.S. Commission on Civil Rights, *Racial Isolation in the Public Schools* (Washington, D.C.: U.S. Government Printing Office, 1967).

9. *Armstrong v. O'Connell*, 427 F. Supp. 1377 (1977).

10. Lauri Steel, Roger E. Levine, Christine H. Rossell, and David J. Armor, *Magnet Schools and Issues of Desegregation, Quality, and Choice* (Palo Alto: American Institutes for Research, 1993). The tabulations presented in this chapter were prepared by the author.

11. *Singleton v. Jackson*, 419 F.2d 1211 (1970).

12. Steel et al., *Magnet Schools*.

13. This concept has been most emphasized in the work of Michael J. Alves and Charles V. Willie; see their "Controlled Choice Assignments: A New and More Effective Approach to School Desegregation," *The Urban Review*, 19:67–88 (1987).

14. The formula for computing dissimilarity for two groups of students, say, black and white, is $D = 0.5 \sum_i |B_i/B - W_i/W|$, where B_i and W_i are the number of black and white students in school i, respectively, and B and W are the total number of black and white students in the system (or at some grade level).

15. The formula for the index of exposure of black students to white students is $E = [\sum_i B_i \times PW_i]/B$, where B_i is the number of black students in school i, PW_i is the percentage of white students in school i, and B is the total black enrollment in the system (or at a grade level).

16. Steel et al., *Magnet Schools*.

17. Another 10,600 school districts with only a single school per grade level were not part of the universe. Aside from the fact that these are very small districts, school desegregation is automatic if there is only one school per grade.

18. The national survey defined a formal desegregation plan as "a formal written plan of student assignment to attain a specified racial/ethnic composition in some or all schools."

19. Small districts with plans accounted for only 514,000 students, and 90 percent of small districts had "Mandatory Other" plans relying primarily on contiguous rezoning techniques.

20. Gary Orfield and Franklin Monfort, *Status of School Desegregation: The Next Generation* (Washington, D.C.: National School Boards Association, 1992); see also Gary

Orfield and Franklin Monfort, with Melissa Aaron, *Status of School Desegregation 1968–1986*, (Washington, D.C.: National School Boards Association, 1989).

21. The relationship between Hispanic and black exposure to whites in the AIR study is not limited to larger school systems. Considering all systems with enrollments greater than 5000, which includes 86 percent of all black students and 90 percent of all Hispanic students, the 1989 black-white exposure index is 54 percent compared to a Hispanic-white index of 57. In general, the exposure indices are higher in smaller school districts, in part because the percent white is higher in these districts.

22. *United States v. Scotland Neck Board of Education*, 407 U.S. 484, 491 (1972).

23. *Spangler v. Pasadena*, 375 F. Supp. 1308 (1974); *Tasby v. Estes*, 572 F.2d 1010 (1978).

24. *Estes v. Dallas NAACP*, 100 S. Ct. 716 (1980).

25. *Carlin v. San Diego School Board*, Superior Court for San Diego County, March 9, 1977.

26. *Crawford v. Los Angeles Board of Education*, Superior Court for Los Angeles County, May 19, 1980, and July 7, 1980.

27. *United States v. Pitman*, 808 F.2d 385, 391 (1987).

28. James S. Coleman, Sara D. Kelly, and John A. Moore, *Trends in School Segregation, 1968–73* (Washington, D.C.: The Urban Institute Press, 1975).

29. For example, see Christine H. Rossell, "School Desegregation and White Flight," *Political Science Quarterly*, 90:675–695 (1975); and Thomas F. Pettigrew and Robert L. Green, "School Desegregation in Large Cities: A Critique of the Coleman 'White Flight' Thesis," *Harvard Educational Review*, 46:1–53 (1976).

30. Reynolds Farley and C. Wurdock, *Can Governmental Policies Integrate Public Schools?* (Ann Arbor: Population Studies Center, University of Michigan, 1977).

31. Christine H. Rossell, "The Unintended Impacts of Public Policy: School Desegregation and Resegregation," Report to the National Institute of Education. Boston University, 1978.

32. Armor, "White Flight."

33. Franklin D. Wilson, "The Impact of School Desegregation Programs on White Public-School Enrollment, 1968–1976," *Sociology of Education*, 58:137–153 (1985).

34. Finis Welch and Audry Light, *New Evidence on School Desegregation*, U.S. Commission on Civil Rights, Clearinghouse Publication 92 (Washington, D.C.: U.S. Government Printing Office, 1987).

35. The data in Figure 4.7 is taken from Welch and Light, *New Evidence*, Table 19, p. 55. All forty-three Post-Swann districts that used pair/clustering were combined, as were twenty-three districts using rezoning techniques only. The voluntary category consists of thirteen districts that were classified by the study as "major voluntary."

36. Christine H. Rossell, "Is It the Busing or the Blacks?" *Urban Affairs Quarterly*, 24:138–148 (1988).

37. Mark A. Smylie, "Reducing Racial Isolation in Large School Districts," *Urban Education*, 17:477–502 (1983).

38. Gary Orfield, "School Desegregation in the 1980s," *Equity and Choice* (February 1988): 25–28 (special issue).

39. Orfield et al., *Status*, 1992.

40. The 1988 comparative analysis also omitted both San Diego and Buffalo, two of the larger and more comprehensive voluntary programs.

41. Christine Rossell, *Carrot or Stick*.

42. Some of the results and analyses discussed in this section are taken from Christine

H. Rossell and David J. Armor, "The Effectiveness of School Desegregation Plans, 1968–1991," Unpublished paper, 1995.

43. Systems that had formal desegregation plans in the past but no longer have them are included in systems with plans.

44. Rossell and Armor, "Magnet Schools."

45. The school district control variables, measured at the school district level, were size, county/central city district, urban/suburban, years since plan (for plan districts), region, percent students on free lunch, and median family income.

46. The reason is that there are some districts (e.g., Dallas, Detroit, Savannah) that operated mandatory plans for many years before converting to voluntary plans during the mid- to late-1980s.

47. School districts that currently have a voluntary plan that formerly operated a mandatory desegregation plan are classified with mandatory plans. Most of the twenty districts in this category implemented mandatory plans as their first major plan and retained them throughout the 1970s and early 1980s. Examples include Savannah, Detroit, Memphis, and Dallas.

48. Since voluntary plans were rare in the South during the 1970s, there were only four southern districts with voluntary plans in the national sample compared to forty-six with mandatory plans, so the differences are based on fairly small samples. In the North, the sample divides into twenty-two with voluntary plans and sixty-six with mandatory plans.

49. Rossell and Armor, "Effectiveness." See n. 45 in this chapter for the control variables.

50. Detailed plan data come from case studies I conducted (including district visits in most cases) for all cities except Buffalo; the latter relies on Christine Rossell, "The Buffalo Controlled Choice Plan," *Urban Education*, 22:328–354 (1987). In Rossell's later work (*Carrot or Stick*), as well as in the Welch and Light study (*New Evidence*), Buffalo is classified as a voluntary magnet plan.

51. Howard Schuman, Charlotte Steeh, and Lawrence Bobo, *Racial Attitudes in America* (Cambridge, Mass.: Harvard University Press, 1985), 74, Table 3.1.

52. I conducted the surveys for school districts designing desegregation plans. See the descriptions for Figures 4.13 and 4.15 for more details.

53. In Norfolk, the higher racial composition was "mostly" black instead of two-thirds black; in Los Angeles, the fifty-fifty question was "half white and half black" and the two-thirds question was "one-third white, one-third black, and one-third Hispanic"; in Worcester the fifty-fifty question was "half white and half black and Hispanic" and the two-thirds question was "one-third white and two-thirds black and Hispanic."

54. A Louis Harris poll conducted for the NAACP in 1988 showed only 57 percent of whites opposed to busing school children for racial balance. Parents with children involved in busing plans showed lower levels of opposition than the national figures, but, of course, those opposed to such plans may be underrepresented due to withdrawal from the school systems in question.

55. In the Los Angeles and Chicago surveys, the question was worded as, "How do you feel about busing children of all backgrounds—white, black, and Hispanic—to achieve school desegregation?"

56. A review of alternative explanations can be found in Schuman et al., *Racial Attitudes*.

57. See Mary R. Jackman, "General and Applied Tolerance: Does Education Increase Commitment to Racial Integration?" *American Journal of Political Science*, 22:203–324 (1978); Mary R. Jackman and Michael J. Muha, "Education and Intergroup Attitudes:

Moral Enlightenment, Superficial Democratic Commitment, or Ideological Refinement?" *American Sociological Review,* 49:751–769 (1984).

58. For a comprehensive statement of the symbolic racism theory, see David O. Sears, "Symbolic Racism," in *Eliminating Racism,* ed. P. A. Katz and D. A. Taylor (New York: Plenum, 1988). See also John B. McConahay, "Self-Interest versus Racial Attitudes as Correlates of Anti-Busing Attitudes in Louisville: Is It the Buses or the Blacks?" *Journal of Politics,* 44:692–720 (1982); David O. Sears, Carl P. Hensler, and Leslie K. Speer, "Whites' Opposition to 'Busing': Self-Interest or Symbolic Politics?" *American Political Science Review,* 73:369–384 (1979); Donald R. Kinder and David O. Sears, "Prejudice and Politics: Symbolic Racism versus Racial Threats to the Good Life," *Journal of Personality and Social Psychology,* 40:414–431 (1981).

59. Seymour Martin Lipset and William Schneider, "The Bakke Case: How Would It Be Decided at the Bar of Public Opinion?" *Public Opinion,* 1:38–44 (1978); Seymour Martin Lipset, "Affirmative Action and the American Creed," *Wilson Quarterly,* (Winter 1992): 52–62.

60. The Housing surveys discussed in chapter 3 revealed that, in answer to an open-ended question about reasons for choosing their neighborhood, a much higher proportion of blacks than whites said they had "no choice."

61. Most studies of symbolic racism argue that self-interest factors are not correlated with attitudes toward various racial policies like busing, but self-interest is invariably measured by broad behavioral factors like whether one has children, length of time in or attachment to a neighborhood, racial composition of a neighborhood, and the like. However, these studies have generally not measured *perceived* self-interests, particularly expectations about the harms or benefits of attending a desegregated school, which would seem especially relevant in theorizing about cognitive phenomenon.

62. McKee J. McClendon, "Racism, Rational Choice, and White Opposition to Racial Change: A Case Study of Busing," *Public Opinion Quarterly,* 49:214–233 (1985).

63. A similar explanation for the phenomenon of white flight has been offered by Christine Rossell, "Applied Social Science Research: What Does It Say about the Effectiveness of School Desegregation Plans?" *Journal of Legal Studies,* 12:69–107 (1983).

Notes to Chapter 5

1. Examples include San Diego, Phoenix, Tangipahoa Parish (Louisiana), and San Jose.

2. San Jose is one.

3. *United States v. Yonkers,* 833 F. Supp. 214 (1993).

4. There are no federal court decisions at present regarding an all-minority school program created on the grounds of educational benefits for the minority child. In principle, the evaluation would be the same as that applied to any racial classification: The school board would have to justify the segregation on the basis of a "compelling government interest" that justified the racial classification (see *Wygant v. Jackson Board of Education,* 476 U.S. 267 (1987), which reviews the standards for racial classifications and compelling government interest). One compelling reason might be improved educational outcomes for black males, if it could be demonstrated convincingly.

5. Press release, National Catholic Educational Association, Washington, D.C., September 17, 1992.

6. The constitutional issues involved here would take this discussion too far afield,

but suffice it to say that the Supreme Court has not ruled on the constitutionality of state-funded vouchers used for parochial schools.

7. To illustrate from the recent metropolitan desegregation case in the Hartford area, more than half of the twenty suburban school systems surrounding the Hartford school system have lower per-capita operating costs than the Hartford city school system.

8. It would enhance white participation in central-city magnet schools if magnet classes or programs were maintained at a fifty-fifty ratio, but it would not have to be a requirement for an equity choice policy.

9. For a discussion and review of evidence that some private schools and some suburban school systems have better educational programs and outcomes than larger urban school systems, see James Coleman, Thomas Hoffer, and Sally Kilgore, *Public and Private High Schools: The Impact of Communities* (New York: Basic Books, 1987); and John Chubb and Terry Moe, *Politics, Markets, and America's Schools,* (Washington, D.C.: Brookings Institution, 1990).

Bibliography

Allport, Gordon W., *The Nature of Prejudice*, Cambridge, Mass.: Addison-Wesley, 1953.

Aloes, Michael J. and Charles V. Willie, "Controlled Choice Assignments," *The Urban Review*, 19:67–88, 1987.

Anrig, Greg, "Test Scores on the Rise for Blacks," *The Trenton Sunday Star-Ledger*, May 27, 1984.

Armor, David J., "The Evidence on Busing," *The Public Interest*, 28:90–126, 1972.

———. "White Flight and the Future of School Desegregation," in *School Desegregation*, ed. Walter G. Stephan and Joe R. Feagin, New York: Plenum, 1980.

———. "An Evaluation of Norfolk Desegregation Plans," Report to the Norfolk Board of Education, December 1982.

———. "School Busing: A Time for Change," in *Eliminating Racism*, ed. P. A. Katz and D. A. Taylor, New York: Plenum, 1988.

———. "Response to Carr and Ziegler," *Sociology of Education*, 64:134–139, 1991.

———. "Why Is Black Educational Achievement Rising?" *The Public Interest*, 108:65–80 (Summer 1992).

Braddock, Jomills H. II, and James M. McPartland, "Assessing School Desegregation Effects," in *Research in Sociology of Education and Socialization*, vol. 3, ed. Ronald Corwin, Greenwich, Conn.: JAI, 1982.

———. "Social-Psychological Processes That Perpetuate Racial Segregation," *Journal of Black Studies*, 19:267–289, 1989.

———. "The Social and Academic Consequences of School Desegregation," *Equity and Choice*, February 1988.

Braddock, Jomills H. II, "The Perpetuation of Segregation across Levels of Education," *Sociology of Education*, 53:178–186, 1980.

Bradley, L. A., and G. W. Bradley, "The Academic Achievement of Black Students in Desegregated Schools: A Critical Review," *Review of Educational Research*, 47:399–449, 1977.

Burton, Nancy W., and Lyle V. Jones, "Recent Trends in Achievement Levels of Black and White Youth," *Educational Researcher*, April 1982.

Chubb, John, and Terry Moe, *Politics, Markets, and America's Schools*, Washington D.C.: The Brookings Institution, 1990.

Clark, Kenneth, and Mamie Clark, "The Development of Consciousness of Self and the Emergence of Racial Identity in Negro Children," *Journal of Social Psychology*, 10:591–599, 1939.

————. "Segregation as a Factor in the Racial Identification of Negro Pre-School Children," *Journal of Experimental Education*, 8:161–163, 1939.

Clark, Kenneth, *Prejudice and Your Child*, Boston: Beacon Press, 1955.

Clark, Thomas A., "The Suburbanization Process and Residential Segregation," in *Divided Neighborhoods*, vol. 32 of *Urban Affairs Annual Reviews*, ed. Gary A. Tobin, 1987.

Clark, William A. V., "Does School Desegregation Policty Stimulate Residential Integration? Evidence from a Case Study," *Urban Education*, 23:51–67, 1988.

————. "Residential Preferences and Neighborhood Racial Segregation: A Test of the Schelling Segregation Model," *Demography*, 28:1–19, 1991.

————. "Residential Segregation in American Cities: A Review and Interpretation," *Population Research and Policy Review*, 5:95–127, 1986.

Coleman, James S., Ernest Q. Campbell, and others, *Equality of Educational Opportunity*, Washington, D.C.: U.S. Government Printing Office, 1966.

Coleman, James S., Sara D. Kelley, and John A. Moore, *Trends in School Integration*, Washington, D.C.: Urban Institute, 1975.

Coleman, James S., Thomas Hoffer, and Sally Kilgore, *Public and Private High Schools: The Impact of Communities*, New York: Basic Books, 1987.

Cook, Stuart W., "Social Science and School Desegregation: Did We Mislead the Supreme Court?" *Personality and Social Psychology Bulletin*, 5:420–437, 1979.

Cook, Thomas, and others, *School Desegregation and Black Achievement*, Washington, D.C.: National Institute of Education U.S. Department of Education, 1984.

Crain, Robert L., and Jack Strauss, *School Desegregation and Black Occupational Attainment: Results from a Long-term Experiment*, Baltimore: Center for the Social Organization of Schools, Johns Hopkins University, 1986.

Crain, Robert L., and Rita Mahard, "Desegregation and Black Achievement, A Review of the Research," *Law and Contemporary Problems*, 42:17–58, 1978.

————. "The Effect of Research Methodology on Desegregation-Achievement Studies: A Meta Analysis," *American Journal of Sociology*, 88: 839–854, 1983.

Crain, Robert L., Jennifer A. Hawes, Randi L. Miler, and Janet R. Peichert, "Finding Niches: Desegregated Students Sixteen Years Later," New York: Teachers College, Columbia University, 1989.

Darden, Joe, "Choosing Neighbors and Neighborhoods: The Role of Race in Housing Preference," in *Divided Neighborhoods*, vol. 32 of *Urban Affairs Annual Reviews*, ed. Gary A. Tobin, 1987.

Deutsch, Morton, and Mary Evans Collins, *Interracial Housing*, Minneapolis: University of Minnesota Press, 1951.

Farley, Reynolds, "Population Trends and School Segregation in the Detroit Metropolitan Area," *Wayne Law Review*, 21:867–902, 1975.

Farley, Reynolds, and C. Wurdock, *Can Governmental Policies Integrate Public Schools?* Ann Arbor: Population Studies Center, University of Michigan, 1977.

Farley, Reynolds, H. Schuman, S. Bianchi, D. Colasanto, and S. Hatchett, "Chocolate City, Vanilla Suburbs: Will the Trend Toward Racially Separate Communities Continue?" *Social Science Research*, 7:319–344, 1978.

Fiss, Owen M., "The Charlotte-Mecklenburg Case—Its Significance for Northern School Desegregation," *University of Chicago Law Review*, 38:697–709 (1971).

Gerard, Harold B., and Norman Miller, *School Desegregation*, New York: Plenum, 1975.

Goodman, Frank I., "De Facto School Desegregation: A Constitutional and Empirical Analysis," *California Law Review*, 60:275–437 (1972).

Green, Robert L., "The Impact of Proposed Changes in the Desegregation Plan of the Public Schools of Norfolk, Virginia," Report to the Norfolk Board of Education, March 29, 1982.

Harding, Robert R., "Housing Discrimination as a Basis for Interdistrict School Desegregation Remedies," *The Yale Law Journal*, 93:340–361, 1983.

Harrison, R. J. and D. H. Weinberg, *Racial and Ethnic Residential Segregation in 1990*, Washington, D.C.: U.S. Bureau of the Census, April 1992.

Hawley, Willis D., and Mark A. Smylie, "The Contribution of School Desegregation to Academic Achievement and Racial Integration," in *Eliminating Racism*, ed. Phyllis A. Katz and Dalmas A. Taylor, New York: Plenum, 1988.

Hawley, Willis D., Mark Smylie, Robert L. Crain, Christine H. Rossell, R. Fernandez, Janet W. Schofield, E. Trent, *Strategies for Effective Desegregation*, Lexington, Mass.: Lexington Books, 1983.

Hirsch, Arnold R., "The Causes of Residential Segregation: A Historical Perspective," *Issues in Housing Discrimination*, Hearings of the U.S. Commission on Civil Rights, Washington, D.C., November 1985.

Jackman, Mary R., "General and Applied Tolerance: Does Education Increase Commitment to Racial Integration?" *American Journal of Political Science*, 22:302–324, 1978.

Jackman, Mary R., and Michael J. Muha, "Education and Intergroup Attitues: Moral Enlightenment, Superficial Democratic Commitment, or Ideological Refinement?" *American Sociological Review*, 49:751–769, 1984.

Jaynes, G. D., and R. M. Williams, eds., *Common Destiny*, Washington, D.C.: National Academy Press, 1989.

Kain, John F., "Housing Market Discrimination and Black Suburbanization in the 1980s," in *Divided Neighborhoods*, vol. 32 of *Urban Affairs Annual Reviews*, ed. Gary A. Tobin, 1987.

Kentucky Commission on Human Rights, *Housing and School Desegregation Increased by Section 8 Moves*, Louisville, 1980.

Kinder, Donald R., and David O. Sears, "Prejudice and Politics: Symbolic Racism versus Racial Threats to the Good Life," *Journal of Personality and Social Psychology*, 40:414–431, 1981.

Koretz, Daniel, *Educational Achievement: Explanations and Implications of Recent Trends*, Washington, D.C.: Congressional Budget Office, 1987.

Lipset, Seymour Martin, and William Schneider, "The Bakke Case: How Would It Be Decided at the Bar of Public Opinion?" *Public Opinion*, 1:38–44, 1978.

Lipset, Seymour Martin, "Affirmative Action and the American Creed," *Wilson Quarterly*, Winter:52–62, 1992.

McClendon, McKee J., "Racism, Rational Choice, and White Opposition to Racial Change: A Case Study of Busing," *Public Opinion Quarterly*, 49:214–233, 1985.

McConahay, John B., "Self-Interest versus Racial Attitudes as Correlates of Anti-busing Attitudes in Louisville: Is It the Buses or the Blacks?" *Journal of Politics*, 44:692–720, 1982.

Mosteller, Frederick, and Daniel P. Moynihan, eds., *On Equality of Educational Opportunity*, New York: Random House, 1972.

Mullis, Ina V. S., and others, *Trends in Academic Progress*, Washington, D.C.: U.S. Government Printing Office, 1991.

Myrdal, Gunnar, *An American Dilemma*, New York: Harper and Row, 1944.

Nearhood, James R., "Foreseeable Racial Segregation—A Presumption of Unconstitutionality," *Nebraska Law Review* 55:144–160 (1975).

Orfield, Gary, *Must We Bus? Segregated Schools and National Policy*, Washington,
  D.C.: The Brookings Institution, 1978.
———. "School Desegregation in the 1980s," *Equity and Choice*, February:25–28, 1988.
Orfield, Gary, and Franklin Monfort, *Status of School Desegregation: The Next Genera-
  tion*, Washington, D.C.: National School Boards Association, 1992.
Orfield, Gary, Franklin Monfort, and Melissa Aaron, *Status of School Desegregation
  1968–1986*, Washington, D.C.: National School Boards Association, 1989.
Pascal, Anthony, *The Economics of Housing Segregation*, Santa Monica, Calif: The Rand
  Corporation, 1967.
Patchen, Martin, *Black-White Contact in Schools*, West Lafeyette, Indiana: Purdue
  University Press, 1982.
Pearce, Diana, *Breaking Down Barriers: New Evidence on the Impact of Metropolitan
  School Desegregation on Housing Patterns*, Final report to the National Institute
  of Education, Washington, D.C.: Center for National Policy Review, November
  1980.
———. "Deciphering the Dynamics of Segregation: The Role of Schools in the Housing
  Choice Process," *Urban Review*, 13:85–101, 1981.
Pearce, Diana, Robert Crain, and Reynolds Farley, *Lessons Not Lost: The Effect of
  School Desegregation on the Rate of Residential Desegregation in Large Central
  Cities*, Washington, D.C.: Center for National Policy Review, 1984.
Pettigrew, Thomas F., and Robert L. Green, "School Desegregation in Large Cities: A
  Critique of the Coleman 'White Flight' Thesis," *Harvard Educational Review*,
  46:1–53, 1976.
Porter, Judith R., and Robert E. Washington, "Black Identity and Self-Esteem," *Annual
  Review of Sociology*, 5:53–74 (1979).
Rabin, Yale, "The Roots of Segregation in the Eighties: The Role of Local Government
  Actions," in *Divided Neighborhoods*, vol. 32 of *Urban Affairs Annual Reviews*,
  ed. Gary A. Tobin, 1987.
Read, Frank T., "Judicial Evolution of the Law of School Integration since Brown v.
  Board of Education," *Law and Contemporary Problems*, 39:7–49, (1975).
Robinson, Anne, "Cooperative Learning and the Academically Talented Student," *Co-
  operative Learning Series*, Storrs, Conn: National Research Center on the Gifted
  and Talented, University of Connecticut, 1991.
Rosenberg, Morris, and Roberta G. Simmons, *Black and White Self-Esteem: The Urban
  School Child*, Washington, D.C.: American Sociological Association, 1971.
Rose, Arnold , *The Negro in America*, Boston: Beacon Press, 1956 (a condensed version
  of *An American Dilemma*).
Rossell, Christine H., "School Desegregation and White Flight," *Political Science Quar-
  terly*, 90:675–695, 1975.
———. "The Unintended Impacts of Public Policy: School Desegregation and Re-
  segregation," Report to the National Institute of Education, Boston: Boston Uni-
  versity, 1978.
———. "Applied Social Research: What Does It Say about the Effectiveness of School
  Desegregation Plans," *Journal of Legal Studies*, 12:69–107, 1983.
———. "Estimating the Net Benefits of School Desegregation Reassignments," *Educa-
  tional Evaluation and Policy Analysis*, 7:217–27, 1986.
———. "Does School Desegregation Policy Stimulate Residential Integration? A Cri-
  tique of the Research," *Urban Education*, 21:403–420, 1987.
———. "The Buffalo Controlled Choice Plan," *Urban Education*, 22:328–54, 1987.
———. "Is it the Busing or the Blacks?" *Urban Affairs Quarterly*, 24:138–148, 1988.

————. *The Carrot or the Stick for Desegregation Policy*, Philadelphia: Temple University Press, 1990.

Rossell, Christine H., and David J. Armor, "The Effectiveness of School Desegregation, 1968–1991," unpublished manuscript, 1995.

St. John, Nancy, *School Desegregation*, New York: Wiley, 1975.

Schelling, Thomas, "Dynamic Models of Segregation," *Journal of Mathematical Sociology*, 1:143–186, 1971.

Schofield, Janet Ward, "School Desegregation and Intergroup Relations: A Review of the Literature," in *Review of Research in Education*, 17:335–412, ed. Gerald Grant, Washington, D.C.: American Educational Research Association, 1991.

Schuman, Howard, Charlotte Steeh, and Lawrence Bobo, *Racial Attitudes In America*, Cambridge, Mass.: Harvard University Press, 1985.

Sears, David O., "Symbolic Racism," in *Eliminating Racism*, ed. P. A. Katz and D. A. Taylor, New York: Plenum, 1988.

Sears, David O., Carl P. Hensler, and Leslie K. Speer, "Whites' Opposition to 'Busing': Self-Interest or Symbolic Politics?" *American Political Science Review*, 73:369–384, 1979.

Sedler, Robert Allan, "Metropolitan Desegregation in the Wake of Milliken—on Losing Big Battles and Winning Small Wars," *Washington University Law Quarterly*, 535–620, 1975.

Slavin, Robert E., "When Does Cooperative Learning Increase Student Achievement?" *Psychological Bulletin*, 94: 429–445, 1983.

————. "Cooperative Learning: Applying Contact Theory in Desegregated Schools," *Journal of Social Issues*, 41:45–62, 1985.

Smylie, Mark A., "Reducing Racial Isolation in Large School Districts," *Urban Education*, 17:477–502, 1983.

Social scientists, "The Effects of Segregation and the Consequences of Desegregation: A Social Science Statement," *Minnesota Law Review*, 37:427–439 (1953), signed by 32 social scientists.

Social scientists, "School Desegregation: A Social Science Statement," in brief of the NAACP et al., as amicus curiae in support of respondents, *Freeman v. Pitts*, U.S. Supreme Court on writ of certiorari to the U.S. Court of Appeals for the Eleventh Circuit, June 21, 1991, signed by 52 social scientists.

Steel, Lauri, Roger E. Levine, Christine H. Rossell, and David J. Armor, *Magnet Schools and Issues of Desegregation, Quality, and Choice*, Palo Alto: American Insitutes for Research, May 1993.

Stephan, Walter G., "School Desegregation: An Evaluation of Predictions made in *Brown v. Board of Education*," *Psychological Bulletin*, 85:217–238, 1978.

Stephan, Walter G., "The Effects of School Desegregation: An Evaluation 30 Years after *Brown*," in *Advances in Applied Social Psychology*, ed. M. Saks and L. Saxe, Hillsdale, N.J.: Erlbaum, 1986.

Stouffer, Samuel A., and others, *The American Soldier*, Princeton, N.J.: Princeton University Press, 1949.

Taeuber, Karl E., "Demographic Perspectives on Housing and School Segregation, *Wayne Law Review*, 21:833–850, 1975.

Taeuber, Karl E, and Alma Taeuber, *Negroes in Cities*, New York: Atheneum, 1965.

Taylor, William, "The Supreme Court and Urban Reality: A Tactical Analysis of *Milliken v. Bradley*," *Wayne Law Review*, 21:751–778, 1975.

Turner, M., R. Struyk, and J. Yinger, *Housing Discrimination Study: Synthesis*, Washington, D.C.: The Urban Institute, 1991.

U.S. Commission on Civil Rights, *Racial Isolation in the Public Schools*, Washington, D.C.: U.S. Government Printing Office, 1967.

Weinberg, Meyer, *Minority Students: A Research Appraisal*, Washington, D.C.: National Institute of Education, 1977.

Welch, Finis, and Audry Light, *New Evidence on School Desegregation*, U.S. Commission on Civil Rights, Clearinghouse Publication 92, Washington, D.C.: U.S. Government Printing Office, 1987.

Wienk, R. E., C. E. Reid, J. C. Simonson, and F. C. Eggers, *Measuring Discrimination in American Housing Markets*, Washington, D.C.:Department of Housing and Urban Development, 1979.

Williams, J. E., and J. K. Moreland, *Race, Color, and the Young Child*, Chapel Hill, N.C.: University of North Carolina Press, 1976.

Wilson, Franklin D., "The Impact of School Desegregation Programs on White Public-School Enrollment, 1968–1976," *Sociology of Education*, 58:137–153, 1985.

Wolf, Eleanor P., "Northern School Desegregation and Residential Choice," *The Supreme Court Review*, 63–85, 1977.

Yudof, Mark G. "School Desegregation: Legal Realism, Reasoned Elaboration, and Social Science Research in the Supreme Court," *Law and Contemporary Problems*, 42:57–109 (1978).

Table of Cases

Index